ECOLOGICAL POLITICS

ECOLOGICAL POLITICS
Different Dimensions

GOPAL BHARGAVA

KALPAZ PUBLICATIONS
NEW DELHI—110052

ECOLOGICAL POLITICS
Different Dimensions
(Poltics)

ISBN : 817835019X

Published in 2001 in India by
Kalpaz Publications
C-30, Satyawati Nagar Ashok Vihar Phase - III
New Delhi—110052
E-mail: kalpaz@hotmail.com

Lesertype setting at : Apex Computers Delhi
Printed at : Mehra Offset Printers

CONTENTS

Foreward 7

Preface 9

1. **Ecopolitics : An Introduction** 13

2. **Agenda of Political Ecology** 49

3. **Mismatch and Risks** 101

4. **Crisis of Nature and Nation - State** 133

5. **Political theories of Ecology** 171

6. **New directions for Ecopolitics** 239

7. **Contemporary Ecopolitics : A case study of india** 253

8. **North - South perspective** 275

9. **Towards a new Ecopolitical order** 291

Bibliography 333

Index 353

Foreword

Now, it is a globally accepted phenomenon that the cardinal purpose and moral obligation of a modern, welfare, democratic state is to provide its citizen with an amicable ambience for leading a happy and peaceful life. Mainly four factors are perceived to be fundamental for a healthy society—ecology as an essential commitment, social responsibility, grassroot democracy and nonviolence.

A large portion of industrial and nuclear units is owned by a few wealthy nations. They, on one end are reaping the benefits from these units, and on the other, the whole world is badly affected by the existence of these pollutant industrial units. Environmental problems have "physical" properties addressed by the natural science and they are shaped by social processes within an international context. There are also the political difficulties in solving environmental problems through any international decision making process dominated by big powers states. These influential nations always come in the way of finding a solution to the environmental problems worldwide.

A nation's environment has a direct bearing on its neighbours. The natural assets like forests can effect the climate of a nation and its neighbouring countries. Political ecology is the study of inter depend among political units and their environment. It is fundamentally concerned with the political consequences of environmental developments in both physical and symbolical senses. It can also be defined as an inquiry into the political sources, conditions and ramifications of environmental change.

In certain contxts, political ecology can be construed as the management of ecological scarcity. *Ecology* scarcity may be defined as the limits to growth and associated costs that appear when human development, amplified by expanding population and technology, emerges from exploitation of biospheres living and non-living resources. Political units are created to direct this exploitation and manage its economic social and environmental consequences.

In this age of rapid industrialisation and nuclear race the third world political ecology should attempt to develop on understanding of how environmental and political forces interact to mediate social and environmental change. We all depend on one biosphere for sustaining our lives. Yet each community and each country strives for survival and prosperity with little regard for its impact on others. Some section emerges community are consuming our earth's resources at a rate that would leave little for future generations. While the rest more in number—consume too little and are left to cape with hunger, squalor, disease and early death.

The ecologists stress that there are natural limits to a society and its political life. There is an intrinsic value in the non-humans who should be considered for moral evaluations.

Let us remember Mahatma Gandhi's words "The earth has enough to our needs, but not our greeds".

JAGMOHAN

Preface

The four fundamental principles by Charline spretnak and Fritjof Capres in their book "Green Politics : The Global Promise" are ecology as an essential commitment social responsibility, grassroots democracy and nonviolence. These fundamental principles are generally embraced by members of green groups. These principles reflect the thinking and spontaneous desire to act of a whole generation committed to the ecological cause share them without 'ever having seen them formally expressed as ideological principles.' The outside ecopolitics : An introduction by Hinstons Wilches—chaux in the book is based on his personal experience in Colombia.

Environmental have "physical" properties addressed by the natural sciences, and they are shaped by the social processes within an international context. Environmental problems also have a political context. These are political difficulties of solving environmental problems through international decision making processes dominated by sovereign states. David Potter in his article "Environmental problem in the political context" addresses two questions like what are the main features of the international political context of an environmental problem ? For answering this question the author makes clear the meaning of a number of rather abstract concepts like "political and power". By discribing the theory of sovereignty and looking at the state as one of the most important environmental change agents David Potter clears the second question. What is the significance of the "sovereign" state in relation to environmental problems ?

Two basic approaches for understanding governance issues are introduced in the chapters "political ecology and political economy". The ecology approach is a relatively new and untested field of inquiry, while the political economy perspective arises from a massive and systematic flowering of literature and analysis. Not surprisingly the dominant framework for understanding global environmental governance is that of International Political Economy (IPE) rather than ecology. The former focuses on the competitive relationships of nation-states, the latter focuses on the interdependence of communities while the study of political economy offers on indispersonable line of inquery for our purposes, it is by no means the only approach needed for understanding the pro and con of global environmental protection. In the broadest sense, political ecology may be defined as the study of interdependences among political units and interrelationships between political units and their environmental.

Raymond L. Bryant in his article "An emerging research agenda in Third World Studies" does a preliminary exploration of Third World political ecology. Throughout the article, it is suggested that third world politics ecology represents an attempt to develop an integrated understanding of how environmental and political forces interact to mediate social and environmental change.

The lack of sufficient correspondence between the legal political structure of world society (which is built out of presumably sovereign nation states) and the structure of the natural and artificial material environmental has become a matter of widespread and urgent concern; for which nature-altering technologies not being employed, humans are drastically affecting the conditions of life on the plannet without being held account for damage they are doing. This chapter (chapter-3) also investigates some dynamics in contemporary environmental politics. It argues that environmental politics now dominated by a discourse that might be labelled ecological lateralization. It presents an outline of this policy or regulation-oriented programme and gives a brief account of its history. Subsequently the chapter presents three ideal-typical interpretations of what ecological modernisation is about.

The attempt of democratic governments to address the environmental problems of great magnitude fills into two stages. The first policies are aimed at conserving wild life and natural resources and will include such measures as setting of hunting seasons and establishment of national parks. As the pace of industrialization intensifies the government will turn increasingly to the problem of air, water and ground pollution.

Chapter five of the book looks for the roots of political ecology, and traces a school of thought up to the present day. Instead of examining the cause of soil infertility or pollution or suggestions for preserving forests the author attempts to trace the reason why it was only from the mid-nineteenth century on that the European "thinking classes" worried about such matters.

Chapter 5 tells about "The development of Modern Ecopolitical Thought". If we look back over the ecopolitical literature of the last three decades, it is possible to discern three major ecopolitical preoccupations that can be encapsulated in themes of participation survival and emancipation. To some extent, these three themes may be seen as roughly characterising the general ecopolitical preoccupations of the last three decades respectively although this temporal association is a loose one only and should not be pressed too far.

Encounter of the ecology with normative political theory is duly dealt with Radical greens devism that ecology constitutes a new perspective in political theory which leaves behind the older longstanding traditions. They argue that there is a green view of society and politics and that specific social and political arrangements can be argued for new green grounds. The main issue in the encounter of ecology with political theory is whether ecology does undermine traditional political theories and constitutes new theory itself.

The world is addressing new issues, using new tools, and beginning to experience a new kind of politics. This shift is perceived to be a broader transformation in how we do the public's business in an increasingly information-based society. The current array of laws and regulations which set limits on the emissions of hundreds of individual chemicals and other pollutions, or they are protecting specific environmental values. Such as wilderness areas, endangered species, or the local quality of air and water. However, the new environmental issues transcend the current array of laws and regulations. The future of individual species and special places deponds on the health of broader ecosystems. The broad ecosystems as well as others that are less peculiar, are threatened by many kinds of pollution simultaneously not to mention the stress of human visitation and occupation. There is still much uncertainty about exactly how ecosystems function, but presently we are in the process of learning to protect them, for that public works, research, education, and public participation should be invested.

The chapter seven is on the ecopolitics in India during 1980's. This chapter concerns about ecopolitics in India which is mainly in the form of government's attitude towards environmental problems and environmentalists and policies they adopt towards the same it also deals with people's attitude towards environmental problems and their response in conserving and protecting sorroundings. The greenpolitics and ecopolitics in relation to India especially in the decade 1980's are discussed in the chapter. The implications are reverborated in the environment sector such as pollution levels touching the stars, forests and natural resources depleting of faster rates, soil erosion increasing in various forms, floods and droughts becoming common features etc.

The chapter eight tells about the North-South links inherent in today's grave environmental and need for an understanding. The need for developing countries except industrial countries to take the first and strongest actions on global warning is duly stressed. The decline of productive natural resources is rapidly emerging as a major threat to development prospects in most part of the third world. Developing countries are many times more dependent than industrial countries on their natural resources—their soils, fisheries, forests and minerals. And within developing countries the poor are dependent of all. Yet this resource source base is rapidly under pressure from unprecedented population growth, deep-seated social iniquities and misguided policies.

The last two chapters tell about he dire need of adopting a new post modernism which not only negates the cultural forms of modernity, but which can replace these forms. The development of postmodern science based on process philosophy which support post-structuralist or postmodernist attacks on the reunification of abstract entities is not enough to defend on new cosmology in opposition to the cosmology which has underpinned modernity. It is necessary to articulate in such a way that it can orient people in practice, in their daily lives, to create an environmentally substantial civilization. To do this it will be necessary to construct a new grand narrative, formulated in terms of cosmology based on philosophy of process.

1

Ecological politic : An Introduction

Ecology is regarded by greens more as an essential commitment and binding philosophy than an academic discipline. This is what I call *ecologism.* Ecologism isn't a science, an ideology, a political party, a new religion or business, much less a passing fashion. It may be better understood to be a certain *attitude* toward the world. It is like a philosophical concept, but also implies conduct consistent with a view of the world not as a collection of relatively abstract and transcendental concepts, but as a tangible reality, as much at the 'cosmic' level as at the level of daily life. Attitudes toward development, power, hierarchy, social conventions and rituals, sex, class struggle, science and technology, God, religion, politics, success, peace, nature etc., are all bound up in this 'green' attitude toward the world.

The fundamental objective of ecologism in the long term is not the conservation of renewable natural resources, nor the survival of endangered species of flora and fauna, nor the purity of rivers, the atmosphere or soil. The objective of ecologism, its reason for existence, is the construction of a more favourable society for human beings; one which is more just, honest and stable.

For such a society to exist it is necessary that there be clean air, water and soil, that the supply of natural resources doesn't expire, and that human happiness isn't built on the merciless destruction of other forms of life. Above all, it requires that the ephemeral economic prosperity of some isn't achieved through the exploitation of others; that the 'development' of some countries doesn't require the bleeding of others; that the construction of human culture doesn't imply the destruction of biological basis for life.

Many experts attempt to reduce the problems of nature to biochemical expressions, or imagine that the contradictions between nature and development can be resolved with short-term technological fixes, rather than by means of the construction of a new society. This is what is described by the Spanish journal *Alfalfa* as 'technobureaucratic ecofascism' : the monopolisation of ecology by the consumer society and its managers.

Ecologism, on the other hand, implies a profound departure from the pathway which has been unilaterally imposed on human beings by the dictatorship of production and consumption within capitalist society, within state capitalism, or within social imperialism under the aegis of the bureaucrats who administer the revolution.

According to Spretnak and Capra 'social responsibility' is the principle which, in Europe, has generated the most disagreement.

For me personally it is clear that if we accept that the environment and human society together form an immense network of interconnected elements interacting dynamically and continuously, we must infer that any group or individual action necessarily produces effects on other groups and individuals, or on the environment and relationships which constitute it.

From this it should be concluded that life in any of its forms has intrinsic value. Even if we deduce statistically and philosophically that in other parts of the universe other civilisations and other forms of life must exist, the Earth is the only planet where we know with absolute certainty that there is life, and we ourselves are part of it. Albert Schweitzer, a profoundly religious man, wrote what I consider to be fundamental to a secular ethic: 'The good consists of that which maintains, promotes and enhances life, and the bad consists of that which annihilates, impedes and damages life.'

Today we know that at least in the countries of the so-called 'Third World' destruction of the environment and its resources in the majority of cases is a result of the absence of economic opportunities for a growing mass of marginalised people from urban and rural zones. As their only means of survival these people transfer to the environment the daily degradation of which they are victims. We must likewise recognise that ecological conservation is a prerequisite for true development, since real long term development cannot be based on destruction of the environment.

According to Manfred Max-Neef there exist two opposing conceptions of development. One is the economists' vision of development, in which aggregate indicators such as Gross National Product (GNP) and the degree of market activity—whether the market transactions be productive, unproductive or destructive—are considered to be positive. The result is that indiscriminate depredation of a natural resource augments

GNP just as a sick population does when it increases its consumption of pharmaceutical drugs and its use of hospital services.

Even wars act to boost GNP, not in those countries where belligerent action takes place, but in those which produce arms, equipment, ammunition, uniforms, victuals, body-bags and everything else consumed by soldiers in combat.

A different approach, 'development at a human scale,' is described in Max-Neef's *Barefoot Economics* as follows:

"The other rationale has as its central axiom neither indiscriminate accumulation nor the improvement of conventional economic indicators—which tell little about the well-being of people—nor an efficiency divorced from the satisfaction of human necessities. This other rationale is oriented towards improvement of the population's quality of life and maintenance of respect for diversity. It renounces the conversion of some into instruments of others and of some countries into instruments of other countries..., to counter the economic logic, inherent in the utilitarian thinking which impregnates modern culture, it is necessary to promote the idea of an ethic of well-being. The development of the people should be put before and in opposition to the fetishism for statistics."

Everything which is said and done in favour of a more pacific cohabitation between the community and nature in Colombia, including ecological education and the protection of society against environmental disasters, is irrelevant if there is no priority given to the re-evaluation of human life. It is irrelevant if no consciousness is acquired of the lamentable fact that in our society violence and horror have become self-justifying processes, ever more distant from the economic and social causes which supposedly explain them.

We must begin to construct a 'society where there is space and fulfillment for all', where we all have the same rights and opportunities—not because we are all 'equal' or because we approach an ideal standard—but precisely because we are different, and because diversity is the source of cultural and evolutionary richness. If we don't attempt to build this new society we remain trapped between uncertainty and the binding spell of our fears.

Focusing on systems and interlinked relationships with human society leads inevitably to the fundamental principle of decentralisation. In an ecologically-based world view the vertical structure of hierarchical power would be replaced by non-linear structures of communication and relationship. The flow of information, and consequently of decisions, would be in different directions. Distinct levels can preserve their identity and autonomy, yet still are able to integrate into the system of which they are a part via common links ofbelonging and purpose. The concept ofhierarchy in terms of power is replaced by one of hierarchy in terms of level of complexity and organisation. With respect to this, Fritjof Capra wrote:

"The traditional symbol for the systems of domination and of control where decisions always flow from top to bottom has been the pyramid. In contrast the majority of living systems exhibit multilevel control in their organisations. They are characterised by the diverse and intricate channels via which the signals of information and transaction flow in a nonlinear fashion, ascending and descending between the different levels. For this reason I have inverted the pyramid and transformed it into a tree, a more appropriate symbol for the ecological nature of the stratification found in living systems. Just as a real tree draws its nutrition from both its roots and its leaves, the power in a tree of systems flows in both directions, without any one extremity acquiring supremacy over the others: all levels interact interdependently to benefit the united whole."

This alternative concept of power necessarily obliges the revision of the roles of, amongst others, leaders and their communities, administrators and their programmes, educators and their pupils, and external agents and the processes in which they intervene.

The political experience of the majority of citizens is limited to the formal right to elect and be elected. However, the political functioning of each individual should include active and critical participation in the life of the community. This requires many things: the creation of conditions which permit and stimulate self management, the generation of alternative values in order to redefine the course of society, the defense of the right to a physically and spiritually sane society, the questioning of the roles and standards assigned to us, the refusal to assume pre-established stereotypes in life, the winning of access to knowledge and to the means of communication, and the possibility to make one's existence a creative exercise and not a mere act of repetition.

Politics is too often confused with the activity of political parties and electoral mechanics; political commitment mistaken for the adhesion to a figurehead; and political ambition confused with access to official positions. Thus, what is known as politics consists exclusively of the professional exercise of politicians, and is no longer a process inherent in the life of society. If we accept that the human habitat is formed as much by strictly ecological relationships as by social and political interactions, we must accept that, in any educational programme with an ecological focus, the social and political should be included.

In Colombia, the constitutional reform of 1968 strengthens local government levels and promotes the active participation of communities, through actions ranging from the popular election of mayors to the formation of Local Administrative Committees in the jurisdictions into which each municipality is divided. This is a sure way to convert political action into a citizen's obligation. Even if the reform began successfully, its complete effectiveness requires a continuous process of reinforcement of civilian society.

Nobody in Colombia doubts that today the main threat to life and the quality of life of Colombians is violence. Statistics show that cardiovascular disease has ceded to homicide its first place in the list of causes of death of adults aged between 20 and 35. This only corroborates the notion that the immediate environment in which we develop our existence is plagued by threats and fears, to the point where one lucid graffitiist forged the concept of *miedo ambiente* (which translates as 'atmosphere of fear') instead of *medio ambiente* (which translates as 'environment').

The causes of violence in Colombia are diverse and sometimes contradictory, and their analysis is not the object of this study. However there is room to comment that although our country is one with great social and economic inequalities, a direct cause-effect relationship between poverty and violence does not necessarily exist. This is demonstrated, for example in Cauca, where in some regions poverty reaches its worst extremes. Yet these aren't the most violent regions. Apart from the objective causes there exist subjective causes embedded in our own cultural patterns, in our prevailing values, and in our vision of the world. To these we should turn to try to understand the self-feeding and to some degree self-justifying process which is bleeding our country.

Together with the more spectacular manifestations of terrorist violence—massacres, assassinations, guerrilla assaults, disappearances and kidnappings—more subtle and disguised forms of violence coexist. Every day there are minor and major acts of violence by the state against the civilian population, by authorities against the citizen, by the professional against the layman, by the political head against the public servant, by men against women and by adults against children.

One especially grave form of violence is that against the natural environment, since it is not just against forests and waters, but against the possibility of future generations to live with dignity and a decent quality of life. The violence against nature is rife in the length and breadth of the country, and constitutes an attempt against the right to life. It may be expressed as the blowing up of oil pipelines, or in the inveterate practice of exploitation of environmental resources, or in what I once named 'Plus Valia Ecologica', to express the practice of empowering oneself for lucrative ends with resources and conditions which belong to the whole community.

The philosophy of nonviolence toward our environment must be accompanied by many practices in daily life: tolerance, cohabitation, respect for others and for the rights of others, valuing diversity, using dialogue as a means of conflict resolution, and rejecting stereotypes and prejudices which impede the discovery of the human beings behind the labels and roles.

These postulates which inspire ecological politics cannot be alien to the principle that 'all is linked to everything... and vice versa.' The holistic vision and commitment of ecology, social responsibility, grassroots democracy and nonviolence are interconnected and interdependent aspects, which contain and are contained by one another. In practice they all act together towards the construction of a real democracy where life—in all its diversity—is respected and valued as a unique phenomenon.

Environmental Problems in their Political Context

Environmental problems have 'physical' properties addressed by the natural sciences, and they are shaped by social processes within an international context. Environmental problems also have a political context.

Two main questions are addressed. The first is: 'What are the main features of the international political context of an environmental problem?' This is a complex question, not least because to answer it requires making clear the meanings of a number of rather abstract concepts like 'political' and 'power'. The second main question considered is: 'What is the significance of the "sovereign" state in relation to environmental problems?'

Lake Toba

An environmental problem is defined as a change in the physical environment brought about by human interferences which are perceived by people to be unacceptable with respect to particular set of commonly shared norms. What has happened at Lake Toba since 1989 is an example of the development of an environmental problem.

Lake Toba is in North Sumatra (Indonesia), an area known for the rich cultural life of the local Batak people and the great natural beauty of the surrounding countryside and its forests. Since 1989 the area has changed in at least four main ways. (What follows in this section is based on WALHI, 1992.)

First, tropical forests have been degraded or destroyed. Aging stands of indigenous *Pinus merkusii* (planted during the Dutch colonial period) and mixed hardwoods have been logged extensively. In some cases, the forest has been clear-cut and replaced by fast growing eucalyptus plantations intended to supply wood for the pulp and paper industry. The former Harianboho Protection Forest near Lake Toba consisting of old growth trees and a rich biodiversity has been divided by a logging road; on one side are lush natural forests full of animal and plant life and on the other side is a dry, silent eucalyptus plantation. The microclimate has already begun to change; particularly around the plantation, the air and soil are becoming noticeably drier, increasing the area's vulnerability to forest fires.

Second, landslides are becoming more common. The watershed around Lake Toba is mountainous and erosion-prone; the forests are extremely important in preventing siltation in the lake and checking erosion in the mountains. Since 1989, landslides have increased with deforestation. Villages and ricefields have been buried and people killed. On the advice of forestry officials, Batak people in some villages have moved from the traditional multiple-family homes to single-family houses in the Javanese style, and in so doing have had their community life disrupted or destroyed.

Third, the water and the air in the region have become polluted. The colour of the River Asahan began to change in 1989 to dark brown, and the river began to stink due to a pulp and paper factory having commenced operations there. One consequence has been that nearby wells have been polluted, and women and children in the area have to travel further from their homes to obtain drinking water. Fish populations have declined sharply, threatening livelihoods. Officials in the factory have expressed concern that the stench so nauseates their employees that it affects their work.

Fourth, livelihoods of the local people more generally have been adversely affected. New laws enabled logging companies to 'own' former community forests, as on Samosir Island; local people were then forbidden to enter the forests and wood carvers found they had to 'steal' from 'their' former forest to keep up their traditional craft and means of existence. Basic family needs in Hutagalung village were threatened because the rattan (stems of climbing palms used to make wickerwork, thongs, etc.) culled from the nearby forest by women and then sold in local markets was no longer available. People in Habinsaran village who used to gather incense from the community forest were no longer able to do so.

Clearly, then this is an example of a developing environmental problem in the sense that there were human interferences in the physical environment perceived by local communities as disrupting commonly shared norms related to work patterns and livelihoods more generally.

What was causing the problem? For the local Batak people what was most visibly disrupting their livelihoods were the men who were cutting down the forests and planting eucalyptus trees. These people worked for a local commercial pulp and paper company called the Perseroan Terbatas Inti Indorayon Utama Ltd. or Indorayon for short. Indorayon was one of 30 such companies owned by the Raja Garuda Mas Group chaired by Sukanto Tanoto, the 'timber king' of Sumatra. Tanoto had rapidly made a fortune through his companies. In 1989 Indorayon alone made profits of $53.6 million; this was helped by the fact that production costs at $226 per ton of pulp were the lowest in the world. International bankers and investors had supported Indorayon from the beginning; a consortium of foreign banks provided commercial loans to aid the original investment and the Swiss Bank Corporation in 1992 approved the issue of convertible bonds worth $43.4 million to provide the finance needed to build Indorayon's pulp and rayon plant on the Asahan River near Lake Toba. Tanoto benefited; so did the banks.

People in the Forest Department and other government officials in the Lake Toba area broadly supported the activities of Indorayon. Such commercial activity was consistent with the broad strategy of the Indonesian government to pursue development for the country principally by providing infrastructure to enable the dynamism of capitalist enterprises like Indorayon to flourish. The results of this strategy prior to developments at Lake Toba had been impressive from the government's point of view. The average annual growth in Indonesia between 1965 and 1988 had been 4.3 per cent (GNP per capita), one of the highest rates in the world at the time (World Bank, 1990). One aspect of that strategy had been to invite private concessionaires, both domestic and foreign, to 'open up' the forests in 1965. Basic Forestry Law No. 5 of 1967 created vast logging concessions and the concessionaires moved in. By 1979 Indonesia had become the leading exporter of tropical logs in the world, with 41 per cent of the market. Logs were also processed into plywood; by 1985 Indonesia was the world's largest supplier of plywood. The forest business attracted international capital needed to spearhead Indonesian development in other spheres. It also provided foreign exchange to service the mounting debt owed to international, commercial and official institutions. The government's national forestry plan was also linked and shaped by the Tropical Forestry

Action Plan sponsored and funded by the World Bank, the UN Food and Agriculture Organisation, bilateral donors including the British government, and others. In all this, the social problems of the indigenous people who had been making a living from the forest received a low priority.

Village people in the Lake Toba region protested to local government officials at the loss of their customary rights of access to the forest and its products, but received little response. They also managed at one point to take Indorayon to court, and unsurprisingly, the court ruled against them. KSPPM (the Community Initiative Study and Development Group), a local non-governmental organisation (NGO), had worked with some of the local people trying to assist them in their struggle. KSPPM was one of hundreds of local NGOs in Indonesia linked to a national umbrella NGO in Jakarta called WALHI (Indonesia Forum for the Environment). WALHI in turn was linked to international NGOs like NOVIB in The Netherlands, Friends of the Earth (with international headquarters in Amsterdam), which worked to shift the forest policies of powerful organisations at international, national and local levels. Local NGOs in Indonesia have had a tough time against a powerful corporation supported by an authoritarian political regime. KSPPM at Lake Toba, for example, was closed down without explanation by the Indonesian government for six months in 1991 and 1992 and was only allowed to resume its activities on condition that it ended its legal aid programme to the local Batak people.

Main Features of an International Political Context

What are the main features of the international political context of an environmental problem like the one at Lake Toba ? Such features can be derived from a consideration of what the concepts 'international' and 'political' mean.

The word 'international' conventionally refers to engagements or interdependencies involving more than one nation state, at a level 'above' the nation state. The word is also used more generally to refer to both international and *transnational* interactions and associations. An international agreement is an agreement between nation states. Transnational linkages can be said to bypass governments because they are society to society relations, many of which are more or less beyond nation state control. There is an incredible array of such transnational relations, from Shell Oil Company to the International Confederation of Free Trade Unions, the World Council of Churches and the International Red Cross. Some people are beginning to refer to a global politics (McGrew et al., 1992) that includes both international and transnational behaviour.

Environmental politics involves both.

There is an ambiguity in the idea of the international context being 'above' the nation state. International contexts of environmental problems include the international/transnational, the national and the local *and the linkages between these different levels.* The environmental problem at Lake Toba brought this out clearly. International processes can also have a spatial dimension; they can press down more or less firmly on different localities at different times.

The key concept in the main question is 'political'. How one uses the concept is of paramount importance in determining what the 'main features' are. Although there is no agreed definition, one can say that, broadly speaking, the political aspect of social life is grounded in the antagonisms and conflicts that are more or less part of any set of social relations and it is about the ensemble of practices, structures, relationships and discourses which establish and maintain some sort of 'order' in such circumstances. Within that general context, for our purposes here, the word 'political' can be said to refer to four main aspects:

- *steering and choosing.*
- such steering and choosing are determined more or less by *conflicting interests and values.*
- they involve *power relations* within and between *agents,* such as organisations, groups and individuals.
- and they are shaped by *structures of power*—economic, social, ideological, cultural.

Defining the'political' that way suggests that a description of the international political context of an environmental problem can be framed in terms of these four main features. We will consider each of these four in the following sections.

The international context of an environmental problem involves steering or governing. The word 'governing' comes originally from the old French *guvernor* which is from the Latin *gubernare* (to steer, pilot, govern), which in turn derived from the Greek *Kybernan* or *Kubernao* (which means 'to steer'). Plato, for example, referred to the process of governing as similar to steering a ship at sea ('the ship of state'). Steering a ship at sea requires a number of things, like trying to stay in control in the midst of turmoil, charting a course and trying to achieve an objective (reach a destination). All these are important aspects of political leadership and to that extent Plato's analogy is quite suggestive. But the people being led are missing from this elitist analogy (rather typical of Plato). We prefer the analogy that has been around in Asia for a long time, of the ruler or political leader being like a person trying to ride a tiger in a particular direction, the tiger being the more or less obedient masses who must be coaxed along and who may, if goaded too hard, turn on the ruler and make big trouble. Steering the tiger involves a series of choices over time. If the tiger starts to become agitated, then the leader may choose to slow the pace for a while (e.g. delay action or amend legislation), let the tiger wander temporarily from its intended trajectory (*e.g.* compromise with the opposition), feed the tiger (e.g. bring out a 'people's budget' just before an election) or get out the whip (e.g. use the police and/or the army to force the people to accept the direction of the leadership). Steering processes are always part of the political context of any environmental problem.

There are always several different sets of organisations, each engaged in processes of steering in accordance with their interests and values, whose actions over time effect the environmental problem in various ways. Three such steering processes were indicated in the Lake Toba case sketched earlier. First, there was the network of institutions (the World Bank, the FAO, the Indonesian government, local government) engaged in trying to steer Indonesian society along a particular course of economic development, the consequences of which were affecting the forests and lifestyles of the Batak people at Lake Toba. Second, there was the network of Swiss Bank, Raja Garuda Mas, Indorayon, and loggers and pulp mill workers steering in accordance with their interests. Third, there was the Friends of the Earth International, WALHI, KSPPM, and local village people who were trying to steer developments in a somewhat different direction.

Steering involves a series of choices over time. Choosing is indeed central to steering. Any agent trying to steer in a certain direction, be it to maintain the status quo or to bring about change, is choosing all the times as it is swept along by the constraints and opportunities that confront it. To choose to steer in one direction inevitably means choosing not to steer in another, and those choices are political because they benefit some people more than others. A set of choices by an organisation, or a network of organisations and groups, over time amounts to a *policy*, defined here as a deliberate course of action by an organisation designed to achieve an objective. Identifying the political context of an environmental problem requires, amongst other things, trying to locate both the relevant agents whose actions or policies affect the problem and the constraints and opportunities that influence the policy choices made.

Politics is not just about processes of steering and choosing at different levels. The content of any particular environmental policy or course of action by an agent and its supporters usually entails a political project or purpose of some kind that expresses the values and interests and ideologies of those doing the steering, and that may or may not be shared by those being steered. The best way to get at the conflicting interests involved in any political context is to ask: who benefits? In whose interests is that particular environmental policy ? Any course of action by a powerful agent that bears on an environmental problem is going to be more advantageous to certain interests and less advantageous to others. For example, take the content of the Indonesian government's policy regarding the forests. Indonesia has the third largest tropical forest area in the world, and the Indonesian government has chosen to use the forests as an important springboard of national development by encouraging policies of large-scale exploitation of the forests for timber with little regard for the economic value of non-timber forest products like rattan and incense or the value of intact forests as a biodiversity bank. The government's policy is to convert the tropical forests into large scale concessions for commercial exploitation by wood-processing firms. Who benefits? Commercial loggers, industrial wood-processing industries, the banks, urban elites in the cities, others. Who loses? People who have depended on non-timber products from the forests, perhaps eventually people in the North and South who will be affected by global warming, future generations denied the biodiversity inherent in tropical forests, others. The matter is not that simple, and this example can be elaborated considerably; the illustration is only meant to underline the important political point that some benefit from the content of dominant courses of action, or policies, more than others. The political context of an environmental problem always involves mainfest or latent conflict between the interests of those who benefit greatly and those who benefit less or not at all.

Conflicts of interest can also divide the North from the South. On the issue of tropical forests, governments in the South are increasingly expressing the view that the North, having historically devastated their own forests and grown rich in the process, are now demanding that the South preserve their forests and stay poor. North-South international conflicts of interest are now a major aspect of the political context of environmental problems. Such conflicts shape policy debates in many settings. For example, at the annual meeting in 1992 of the International Tropical Timber Organisation, comprising representatives of the main producing and consuming states accounting for over 95 per cent of the international trade in tropical timber, there were major disagreements between northern and southern states over a proposed policy to regulate the cutting of timber. The South wanted an 'all-timber' agreement affecting northern and southern forests, the North wanted only a tropical timber agreement.

Political processes of steering and choosing at different levels are shaped by the conflicting interests of those involved. Ultimately, such processes are informed by values. Values are preferences and moral assumptions about what is good or desirable. Any course of action related to an environmental problem is going to reflect certain dominant values and not others. The course of action pursued by the Indonesian government *vis a vis* the forests at Lake Toba rests on a whole set of value preferences which have to do with competition, economic efficiency, the free market, and so on as the desirable way forward for national development and well-being, and at bottom the whole strategy may be said to rest on some moral conception about the value of individual freedom for entrepreneurs and others. Another strategy of development with rather different environmental consequences for the Lake Toba region would de-emphasise such values and give much more weight to sustainable forestry, collaboration, grassroots empowerment, the rights of local communities, and so on. This would amount to a different political project grounded fundamentally in a more egalitarian moral premise.

Naturally, political leaders and other involved in political processes will 'claim to be taking all factors into account when trying to reach a reasonable trade-off between conflicting values and interests' (Goldsworthy, 1998). They will say they are of course 'for' both freedom and equality, 'for' both enterpreneurial enterprise and grassroots empowerment, and so on. But no course of action can be anything like optimal for all the individuals, groups and social classes involved. What is optimal depends on the values you entertain and these differ between agents. Therefore, biases in favour of certain people and not others are necessarily embedded in environmental policies. That is why the environment is an intrinsically political subject.

Various organisations and other political agents inhabit the international political context of an environmental problem. Each agent is engaged in processes of steering and choosing as framed by conflicting interests and values, and each is also more or less powerful.

Power is like the air we breathe; it is everywhere and invisible. There is no universally agreed definition. There are instead a range of related but different definitions (Lukes, 1986); Robert Dahl, for example, defined it as the ability of A to get B 'to do something that B would otherwise not do' and Nicos Poulantzas said it was 'the capacity of a class to realise its specific objective interests'. What these different definitions share perhaps is the sense that individuals or organisations have power if they have the capacity to shape action. We shall use the word 'power' in this general way in this chapter.

Notice the word 'capacity'. A may have the capacity to shape the action of B, but A may actually do nothing; B's actions are nevertheless shaped by A because of what B thinks A could do. For example, a motorist, B, stops at a red light; the action of the driver is shaped by the power of the state, A, as represented in various ordinances and laws. No police or other state officials are in sight, the state does not act, but the power of the state nevertheless shapes the action of this motorist because of what the motorist thinks might happen if he or she breaks the law. This is what Poulantzas implies when he suggests that the structures of society can give a social class or other social organisation like the state the capacity to realise its objectives without actually 'doing' anything.

In any social context all agents, individuals and groups, may have some power, but of course some have it more than others. The more powerful usually have more, easier access to, political resources, e.g. physical strength, arms, wealth information, expertise, organisation, charisma, legitimacy, sanctions that can be applied to others, and so on. Measuring precise amounts of power is virtually impossible, but general evaluations of the relative power of any individual or organisation in relation to political resources are feasible.

The international political context of an environmental problem will comprise an extravagantly complex array of agents at various levels whose power, and the interests and values that give it direction, impinges on the problem. These agents comprise groups or organisations which either impact directly on the problem or shape the actions of others who are also directly involved. Moreover, these agents are located at different levels throughout the world and linked together by complex networks of communication and affiliation. Some organisations, like the World Bank, are fairly durable whereas others, for example, the Rio Earth Summit (though not the subsequent so-called 'Rio-process'), are more transitory. Some have full-time employees organized in bureaucratic hierarchies (e.g. governmental departments), others are informal groupings of volunteers animated by a common concern (e.g. Earth First! in the USA, the Chipko movement in India). There are also influential individuals who belong to no group or organisations.

To identify and delineate the relative power relations among all the individuals and informal groupings and organisations throughout the world that impinge directly or indirectly on environmental problems is beyond the capacity of anyone's political understanding, even in principle. However, it is possible and important to be able to identify prominent features of the international political context of any particular environmental problem.

A useful approach to understanding the international political context of an environmental problem is to start by trying to identify prominent organisations and groups and their relative power at local, national, and international levels and to notice the interdependencies between them. Each organisation or group will be steering and choosing in accordance with their particular interests and values, the consequences of which bear directly or indirectly on the international problem. At each level one should start by locating relevant organisations or groups in at least four different worlds; the world of government organisations; the world of business—industrial, financial and other economic organisations; the world of NGOs—organisations that are non-governmental and non-profit; the world beyond formal organisations, e.g. environmental movements, protest groups, voters.

Take Lake Toba. At the local level, organisations and groups in all four worlds were pursuing courses of action, in co-operation or conflict with each other, that shaped the problem there. From the world of business, Indorayon steered a course of action in pursuit of their interests in making profits from their logging, pulp and paper activities. Indorayon's interests were in conflict with the interests of local people wanting to use the forests in other ways. Indorayon was able to shape local activities to its advantage in this conflict because it had more power due to its command over substantial political resources in comparison with the limited resources of the unorganised Batak people. It also had the support of the State. Local officials of the Forestry and other departments of the Indonesian government administered the law, including Law No. 5 of 1967 making legal the forest concessions which Indorayon were using to their advantage. The local district court and the High Court ruled in favour of Indorayon when local people brought a case against them. The local police moved in and closed down KSPPM, the local NGO working for the local people against Indorayon, thereby tilting the balance of power even more towards Indorayon. Understanding the local political context, and the power relations involved helps to explain why the forests around Lake Toba were being adversely affected.

Such actions, conflicts and power relations that make up the political context locally do not take place in a vacuum. They are shaped by power relations of the four different worlds of organisations and groups at national level. For example, Indorayon's power locally is much enhanced by its being one of the companies in Tanoto's larger Raja Garuda Mas Group. The government of Indonesia's broad economic strategy, backed by the considerable power of the state apparatus, provides a favourable context for the Group's activities and Indorayon's actions at Lake Toba. The government of Indonesia, however, is not a monolith. It is a very large organisation, or rather set of organisations, and there are conflicts and inconsistencies within it. Thus, Emil Salim, a well-known Minister for Population and Environment for many years (until 1993), used to express himself fairly freely in Cabinet on behalf of environmental concerns and, although he was highly regarded, he was also regularly overruled by the Ministers for Forestry, Industries and others. Some progressive environmental legislation gradually found its way into the statute books. Emil Salim actually had good connections with all the environmental NGOs in the country, sometimes supporting their activities, at other times disagreeing sharply with them. Such national level tensions and inconsistencies among different Ministries within the government had an effect locally and compromised somewhat the overall power of the local state.

Two NGOs in Jakarta were also prominent at the national level of the political context. One was SKEPHI, a forest specific NGO. The other was WALHI, an umbrella organisation linking hundreds of local NGOs throughout the country; one of these local NGOs was KSPPM at Lake Toba. WALHI, represented by the Indonesian Legal Aid Foundation, brought a court case against Indorayon, the national ministries for Population and Environment, Forestry and Industries, the National Investment Co-ordination Board and the Governor of North Sumatra arguing that the Indorayon factory had been licensed without completing an Environmental Impact Analysis required by Indonesian law. WALHI lost the case, but won the right to stand for the environment, thereby setting a useful precedent in environmental law. Through these and other actions by local and national NGOs, the local Batak people could be said at least to have some representation in the Indonesian political arena.

Such representation, even if only rather marginal, is important given the authoritarian character of Indonesia's political regime. Indeed, WALHI and SKEPHI and other NGOs are tolerated by the Indonesian state as useful 'pressure valves' enabling middle class people to let off steam and ventilate their grievances; they are useful precisely because the Indonesian state does not permit competitive elections enabling voters from time to time to shape the compositions of the government. Also, civil and political rights appropriate to democratic regimes are severely compromised in Indonesia. Individual citizens have difficulty forming associations of like-minded people to lobby the government. Most people at Lake Toba, in short, have little influence, and this is an important aspect of the distinctive political context of the environmental problem there. Indorayon and the state do not rule supreme, but their capacity to shape action locally to suit their interests is impressive. The political context of, say, a local forest problem in a more democratic setting might look a little different.

Indorayon and the Indonesian state also do not reign supreme because their actions are shaped by the power of organisations at the international level. Indorayon's behaviour at Lake Toba, for example, was shaped by the need to service the loan from the Swiss Bank Corporation; and the Indonesian state forest policies that affect Lake Toba so profoundly, are shaped by a large and complex array of organisations and processes in the international arena. The most important international processes affecting the national state and the company relate to international debt, trade and aid.

As for debt, the data in Table 1 show that Indonesia owed over $53 billion to external creditors in 1989 (see column 5); of the ten main rainforest countries in Asia, only India, because of its great size, comes out in the table as more heavily in debt.

The problem for the Indonesian government of servicing that debt jumped substantially between 1980 and 1989 as columns 6 and 7 of Table 1 suggest. The Indonesian government has had to find a way to earn foreign exchange to repay rising debts. One thing the government has done is to exploit the large tropical forest (see columns 1–4) for timber and timber-based products, for which there is a substantial demand internationally. Overexploitation is the more appropriate word; Indonesia's deforestation rate of 12,000 square kilometres per year (see column 1) was by far the highest in Asia, and indeed in the world after Brazil. The connection between deforestation and debt has been widely acknowledged; for example, the EC said in 1989 that 'international debt obligations... can lead developing country governments to accelerate the rate of forest exploitation in order to earn needed foreign exchange' (reported in FOE, 1992,), and the Forest Principles agreed at the Earth Summit at Rio in 1992 recognised 'the importance of redressing external indebtedness'. Others dispute that there is a causal connection between international debt and deforestation.

Table 1. Deforestation and debt service ratios in some Asian countries; the 1980s Source; FOE (1992). Note: the debt figures were taken from World Bank (1991). The figures related to forest loss are from Myres (1989).

Country	*Annual deforestation rate (square kms) 1989*	*Forest already lost (square kms) 1989*	*Remaining forest (square kms) 1989*	*Percentage origianl forest remaining 1989*	*Total external debt 1989*	*Debt as a percentage of exports 1980/1989*	
Burma (Myanmar)	8.000	225.000	245.000	52	1.761	25.4	30.4
India	4,000	1,435,000	165,000	10	62,509	9.1	26.4
Indonesia	12,000	360,000	860,000	70	53,111	13.9	35.2
Kampuchea	500	53,000	67,000	56	nd	nd	nd
Laos	1,000	42,000	68,000	62	949	nd	15.6
Malaysia	4,800	148,000	157,000	51	18,576	6.3	14.6
Papua New Guinea	3,500	65,000	360,000	85	2,496	13.8	34.3
Philippines	2,700	200,000	50,000	20	28,902	26.5	26.3
Thailand	6,000	361,000	74,000	17	23,466	18.7	15.9
Vietnam	3,500	200,000	60,000	23	nd	nd	nd

The Indonesian government's rising debts are owed to private creditors, commercial banks, other governments (bilateral debt) and international organisations like the World Bank (multilateral debt). These organisations do not tell the Indonesian government to destroy the tropical forests, but the political leverage they have through Indonesia's debt obligations and the conditions attached to loans shapes the policies of the Indonesian government in the direction of exploiting a primary natural resource valued in the international market. Such international organisations are part of the international political context that affects the thinking of Indonesia's political leadership when they consider the forests in relation to national development strategy.

The Indonesian government also has had to contend with the politics of the international trade in tropical timber governed by the General Agreement on Tariffs and Trade (GATT), the ITTO (International Tropical Timber Organisation), northern governments and intergovernmental bodies. For example, in the decade or so after the Indonesian government promulgated the Basic Forest Law of 1967, many of the forest concessions from which logs were exported were dominated by large multinational corporations, e.g. Weyerhauser, Georgia Pacific, Sumitomo, Mitsubishi.

The economic benefits of these activities for the Indonesian government were modest. In consequence, the government decided in 1980 to ban the export of raw logs from 1985 onwards; they wanted to reap more benefit from the logging industry, build up their pulp and paper industries (which led to the establishment of Indorayon), and capture a larger share of the world plywood market. They also said the ban was environmentally sound. Fewer logs would be needed to earn the same amounts of hard currency. Most of the multinational companies left Indonesia in the next few years for easier profits in Papua New Guinea or eastern Malaysia.

Indonesia's plywood business boomed, most of it involving indigenous companies. In 1987, however, the EC complained to GATT that Indonesia's ban on the export of certain tropical hardwoods violated GATT rules. Eventually, the Indonesian government had to reverse its policy, notifying GATT in 1992 that the ban had been revoked and at the same time announcing also higher taxes on exports of raw timber. Once again, we see the national government's policies in relation to the forests being shaped by the power of international organisations and processes.

As for international aid, probably the most significant instrument affecting the Indonesian government's forest policy has been the TFAP (Tropical Forest Action Plan) under the direction of the World Bank, the FAO (United Nations Food and Agriculture Organisation), UNDP (United Nations Development Programme), and the WRI (World Resources Institute—a think tank in Washington DC). TFAP is a global mechanism meant to address the problem of deforestation by identifying priorities for action in individual developing countries that aid donors (including foreign governments) can target. About $8 billion was to be spent on such projects from the mid-1980s. Each national plan was to be worked out over a period of time by consultation between foreign experts and international donor agencies together with government officials in the country concerned. The Indonesian National Tropical Plan has not been made public but it is known that the main assumption of the plan is that the forest people, like the Batak at Lake Toba, are targetted as the main problem, not logging companies. There is no mention of the fact that the Batak people have been engaged in sustainable use of the forests for centuries. Here we have an example of international aid flowing in support of a particular view of the environmental problem in the forests that shapes and reinforces the national government's view of it. Such processes are therefore also part of the international political context.

NGOs, North and South, are also part of the international political context affecting national government policy and the actions of companies and corporations working in the forests. Reference was made earlier to such NGOs in the Lake Toba case, e.g., NOVIB in The Netherlands and FOE (International). NGOs and North-South coalitions have continued to press for changes in environmental policy at international levels. They have, for example, been critical of TFAP, e.g., 'the plan not only is failing dismally to meet its objectives, but will actually accelerate the already catastrophic rate of forest loss world wide' (Lohmann and Colchester, 1990); and 'an ecological Frankenstein has been unleashed' (Rich, quoted in Ekins, 1992). NGOs have also proposed alternatives, e.g. TFAP should be a bottom-up process involving centrally the people who live in the forests, not a top-down process controlled by northern and southern elites. NGOs lobby at meetings of GATT, ITTO, the World Bank, northern governments. They attempt to shift the activities of companies and corporations; RAN in San Francisco, for example, regularly demonstrates against the Mitsubishi Corporation at trade fairs in the USA, drawing attention to destructive practices of Mitsubishi companies in tropical forests. Such NGOs and NGO coalitions have fewer political resources than governments and corporations and are therefore less powerful, but they do have some influence at times in limiting damage or hastening environmentally friendly decisions which would otherwise have taken longer.

The previous sections have emphasised that the international political context of an environmental problem involves the *actions* of four worlds of political organisations (government, business, NGOs, social movements) and other political actors who, as agents, are more or less powerful at international, national and local levels. This aspect can be referred to as the *agency* of power—the actions of specific organisations or groups that shape behaviour and choices affecting the environment. Dahl's definition of power, referred to earlier, is mainly about this aspect of power—'the ability of A to get B to do something that B would otherwise not do,

There is, however, another aspect of power. The contemporary international political context of an environmental problem involves structures of power inherited from the past, accumulated legacies of past practices and beliefs and past privilege. Poulantzas' definitions of power— the capacity of a class to realise its specific objective interests'—is more in keeping with this aspect. He is implying that the structure of society generally can enable a social class, e.g., a capitalist class, to benefit without it actually 'doing' anything. Identifying the international political context of an environmental problem requires being alive both to the agency and structure of power relations bearing on the problem.

Structure and agency are intimately related. Political organisations and groups as agents adopt policies, pursue courses of action, co-operate or run into conflict with each other. Their actions as agents are shaped by structure of power or underlying processes of a more enduring kind over which they have little or no control. For example, WALHI and SKEPHI in Indonesia pursue policies meant to safeguard the tropical forests there and the interests of people who live in them. These NGOs are in conflict with other political organisations and groups, like Indorayon and the Indonesian government, in ways which also have consequences for the forests and the people in them. But this interorganisational activity does not take place in a vacuum. It is framed by structures of power which help to determine the outcomes of political struggles between the groups and organisations by being more favourable to some groups than others.

Four dimensions of power structure can be identified: the economic, the social, the ideological and the political:

- *Economic structure of power* : All political struggles inhabit, for example, a global economic structure of power, a dynamic world of global capitalism dominated by private ownership, production for profit, the accumulation of profit, competitive struggle between large corporations and companies, reliance by such organisations on wage labour and continuing tensions between owners and workers in such organisations. The Indonesian state is powerfully influenced to manage its economy within that context for that is the world it inherited from the past and inhabits now. Its policies in relation to its tropical forests are shaped profoundly by the constraints of that economic structure. Also, capitalist organisations like Indorayon using the forests for capital accumulation and profit are, broadly speaking, advantaged by that economic structure more than environmental NGOs (which are non-profit) and local people using the forests for their own needs.

- *Social structure of power* : That general way of organising economic production tends to create and sustain particular social structures of power—class, gender, ethnic and other interlocking inequalities which are relatively entrenched. Powerful interests are served by, and organised in relation to, these structures from which they benefit. By enhancing their power, the social structure enables such interests to have a disproportionate influence on environmental policy.

- *Ideological structure of power* : Dominant ideologies—sets of collective beliefs—can also be said to form a structure of power. Such ideologies help people to make sense of, and accept, the prevailing social structure from which ruling groups and other powerful interests benefit. There can also be counter-ideologies which question the existing structure and serve the interests of subordinate groups (Ekins, 1992). Environmental movements and NGOs representing them may be said to be advancing new ideologies—new ideas about the forests, for example, which see them not as a resource to be plundered for profit by the few but as a precious asset to be sustained for all for the benefit of present and future generations.

- *Political structure of power* : Environmental policy makers also must work within the constraints and opportunities provided by political structures of power. An environmental NGO, for example, is confronted by an international system of nation states and other international organisations: even if many NGOs get together they cannot immediately get rid of that system and replace it with, say, an environmentally-friendly world government. Governments, corporations, NGOs and other political organisations and groups must work within that political framework and understand its particular configurations of power in order to advance their particular interests. Similarly, within particular societies, politicians and other political actors inherit a political structure and set of political processes which they cannot do much about, at least not immediately.

So far it has been suggested that identifying the international political context of an environmental problem requires paying attention to four main features:

- There are those general processes of steering and choosing by governments, economic organisations, NGOs and other political organisations at international, national and local levels. Such processes produce, amongst other things, environmental policies or courses of action by organisations that cause or otherwise affect the environmental problem.
- There are the interests and values expressed in the content of such policies affecting the environmental problem and other conflicting interests and values not expressed there. Identifying a political context means comprehending such conflicting interests and values related to the policies of various powerful organisations, and recognising whose interests are better served by those policies.
- There are the myriad political organisations and other political agencies whose actions affect the environmental problem, each of which is more or less powerful. They can be grouped roughly into the worlds of government, business, NGOs, and social

movements at local, national and international levels.

- There are more enduring structures of power that shape the power and actions of political organisations, determine whose interests and values prevail, and frame the processes of steering and choosing at different levels.

Political Contexts: Variation and Change

The story of the deforestation at Lake Toba provides four abstract features of the political context of an environmental problem. Of course, deforestation is only one environmental problem. All environmental problems have political contexts containing processes of steering and choosing at different levels, conflicting interests and values and relations of power. But each political context has distinctive features. In the following section a wider array of examples is used to demonstrate four different dimensions which help differentiate the political context of environmental problems:

- *Scope and scale of the environmental problem* : First, political contexts vary depending on the scope and scale of the environmental problem. Some problems are global, e.g. depletion of the earth's ozone layer ; others are local, e.g. pollution of Brighton beach in southern England. The political context of the former is distinct from the one at Brighton beach because of the sheer number of political agencies involved and the greater complexities of reaching agreed courses of action due to the wider array of values and interests that need to be accommodated. What makes ozone a global environment problem (and pollution at Brighton beach not a global problem)? One of two criteria must be satisfied (Porter and Brown, 1991): either the environmental consequences of an economic activity (e.g. producing CFCs and halons) are global or the political actors (state and non-state) involved transcend a single region of the globe. Deforestation at Lake Toba is therefore also a global environmental problem because the political actors involved certainly transcend a single region and the consequences of the activity there have at least a marginal impact on the loss of biodiversity and global warming.

- *Control of environmental problem* : Political contexts also vary depending on whether or not the activity producing the environmental problem is considered to be under the control of a nation state. Some activity takes place in areas not under such control, like the atmosphere, the oceans and the deep sea bed. Such areas are part of the so-called global commons, and there are distinctive political features of international efforts by so many states to manage the commons (Vogler, 1992). The political context of such problems in the global commons is distinctive by virtue of the relevant conventions and protocols that have been agreed or by the efforts to reach such agreements. We will come back to such agreements in a moment. Other global environmental problems not part of the commons are more firmly under the jurisdiction of nation states. Tropical forests and land degradation are examples. The political context of such problems is distinguished by the greater prominence of states trying to insist on their 'sovereign' right to control their forests or land for their own benefit rather than necessarily in accordance with the interests of some global constituency.

• *Advancement on the environmental agenda* : Political contexts also vary depending on the extent to which the environmental issue has advanced on the global environmental agenda. That agenda has now been agreed, at least in principle, by virtually all of the nation states when government leaders accepted Agenda 21 at Rio de Janeiro in 1992 (see Chapter 1 and Box 1).

Some of the issues in Agenda 21 are further advanced than others, in the sense that they are the subject of multilateral conventions and protocols among at least some nation states. (For detailed discussion on conventions, protocols and other legal instruments). Furthest advanced, perhaps, by the mid-1990s was ozone; fairly tough multilateral agreements had been reached. Other issues were less well advanced. For example, there were no agreed conventions or protocols on fresh water resources and water quality, land degradation and desertification or deforestation and degradation of forests; and there was only a Framework Convention on Climate Change, agreed at Rio. Once conditions and protocols are agreed, then there are implementation stages involving monitoring and verification and political actors working to bring other relevant actors into the agreements in order to strengthen them. The political context of environmental problems can vary depending on whether multilateral agreements are strong, weak or non-existent. Explaining why an environment issue moves from one stage to another involves identifying and analysing its political context, including the transnational political processes relating to that issue.

• *The 'level' of democracy* : Lastly, the political context of an environmental issue can vary depending on whether the political regime involved is more or less democratic (see Box 2).

Democratic regimes may be more open and less secretive, with more independent and outspoken media, and are therefore more willing to accept the monitoring and verification procedures that are an essential element in implementing and ensuring the credibility of multilateral environmental agreements. Democratic regimes are also more likely to enable environmental NGOs to flourish, and to be allowed to participate in environmental policy making. Democratic regimes, however, do not necessarily always provide environmentally advantageous political contexts. Also environmental disasters may be so palpable that they will achieve prominence on the political agenda regardless of whether a regime is democratic or not. Despite such ambiguities regarding the general relationship between democracy and the environment, it is clear that the political context of an environmental problem, including the relative power of different political organisations and groups, will look somewhat different depending on whether relevant political regimes are more or less democratic.

Box 1

Environmental issues in Agenda 21

Agenda 21 is a long document but one can say that there are broadly ten issues on the global agenda:

- atmosphere pollution
- ozone depletion (in the stratosphere)
- climate change
- marine pollution
- freshwater resources and water quality
- land degradation and desertification
- deforestation and degradation of forests
- loss of biological diversity
- environmental disasters
- environmentally sound management of toxic, hazardous and radioactive wastes.

See: Tolba (1992).

A point which needs to be emphasised is that political contexts change through time. Take, for example, in reverse order the four points just made about the variability of political contexts.

Box 2

What is a democratic regime ?

Democratic regimes are distinguished by at least the following: rulers are accountable to the ruled through representative assemblies and governments formed at regular intervals through competitive elections based on universal adult suffrage involving multiple political parties providing reasonable choice for the voters; there is a diversity of power centres within the state and in society generally; there are guarantees in law of civil and political rights and freedoms; there is political participation by people throughout society in collective decisions that directly affect their lives. Democracy has historically been about lessening the unequal distribution of power, about the empowerment of subordinate classes and groups through the vote, representation and increased political participation in the collective concerns of society (Rueschemeyer *et al.*, 1992).

First, political regimes can change as authoritarian regimes move in a more democratic direction, a process of political change called democratisation. In the 1990s democratisation has been occurring in a number of countries in Eastern Europe, Asia and elsewhere, and there have been a number of attempts to explain this phenomenon (*e.g.* in Held, 1993). It is possible that the potential for more effectively tackling environmental problems in these regions may be enhanced as democratisation proceeds. Then again, it may follow that environmental problems will not be tackled, at least not at first.

Second, political contexts change when conventions and protocols are agreed. Parties to such agreements then begin to meet on a more regular basis to discuss both the implementation of the environmental agreement and strategies for getting other relevant political actors to join. Changing legal and other constraints also changes the political context. For example, the Montreal Protocol on Ozone in 1987 committed signatories to specific reductions in CFC and halon manufacture. The 1990 London Conference then tightened these regulations, committing developed country signatories to a complete phase-out by the year 2000 and the possibility of economic sanctions in cases of non-compliance. The political context of the ozone problem by the mid 1990s had changed considerably from what it was only ten years previously.

Third, political contexts of environmental problems in the global commons change as the technological capability to exploit the commons increases. For example, traditionally the ocean commons were open to all for use beyond the famous 'three mile limit', the reason being that the prevailing technology was such that anyone's cannon shot could not travel further than about three miles. More recently, new technologies have changed the nature of the ocean commons and the uses made of it, some of which are polluting, and these dangers have stimulated multilateral conventions and protocols regulating activities at sea, e.g. the 1972 Convention on the Prevention of Marine Pollution by Dumping of Wastes and other Matter; the 1976 Convention for the Protection of the Mediterranean Sea against Pollution, and several related protocols.

Fourth, the political context of environmental problems is changing as the scope and scale of economic and technological activity, and its adverse environmental consequences, are increasingly globalised. This has led to the increasing globalisation of environmental politics. One consequence of this is that there has been a marked increase lately in co-operative endeavour by states and international agencies in the form of agreed conventions and protocols, which are seen as necessary to deal effectively with many contemporary environmental problems. In short, political contexts are changing as 'sovereign' states acting alone find themselves unable to cope with environmental problems having global causes and consequences. This leads to the subject of the final main section of this chapter.

Sovereignty and the State

The nation state (and its power) has figured importantly in the discussion so far. Notice that the state's power is conditional (see Box 3). The state *seeks* predominance and *aims* to institute binding rules. What this underlines is that the state's predominance may be strong and effective, but it may also be weak and reflexive, so weak indeed that the state's power may really be of little consequence beyond the walls of the political leader's compound.

Conventionally allied to the idea and reality of the state, but distinct from it, is the theory of *sovereignty*. This amounts to a claim by the state to supreme authority over the people within its jurisdiction and over the course of events (both social and physical) within its domain (Camilleri and Falk, 1992). This claim by each state is legally recognised in principle by all the others, creating a world partitioned into separate domains with (in principle) uncontestable physical boundaries, each sovereign state having supreme authority over its particular society, economy and ecology.

Box 3

What is the state ?

The state is an ensemble of political institutions—coercive, administrative, legal—distinguished from other organisations in society in 'seeking predominance over them and in aiming to institute binding rules over the activities of other organisations within its boundaries' (Azarya, 1988). Each state also aims to provide security from foreign intervention for people within its boundaries by conducting relations, both peaceful and warlike, with other states. A state also seeks continually to promote a sense of national identity and common citizenship in order to have its rule accepted by the people (or at least some of the people) as legitimate, and in doing so to define away or suppress competing ideologies subversive of the state's rule and what the state defines as 'the national interest'. This process of legitimation is central to the reproduction through time of any state form.

The theory of sovereignty not only sharply delimits space in this way; it also presupposes that the state's supreme authority extends indefinitely backwards and forwards in time. State leaders have regularly proclaimed their 'sovereign right' historically to such control, free from 'outside interference' in the country's internal affairs. Over time, these ideas have become an important ingredient of the state's political consciousness, invoked frequently by political leaders to explain and justify state policies and actions and widely believed in society more generally.

Despite the power of the idea, the theory of sovereignty has always been a legal fiction. Historically, powerful states have intervened repeatedly in the affairs of weaker states; and the legal sovereignty of a state has always been more or less compromised in practice by transnational economic and social processes. Although thoughtful observers have always recognised the 'tensions between interdependence and sovereignty in world politics' (Di Muccio and Rosenau, 1992), by the 1990s the mismatch between the theory of sovereignty and the political reality of the modern world was becoming increasingly obvious. President Bill Clinton remarked in his Inaugural Address in January, 1993 that 'there is no clear division today between what is foreign and what is domestic'. In Europe in the 1990s, it has been argued that 'all *significant* societies are either larger or smaller than the nation state' (Mulhern, 1993). The mismatch is nowhere clearer than in the difference between the description of reality implied in the theory of sovereignty and the dynamics of the environment.

It is transparently clear that environmental problems, their causes and consequences do not come tidily packaged within the confines of states. Even the problem at Lake Toba, seemingly a very local affair within a nation state, is seen upon careful examination to be shaped by an international political context. States rarely have 'supreme authority' over environmental problems, as the theory of sovereignty presupposes, because their environmental policies are determined more or less by international debt obligations, international trade arrangements, other international economic agreements and conditions, international security arrangements, international environmental conventions or protocols broader class structures as well as domestic political considerations.

This does not mean that power is of no consequence. Indeed, states are still more or less autonomous and powerful within the international political context and what they do or fail to do can have major positive or negative impacts on environmental problems. But states are not sovereign even though state leaders still like to proclaim that they are. Even with regard to those environmental problems, where the state apparently rules supreme, the theory of sovereignty is misleading (see Box 3).

Nuclear power provides a good example. This would appear to be pre-eminently a matter in which each state has had 'supreme authority' (sovereign power) to opt for a nuclear industry, develop it, control crucial aspects of the nuclear fuel cycle even after transferring some aspects of it to private companies, defend nuclear power by obscuring from public view its environmental hazards, and so on. Yet even nuclear power has an international political context. For example, the apparent freedom of the state to determine a 'need' for nuclear power has often been shaped by strong pressure from external nuclear vendor companies, who work with international banks to provide low-interest loans to enable states to purchase nuclear reactors on favourable terms. Such foreign technologies, once obtained, can lead to the receiving state relying increasingly on international vendor companies for expert advice, replacement parts, maintenance and so on (Camilleri and Falk, 1992). Attempting to understand the causes of state decisions about nuclear power is not helped by a theory of sovereignty which ignores the international political and economic context in which the state acts.

Nuclear power also provides a classic example of how the theory of sovereignty fails to cope with environmental consequences. As it shows, when the Chernobyl reactor near Kiev caught fire on 26 April, 1986, it spewed clouds of radioactive gases into the air for ten days which drifted easily across many states in Europe and elsewhere causing significant increases in radiation levels and threatening the lives of state citizens. It was a stunning demonstration of the mismatch between the theory of sovereignty and the reality of modern technologies which can pose environmental risks beyond the control of any one state.

Generally, then, the theory of sovereignty is a poor guide to the role of the state in environmental problems. More than that, it is actually misleading because it can obscure both the causes and the consequences of such problems. In addition, according to Camilleri and Falk (1992), there are at least three other implications to be drawn from the theory of sovereignty that have adverse consequences for environmental problems and political efforts to cope with them.

First, the theory insulates the state from the internatioanl environmental consequences of its actions. Each state claims the 'sovereign right' within its domain to make decisions on complex environmental problems. Such decisions may have appalling environmental consequences for people living beyond the state's domain but the theory of sovereignty enables that state of defend such decisions as legitimate choices by a sovereign power with supreme authority. Furthermore, other states in principle respect their sovereignty.

Second, the world being divided into many sovereign states, each respecting the sovereign right of others, makes for a formidable impediment to concerted action to meet environmental challenges transcending state boundaries. Anyone who has been involved in trying to orchestrate interstate agreements in the form of environmental conventions and protocols can attest to the difficulties posed by representatives of states insisting on not compromising their 'sovereign rights' over activities within their domain. The history of such agreements that have been reached has been marked by efforts to overcome what can be called the discourse of sovereignty. For example, the negotiations between France, The Netherlands and Germany on measures to protect the Rhine against pollution eventually had to rise above the sovereignty discourse; according to that discourse, France, for example, could do what it liked in relation to a river flowing through its domain. As one expert remarked after an interstate agreement about the Rhine had been reached, 'legal developments concerning protection of the Rhine against pollution show that nothing can be done in this field at the national level. Pollution control in Europe requires international co-operation...' (Kiss, 1985).

Third, a collection of many sovereign states each with their own laws and regulations enables organisations whose activities are polluting or otherwise environmentally damaging to move from countries that adopt strict environmental controls to other countries whose laws are less strict. In this way, the theory of sovereignty serves the interest of a transnational polluting industry, for example, by enabling it to argue that the state to which it has shifted its operation has the sovereign right to decide what laws and regulations are best for its particular domain, and that we, the polluting industry, are merely pursuing our legitimate interest within the laws of that state. An example is Union Carbide locating one of the dirtier aspects of their pesticides business in Bhopal, India, where enforcement of national legislation to regulate safety measures at pesticides factories was not rigorous. In 1984 an emission of lethal gas at the Union Carbide plant in Bhopal killed an estimated 3000 people (at least), injured at least 200,000 more, and had devastating environmental consequences (Shrivastava, 1992).

The theory of sovereignty—that states have 'supreme authority' within their boundaries—is both a legal fiction and a powerful idea with important environmental consequences. It is fiction because the state has never had such supreme authority and people and environments within states have always, and increasingly today, been affected by transnational processes over which states have little or no control. It is still a powerful idea, however, because many state leaders regularly proclaim as real their sovereign right to determine the destiny of the national community (even through they know better), many people still actually assume (without really thinking about it) that states have such supreme authority, and leaders of other states continue to respect (or at least pay lip service to) the claim because it strengthens their own claim and sense of self-importance. As the 20th century draws to a close, the charade of sovereignty is being increasingly exposed by global economic processes of production and exchange beyond state control, by global political processes that shape what states can and cannot do, by modern technologies that 'shrink the globe' and ignore the state, by environmental problems whose causes and consequences implicate many states, and by other globalising processes.

It does not follow from this expose of the theory of sovereignty that the state itself is becoming increasingly unimportant. The idea of the state and the theory of sovereignty are two quite separate things, as was made clear earlier. States are not sovereign but they are powerful, and in some setting very powerful, within international political contexts. Indeed, a smaller or weaker state may actually become more powerful or influential when it abandons the pretext of sovereignty and joins other states in forming interstate agreements binding on all of them.

Within international political contexts the state can be profoundly important in relation to environmental problems in three general ways. First, the state as a *powerful agent* in society can adopt and implement policies nationally or locally that directly cause environmental problems or exacerbate ones that already exist. The British government during the 1980s and early 1990s, for example, pursued a policy (pressed on it by the Central Electricity Generating Board) of not fitting antipollution equipment to its largest power stations. The possible effects on trees in Norway, Germany and other European countries downwind of these power stations had been widely publicised for years. Less well known until recently was the effect on British trees; a joint survey in 1993 by the EC and the UN Economic Commission for Europe reported that the proportion of trees moderately or severely affected by 'blight' was higher in Britain than in any other of the 34 European and former Soviet countries surveyed, and that virtually all scientific and other experts in Europe (apart from the state-owned British Forestry Commission) were now almost certain that the 'blight' throughout Europe was caused principally by that noxious brew of pollutants to which the British power stations made such a significant contribution (Lean, 1993).

Of course, the state as a powerful agent in society can also adopt and implement policies that directly contribute to the solution of environmental problems or result in distinct improvements. For example, the implementation of the Clean Air Act passed by the British Parliament in 1956 contributed (along with changes in central heating fuels, fewer sources of industrial pollution and lower density developments) to the gradual reduction in levels of coal dust that had hitherto afflicted the people of London.

Second, the state can deliberately provide an *enabling structure* for other organisations and groups in society whose actions directly affect environmental problems. One such enabling structure is the particular content and character of the law and of law enforcement agencies administered by the state which non-state economic organisations, NGOs and others can use in various ways which have direct consequences for the environment. Another enabling structure may be said to be the set of economic policies favourable to capitalist accumulation, including policies to control the labour force, which provide essential infrastructure for capitalist economic development which may or may not be environmentally sustainable. An illustration from this chapter of how important both these enabling structures in combination can be is the way in which the Indonesian government in 1967 created vast logging concessions in much of the country's tropical forest which enabled private capitalist logging companies to move in and make huge profits with devastating environmental consequences at Lake Toba and elsewhere.

Third, the state can be a *structural obstacle* blocking advances towards more environmentally sustainable forms of development. In this aspect, the state neither deliberately creates enabling structures nor actively makes environmental policy. Instead, it does nothing (structural power), but its sheer presence blocks avenues of advance for people whose livelihoods are threatened by disturbances of physical resource upon which they depend and who want to do something about it. When the state is perceived by ordinary people—peasants, workers, others—as such an obstacle, then forms of collective struggle may be generated which combine defense against further threats to their livelihoods with resistance to the structures of the state and the power of capitalists and landlords who benefit from those structures (see Box 4 for an example).

This example of Chipko shows that the three aspects of state power are not mutually exclusive; through time the Indian state moved from being a structural obstacle to initiating as an agent a particular course of action. Furthermore, a state can even be simultaneously a powerful agent regarding environmental problem A, provide an enabling structure for environment problem B, and be a structural obstacle for environmental problem C. Whatever the combinations, it is clear that the power of the state in relation to environmental problems is such that it can both be a major part of the problem and provide a major part of the solution. The state through its actions or sheer presence can do great environmental damage, but state policies can also be environmentally beneficial and when international environmental protocols are agreed to control certain activities having adverse environmental consequences, it is currently only the state which is in a position to enforce such agreements.

This chapter has dealt with two main questions:

- What are the main features of the international political context of an environmental problem ?
- What is the significance of the 'sovereign state' in relation to environmental problems ?

Box 4

The emergence of Chipko Aandolan (literally translated as the 'hugging' movement) in the foothills of the Garhwal Himalaya

In India in the 1970s, in response to growing threats to their livelihoods from logging operations and growing dissatisfaction about the distribution of profits from forest resources to forest contractors through the 'contract system' maintained by the state, village people, especially women, began to hug trees identified for the chop and these actions were so successful that they spread more widely in the Himalaya and elsewhere in India (Khator, 1991; Guha, 1991). The targets of the movements included state officials, who were perceived as in alliance with the contractors. Chipko became an environmental movement, a struggle against economic exploitation, and more generally an effort to undermine the structural obstacle of the Indian state. Eventually, in 1980, the state stopped being an obstacle and acted (a little). The Prime Minister (Indira Gandhi) declared a temporary ban on logging in the Gardwal Himalaya.

In approaching the first question it was necessary to define the word 'political' and then to use the definition to suggest that an environmental problem always has a political context because it is affected by processes of steering and choosing which are favourable to certain interests and values (and not others) and which involve relations of power. In dealing with the first question it was suggested that the tough business of identifying the international political context of an environmental problem means paying attention to those four main features in the definition of the word 'political' as they relate to the problem. The example of the environmental problem at Lake Toba was used here.

As for the second question it was argued that states are not 'sovereign' in the sense of having supreme authority over people and events within their boundaries, even though many people still believe that states are sovereign and this belief has environmental consequences. But although not sovereign, states are certainly more or less powerful and autonomous within international political contexts, and they have the capacity to affect environmental problems positively or negatively in profoundly significant ways by virtue of their power as agents and structures.

So what ? Does knowing about the political context of environmental problems actually matter to anyone besides academic people who write chapters in books ? The answer is that it matters very much to anyone wanting to understand who or what is causing an environmental problem. If people in an NGO, for example, understand that the causes are at least partly political, and if they perceive correctly who or what they are up against politically and who or what to target, then they are more likely to work collectively in ways that may result in their being more successful in achieving their objectives.

2
Agenda of Political Ecology

Let us examine the institutional design questions that arise in changing that process in order to construct more effective environmental policies and regimes. Two basic approaches for understanding governance issues are political ecology and political economy. The ecology approach is a relatively new and untested field of inquiry, while the political economy perspective arises from a massive and systematic flowering of literature and analysis. Its origins can be traced to Adam Smith's *Wealth of Nations* (1776) and perhaps even earlier. Not surprisingly, the dominant framework for understanding global environmental governance is that of international political economy (IPE) rather than the ecology. The former focuses on the competitive relationships of nation-states; the latter focuses on the interdependence of communities.

While the study of political economy offers an indispensable line of inquiry for four purposes, it is by no means the only approach needed for understanding the ebb and flow of global environmental protection. Another and perhaps deeper basis for understanding can be found in the application of ecology to the art of governing. In the broadest sense, political ecology may be defined as the study of interdependence among political units and of interrelationships between political units and their environment. It is fundamentally concerned with the political consequence of environmental change—in both a physical and a symbolic sense. A second more restrictive definition renders political ecology as "an inquiry into the political sources, conditions, and ramifications of environmental change" (Brayant, 1991 : 165). Here, the direction of inquiry is reversed and the emphasis is placed in the physical environmental consequences of political decision making. In this second definition, the goal of political ecology can be construed as the management of ecological scarcity. Ecological scarcity may be defined, following Ophuls and Boyan (1992 :

175), as the limits of growth and associated costs that appear when human development, amplified by expanding population and technology reaches diminishing returns from exploitation of the biosphere's living and nonliving resources. To larger extent, political units are created to direct this exploitation and to manage its economic, social, and environmental consequences.

Today, the only political unit considered important in this regard are the 189 or so nations that declare a sovereign right to transform that portion of nature lies within their territories into the resources for consumption or trade. In political economy terms, these nations ultimately determine the property right in natural capital (e.g., forests) and, through their control over the domestic use or exchange of this natural capital in international trade they help to manage the production of man made capital (*e.g.*, paper). While the worst environmental impacts of this arrangement are becoming visible in one ecological disaster after another the political momentum behind almost four centuries of nation states dominance makes it very hard to imagine an alternative system of governance by which to ensure global environmental protection.

In conventional political economy terms, a nation's power and wealth are positively related to its "factor endowments"—labor supply, natural resources, favorable climate, availability of man made capital, and so forth. When combined with information about cultural factor, intellectual capital, innovation rates, and political or military capacity, these endowment characteristics can reveal a great deal about a particular nation's policy preferences and political behavior. Since the standard unit of analysis for comparing endowments remains the nation-states, political economists tend to regard nationalism as one of principal driving forces in world politics. Many view the pursuit of national competitive advantage as the principal source of both progress and conflict in international affairs. In their estimation, any collective action on the global environmental front will have to be achieved with little or no net loss in a participating nation's economic competitiveness.

Political ecologists start with a different view of endowment characteristics and a different unit of analysis. Endowment is measured as a function of ecological wealth—for example, the availability of clean drinking water or, more generally, a healthy biosphere (and, by extension, climate). Such ecological assets are deemed to be far more valuable, ultimately, than all the factories, farms, and productive workers that can be concentrated within a nation's boundaries. Rather than focusing on nation states, students of political ecology pay greater attention to interaction of smaller units of political organization, particularly those that serve as the constituent parts and mediating institutions of grassroots political action. It is people's primary group affiliation or community identity that matter most in determining their attitudes toward the environment. The nation state is viewed predominantly as an aggregation device for power and security. What makes politics personal and at the same time transcendent is the link to community. "All politics is local", noted the late Tip O'Neill, former speaker of U.S. House of Representatives. In keeping with this thought, many political ecologists attempt to combine a global perspective with local community focus, leaving others to scrutinize national politics. In contrast, political economists, by focusing on state-sponsored or state managed trade and development issue, leave it to political ecologists to worry about the repercussions of national policies at the global and primary community levels.

Glocalization

This dual concern with global and local politics is derived from the "glocal" perspective introduced in chapter 2 Political ecologists argue that we must think "glocally" in order to develop the environmental understanding and response measures needed to avert widespread ecological disaster. Although political ecology runs the risk of being construed as an ideology of glocalism, it is in fact no more ideologically driven than are conventional schools of political thought, which uncritically accept the nation-state system as the baseline from which all major political ideas are to be measured and interpreted. Taking a glocal perspective does not mean ignoring the nation-state, but merely downgrading its importance in addressing the ecological challenges of this planet.

One need not be an environmentalist to see that glocalism is gaining on nationalism. In fact, one need only be a modern consumer to appreciate that it is economic and technological factors, more than environmental ones, that lie behind its accelerating pace. A provocative examination of the economic and technological driving forces behind glocalism is provided by Kanichi Ohmae in his book *The Borderless World* (1990). Ohmae argues that the development of an interlinked economy is simultaneously elevating the importance of global, regional, and community affairs, while at the same time undermining the ability of national governments to serve the interests of their citizens. According to Ohmae, the need for strategic alliances among nations is being rapidly diminished by the rise of global strategic alliances among corporations and local consumer groups. Global markets and the phenomenon of "nationality-less" young consumers are combining to challenge and mock traditional notions of state sovereignty. And the rise of the global marketplace is influencing regional and local political economies to a greater degree than the actions of national economic planners. Addressing the next generation of consumers, Ohmae describes a world economy that is already subverting the principles on which nationalism rests:

At the cash register, you don't care about country of origin or country of residence... It does not matter to you that a "British sneaker by Reebok (now an American owned company) was made in Korea, a German sneaker by Adidas in Taiwan, or a French ski by Rossignol in Spain (1990:3).

While such views may underestimate the potency of parochial thinking and the influence of nationalistic pride on future economic development, the latest sales and distribution figures from companies such as Reebok, Adidas, and Rossignol suggest that many of today's youthful consumers behave as if they already live in a borderless world. It is their parents and grandparents who have not yet fully discovered how the logic of consumption is rapidly erasing the geographic boundaries of citizenship. Critical theorists understand this as the inevitable result of world capitalism flourishing in an age of instant communication.

For the political ecologist, the implications of economic glocalization, or what Sony's Akio Morita terms "global localization", are perhaps most apparent in the development of fledgling periodicals such as the *Journal of Municipal Foreign Policy* and the creation of foreign trade offices and bilateral international initiatives by large city governments (Shuman, 1992). Given the increasing need for global policies and institutions, political ecologists might do well to focus on how to shift the revenue and spending streams of national governments to support greater involvement of local and supranational entities. Those who have recommended sweeping reallocations argue that we should begin with the revenue side. Ohmae, for example, offers an appealingly simple, if simplistic, formula for government taxation:

If I had my way, I'd pay a third of all my taxes to an international fund dedicated to solving world problem, such as the environment and famine. A third to my community, where my children are educated and my family lives. And then a last third to my country, which each year does less and less for me in terms of security or well-being and instead subsidizes special interests. (1990 : 215).

The Political Ecosystem

In order to maintain a sense of both global and local political relationships, students of political ecology employ the concept of an ecosystem to describes and explain the interplay of various political entities. They portray the global political order as an ecosystem consisting of ten thousand human societies spread across more than fourteen major biomes (ecological regions) and eight zoogeographical realms (Lean and Hinrichsen, 1992 : 12-13). Organized with in this political ecosystem can be found more than 180 nation-states, approximately two thousand intergovernmental organizations, the United Nations system, and nearly eighteen thousand transnational NGOs operating at the intersections of state power (Boulding 1993 : 167). These interstitial organizations attempt to provide improved communication interest-group representation, conflict resolution, and greater economic opportunity both within and across nation-state boundaries. Providing legal authority and rules for exchanges and relationships between state actors are approximately sixty-two thousand international treaties, most of them bilateral or regional. Although the nation-state remains the dominant "species" within today's political ecosystem, political ecologists would say it is undergoing an evolutionary transformation toward glocal forms of governance that portend greater interdependence between local, national, and supranational forms of authority.

The essence of political ecology can be found in this concept of interdependence and its relationship with diversity. To ecologists, interdependence is the fundamental basic for community. Its meaning is perhaps best captured in the poet Francis Thompson's expression, "thou canst not stir a flower without troubling a star," or in John Muir's simple observation, "when we try to pick out anything by itself, we find it hitched to everything else in the universe." Ecological diversity refers to the variations in genes, niches, food supplies, and adaptive traits that facilitate species survival (and, by extension, biodiversity) in the face of pathogens of epidemics, increased predator population, and sudden climate change. It is expressed in the law of heterogeneity—that there is safety in numbers of species and subspecies traits, or for that matter, in numbers of democratic interests (e.g., pluralism). It is also evident in the postmaterialist idea of progress, with its emphasis on the qualitative growth through differentiation (e.g., the acorn's future as an oak tree, as contrasted with the undifferentiated growth of cancer cells).

The organizing principle on which the political ecosystem rests is *asymmetric interdependence*. All political units are interdependent to some extent. What is striking about the new era we are entering is that interdependence is growing as a result of advances in information technology and global communication, rapid growth in population and migration, heightened global risks of terrorism and nuclear proliferation and accelerating rates of transboundary pollution and nonrenewable resource consumption. Meanwhile, the asymmetrical properties of the relationships are growing stronger in some ways (e.g., gaps between rich and poor) and weaker in others (*e.g.*, greater parity in access to weapons technology that can disrupt or destroy societies). The asymmetry arises from the fact that almost all interdependency relationship tend to be stronger in one direction than another. Moreover, those in the stronger position often fail to recognize their own forms of dependency. These differences in dependency—real or falsely perceived—greatly influence the basic power and interest structures that govern competing political units. Some scholars, in fact, define power as a function of asymmetrical interdependence (e.g., Knorr, 1977 : 102). These asymmetries also account for the basic inequities in the allocation rules that govern international trade, development, and the inhibit the cooperation needed for coordinated responses to global environmental change.

As a complement to the international political economy focus on competition, political ecology's emphasis on asymmetrical interdependence aids in understanding why the state-centric world of today is so poorly equipped to foster the cooperation that is needed for genuine human progress. It reveals the inadequacy of territorial governance in an increasingly borderless world. With nearly two hundred primary territories and several thousand subsidiary jurisdiction, the earth's political geography bears no resemblance to its appearance from space—a solitary blue planet, with a single ocean and seven large land masses. To point out the obvious, however, does little to change people's comfort levels with the political systems under which they are governed. Many still profess a willingness to defend their nation's sovereignty with their lives. Clearly—the political ecology view is unlikely to engage the attention of large numbers of people in the near future unless opinion leaders recognize, and begin to admit publicly, that the fundamental environmental and economic security interests of citizens have transcended the political boundaries of the nation-state. Eventually, of course, the interactive media being developed as part of the information technology revolution will make this fact obvious to all but those who are unable to gain access to computer and to be the global networks of digital technology. In the meantime, visionary leadership is called for.

The most ambitious, if short-lived, development in this direction occurred in 1989 with the signing of the Hague Declaration, which called for bold new international environmental institutions and an expansion of U.N. authority to deal with global environmental problems. Led by the prime ministers of France, the Netherlands, and Norway, heads of twenty-four nations agreed to support proposals for international environmental enforcement based on "nonunanimous decisions of supranational entities" (French, 1992b : 35). Other provisions called for new legislative mechanisms and new powers for the International Court of Justice to impose its jurisdiction over the implementation of U.N. environmental treaties, Although nearly forty nations eventually signed the declaration, the impact was small. The conference in March, 1989 that created the declaration was marked by the conspicuous absence of the United States, China, Britain, and the former Soviet Union, ensuring that little momentum would develop for a power transition. The implied rebuke by key members of U.N. Security Council seemed to suggest that the only environmental reforms that were likely to emerge were those they supported or acquiesced in as part of a state-centric system of governance.

Whither the Nation-State?

If the nation-state in its present form is the only viable basis for governance, then the prospects for sustained environmental improvement appear to be very poor. The reasons have less to do with leadership and administrative capacity than with structural design flaws. As we have seen, the modern state is product of territorial thinking. It is by definition an autonomous part of the earth wherein citizens openly declare their independence from other parts and from the planetary whole. Although it is ecologically untenable to conceive of sovereign parts in an interdependent world, the concept has managed to flourish in its secular form since at least the Treaty of Westphalia in 1648. The need to manage and coordinate larger population, economic trade, and technological innovation has seemingly cemented the nation-state as the ultimate successor to tribal, feudal, and city-state forms of political organization. Because of its amazing capacity for organized power and geopolitical differentiation, the state has become the most widely accepted instrument of group identity outside the family.

The state derives its power ultimately from the struggle to control land and other resources through the bureaucratic imposition of law and political will, backed by the threat of force. As the supreme power within a territory, modern states perform at least three key functions (Clark and Dear, 1984 : 43) : (1) forging social consensus and integration, (2) securing the means or conditions of production through social investment practices and the regulation of consumption, and (3) protecting the accumulation of wealth (i.e., ensuring property rights); while providing for the welfare of those at the bottom of the income distribution. Although the effort expended on each of these functions differs markedly from democratic to authoritarian states, and from capitalist to socialist states, the rationale for their inclusion is almost always the same: to manage foreign and domestic conflict arising from differences in ideology, race, ethnicity, territorial ambition, class, and economic competitiveness. Management of conflict in this case means everything from prevention to outright encouragement of violence, depending upon the shifting interests and capabilities of a particular states.

In the past, the legitimacy of a state has depended largely on its ability to provide military and domestic security, enforce contracts, and represent the interests of its citizens in foreign affairs. For the most part, environmental threats that transcended state boundaries became the subject of international attention only insofar as they affected the perceived economic, health, or security interests of powerful nations or their leaders. Since neither domestic nor supranational costs of environmental destruction have been effectively accounted for in national development budgets, international environmental protection today is dependent on the ability of a nation, or coalition of nations, to prove that their territory or citizens have been harmed by the environmentally unsound practices of one or more nations with whom they share a common physical or biological medium (e.g., air, water, migratory wildlife). Where the scope of environmental risk becomes truly global, as in case of atmospheric change, nation-state system is put to the severest test. In most cases, it presents member states with an unsavory choice between unilateral action to protect the environment, which often places the eager nation at a competitive disadvantage, or large-scale collective action, which is usually subject to the "slow boat" rule (the rate of progress is set by the least enthusiastic party) and therefore too cumbersome in many instances to permit timely international responses.

According to Mische (1993), and many other environmentalists, the nation-state has become the principal obstacle in securing global environmental protection:

When we try to approach a resolution of today's ecological crises, we soon run into a central dilemma: The Earth does not recognize sovereignty as we now know it. Existing concepts of state sovereignty are incongruent, even antitetical, to the prerequisites for global ecological security.

Critics of the state argue that whatever authority and legitimacy it may have once had, a tide of globalism is eroding away its hold on power. Some want to see the state wither away completely. For example, Edward Goldsmith (1994) editor of *The Ecologist*, asserts:

The state is foreign to society. It is a gesellschaft— a single purpose association concerned almost exclusively with its own short-term interests and almost invariably to the real needs of those it has been called upon to govern. There is no place for the state or its specialized institutions in a society that seeks to recreate for itself a sustainable existence on a sustainable planet.

Another British environmental author, R.J. Johnston, argues that be - cause the modern state promotes accumulation and environmentally destructive modes of production, it has precipitated a potential crisis of legitimacy and rationality, brought on by increasing scientific evidence that the accumulation and production it sponsors are irreversibly destroying the earth. In Johnston's view (1989), the dilemma is not likely to be resolved by appealing for international cooperation:

[T]he creation of environmental problems is a product of the dominant mode of production in the world today, and the solution of those problems is difficult because the only institution within which the necessary collective action could be mobilized exist to promote the interests of that mode of production.

Defenders of the nation-state are apt to apply Churchill's sentiments about democracy to the modern state system: the worst form the government except for all the rest. They acknowledge many of the flaws and limitation of the present system but doubt the promise claimed for alternative forms of political organization. Most reject the notion that a global, regional, or other supranational system of governance is feasible and desirable. Among scholars who study the issue, the prevailing concern is not so much with the state-centric structure of political life as with the way in which state power is concentrated or dispersed within the system. Many students of international relations believe that power convergence is needed for the international system to maintain stability. So called "hegemonic stability" theorists (*e.g.*, Gilpin, 1981; Keohane, 1984) posit that the system is only orderly when there is a clearly recognized leading state (or in some variants a bipolar power distribution) to encourage orderly alignment of other state actors. According to those who hold this view, global environmental cooperation has a better chance of developing and surviving if a hegemon exists whose perceived interests are served by collective action. Without a hegemonic leader, wide-open military competition may ensue, resulting in reduced investment in cooperative activities, such as environmental diplomacy.

Because of the sweeping changes in world power and interests triggered by the end of the Cold War, hegemony has become, like (revisionist) history, "not what it used to be." Superpower bipolarity has been pronounced dead and condominium appears to be the order of the day. Given the string tendency in contemporary world affairs to assume a tripolar regional structure— North America, Europe, and East Asia—the role of hegemonic states and their influence on environmental diplomacy are likely to become increasingly difficult to define and assess. As the unexpected and unprecedented events of world politics continue to unfold in the final years of this century, some political ecologists are beginning to ask whether a viable alternative to state-centric governance may yet emerge.

Prospects for Supranational Governance

Whatever the flaws of the nation-state system, most political observers argue that it is here to stay. Only a small group of planetary thinkers seriously entertain the possibility that the world is undergoing a transition to some form of world government, "global constitutionalism," or world federalism (e.g., Falk and Kim, 1982). Those in the middle of the spectrum, the "practical internationlists" as Richard Gardner (1992b) calls them, are prone to argue that a larger confederal system of national and supranational gcvernance is the most likely outcome of present trends. They imagine an increasing number of interstate regimes that can somehow complement the environmental programs of individual states without threatening their sovereign claims.

These three visions of future environmental governance—continuation of the status quo, world government, and some mixed form of nationalism and nascent supranationalism—are frequently presented as the leading options available for the twenty-first century. Other authors have labeled these approaches "incrementalism", "global governance," and "global partnership" (Porter and Brown, 1991: chapter 5), but the basic distinctions between content remain the same. So do the rank-order preferences of many international relations specialists who have evaluated the three options. Maintenance to the state-centric status quo appears doubtful in the face of globalizing and regionalizing forces, such as transboundary environmental protection, the growth of free-trade zones, and European political integration. Even less promising, however, is the hope that nation-states will somehow voluntarily surrender their sovereignty to a central world authority in exchange for untested assurances of collective security. Not surprisingly, many scholars conclude that hybrid variety of compromise between the other two options remains the best bet, although most expect the outcome to be much closer to the status quo than to a unitary world government. The order in which these analysts present their evaluations and their framework for choosing among options resemble what might be called the "Goldilocks principle" of world politics: The first approach is too "cold", the second too "hot", but the third seems "just right".

For the planetary thinkers who like their porridge hot, the conventional wisdom about future governance structures is just another expression of postmodern pessimism. It serves as a self-fulfilling prophecy, promoting a future of incremental change and timid politics—a future of "the bland leading the bland." Critics of the conventional wisdom argue that a global transformation of political institutions is overdue and likely to occur sometime in next century, whether we plan it or not. For example, Saul Mendlovitz (1975: xvi), director of the World Order Models Project, argues that the key question about global level governance is not if but how it will develop—"by cataclysm, drift, more or less rational design"—and what form it will take—"totalitarian, benignly elitist, or participatory (the probabilities being in that order)." While not advocating world government *per se*, Mendlovitz and many of his colleagues favour a transformation to a constitutional form of world order, one that makes possible the collective realization of five basic goals or values: peace, ecological balance, social justice, economic well-being, and positive personal identity. Some one-world thinkers argue that such goals and values are best realized in a political system that strategically redistributes increments of power from the state to the global and the local levels of human community. In that respect, they think like political ecologists.

Advocates of "postinternational politics" (e.g., Rosenau, 1990) have argued repeatedly that there are at least two policy domains—environment and security—in which global or supranational forms of governance are needed to augment national ones. They call for a selective relaxation of national sovereignty in the interest of protecting the biosphere and strengthening global peacekeeping. Ervin Laszlo, a prominent futurist, uses the term "cooperative governance" to describe this two-pronged approach to changing the state-centric system. Central to his political vision is the argument that traditional notions of sovereignty are obsolete:

In the last analysis, decision-making can grow to the international dimension if, and only if, the sacrosanct nature of national sovereignty is surrendered. A full recognition of the historical obsolescence of that principle is the single greatest precondition of recovering the governability of contemporary societies in regard to the two most pressing issues of our times: world security, and biospheric sustainability. (Laszlo,1991 : 221)

Laszlo proposes that cooperative governance, which is similar to the concept of glocalism, be applied solely to international security and environmental issues, at least initially. Nation-states would retain their sovereign powers in all other areas of social and economic life. By carefully delineating what Robert Keohane (Hass *et al.*, 1993) calls "formal" sovereignty (legal independence) from "operational" sovereignty (degrees of freedom under international law), what was previously a dichotomous variable (i.e., sovereign or not) can be turned into a continuous one, (i.e., degree of sovereignty). The problem with such apportionments, of course, is that many types of social and economic intervention could theoretically be justified on grounds of security and environmental protection. Perhaps the most sensitive grounds for such intervention involves the protection of basic human rights, which more than any other issue, has been repeatedly invoked to justify proposals for international intervention.

The movement to develop a supranational authority to protect basic human rights has accelerated in the wake of so-called "crimes against humanity" that have taken place in the past five to ten years in South Africa, Tianamin Square, Bosnia, Somalia, Haiti, and parts of the Middle East. Rather than focusing on the security of states and regions, human-rights advocates have sought to protect individuals through the establishment of certain universal rights (e.g. protections against torture and slavery) that are enforceable across territorial and cultural boundaries. Organizations such as Amnesty International have played an influential role in uncovering the systematic abuses that have been committed in the name of state security and economic development. Only recently, however, have environmental quality issues become interwoven with human rights campaigns. Increasingly, access to safe food and drinking water have appeared on the lists of demands by human rights activists. Authoritarian national governments that have been accused of gross abuses are vilified as enemies of the people by these activists, but the cloak of sovereignty ultimately protects the governments from meaningful censure. As a result, some activists are pushing for a binding universal declaration of basic rights, backed by an agreement among nations to permit supranational intervention whenever gross abuses of those rights are documented.

Leaving aside the obvious difficulties in arriving at a universal definition of rights in the midst of ethnic, cultural, and national diversity, the prospect of supranational intervention in what is widely perceived to be the internal affairs of notions invariably provokes strong opposition. The key challenge in any architectural design for a new global politics is how to devise safeguards that will induce individual states to relinquish a portion of their sovereignty in return for the benefits of enhanced international security and quality of life (Myers, 1993a). To the political ecologist, this is the dilemma of preserving autonomy in the midst of interdependence.

The Federal Option

Throughout much of modern history, the response to such dilemmas has been to design a federal system of governance—a constitutionally guaranteed balance of power between a political center and its peripheral units. For many observers, the greatest challenge of global environmental governance will be to accomplish a peaceful transition from statism to world federalism, relying on regional and global confederations along the way. Federalism applied on a global basis offers, in their view, the most promising way of limiting national sovereignty while still preserving the modern state's unrivaled capability for extracting collective action out of the competing primary group affiliations of its citizens.

The essential feature of federalism is the division of formal authority over people or territory into two levels of governance—central and constituent—with the sharing of power between the two specified in such a way that neither may legally dominate the other in an overall sense (Watts, 1981). Federalism is thus a compromise between autonomy and interdependence; between primary group identity and national or supranational identity. In the past, federalism has invariably functioned as a form of territorial political organization in which power or sovereignty was constitutionally distributed between center and periphery in the hopes for achieving some optimal level of national political integration. Federal arrangements were usually the result of a trade-off between statist demands of central authority to manage for coordinate large-scale business and defense enterprises, and community demands for smaller political units that would foster participation and permit self-expression by sub-national ethnic, religious, and other interest groups. Regardless of the balance struck between centralized and decentralized authority, the units of political organization were defined territorially. In a global experiment, however, the chief function of federalism would be to allocate power between territorial and non•territorial instruments of governance, with the constituent units in this case being nation-states, and the central or nonterritorial institution being some form of constitutionally limited world legislature or governing council.

In the debate about global environmental governance, world federalism remains a troubling concept for many participants. Some fear that progress on the environmental front would be achieved at the expense of democratic reform. As nations reluctantly transferred authority for the management of global commons and transboundary pollution, they would be establishing a "slippery slope" precedent for transfers in other areas. The ultimate test of federal power—the control of military forces–would arise when the questions of enforcement and intervention were addressed. At that point, critics argue, world federalism could become a dangerous end in itself, rather than a means for combating global environmental destruction.

For James Madison, ironically, national federalism was not an end but a means by which to extend democracy for purposes of large-scale governance. It was, in a sense, an inventive political response to the consequence of population growth and technological innovation. Federalism made possible the retention of decentralized political power in midst of driving forces that constantly increased the scale of economic and social interaction. The question today is whether federalism can (or should) facilitate the transition already underway from a national to global scale of interaction and interdependence.

Declaring in the 1930s that federalism was obsolete, the political scientist Harold Laski (1939 : 367) argued that rather than a means to create large-scale democracies, as Madison had hoped, federalism had become the lackey of large-scale capitalism. "Giant capitalism", as he termed it, was showing signs of incompatibility with democracy, and federalism was no longer able "to keep peace" with its growth and its demands on the political system. Imagine Laski's astonishment were he alive to witness today's influence of global capital. The critique he made of American federalism could easily apply to present proposals for world federalism; one has only to substitute the term nation-state for Laski's reference to a subnational state in order to appreciate the potential limitation of federalism in global system of capitalism, particularly one that is characterized by strong asymmetries in wealth:

The poor state is parasitic on the body politic. It offers privileges to giant capitalism to obtain its taxable capacity, offers escape from the imposition of rich states, in order to wrest from the wealthy some poor meed of compensation for its backwardness. It dare not risk offending the great industrial empires—cotton, coal, iron and steel, tobacco—lest it lose the benefits of their patronage. Their vested interests thus begin to define the limits within which the units of the federation may venture to move. And since the division of powers limits, in its turn, the authority of the Federal government to intervene — the latter being a government of limited powers—it follows that the great industrial empires can, in fact, prevent the legislation necessary to implement the purpose of a democratic society. (Laski, 1939 : 368)

Clearly an adequate system of governance for the twenty-first century would address both the power and the interests of nationalism and transnational corporations (TNCs)—a subject that is addressed in the next chapter. Federalism, according to Laski's logic, might merely speed the global rise of corporate capitalism, making it for all practical purposes the new hegemony, while subjecting previously sovereign states and their central governing institutions to a debilitating struggle for what is left of the political power. World federalists might object that the power of TNCs has already grown enormously under the state-centric system, and they would argue that a federal system would offer significant advantages in regulating the activities of TNCs; but the fact remains that federal structures could be used to frustrate control of TNC power just as easily as to enhance it.

Today, only about 20 per cent of the world's people live in national federations or in nations claiming to be federalist. Even among this 20 per cent or so, few citizens appear to be strong advocates of federal arrangements. Perhaps they are convinced that too many clumsy, competing layers of government bureaucracy result. Or perhaps they doubt that federalism can survive the asymmetries of power that typically exist between the center and the periphery. In India, for example, the central government has invoked emergency powers more than ninety times in the past fifty years in order to disband state governments, raising the question of whether India is truly a federal entity. Because of perceptions and experiences like this one, there is little reason to believe that most citizen would prefer supranational federalism over nationalism, even in the interest global environmental protection. Given the vigor with which national pride is exhibited in many parts of the world, about the most that can be hoped for in the short-term—or tolerated, according to today's neorealists—is a stronger confederation of nation-states organized around the existing U.N. system. While supranational federalism appears to offer a very attractive model for building glocal forms of governance, a strengthened U.N. system may well provide the intermediate step needed to facilitate its development.

United Nations Reform

The United Nations represents a half-century experiment with a weak form of world confederation. Although its record of achievements in security and environmental affairs is decidedly mixed, the U.N. system has become, almost by default, the last, best hope of many green globalists. Many have regarded its fragile institutions as potential stepping stones to world federalism or some other kind of constitutional world order. Others, seeing little prospect for effective world government, have opted for a more pragmatic and incremental course of action. They have argued that the U.N. represents the promise of world governance without the risks of world government. Through selective reform and strengthening, the U.N. is capable in their view, of becoming a strong and effective confederation— one that can live with the continuing paradox of state sovereignty in an era of interdependence.

As the scale and significance of supranational problems and opportunities have grown, the limits of cooperation between U.N. member states have become more pronounced. Frustrated diplomats guardedly admit that the environmental and peacekeeping benefits that could flow from stronger U.N. interventions are potentially enormous, but so are the risks of tyranny. Global fascism is the fear lurking behind almost every futuristic image of a powerful United Nations. Meanwhile, progressive states are being confronted as never before with the painful trade-offs that arise when respect for national sovereignty conflicts with respect for human dignity, ecological integrity, and economic efficiency. The peacekeeping challenges encountered in 1994–95 in Bosnia, Cambodia, Somalia and Haiti, like Western Europe's encounter in 1986 with the fallout from Chernobyl, demonstrated that neither self-reliant unilateralism nor weak collectivism on the part of the U.N. is adequate to contain today's sources of political and ecological danger. The U.N. remains a "paper tiger" when it comes to enforcement. Despite undertaking the three largest peacekeeping missions in its history, all since 1991, the U.N. has gained little respect for its efforts. It may, in fact, have managed only to strengthen the conviction of its critics that a return to hegemonic state intervention offers the surest way to suppress violent nationalistic and ethnic conflict. And when it comes to enforcement of environmental accords, the U.N.'s capability in this area appears even weaker than its peacekeeping powers.

If supranational governance is unlikely and we wish to avoid a return to the risky practice of unilateralism, the U.N's authority and capacity for peacekeeping and "earthkeeping" must be strengthened to the point where its agencies can effectively intervene in trouble spots on behalf of the community of nations. Within the environmental movement, reformers have urged that the U.N.'s policy-making apparatus be fundamentally restructured in order to treat ecological security on a par with military and economic security. Among their most ambitious proposals have been plans to create an ecological security council to mirror the existing Security Council or, failing that, to redesign the present council to incorporate transboundary environmental risks as a major part of its purview. Others, perhaps forgetting why supranational governance is so difficult to achieve, have suggested the creation of a standing U.N. peacekeeping force that would also be empowered to enforce trade sanctions or other penalties against those who violate international environmental treaties. Appeals by states accused of violating major treaty provisions would be reviewed under the mandatory jurisdiction of a strengthened International Court of Justice. Some reformers have even proposed that the interests of future generations be given official U.N. representation. For example, one of the more ambitious proposals, suggested that members of the General Assembly be elected and then assigned by lottery so that two-thirds of those elected represent current generations and one-third explicitly align themselves with the interests of future generations, assuming that those interests can be foreseen. Celebrating the fiftieth anniversary of the U.N. in 1995, many of these reformers called for global summit to consider these and other proposed changes.

The most prominent reform effort to date was launched in late 1992 with the creation of the commission on Global Governance, an independent study group composed of twenty-eight international diplomats, scholars, and NGO leaders who were asked "to explore opportunities created by the end of the Cold War to achieve common security and sustainable development through better global governance" (Commission on Global Governance, 1994 : 6). The commission released its first report in January 1995. Building on its members' vision of "global neighourhood" and "planetary security", the commission called for phased reforms of the U.N. system to promote expanded humanitarian relief, demilitarization and greater conflict provention, elimination of permanent membership and veto powers on the Security Council, creation of an "apex" global economic council within the U.N., expanded and compulsory jurisdiction for the World Court, a strengthened international civil service, and the establishment of strict U.N. custodianship of the global commons (Commission on Global Governance, 1995).

A summary of proposed reforms of the U.N. system and its environmental policy mechanism is provided in Table 1. While some of the proposals border on utopian visions, it is important to note that many ideas that seemed outlandish less than a decade ago now wear the look of respectability, plausibility and, their supporters would even say, logical inevitability. What imperils their development is not some massive denial of status quo deficiencies, but rather disarray about what can be done to repair them. Despite a flurry of suggested changes, there is no elite or mass consensus to propel major reforms at the present time.

Consider the evidence from a 1993 *Los Angles Times* survey of 649 elites representing high level positions in American government, business and finance, academia, religion, science and engineering, foreign affairs, the arts, and the news media (McManus, 1993 : H3). Each interviewe was asked to choose which of six challenges facing the world—nationalism and ethnic hatred, proliferation of weapons of mass destruction, international trade conflicts, environmentional pollution, religious fanaticism, and overpopulation—was the most dangerous to world stability. Only members of one elite, science and engineering , were able to reach a bare consensus (51 per cent) on the most important issue—in their case, overpopulation. No other elite managed a 50 per cent vote on any of the six issues tested. A parallel survey of the American general public by Princeon Research Associates revealed even less consensus than was achieved among elites (McManus, 1993 : H2). While it is possible that both surveys overlooked more important issues, and that the subjects surveyed were not representative of either elite or non-elite world opinion, one potential lesson for would-be reformers seems clear: Where there is no consensus on the priority of needs, it will be difficult to find consensus on the direction of reform. Without that consensus, the entrenched power of sovereign states and U.N. bureaucracies is likely to make institutional reform at best an ad hoc and incremental process.

In trying to strengthen the U.N., reformers must bear in mind that a state's right of secession will act as an ever-present check on the scale and pace of political change that can realistically occur. Even a crisis-driven transition to a world constitutional order would presumably be tempered (initially, at least) by the right of secession of any member state.

While concerns about issue linkage and lost political leverage may make the option to defect very difficult for some states to exercise, the mere

TABLE 1. Proposed Reforms of the United Nations by Major Function

Generic Policy Making

- Alter the Security Council by expanding or changing its membership, and limiting the five permanent member's veto power
- Create a U.N. federation with a bicameral world legislature composed of a House of States (appointed government representatives) and a House of Representatives (citizens who are directly elected)
- Create a second U.N. Assembly, subsidiary to the General Assembly, composed of representatives from nongovernmental organisations
- Form a World Consultative Council composed of leading world citizens appointed on the basis of their prominence outside of government
- Arrange a global summit for the purpose of systematic U.N. charter reform
- Extend limited mandatory jurisdiction of the International Court of Justice

Environmental Policy Making

- Elevate the Commission on Sustainable Development (established in 1992)
- Establish an Environmental Security Council, or add global environmental protection as one of the existing council's chief security functions
- Establish a permanent intergovermental panel of global environmental experts
- Strengthen environmental treaty secretariats, including the right to perform independent monitoring of national implementation efforts

Environmental Funding and Capacity-Building

- Achieve the U.N.'s goal of persuading donor nation to give 0.7per cent of their GDPs for official development assistance
- Expand the Global Environmental Facility to increase environmental funding under the direction of UNEP, UNDP, and the World Bank
- Elevate the role of CIDIE in development assistance
- Create limited U.N. taxing authority (e.g., taxes on international sales of cigarettes, transfers of hazardous materials, etc.)
- Create regional environment and development agencies

Environmental Monitoring and Analysis

- Establish at U.N. headquarters a Center for Environment and Development Analysis
- Strengthen UNEP's Earthwatch Program
- Develop a U.N.-level "Mission to Planet Earth," based on the US model
- Expand the use of GIS and computerized data retrieval systems, and provide improved links between U.N. and nongovernmental organisations

Intergovernmental Environmental Coordination

- Expand UNEP's role as a clearinghouse and organizer of international fora
- Increase the contact and communication levels of the interagency program for Designated Officials on Environmental Management

---

Marc Nerfin. "The Future of the United Nations Systems: Some Questions on the Occasion of an Anniversary." Development Dialogue No. 1 (1985)

threat of defection is nevertheless a powerful limiting factor in attempts to strengthen international environmental institution. Such conditions of political feasibility may weaken over time, but for the foreseeable future, reform will be limited by the potential of any state to reassert its formal sovereignty whenever international institutions are perceived to threaten one of its core interests. Hence, global environmental governance may remain a function of national foresight and voluntary international cooperation well into the next century, and perhaps beyond.

For those who are convinced that this will be the case, a strategic retreat from world order objectives is necessary. In their minds, the appropriate goal of environmental design or intervention must be much smaller and simpler than world federalism or reform of the U.N. system (French, 1992a, b). It is a goal that is much more likely to be achieved by piecemeal engineers than by the global systems architects. In its most common depiction, the goal is to expand and strengthen the use of issue specific, negotiated regimes for environmental management. Such regimes form the backbone of today's system of international environmental governance.

Green Regimes

While planetary thinkers worry about reforming a complex, interlinked set of international institutions, political pragmatists (pessimists?) focus on multilateral policy responses to particular problem. For those interested in environmentally pragmatic action, regime formation and maintenance have become the key objectives of multilateral policy making. A regime, as defined by Gareth Porter and Janet Welsh Brown (1991:20), is a "system of norms and rules that are specified by multilateral legal instrument [e.g., treaty] among states to regulate national actions on a given issue." Regimes that are principally designed to regulate national environmental behavior that affects other nations or the global commons can be defined as "green" regimes. Some of the most important of these regimes are derived from the environmental treaties listed in table 2. At present, approximately 150 green regimes are in operation. This is in addition to more than 500 bilateral environmental agreements that have been successfully negotiated during this century.

Unlike an international governing institution with broad authority over issues of transnational environmental quality, green regimes are constructed to deal with one issue at a time. Because they often function more like marginal adjustments than structural reforms, regimes constitute a less threatening political means for strengthening environmental governance. They arise in ad hoc proceedings, under the design of ad hoc bodies of negotiators, and develop as outgrowth of existing international law. They address transboundary threats from pollution, resource consumption, and ecosimplification without directly challenging the state centric system. For all of these reasons, self-proclaimed pragmatists argue that the path to an improved global environment is through stronger. policy-driven regimes, not through fundamental changes in political institutions.

Table 2. A Chronology of Major Multilateral Treaty Instruments Used in the Creation of Green Regimes.

1911	"Big Four" Convention for the preservation and protection of North Pacific Fur Seals (Russia, Great Britain/Canada, United States, Japan)
1940	Washington-OAS Convention on Nature Protection and Wild life Preservation in the Western Hemisphere
1946	Washington Convention for the Regulation of International Whaling
1949	Rome Agreement for the Establishment of the Central Fisheries Council of the Mediterranean
1950	Paris Convention of the Protection of Birds

1951 Rome International Plant Protection Convention

1954 London Convention for the Prevention of Pollution of the Sea by Oil

1957 Washington Interim Convention on North Pacific Fur Seals

1957 Geneva-European Agreement Concerning the International Carriage of Dangerous Goods by Road

1958 Geneva Convention on Fishing and Conservation of the Living Resources of the High Seas

1959 Washington Antarctic Treaty

1963 Vienna Convention on Civil Liability for Nuclear Damage

1963 Moscow Treaty Banning Nuclear Weapon Tests in the Atmosphere, in Outer Space, and Under Water

1964 Copenhagen Convention for the International Council for the Exploration of the Sea

1966 Rio International Convention for the Conservation of Atlantic Tunas

1967 Treaty on Principles Governing the Activities of States in the Exploration and Use of Outer Space (London, Moscow, Washington)

1968 Algiers African Convention on the Conservation of Nature and Natural Resources

1969 Brussels International Convention on Civil Liability for Oil Pollution Damage

1969 Brussels International Convention Relating to Intervention on the High Seas in case of Oil Pollution Casualties

1969 Bonn Agreement on Cooperation for Control of North Sea Oil Pollution

1971 Ramsar Convention on Wetlands and Waterfowl Habitat

1971 Brussels International Convention on the Establishment of an International Fund for Compensation for Oil Pollution Damage

1972 London Convention on the Prohibition of the Development, Production, and Stockpiling of Bacteriological and Toxin Weapons, and on their Destruction

1973 Washington Convention on International Trade in Endangered Species of Wild Fauna and Flora

1973 London International Convention for the Prevention of Pollution from Ships (MARPOL)

1974 Geneva Convention Concerning Prevention and Control of Occupational Hazards Caused by Carcinogenic Substances and

Agents

1974 Paris Convention for the Prevention of Marine Pollution from Land Based Sources

1976 Convention on Protection of the Rhine Against Chemical Pollution

1976 Barcelona Convention for the Protection of the Mediterranean Sea Against Pollution

1977 Geneva Convention Concerning Protection of Workers against Occupational Hazards in the Working Environmental Due to Air Pollution, Noise, and Vibration

1978 Nairobi-Principles of Conduct in the Field of the Environment for the Guidance of States in the Conservation and Harmonious Utilization of Natural Resources Shared by Two or More States

1978 .Ottawa Convention on Future Multilateral Cooperation in the North-west Atlantic Fisheries

1979 Geneva Convention on Long-Range Transboundary Air Pollution

1971 Bonn Convention on Conservation of Migratory Species of Animals

1980 Nairobi Provisions for Cooperation between States on Weather Modification

1980 Canberra Convention on the Conservation of Antarctic Marine Living Resources

1981 Abidjan Convention for Cooperation in the Protection and Development of the Marine and Coastal Environment of the West and Central African Region

1982 Montego Bay Convention on the Law of the Sea (not in force)

1983 Geneve International Tropical Timber Agreement

1983 Rome International Undertaking on Plant Genetic Resources

1983 Bonn Agreement for Cooperation in Dealing with Pollution of the North Sea by Oil and other Harmful Substances

1984 Geneva Protocol (1979 LRTAP) for Long-Term Financing of Monitoring and Evaluation Programs

1985 Nairobi-Montreal Guidelines or the Protection of the Marine Environment against Pollution from Land-Based Sources

1985 Vienna Convention for Protection of the Ozone Layer

1985 Helsinki Protocol (1979 LRTAP) for Reduction of Sulfur Emissions

1985 Rome International Code of Conduct on the Distribution and Use of Pesticides

1986 Vienna Conventions on Early Notification of a Nuclear Accident, and on Assistance in the Case of a Nuclear Accident or Radiological Emergency

1986	Geneva Convention Concerning Safety in the Use of Asbestos
1987	Nairobi-London Guidelines for the Exchange of Information on Chemicals in International Trade
1987	Montreal Protocol (1985 Vienna Convention) on Substances that Deplete the Ozone Layer
1988	Sophia Protocol (1979 LRTAP) for Control of Nitrogen Oxide Emissions
1989	Basel Convention on the Control of Transboundary Movements of Hazardous Wastes and their Disposal
1990	London Amendments to 1987 Montreal Protocol
1991	Bamako Organisation of African Unity Convention on the Ban of the Import into Africa and the Control of Transboundary Movement and Management of Hazardous Wastes within Africa (not in force)
1992	Rio Biodiversity Convention
1992	Rio Climate Change Convention
1993	Copenhagen Amendments to 1987 Montreal Protocol
1993	London Dumping Convention to Ban Nuclear Waste Disposal in Oceans (replaces voluntary moratorium adopted in 1983)

presents a simple conceptual model of international regime formation and adjustment, based on a cyclical process of problem recognition, interest articulation, national response, coalition building, application of international norms and voting rules, policy adoption and financing, ratification, implementation, and enforcement. The swirl of activity portrayed in the models takes place around a secretariat that is responsible for arranging meetings of the parties, coordinating implementation, and serving as regime's "headquarters" or information clearing-house. The cyclical portrayal is necessary because many regimes have to be renegotiated at the margin as new protocols and new interpretations of regime authority are proposed.

The process of regime formation, like all voluntary attempts at collective action, permits state actors to adopt one of three basic roles: to lead, follow, or oppose proposed agreements. Some actors may initially choose to be "swing states" (Porter and Brown, 1991 : 36), taking no position in support or opposition until other actors have given them a good reason to do so. Because most proposed regimes represent very modest concessions of state power, the stakes in regime negotiation often have more to do with national prestige, strategic posturing, and avoidance of "slippery-slope" precedents than with substantive environmental problem solving.

In the case of the 1992 biodiversity convention, for example, many negotiators from industrial countries shared the U.S. government's concerns about the treaty's provisions for intellectual property and financing mechanisms, but unlike the United States they chose to support the regime at the Earth Summit, calculating perhaps that the potential gains in cooperation and national prestige would more than offset the political and economic concessions implied by the treaty.

The question of how to create stronger international regimes in a community of sovereigns states has been vigorously debated in recent years (Camilleri and Falk, 1992; French, 1992b; Lipschutz and Conca, 1993). There appear to be many ways to accomplish this objective, some that seem anathema to a strict interpretation of national sovereignty. The most important approach, perhaps, centers on the voting rules that are adopted for bringing a particular regime into existence. The old approach of requiring unanimity among participating states virtually ensured that regime formation would be shaped by lowest-common–denominator politics. Increasingly, however, qualified majority voting (e.g., agreement by two-thirds of the nations participating) has been adopted to prevent one or a few blocking states from continually steering policy. The 1992 convention on biodiversity, for example, went into force upon ratification by thirty states. The 1992 climate convention required only fifty state ratifications to take effect. Although states refusing to sign initial agreements often declare their immunity from majoritarian regimes, in practice, many continue to comply out of concern that they will be perceived as outcastes or penalized indirectly in lost political leverage or credibility. In the International Whaling Commission, which uses qualified majority voting, Japan, Norway, the former Soviet Union, and Peru all said they would defy the 1986 moratorium on harvesting, but none of the states openly followed through on their previous declarations of immunity.

Additional ways to strengthen regimes include development of (1) innovative financing mechanisms, such as earmarked environmental trust funds; (2) the creation of standing international bodies to replace ad hoc negotiators; (3) development of trade sanctions for noncompliance; and (4) monitoring and evaluation programs that require regular reports by states, while permitting unintrusive, independent inspection by representatives of treaty secretariats. The idea here is to have sufficient data to undertake state by state performance and compliance evaluations, with any poor showings brought to the attention of the world press and appropriate NGO watchdogs. If we have learned anything about what makes regimes work, it is that a state's concern with its international image (e.g., avoidance of embarrassment) may be at least as important as its respect for international law, thus inviting grudging state participation in regimes that it does not truly favor.

The theory behind international environmental regime formation is relatively straightforward, since it is derived from theories of the state. The multilateral norms and rules that make up green regimes create obligations on behalf of states and their agents to limit or prevent certain types of environmental harm. Such arrangements become necessary to reduce transboundary environmental impacts and the political conflict that such impact generate. In political ecology terms, green regimes help determine the degree to which homeostasis or ecological balance will be legally recognized and protected across states or the commons they share. The regimes also help determine what might be called the economic "trophic" levels that competing states, as natural resources consumers, will be allowed to occupy. Most important of all, they help determine how asymmetries in political interdependence and in environmental relations between states will be redressed.

For instance, consider states whose quality of surface water or air depends heavily on the pollution-prevention practices of their upstream or upwind neighbours. Next consider a world in which all states are vulnerable to global pollutants that each state emits in varying amounts. In the first case, regional regimes, such as river-basin authorities, can redress the asymmetry of state relationships with respect to the environment by allowing injured or potentially injured states to invoke previously agreed upon and codified norms and rules, in the form of multilateral treaties. These treaties protect them from such harm or at least provide grounds for seeking compensation if it occurs. In the second case—global emissions of carbon dioxide, for example—comprehensive regimes must include all states as both causes of injury and as potentially injured parties.

To properly address differences in state contribution and in their environmental risks, a globally effective regime would have to incorporate the historical emissions record of each state, the per capita emissions record, and perhaps the population growth record. It would then have to deal with the political and economic asymmetries that arise when states suffer different levels of absolute loss due tc global environmental changes, leaving some states to conclude that they are in a position of relative gain with respect to their competitors and potential enemies. For example, conventional notions of national security and prestige may encourage some states to perceive global damage from climate change as an acceptable cost if it is disproportionately concentrated among their enemies. Under these circumstances, global regimes are likely to form only where environmental crises impose absolute losses on a state that appear greater, in the near term, than the sum of relative gains (*e.g.*, trade and security advantages) created by the losses experienced by competing states. In other words, as long as nations value their futures in the immediate terms of international political economy, instead of in the long-range terms of political ecology, there can be little prospect that sufficient portions of state sovereignty will be surrendered to provide for the common good.

We began this assessment of environmental governance with bold visions what could be and ended with incremental variation of what is. The apparent staying power of nationalism seems to drive thinking in that direction. It would be unwise, however, to argue that what is past will continue to be prologue. Institutions and policies can change in unexpected and nonincremental ways, as recent studies of "punctuated equilibria" in politics make clear (e.g., Baumgartner and Jones, 1993). Moreover, the pragmatic preference for policy reform over institutional reform relies on a distinction that is much sharper in theory than in practice. Policy changes are necessary, but not sufficient, elements of effective global environmental governance. They must be combined with institutional reform and innovation.

Environmental treaties offer disoriented reformers a means of sharp focus, timely response, and sometimes a rewarding sense of closure. Although they are accorded most of the attention by today's scholars, practitioners, and advocacy coalitions, attempts to design new institutions and political orders, however scattered and open-ended they may seem are probably much important in the long run. Granting that state-level adjustments at the margin are, and will continue to be, the most favored response of governments, the task for environmental NGOs will increasingly become one of persuading their governments and fellow citizens that the most pressing challenges we face are largely glocal problems that require nonincremental, glocal responses, if the precepts of political ecology are correct, neither unitary world government nor nation-state confederations will be adequate for meeting those challenges.

The design of stronger confederations through a revitalized United Nations and World Court offers a promising way in the short run to elevate the rule oflaw in international relations, but it is unlikely to prove any more sustainable in the long run than the economic development plans of its sovereign members. Utopian as it may seem, a constitutionally based world federation that can link communities and regions, without either decimating or strengthening nation-states, may be the only way to ensure that the policy and institutional responses needed for effective global environmental governance do not undermine the world's growing but fragile impulse for democracy.

An Emerging Research Agenda in Third–World Studies

In the future, the interaction between environmental and political forces will mediate Third-World development in unprecedented ways. Thus, as environmental problems assume greater political significance, the need for an analytical approach integrating environmental and political understanding becomes more pressing. In the 1980s, scholars from diverse academic and institutional background began to examine the links between environmental and political activities in parts of Asia, Africa and Latin America. Correspondingly, a body of work that may be termed Third-World political ecology emerged. Such work suggests a fruitful research agenda in Third-World studies.

Diverse scholarship has highlighted aspects of this agenda. Emel and Peet (1989), for example, review work on resource management and natural hazards. Watts (1989) and Berry (1989a) consider the literature ofthe African agrarian studies movement. Beinart (1989,1990) addresses recent research on hunting and conservation in colonial Africa. Redclift (1984,1987), Blaikie and Brookfield (1987b), Blaikie (1988b, 1989b) and Adams (1990a) also explore aspects of Third-World political ecology. These works offer a tantalizing glimpse of how political and environmental understanding is being integrated in diverse settings. They do not, however, provide a general treatment; consequently, the parameters of the emerging research agenda have not been systematically examined.

A preliminary exploration of Third-World political ecology, emphasizes analytical clarification over critical evaluation. In discussing such research, the objective is not to exaggerate the coherence of this emerging agenda, but to highlight common themes and suggest areas for further exploration. With such caveats in mind, the structure of the argument may be summarized as follows. First, after a preliminary introduction to Third-World political ecology, a framework for understanding the emerging research agenda is developed, embracing three critical areas of inquiry: the contextual sources of environmental change; conflict over access; and the political ramifications of environmental change. In examining each area, a two-fold strategy is adopting, reviewing the relevant literature, and then exploring central analytical issues. In so doing, the central objective is to analyse these three key aspects of the emerging agenda.

In reviewing the human environmental literature, Deutsch (1977:359) lamented that political processes and institutions are rarely mentioned directly and even more rarely analysed in details. And yet, the substance of politics... is inescapably implied in almost every ecosocial problem. This dynamic interaction of environmental and political forces has but recently received scholarly attention. It was only in the 1980s, that Third-World political ecology emerged as a research agenda. As the framework is developed, key elements of this agenda will be discussed. First, however, the general approach of Third-World political ecology must be addressed, and its possible interpretations considered.

Broadly, Third-World political ecology may be defined as the attempt to understand the political sources, conditions and ramifications of environmental change. Specifically, Blaikie and Brookfield (1987b:17) offer a useful working definition:

> The phrase 'political ecology' combines the concerns of ecology and a broadly defined political economy. Together this encompasses the constantly shifting dialectic between society and land-based resources, and also within classes and groups within society itself:

Such a definition has much to commend it, particularly when extended to encompass not only 'land', but more generally 'environment'. In utilizing this interpretation, however, *economic reductionism* must be avoided. As such *reductionism* has been a recurrent feature in Third-World political ecology, it is therefore important to review briefly the ways in which economic reductionism simplifies reality, diminishing analytical accuracy.

Economic reductionism can weaken research in *Third-World political ecology* in at least three ways. First, reductionism fails to attribute *explanatory significance to ecological factors*. Thus, as Blaikie (1989a:22) notes in the context of African desertification:

> any attempt to attribute desertification to natural forces' other than the penetration of capitalism is written off in some quarters as merely a bourgeois red herring. This is a simplistic and unnecessary polarisation since it is the dialectic between environmental and social change which must provide the context in which land degradation is discussed.

Secondly, economic reductionism neglects other sources of environmental change. By equating social action with capitalist development, it not only neglects ecological factors, but also *devalues the role and importance of state and interstate forces*. Hence, it impoverishes understanding of the complex interaction of contextual sources which together, but in differentiated and often contradictory ways, relate to and are affected by environmental change.

Finally, economic reductionism also excludes from serious consideration those *without power*—peasants and other socially-disadvantaged groups. As with the environment and the state, the role of peasants is dismissed as analytically insignificant. And yet such premises are ill-founded—those 'without' power are not always as incapable of resistance as reductionist accounts might imply. As Giddens (1979:149) reminds us: 'all power relations, or relations of autonomy and dependence, are reciprocal: however wide the asymmetrical distribution of resources involved, all power relations manifest autonomy and dependence "in both directions".'

The preceding discussion highlights the dangers of economic reductionism. Third-World political ecology is understood as inclusive, premised on the view that it must be sensitive to the *interplay of diverse socio-political forces, and the relationship of those* forces to environmental change. The following framework explores the complexities of political and environmental interaction; consequently, its approach 'aims to unify but through an appreciation of plurality of purpose and flexibility in explanation' (Blaikie and Brookfield,1987b:25).

Taking first the *contextual sources* of *environmental change*, then, the following topics can be identified: *interstate relations*, and global *capitalism*. Such topics reflect the growing impact of national and transnational forces on the environment in a world of increased political and economic interdependence. In contrast, the second element of the framework addresses conflict over access, and *emphasizes location-specific struggles over the environment*. Embracing both the historical and contemporary dynamics of conflict, this research area illustrates how those 'without' power fight to project the environmental foundations of their livelihood. The final area of inquiry considers the political ramifications of environmental change. By addressing issues of socio-economic impact and political process, this element of the framework focuses on an often neglected area of human-environmental interaction: namely, the important effects of environmental change on socio-economic and political relationships.

In addressing the political ramifications of environmental change, however, caution must be exercised. Analyses of how environmental change may effect diverse socio-economic groups and concrete political processes differ, and must never be confused with *environmental determinism*. As Peet (1985) and others have shown, environmental determinism is better understood as an expression of *racist sentiments* than as an example of serious geographical research. In contrast, discussion of political ramifications of environmental change is designed to complement understanding of the other elements of the framework—the contextual sources of environmental change and conflict over access.

Juxtaposing these areas of inquiry in a single framework underscores the scale-dependent nature of research in Third-World political ecology. Discussion of *contextual sources*, *location-specific conflict over access*, and *political ramification*, must embrace recognition of the different *socio-political, economic* and *ecological scales* of an area or the nation.

Contextual Sources of Environmental Change

In Third-World political ecology, research has examined extensively, if somewhat unevenly, the contextual sources of environmental change. The identification of such sources constitutes the first element in the framework. Correspondingly, environmental change needs to be related to *state policies*, *interstate relation* and *global capitalism*.

One contextual source extensively canvassed in the literature is that of states policies. As Walker (1989:32) notes, there is 'an inherent, continuing potential for conflict between the *state's roles as developer* and as *protector* and *steward of the natural environmental on which its existence ultimately depends*'. A variety of regional and thematic studies have documented this ambiguity. In Repetto (1988a). Repetto and Gillis (1988) and Hurst (1990), for example, state policies are linked with processes of deforestation. Making reference to Indonesia, Malaysia, the Philippines and Brazil, Gillis (1988a, 1988b), Boado (1988) ad Browder (1988b) cite the trade taxation and industrial as well as forestry policies that have fostered policy contexts detrimental to the sustainable use of forest resources. McDowell (1989), Bautista (1990), Porter (1990), Anderson (1987), Guha (1985, 1990). Hirsch and Lohmann (1989), Kulkarni (1983) and Smil (1984,1987) also relate state policy to forest use in different Third-World countries In recent years, several states have belatedly attempted to reverse proceses of forest decline. Peluso and Poffenberger (1989) and Hafner and Apichatvullop (1990) examine such efforts in Indonesia and Thailand.

The Brazilian Amazon is particularly rich in case-study material.

Although long subject to exploitation, political and economic forces set in motion by the 1964 military coup accelerated Amazonian change, contributing to 'Brazil's social and environmental mortgage' (Guimaraes, 1989, 99). Hecht (1984,1985), Repetto (1988b), Pompermayer (1984), Myers (1984), Branford and Glock (1985) and Browder (1988a, 1988b) document the credit and infrastructural inducements used to promote large-scale investment in ecologically and economically dubious cattle-ranching in the eastern Amazon. Bunker (1980), Schmink (1988a) and Wood and Schmink (1979) note the adverse impact on activities (extraction; small scale farming) previously encouraged by the state. As manifested in the Greater Carajas programme, Hall (1987,1989), Fearnside (1986) and Anderson (1990) examine the state's role in continued regional upheaval, while cummings (1990) addresses the controversial energy policies designed to exploit the region's enormous potential for hydro-electric power, but which are irrevocably transforming its social and ecological character.

The Brazilian state persists with such disastrous policies, but in addressing this issue. Hecht and Cockburn (1989), Schmink and Wood (1987), Bunker (1985a) and Hall (1989), amongst many others, emphasize the inter-linked nature of state and commercial interests. Moreover, as Bunker (1982, 1985b) and Guimaraes (1989) suggest, internal divisions and the imposition of inappropriate bureaucratic procedures on the region may also impair the state's ability to develop coherent policies. Brazils has not been alone, however, in perpetuating deleterious social and environmental policies. Collins (1986) and Painter (1987) make note of similar policies in neighbouring countries.

The state influences environmental change in other ways too. The manipulation of water suppliers and pastoralist-farmer relations in Africa is particularly illustrative. Peters (1984), Cliffe and Moorsom (1979), Hedlund (1979), Worby (1988) and Toure (1988) relate the state-led introduction of boreholes in Botswana, Kenya and Senegal to transformed pastoralist lifestyles and environmental degradation. Horowitz and Salem-Murdock (1987) explore the socio-ecological impact of a state-sponsored dam and mechanized irrigation. State intervention in pastoralist-farmer relations also contributes to environmental change. Bassett (1988) examines the socio-ecological complexities of state support for Fulani pastoralists in the Ivory Coast. Typically, however and even in ecologically fragile areas, the state has favoured settled agriculture over pastoral activities, intensifying processes of environmental degradation. In diverse African settings, Thompson (1985), Horowitz (1986), Ahmed (1987) and Horowitz and Little (1987) highlight some of the consequences of such intervention.

While the state environmental performances has been extensively examined, interstate sources of environmental change have yet to be fully addressed. Walker (1989) and Mische (1989) note how the interaction between sovereign states can militate against long-term environmental stability. Inter:state warfare is the most obvious facet of this interaction to receive attention. Drawn from the Vietnam war experience (Westing, 1976; Neilands *et al.*, 1972), such research addresses the ecological impacts of the use of herbicides high-explosive ammunitions and other weaponry. Lauren (1982) offers an introduction to this material, but a series commissioned by the Stockholm International Peace Research Institute (Westing 1980, 1984a, 1984b, 1985), constitutes a more ambitious treatment of the subject. Although most research on interstate, warfare examines the environmental consequence of nuclear war, Pittock *et al.* (1985) and Ambio (1983) provide two of the more comprehensive efforts. Integrating diverse aspects of the literature, Galtung (1982) analyses the impact of military activity on both environmental and developmental processes.

Much of this research, however, is general; consequently, there is need for regional and national-oriented analyses. Hjort af Ornas and Mohamed Salih (1989) provide one, albiet uneven, example in an African setting. In diverse national and regional contexts, essays in this volume explore the contemporary social and ecological implications of recurrent warfare and endemic personal and group insecurity. In contrast, Kemf (1990) combine personal narrative with scientific investigation in order to assess the lingering social and ecological effects if American environmental warfare in Vietnam. This research, however, only pans the surface of salient issues, and much more work needs to be done.

While warfare is undeniably important, environmental change may also result from the peaceful interaction of states. Two quite different examples illustrate this point: the link between international aid and environmental change, and international watershed management.

The link between international aid and socio-ecological disruption has been the focus of mounting concern and criticism. Through national and multi-lateral agencies, First-World states have facilitated socially and environmental disruptive policies and practice in diverse Third-World settings. Many of environmental changes associated with state policies may also be partially attributed to such interstate cooperation. This cooperation, for example, has disrupted pastoralist-farmer relation with local ecosystems (Horewitz, 1986; Ahmed, 1987), and through support for transmigration schemes (Le Prestre, 1989; Hurst, 1990; Colchester, 1986), and large-scale hydro-eletric projects (Goldsmith and Hildyard, 1984, 1986; Cummings, 1990), has contributed to deforestation. Undoubtedly important, the contribution of aid agencies to environmental change must not be overemphasized: 'it remains an open question... as to how much influence aid agencies actually have on the nature and course of development projects. The power of aid donors is often exaggerated, and of course varies a great deal' (Adams, 1990a: 166). Moreover, in an era of heightened environmental awareness in both the Third and First Worlds, the possibilities for both socially and ecologically more sensitive interstate cooperation—or what has been termed *the greening of aid* (Conroy and Litvinoff, 1988)—should not be discounted.

Peaceful cooperation between states also contributes to environmental change in other ways—international watershed management being an example. As the literature on the Nile watershed illustrates, however, such cooperation remains tentative and, in a world of sovereign states, ever subject to disruption. The Nile has been affected by what Waterbury (1979) terms *hydropolitics*, and Collins (1990) and Godana (1985) examine the colonial antecedents to modern riparian cooperation. Waterbury (1979), Haynes and Whittington (1981), Godana (1985), Collins (1990), Whinttington and Haynes (1985) and Beshir (1984) explore contemporary processes of cooperation between Egypt and the Sudan. Collins (1990) and Howell *et al.* (1988) offer detailed analyses of the ill-fated Jonglei Canal project. These and other, more general, works (*e.g.*, Myers, 1989), emphasize how socio-economic and ecological changes in the region indicate the need for expanded interstate cooperation, while highlighting the political difficulties associated with it. As Godana (1985) points out, however, the political difficulties associated with international watershed management are hardly unique to the Nile. The internal and interstate antipathies that often lead to war are a powerful and enduring obstacle to the cooperation that international river management requires.

If these interstate sources have yet to receive adequate attention, the links between global capitalism and Third-World environmental change have been extensively examined. Redclift (1984,1987), O'Connor (1989) and Shanmugaratnam (1989) broadly relate such change to patterns of First-World development. Other studies explore this relationship in greater depth. Thus, Mekvichai (1988) and Lohmann (1990) examine the environmental consequences of commercial forestry in Thailand. Schmink (1988b), Branford and Glock (1985), Hecht (1984,1985), Schmink and Wood (1987), Bunker (1980,1984, 1985a), Wood and Schmink (1979) and Hecht and Cockburn (1989) assess the impact of capitalist development on

Amazonian ecosystems.

It is in the African context, however that capitalism, environmental degradation and poverty have been most systematically inter-related. Watts (1983b) and Franke and Chasin (1980) examine the links between expanded groundnut and cotton cultivation and West Africa's increased vulnerability to drought. O'Brien (1985) shows how Sudan's shift to export–crop production in the 1970s intensified environmental degradation and undermined national food security. Kjekshus (1977), Vail (1977) and McCracken (1987) offer contrasting perspectives in the impact of colonialism and capitalism on people and environments in East Africa. Garcia (1981), Horowitz and Little (1987), Wijkman and Timberlake (1984), Timberlake (1988) and Cliffe and Moorsom (1979), amongst others, also explore the relationship between capitalism and environmental change in Africa.

In recent years, area studies have been complemented by research relating transnational cooperations (TNCs) to environmental change. Pearson (1985) and Leonard (1988) examine the interaction among TNCs, Third-World governments, and people and environments. Combining thematic and case-study approaches, Pearson (1987) explores this interaction at greater length. Pintz (1987) and Gillis (1987), for example, study TNC operations in Papua New Guinea and Indonesia, while Gladwin (1987) offers a general review paper.

Of particular interest is research linking global agribusiness with biotechnology. Although biotechnology's 'epoch-making' role should not be exaggerated (Buttel, 1989), the ability to manipulate genetically plants and animals represents apotent means by which TNCs can effect environmental change. Kloppenburg (1988), for instance, notes how herbicide-resistant crop could increase herbicide use, thereby accelerating social and ecological degradation. As Bull (1982) observes, such degradation is already pervasive. Moreover, as Buttel (1990) notes, a growing demand of feedstock materials by First-World biotechnology industry might increase the burden on already threatened Third-World ecosystems. Goodman *et al.* (1987), George (1985), Franke and Chasin (1980), Dinham and Hines (1983), Kenney and Buttel (1985) and Redclift (1987) explore other aspects of this important relationship.

While the preceding review has documented the extensive, albeit uneven, literature on the contextual sources of environmental change, it remains to explore analytically the themes that have been raised. Addressing state policies, interstate relations, and global capitalism, in this manner, will help to clarify the nature of the framework's first area of inquiry.

State policies play a pivotal role in contemporary human-environmental interaction. As well as suggesting the priorities and practices of the state, such policies help to structure social discourse about environmental change, and are crucial to a broada understanding of the politics of such change. Thus, their origins, content, implementation and impact require analysis.

State policies are not developed in a political and economic vacuum. Rather, they result from struggle between competing actors seeking to influence policy formulation. Given that sundry policies have environmental implications, the number of actors involved can by great, including government departments and agencies, national and transnational corporations, non-governmental organizations, multilateral agencies and foreign governments. The challenge is to identify the different and often conflicting pressures on policy-makers in order to understand a particular policy outcome. How previous policy choices contributed to environmental change, and how much change in turn affected the decision-making process, must also be explored.

Research could then address all relevant policy content. The complexities of such research are as formidable as the diverse and often contradictory objectives of state policy itself. If the state is 'a theatre in which resources, property rights and authority are struggled over' (Watts, 1989 : 4), then state policies embody that struggle, often facilitating the interests of powerful economic elites, and inculcating both social unrest and ecological degradation. State policies, however, also promote non-economic objectives, and, as Hecht and Cockburn (1989) and Budiardjo (1986) note, national security questions impinge in the policy process. More prosaically, state policies may simply reflect a desire on the part of political elites to assert control over individuals and groups. From this perspective, economically disastrous policies and projects may serve other, un-stated ends—for example, serving as 'a rural manifestation of the states' active presence' (Hart in Adams, 1990a: 157).[10]

State policies then, are an embodiment of societal divisions and struggle and the narrower interests of the state itself. Such policies, however, cannot be understood in isolation. Not only do policies embody conflicting aims and objectives, but their fate may concurrently be linked with those of other policies removed from the environmental arena. Forest policies, for example, may attempt to reconcile an interest in conservation with pressures for commercial and non commercial use, within broader context where tax, trade and industrial policies often prejudice the outcome (Gillis and Repetto, 1988). Since many Third World states lack the requisite coordinating mechanisms, policy fragmentation compounds the research problem. How do diverse groups in state and society fare under such conditions? What role do organizations like the World Bank and the International Monetary Fund play in this process ? (Le Prestre, 1989) Such questions highlight the importance of process as well as content in policy analysis.

Attention could then be directed towards exploration of policy implementation. A policy's impact may well derive more from the manner in which it has been implemented than from its content, thereby highlighting the important role of local officials. Does policy interpretation balance local expectations with official views? Are officials subject to pressure from local elites, transnational corporations or peasant organizations? What role does corruption play in policy implementation? To what extent are standardized bureaucratic procedures attempt to minimize policy 'leakage'? As Bunker (1982,1985b) notes, however, the application of such procedures to socio-economically and ecologically underdeveloped regions may in itself be problematic. How successful, then, are bureaucratic structures in controlling the many location specific policy expressions? These questions highlight the importance of the implementation stage, local officials, and the bureaucratic structures within which they operate.

Finally, the environmental impact of state policy should also be addressed. Does the nature and extent of environmental change vary according to whether policy is implemented directly by the state, or indirectly, through other social groups? Can policy have an 'environmental multiplier effect', accelerating certain processes of human-environmental interaction at the expense of others? How do different political economic and ecological settings influence policy impact?

While discussion has focused on the role of state policies in shaping environmental change, states do not formulate policies in isolation from each other. As Skocpol (1985:8) observess, 'the modern state... has always been ... part of a system of competing and mutually involved states'. Thus, conflict and competition between states has long contributed to environmental modification. And yet, as the review highlighted, research in this area is underdeveloped. How might the interstate dimensions of environmental change best be approached? A useful beginning would be to distinguish between its peaceful and violent variants, as they impinge on land, water and forest conditions.

As the literature highlights, violence between states often contributes to environmental change. In exploring this relationship at greater depth, it was suggested that scholars need to devote increased attention to the national and regional dimensions of such violence. Recent international developments reinforce this point, as—East-West rapprochement notwithstanding—the diffusion of military hardware, including nuclear weapons, to the Third-World, continues. Gill and Law (1988:370) note that East-West rapprochement may in fact encourage this trend; in the context of substantial reductions in domestic military expenditure, the superpowers may attempt 'to maintain their economies of scale in certain types of military production.' How would this greater availability of armaments alter the kind, extent and intensity of Third World interstate violence and environmental change?

The peaceful interaction between states is also laden with environmental implications. Such interaction may accelerate development of non-state sources of environmental change—global capitalism, for example. As the discussion of international aid and watershed management highlighted, however, peaceful relations between states contribute directly to environmental change. In the process, the costs and benefits of such change may be inequitably distributed between states. Thus, does the political dependence of one state on another translate into increased environmental degradation? Conversely, may a politically ascendant state avoid such degradation by 'exporting' it to client states? Do power imbalances among states arise, in part, from differential control over environmental resources? Can disadvantaged states use internal processes of environmental change—tropical deforestation. For example, to strengthen their position *vis-a-vis* other states? In recent years, concepts such as 'debt-for-nature' swap, and 'global bargain' have entered the international political vocabulary. Motivated by a perceived 'crisis of the commons', First-World states have begun to consider making economic concessions to ensure Third-World environmental conservation. To what extent such concessions would offset long-standing power imbalances between 'developed' and 'developing' countries remains uncertain.

Both interstate and state sources of environmental change, however, must be situated in a broader context that embraces the role of global capitalism. As increasingly embodied in the transnational corporation (TNC), global capitalism is a powerful source of environmental change. Seeking profit maximization, corporate growth and market control, TNCs have contributed to virtually every form of environmental change. Such corporations, however, effect the environment differently. An examination of the link between global capitalism and environmental change, then, might begin with an analysis of the individual firm, move to the broader economic context and conclude with an assessment of the general socio-political milieu within which TNCs operate.

The relationship between the individual firm and environmental change raises a variety of issues (Pearson, 1987). How does the structure and organization of a transnational firm affect its role and performance as an environmental manager? Does the degree of corporate centralization or decentralization influence its environmental record? How may a corporation's size, history, country of origin and operational distribution affect its environmental actions?

A TNC is not a monolithic entity and, as with other social organizations, its conduct reflects the interaction between numerous individuals and groups. Consequently, there is a need to 'unpack' the corporation, exploring the attitudes and practices of its employees. In particular, attention should be directed toward individuals at the environmental 'interface', responsible for implementing corporate policy. How important are the opinion of local managers, for example, in the implementation of a firm's environmental policies and practices? Is the corporation's local reputation considered significant?

In understanding this link between TNCs and the environment, attention must also be directed to the socio-political and economic factors impinging upon an individual firm's actions. What characterizes the industry within which a TNC operates? Do small and large firms co-exist or do technological and financial barriers encourage oligopolistic conditions? If such conditions prevail, what are the implications for TNC environmental interaction? Conversely, how does competition affect a firm's environmental practices? As they do business in diverse national setting, the possibility that firm will face a combination of these conditions should also be considered.

Such characteristics indicate the multifarious ways in which TNCs differ in their operations and, hence, in their environmental relationship. TNCs are not independent of the societies in which they operate, though, and in understanding how firms contribute to environmental change, it is also important to understand the socio-political context of their activities, in both the 'host' and 'home' countries.

In this sense, the relationship between TNCs and the state is particularly significant. In Third World 'host' countries, are state policies based on economic nationalism? If so, how may such policies affect TNCs and their environmental practices? Moreover, although they will clearly vary between countries, what factors affect bargaining power between host states and TNCs?

In recent years, however, a conservative revolution in the international community has reversed policies of economic nationalism. Burdened with debts they are often unable to repay, many countries adopted structural adjustment policies favouring private sector export activities (George, 1988; Watts, 1990). Do such policies constitute a *carle blanche* for TNCs in their use and misuse of the environment? Or, by contrast, has a growing concern about ecological degradation in many parts of the Third World fostered a policy milieu conducive to more stringent environment regulations?

TNCs must also be sensitive to the socio-political conditions in their 'home' countries. Typically located in the First World, home countries—and more particularly their states—may also influence how TNCs affect Third World environments. As in the Third World, however, governments have shown less interest in regulating TNC practices. Thus, to what extent have pro-business governments in the First World relaxed supervision of TNCs? Moreover, how has a more competitive global business environment, and the growing power of Japan and the newly industrializing countries, affected home supervision? Conversely, what are the implications of the re-emergence of environmental concerns (global warning, ozone depletion, etc.) on national and international political agendas for relations between the home state and TNCs?

If attention so far has centred on the TNC-environmental relationship, a comparable set of questions could inform analyses of national corporations and Third World environmental change. The differing constraints and opportunities facing national, as opposed to transnational, corporations, must be addressed. Do national corporations have greater freedom to manipulate the environment, while technologically more advanced TNCs are expected to meet more exacting standards? Further, the ability of TNCs to move into and out of a country may confer certain advantages not enjoyed by national corporations. How, then, does mobility affect a corporation's interaction with state, society and environment?

These questions underscore the complex links between global capitalism and Third World environmental change. While transnational and national corporations play a critical role in environmental transformation, the multifarious nature of that role must not be forgotten. Moreover, this role must not only be understood in relation to other contextual sources (state policies, interstate relations), but also the location-specific dimensions of environmental change. Research addressing conflict over access, the framework's second area of inquiry, may further such understanding.

Conflict Over Access

Research into question of conflict over access examines the relationship between access rights, local struggle and ecological transformation (Peluso, 1988; Hirsch, 1990). Thus, the second element in the framework is concerned with the constraints and opportunities facing peasants and other socially disadvantaged groups in struggle to protect the environmental foundations of their livelihood. Specifically, in seeking to understand conflict over access, both the historical and contemporary dynamics of struggle must be addressed.

While much of the literature on conflict over access focuses on contemporary debates, a number of scholars have adopted an historical perspective. To illustrate elements of continuity and change in local struggle, several studies compare and contrast the colonial and post-colonial experiences. Peluso (1988), Watts (1983b), Guha (1989a), Guha and Gadgil (1989) and Nadkarni (1989) do so in the Javanese, Nigerian and Indian settings. Peters (1984) and Worby (1988) examine the struggle for land water rights in Botswana. In different socio-political and ecological setting, these studies nevertheless pinpoint the major transformation wrought by colonial rule, and the bitter legacy of state-peasant antagonism over control of environmental resources that, even today, shows few signs of dissipating.

For the post-colonial era, the nature of state —peasant and other types of conflict over access has been extensively reviewed. Work by Shiva (1987), Agarwal and Narain (1985), Fernandes (1990), Jodha (1986), Lohmann (1990), Leonard (1985), Thomson (1985) and Schmink (1982) illustrates the breadth of issues addressed. The following review, then, highlights only selected themes.

Conflict pitting peasants against state or economic elites not only involves questions of 'land', but may embrace the struggle over flora and fauna (Peluso, 1988; Mackenzie, 1988; Dogra, 1985: Saldanha, 1990), soil conditions (Hirsch and Lohmann, 1989), and water supplies (Peters, 1984). More work, however, needs to consider the roles that these and other environmental resources play in the livelihoods of the rural poor (Chambers and Leach, 1989: Hecht *et al.*, 1988). Concomitantly there is a need for greater knowledge of how such groups interpret these roles (Chamber, 1983; Richards, 1985; Blaluert, 1988).

The complexity of conflict over access is partially attributable to tenurial systems and social institutions regulating access, control and use of environmental resources. Recent work on the sociology of access in Africa is illustrative. As pertaining to an understanding of broader agricultural and ecological issues, Okoth-Ogendo (1989), Blaikie (1989a) and Berry (1989b) offer contrasting perspective on resources access and use. Mackenzie (1986, 1989), Haugerud (1989). Carney and Watts (1990), Becker (1990) and Davison (1987), provide empirical case-studies examining many of the ideas developed in these papers. In this research, complexity of access is emphasized; multiple and overlapping rights combine with formal and informal tenure to produce a complex web of dependencies. Similarly, as Peters (1984) and Berry (1988) point out, struggle is equally complex. Given the importance of social identity, for example, in the determination of access right, 'struggles over meaning are as much a part of the process of resource allocation as are struggles over surplus or the labor process' (Berry, 1988:66). As Berry (1988) and Haugerud (1989) emphasize, this complexity has important implications for both public and private efforts to regulate land use.

The role of women in conflict over access is crucial, and yet, has typically been neglected. Only recently has gender begun to receive systematic attention. Shiva (1987,1988), B. Agarwal (1988a, 1988b, 1989), Mies (1984), Jain (1984) and A. Agarwal (1988), for example, consider the role of Indian women in struggles to retain access to land, water and forest resources. B. Agarwal (1990) analyses the relationship between such struggles and individual/family security in the face of seasonality and calamity. In the Kenyan context, Davison (1987), Mackenzie (1986,1989) and Maathai (1986) examine questions of tenure, ecological change and women's politicization. Similarly, Dankelman and Davidson (1988) and Carney and Watts (1990) explore aspects of women's struggle. Focused on gender-derived inequalities, this research views household relations as a 'deeply contested terrain' (Watts, 1989: 12) in which access to environmental resources remains a bitter source of conflict.

As illustrated, conflict over access to environmental resources is a powerful source of social division. Apart from the household, however, conflict between socially disadvantage and 'contextual' groups is also significant. Embracing 'peasant' relations with political and economic elites, this conflict may be formalized with the development of environmental movements. As discussed below, environmental movements are an important strategy for the poor attempting to preserve the environmental foundations of their livelihood.

The preceding review highlight the complexities of conflict over access, as well as literature only beginning to recognize that complexity. Analytically, however, the framework's second area of inquiry may best be approached by pursuing themes in the historical contemporary dynamics of conflict.

Adopting an historical perspective serves as a useful reminder that conflict over access is intrinsic to human development. Shaped by diverse political, social and ecological factors, it has been expressed in innumerable location-specific ways. As such, the struggle for access did not originate with capitalism and colonialism—the latter being simply the most recent in a recurring motif of human struggle over the environment.

And yet the advent of colonialism and capitalism marks a qualitative change in the history of Third World struggle. Whereas pre-colonial conflict over access was tempered by decentralized power relations, and by a relatively low level of technological development, colonial and post-colonial struggle has faced few such constraints. How has this transformation of political, economic and technological capabilities affected traditional conflict patterns? To what extent have new patterns emerged, or traditional practices been invoked?

As appreciation of the historical dimensions of conflict over access is essential to a understanding of contemporary struggle. Inherently location specific, such conflict nevertheless brings together national and international, as well as local actors, and embodies the struggle between diverse political, social and economic interests. The management of such competing interests is as integral research theme.

In understanding the contemporary dynamics of conflict, however, a spatial distinction should be drawn between actors at or near the conflict site, and those elsewhere—at regional, national or international centres. How may this pattern influence the nature and outcome of struggle, and be reflected in coalitions amongst actors? How are coalitions constructed? What impact does the spatial fragmentation of 'contextual' actors, the state and TNCs, have on location specific conflict?

Spatially differentiated, actors also differ in their access to strategic resources. TNCs and the state, for example, typically possess greater informational and technological resources than local villagers. How these contextual actors deploy much resources in location-specific struggles is among the more crucial research questions. To what extent may imbalances in technological and informational capability affect the outcome? Is superiority in strategic resources offset by other, perhaps intangible factors? In the Malaysian context, for instance, Scott (1985) has shown that the 'weapon of the weak' are not inconsequential in the conflict over access. When combined with overt resistance, the tenacity and desperation of those faced with the loss of critical environmental resources may, to some extent, counteract the forces of the powerful (Anderson and Huber, 1988; and below).

Recognizing the spatial, technological and informational differentiation between actors is but a preliminary step towards understanding the contemporary dynamics of conflict over access. Although helpful, details of differentiation and conflict—prerequisites for a more comprehensive treatment of access conflict —are not considered. A more adequate inquiry, then, must deconstruct commonly used terms that typically conceal more than they reveal ('peasant', 'state', 'TNC') in order to expose the complex reality embedded in them.

An examination of the specific rather than generalities, of conflict over access, brings into question widely-held beliefs about Third World human-environmental interaction. Conflict between poor villagers dependent for their well-being on local land, water and forest resources, and various powerful coalitions attempting to deprive them of access to those resources, recurs in the literature. And yet, this dichotomy masks a web of complex power relations (Hirsch, 1990; Bernsterin, 1990). To what extent, for example, are villagers an undifferentiated mass, united in their destitution? Are they not also caught up in differentiated relations with the powerful and with each other, and does this not translate into differing interests and objectives in conflict over access? In this sense, the role of women merits particular scrutiny. In the household, how do gender-based, and often unequal divisions of labour contributte to the complexities of social struggle for land, water and forests? Comparable questions may be asked about contextual actors. Do political and economic elites act unanimously? Is state unity jeopardized by divergent personal and bureaucratic interests, and do TNCs and the state always concur?

Not only do these questions highlight the complexities of conflict over access, they also indicate the difficulties associated with its management. Although the state plays a central role in conflict management, its role is circumscribed by at least two factors. First, the state is not an impartial observer in such struggles — indeed, it is often a leading participant. Secondly, the state is often riven by conflicting interests.

Given these circumstances, what roles do other actors play in conflict management? To what extent do intimidation, coercion, avoidance behaviour, organized protest, theft and bribery regulate the struggle for access? Moreover, how should TNC efforts to cultivate local goodwill be interpreted? Research needs to be sensitive to the complexities of conflict, the multifarious ways in which such conflict is managed, and ultimately, the political ramifications of environmental change.

Political Ramifications of Environmental Change

Research into the political ramifications of environmental change, the framework's third area of inquiry, explores the ways that environmental change influences socio-economic inequalities, and by extension, political processes. Thus, it acknowledges an often overlooked dimension. Just as political forces contribute to environmental change, the modification of land, water and forests has important political ramifications. To appreciate better those ramifications, however, attention needs to be directed to socio-economic impact and political process.

The diverse literature on political ramifications has been guided by two basic questions. First, to what extent are the costs of environmental change borne by socially-disadvantaged groups, and how does this unequal distribution of costs mediate existing socio-economic inequalities? And secondly, under what circumstances does unequal exposure to environmental change modify political processes?

In the literature, questions of socio-economic impact recur, and have been addressed differently. Blaikie (1985) notes that soil erosion adversely affects both small rural producers and the urban poor. Thomson (1985) explores how desertification in Niger reinforces inequalities among the Tuareg, and Zaman (1989) examines how riverbank erosion in the Brahmaputra-Jamuna floodplain of Bangladesh strengthens the dependency of landless peasants and displaces on rural elites. Agarwal and Narain (1985) and A. Agarwal (1988) survey the effects of ecological degradation on India's poor. Amongst many others, Hecht and Cockburn (1989), Ramos (1984), Bunker (1985a), Hecht *et al.* (1988) and Cummings (1990) highlight the impact of resource extraction in the Amazon on the area's socially-disadvantaged groups.

Not surprisingly, this literature emphasizes the poor's particular vulnerability to ecological degradation: social erosion, desertification. But they are also threatened by changes which, superficially, might be considered environmentally beneficial. Commercial tree plantations are a case in point. Lohmann (1990), Hirsch and Lohmann (1989). B Agarwal, (1988a) and Agarwal and Narain (1985), for example, observe how eucalyptus plantations in Thailand and India may eliminate opportunities for grazing and collection of minor forest produce, even jeopardizing local soil and water regimes. As A. Agarwal (1988) notes, even planting eucalyptus on 'barren' lands implicates the poor, who may require the weeds on such lands for fuel.

The literature addressing political ramifications of environmental change underscores the serious plight of those who are socially and ecologically disadvantaged. For some, the lesson seems clear: 'poverty and environmental degradation form a trap from which there is little chance of escape' (Adams, 1990a: 87). And yet, paradoxically, environmental degradation may also assist the poor. As Chambers (1987) notes, degraded land of low monetary value may yet provide 'sustainable livelihoods', particularly when combined with non-agricultural income (Blaikie, 1998a). Although it must not be exaggerated, adaptation to changing circumstances, impelled by the sheer quest for survival, should not be summarily dismissed (Mortimore, 1989). The resilience of the land, and the poor drawing sustenance from it, cannot be underestimated, nor the political obituary of the Third-World peasantry read (Hall, 1989; Browder, 1989; Richards, 1990).

In examining the political ramifications of environmental change, moreover, the willingness and ability of the poor to contest their plight should not be forgotten. Research on peasant protest often emphasizes the clandestine nature of such resistance (Scott, 1985), and evidence of this covert activity appears in several sources discussed herein. Guha (1989a, 1989b), Peluso (1988) and Hafner and Apichatvullop (1990) cite arson and theft as examples of everyday resistance, but as Scott (1985: 29–30) observes, these 'weapons of the weak' should not be exaggerated: 'they are unlikely to do more than marginally affect the various forms of exploitation that peasants confront.'

It is hardly surprising that peasants faced with a threat to the environmental foundations of their livelihoods, have often resorted to overt collective resistance. As Guha (1989a, 1989b) shows, such resistance is not new. Nevertheless, it is only over the last two decades that Third World environmental movements have gained momentum.

A number of scholars have examined the emergence of environmental movements in Africa, Latin America and Asia. Although these groups differ, important similarities exist between them. As Redclift (1987: 159) notes, environmental movements in the South must be differentiated from their Northern equivalents:

The two principal components of environmental movements in the South are of marginal importance to most movements in the developed countries. They are that those who constitute the 'movement' are engaged in a livelihood struggle and, secondly, that they recognize that this livelihood struggle can be successful only if the environment is managed in a sustainable way.

These 'livelihood struggles', then, have been the focus of much attention. Redclift (1987) provides a useful introduction to Third World environmental movements. In the Indian setting, Agarwal and Narain (1985) and Omvedt (1989) survey the plethora of movements that have emerged. In particular, Shiva (1987), Shiva and Bandyopadhyay (1988), Weber (1987). Bahuguna (1985) and Guha (1989a) outline the development of India's renowned Chipko movement. Hirsch and Lohmann (1989) and Lohmann (1990) study various movements launched by Thai people to contest eucalyptus plantations and hydro-electric dams. Maathai (1986) traces the evolution of Kenya's Green Belt Movement. Redclift (1987) examines Mexican environmental movements, while Hecht and Cockburn (1989) and Schwartzman (1989) discuss the rubber-tappers' movement in the Brazilian Amazon.

Much of this research focuses on the livelihood struggles of ethnically-dominant, albeit economically-subordinate, groups. But what of ethnic minorities and attendant forms of protest? The link between ethnicity, ecological change and political protest awaits adequate exploration. Several studies, however, suggest the research possibilities. Hong (1987) provides a detailed study of deforestation and indigenous protest in Sarawak. Drucker (1985), Porter (1990) and Hurst (1990) also explore ethnic-minority resistance in Southeast Asia. Hecht and Cockburn (1989) and Cummings (1990) briefly document the genesis of Indian struggles in the Amazon. Blaucert (1988) discusses emerging autochthonous resistance in southern Mexico, and Anderson and Huber (1988) offer a case-study of similar protest in central India.

The preceding review of work on the political ramifications of environmental change emphasizes that such change not only exacerbates socio-economic inequalities, but also serves as a catalyst for political protest, notably as manifested in environmental movements. In analysing this third element in the framework, therefore, there is a need to differentiate between socio-economic impact and political process.

An appreciation of the political ramifications of environmental change typically necessitates location-specific understanding. As Blaikie (1985), Blaikie and Brookfield (1987a) and others have noted, such understanding must be sensitive to the physical and biological processes specific to a given locale. However, development of a location specific and technical approach is unnecessary In exploring the political dimensions of environmental change, a more general scheme is appropriate. Thus, in referring to environmental change, a broad distinction is made between episodic and everyday changes. Episodic change includes flooding, drought and similar disasters, while the everyday embraces soil erosion, salinization, deforestation and various types of pollution. Although these two forms of environmental change may be interrelated, this interrelationship remains open to debate (Hamilton and Pearce, 1988; Messerli. 1990).

Everyday forms of environmental change are, as their name would suggest, temporally and spatially ubiquitous, having a gradual and cumulative impact on human communities which may long go unrecognized (Blaikie, 1985). When such change is recognized, it may then mingle with human interests, yielding competing perceptions and definitions (Blaikie and Brookfield, 1987b). The complexities of everyday forms of environmental change, however, should not obscure their differentiated socio-economic impact.

In addressing that impact, research should be sensitive to the social and ecological marginality of the poor (Blaikie and Brookfield, 1987b). How do land managers, for example, become, spatially and economically marginalized? How does such marginalization relate to ecological marginality—that is, lands of low and/or erratic capability? Moreover, how do these forms of marginality interact to produce 'socio-ecocide'—or a downward spiral of human and environmental degradation? Most importantly, how can individuals and groups caught in this trap organize resistance?

Everyday forms of environmental change must also be related to episodic forms of change—the droughts, floods and other disasters that periodically threaten human existence. Although episodic change occurs independently of human design, its impact on social communities is by no means exclusively or even predominantly 'natural' (Watts, 1983a; Susman *et al.*,1983). Processes of social and ecological marginalization noted above with respect to everyday change are also crucial to an understanding of the impact of episodic change. Marginalization typically increases the vulnerability of the poor to episodic change, breaking down previous defence mechanisms against ecological stress (Shenton and Watts, 1979; Watts, 1984). As the recent history of famine in Africa attests, the interplay between processes of marginalizations, and everyday and episodic forms of environmental change can have tragic human consequences.

As illustrated in the discussion of socio-economic impact, the unequal exposure of groups and individuals to environmental change is imbued with political significance. Environmental change may not only reflect existing inequalities, but it may also insidiously reinforce them in the long-term. As Durning (1990:135) says 'poverty's profile... has become increasingly environmental'.

Unequal exposure to environmental change may also modify political processes—and yet, this relationship is not self-evident. Even if political change occurs, it cannot be assumed that such change is designed to reverse ecological degradation or to assist those individuals and groups adversely affected by such degradation. Thus, just as socio-economic impact resonates with ambiguity, so too does its political outcome.

To yield a clearer picture of how environmental change affects and is absorbed into political processes, the network of power relations must be understood. In the face of environmental crises, do such relations facilitate or block social mobilization? Put differently, are power relationships reinforced by environmental changes? And if so, how are they reinforced? What opportunities do oppressed groups have for protest and resistance?

As the literature specifies, the socially-disadvantaged in many parts of the Third World are increasingly turning to overt strategies of collective resistance and, as manifested in environmental movements, such strategies represent a potentially potent challenge to local, national and even international political processes. How successful is such resistance in overcoming political and economic power configurations disposed to perpetuating the *status quo*? Further, how do political and economic elites attempt to defuse protest, emasculate resistance, and reaffirm extant power relations (Cummings, 1990) ? Are Third World environmental movements, often coalitions of diverse and potentially contradictory interests, vulnerable to subversion by such elites? How may such movements guard against internal divisions? As Guha (1989a), Weber (1987) and B. Agarwal (1988a) illustrate, environmental movements like the Chipko movement may be differentiated according to philosophy, gender and resistance strategies. Ironically, the location-specific focus of environmental movements weakens, and may ultimately limit, their ability to re-define prevailing power structures.

These issues are central to an understanding of the political ramifications of environmental change. By critically focusing on the relationship between environmental change, socio-economic impact and political process, such research addresses often neglected issues. It rejects facile assumptions about environmental change and human welfare—for example, that ecological degradation is a universal evil befalling rich and poor alike. Rather, it explores how such change is incorporated into concrete political and economic relationships, and the ways that it may then be used reinforce or challenge those relationships. As such, research into the political ramifications of environmental change constitutes an integral part—along with analyses of conflict over access and the contextual sources of environmental change—of a more general inquiry into the politics of environmental change.

Synopsis and Implications

This paper offers a preliminary exploration of Third World political ecology and, to this end, a framework comprising three areas of inquiry has been developed. Although related, the contextual sources of environmental change, conflict over access, and the political ramifications of environmental change, were disaggregated in order to appreciate the specific processes involved. In each case, the relevant literature was reviewed, and the central analytical issues examined. It should be reiterated, however, that neither the review nor the analytical components purports to be comprehensive.

As embodied in this paper's framework, the agenda for Third World political ecology is both complex and challenging, requiring analytical refinement as well as empirical exploration. How may such work be encouraged? A first step must recognize that Third World political ecology does indeed constitute an emerging research agenda. Such recognition, however, is hindered by low levels of awareness. Divided by disciplinary and institutional affiliations, many scholars have been further isolated by the empirical and policy-oriented bent of the research community. Where scholarly exchanges has occurred, it has tended to remain regionally based with comprehensive Third World exchange more the exception than the rule (*e.g.* Little and Horowitz. 1987; Repetto and Gillis, 1988). A growing sense of community, sustained by knowledge of a common research agenda, might remove some obstacles to cooperation, and set the stage for a more intensive phase in the development of Third World political ecology.

As this agenda emerges, new issues will need to be addressed—the role of ideology and culture in environment at change seems particularly important.[18] How the environment and environment at change are perceived, and related to different aspects of human development, influences the nature and extent of such changes. Correspondingly however, these factors need to be integrated with the contextual and location-specific forces discussed above.

Ideas are never 'innocent' Mental conceptions, including belief systems, morality, philosophy; and law, either reinforce or challenge existing social and economic arrangements. And they do so actively, as biased participants in sociopolitical intercourse (Schmink and Wood, 1987: 51)

In exploring these and other issues, political ecology must be situated in the broader context of Third World studies. Such integration will benefit the latter (Hettne, 1990), while promoting more rigorous development of the former. Third World political ecology might be enriched by recent work in contiguous and often overlapping research agendas: peasant studies and power analysis (Scott, 1985; Colburn. 1989; Hart *et al.*, 1989); household and gender studies (Watts, 1989; Whitehead, 1990); and the literature on the politics of hunting and implications need to be systematically incorporated into Third World political ecology, with particular reference to conflict over access and the political ramifications of environmental change.

A more systematic definition of the research agenda is thus urgently required. Emerging at a time of intense environmental change, Third World political ecology attempts to integrate environmental and political analysis to illustrate how these two activities, both helping to shape human destiny, are interrelated, and more importantly, how the one cannot be fully understood without the other. It is in the recognition and analysis of this interdependence that Third World political ecology could make its most crucial contribution.

3
Mismatch and Risks

The lack of sufficient correspondence between the legal-political structure of world society (which is built out of presumably sovereign nation-states) and the structure of the natural and artificial material environment (which is unavoidably transnational in many of its dimensions) has become a matter of widespread and urgent concern; for with nature-altering technologies now being employed, humans are drastically affecting the conditions of the life on the planet without being held accountable for the damage they are doing. The 1987 report to the United Nations by its specially appointed distinguished persons World Commission on Environment and Development stated what is now commonplace recognition of this planetary incongruence:

> The Earth is one but the world is not. We all depend on one biosphere for sustaining our lives. Yet each community, each country, strives for survival and prosperity with little regard for its impact on others. Some consume the Earth's resources at a rate that would leave little for future generations. Others, many more in number, consume far too little and live with the prospect of hunger, squalor, disease, and early death.

The report of the World Commission (often called the Brundtland Commission, after its chairperson, the former prime minister of Norway, Gro Harlem Brundtland) was a landmark in the building of a basic world consensus on the essential characteristics of the global ecological/ environmental predicament and on basic policy imperatives for dealing with this predicament. As such it reflected and helped shape the growing consciousness among statespersons that urgent, and probably radical, departures from the business as usual, international economics as usual, world politics as usual approaches may be required to assure the healthy survival of the human species.

A principal contribution of the Brundtland Commission was to challenge the presumed antithesis between economic development and environmental care—a concern of many Third World economists, worried that the new ecology-preservation imperatives being touted by environmentalists in the United States and Europe would slow down and make more costly the industrialisation of their countries. The Brundtland Commission's central concept of *sustainable development* was directly responsive to this concern. The imperative for affluent as well as poor countries, industrial as well as primarily agricultural societies, said the Commission, was "the integration of environment policies and development strategies." Far from urging a cessation of economic growth, the Commission called for "a new era of growth in which developing countries play a large role and reap large benefits." In particular, "development that is sustainable has to address the problems of the large number of people who live in absolute poverty... [for] poverty reduces people's capacity to use resources in a sustainable manner; it intensifies pressure on the environment." But policymakers guided by the concept of sustainable development "will necessarily work to assure that growing economies remain firmly attached to their ecological roots and that these roots are protected and nurtured so that they may support growth over the long term."

Though recognising that economic and social systems and ecological conditions differ widely among countries and that each nation will have to work out its own sustainable development policy, the Brundtland Commission was equally insistent that no country can develop in isolation from others. The pursuit of sustainable development, it concluded, "requires a new orientation in international relations."

Following the Commission's recommendations the United Nations called a World Conference on Environment and Development, to convene in Rio de Janeiro in June, 1992. The Conference Secretary General, Maurice Strong, articulated the Conference mandate:

> The Earth Summit will be asked to adopt an Agenda for the 21st Century, setting out an internationally agreed work program, including targets for national and international performance... [and] new international conventions on climate change, forestry, and biodiversity... The summit will be asked to provide developing countries with access to additional financial resources... and environmentally sound technologies to enable them to implement the conventions and to integrate environment into their future development. *It will also be asked to consider far-reaching reforms*

of the international system [my emphasis].

Traditionally, when humans consumed, took possession of, or altered nature's "givens," these actions, even though often constrained by national or local community interests and laws, typically were characterised by indifference to the well-being of outsiders (human and non-human), particularly those outside of the national community. Moreover, the international indifference was legitimized by the dominant norms and institutions of the world polity.

Despite national variations in the amount of governmental regulation of private action and in the extent of devolution of regulatory authority to local subdivisions of government, countries the world over lodged ultimate responsibility for assuring prudent private and community use of natural resources in their national governments. If countries got in each other's way in the use of natural resources, they would negotiate or fight to determine access or shares; and that, for the time being, would be that. But the traditional lack of continuing international monitoring and control of natural resources is coming to be seen by more and more people as a luxury dangerous to the affluent as well as an unjust infliction on the poor.

Much of the contemporary consciousness can be traced to the work of marine biologists in the 1950s, reflected in Rachel Carson's 1962 best selling book *Silent Spring*. Carson reported in evocative prose how mindless and narrowly self-interested uses of the seas were profoundly disturbing the ocean's natural ecologies in ways that could jeopardize the food supplies and health of large segments of the Earth's human population. By the end of the 1960s, a full-blown environmentalist movement had arisen, galvanised by two shocking accidents: the widespread death of aquatic animals and plants resulting from the 1967 oil spill of the super tanker *Torrey Canyon* as it ran aground, and the devastation to ocean and coastline ecologies caused by the 1969 leak in the Union Oil Company's rig in the Santa Barbara Channel. Over the next few years numerous publications, television documentaries, and legislative hearings alerted newly attentive publics worldwide that not only accidents, but "normal" activities—fishing, beachfront residential and recreational development, the dumping of wastes, the tank-washing procedures of oil tankers, drilling in the seabed seismic, explosions, thermal heat transfers from power stations, and the atmospheric transfer to the oceans of agricultural pesticides—were despoiling the seas. Meteorologists, aware of the crucial function the great world ocean (covering 70 per cent of the Earth's surface) plays in absorbing carbon dioxide from the atmosphere, began to worry about the effects of widespread marine pollution on the Earth's climate. A

Resources for the Future study expressed the growing concern: "We know all too little of how the sea and its biotic communities impinge on global ecology, but there is every reason to treat this relationship with great respect. Instead we utilize the sea thoughtlessly as the ultimate sink for all sorts of debris and chemicals generated on land and transmitted by air and water." Meanwhile, the United Nations Conference on the Environment, meeting in Stockholm in 1972, elevated the protection of the Earth's basic ecologies to a primary concern of international statecraft and authorised a new permanently sitting global agency, the United Nations Environmental Program (UNEP), to stimulate international cooperation in this field. But the UNEP, despite the vigorous leadership of its first Secretary General Maurice Strong, was provided with few carrots (financial resources) and no punitive sticks whatsoever with which to induce adherence to its resolutions. The most important function of the UNEP has been as a catalyst and clearinghouse for environmental scientists and other professionals to interact as an "epistemic community" of common knowledge and commitment and to reinforce one another's influence within their respective countries.

By the 1980s, the world media were full of reports of unhealthy air pollution levels, acid rain, oil-drenched coasts, dying seas and lakes, poisoned fish, and contaminated food chains—all of this symptomatic of the transborder communities of mutual vulnerability wrought by the industrial and technological revolutions. But there did not seem to be much progress in closing the gap between the harms people can suffer across international boundaries and human society's means for assuring the accountability of those responsible for the injuries. This gap was further exposed by the explosion and meltdown at the Soviet Union's Chernobyl nuclear plant in April, 1986. Neighbouring countries in the path of the radioactive cloud escaping from the fire in the nuclear facility did not even know that a terrible accident had occurred until two days after the explosion, when scientists in Sweden and Finland discovered abnormal levels of radioactivity in their own atmosphere.

Finally, in the late 1980s, the dissemination of startling scientific findings on the depletion of the Earth's protective ozone layer and the buildup of greenhouse gases began, at last, to stimulate a *do something*! attitude on the part of publics and elites—portending, perhaps, a larger cultural shift at the level of socio-political community to match the factual global community of common vulnerability being experienced at the material— ecological level of human existence.

Increasingly, given the new consciousness of common ecological vulnerability, many of the reasons that have been found compelling for regulation, even common management, of natural resource use *within* countries are coming to be accepted as compelling for such regulation and management *among* countries. As put by Jessica Tuchman Mathews, vice—president of the World Resources Institute, "The majority of environmental problems demand... solutions which encroach upon what we now think of as the prerogatives of national governments. This is because the phenomena themselves are defined by the limits of watershed, ecosystem, or atmospheric transport, not by national borders." The fish, it has been frequently observed, refuse to read the political maps.

People attentive to international issues, however, do read the political maps; and more and more of them are concerned that the sacrosanct quality statespersons and publics have heretofore accorded to the thick lines demarcating countries may be inhibiting the kinds of cooperation needed for humankind to deal adequately with the growing environmental threats to the well-being of people. Echoing concerns being voiced in similar gatherings in policy communities of countries around the world, the Final Report of the April, 1990 American Assembly found that.

> Three indivisibly linked global environmental trends together constitute an increasingly grave challenge to the habitability of the earth. They are human populations growth; tropical deforestation and the rapid loss of biological diversity; and global atmospheric change, including stratospheric ozone loss and greenhouse warming. These trends threaten nations, economic potential, therefore their internal political security, their citizens' health (because of increased ultraviolet radiation), and, in the case of global warming, possibly their very existence. No more basic threat to national security exists [my emphasis].

All nations, concluded the American Assembly report, are bound together in a new condition of "collective insecurity," which, in turn, calls for "an unprecedented strategy of international cooperation"—particularly cooperation between the industrial and developing countries that will include, unavoidably, substantial financial assistance by the rich to the poor.

The potentially massive political implications of the new ecological consciousness were pointed to by the prestigious Brundtland Commission:

> The mechanics of increased international cooperation required to assure sustainable development will vary from sector to sector and in relation to particular institutions. But it is fundamental that the transition to sustainable development be

> managed jointly by all nations. The unity ofhuman needs requires a functioning multilateral system that respects the democratic principles of consent and accepts that not only the Earth but also the world is one.

If "democratic principles of consent" were indeed to be applied "multilaterally" to human groups that are ecologically dependent on one another—that are, in other words, joint users of the planet's natural "commons"—the implications for the world polity would be nothing short of revolutionary.

The multilateral accountability arrangements, if they are to be congruent with the natural commons, in many cases will need to traverse the territorial boundaries of the existing nation-states. This is obviously the case for the *global* ecological commons (the biospheric envelope of the Earth, its climate and weather systems, and the great world ocean). Transborder arrangements are also required for many localized biotic, geologic, and atmospheric commons. And if such multilateral accountability arrangements are truly to be designed in accord with "consent of the governed" principles analogous to those that apply within most representative democracies, the sovereign authority of the existing nation-states will in many cases be challenged, if not supplanted by, new transnational authorities representing ecologically defined rather than territorially defined communities.

"The political organisation of the world is undergoing reconstruction," writes Lynton K. Caldwell. "The *de facto* sovereignty of the `sovereign nation state' is being modified by new concepts of political responsibility in which environmental imperatives—changes impacting on human welfare—are becoming compelling forces." Similarly, the authors of a 1991 textbook on the political dimensions of environmental problems reflect that a degree of "global governance, which seemed hopelessly idealistic only a few years ago, has been given legitimacy" in the environmental field. UN resolutions and international covenants such as the 1987 Montreal Protocol on Substances That Deplete the Ozone Layer, and the treaty on global warming being prepared for the 1992 Earth Summit mark the "development to legal concepts that... reduce the zone of absolute sovereignty of individual states in issues affecting the global environment." These developments anticipate a more comprehensive

> global governance approach [that] would... make the "common heritage of mankind" and "intergenerational equity" legal principles applicable to all global environmental issues that touch on threats to the global commons or natural·resources

affecting the interests of future generations. Such a revolutionary development in international law would presumably go hand in hand with the transformation of the international system by the creation of a global environmental authority.

To recognize the revolutionary political implications of the growing ecological consciousness, however, is not to predict that these political implications are anywhere near being acted upon in most places nor even to say that they are widely understood. Indeed, as the larger economic and political implications become more widely understood, the likelihood is that they will generate powerful backlashes against the ecological ethos by groups emotionally and/or pragmatically attached to the existing state-sovereignty norms.

Movement toward the degree of global accountability that is needed—which may well eventually involve a revolutionary transformation of the world polity—will therefore probably take place gradually, in small steps that at the outset impinge only minimally on the legal and political autonomy of countries. The outline of such a step-by-step approach presented in a 1976 Brookings Institution study on international commons regimes rather closely approximates what is now taking place in the environment field. The Brookings study contemplated at least two stages preliminary to any substantial sacrifice of national sovereignty.

1. *The international empanelling of scientists to gather and assess information about regional and global commons and to provide the international community with authoritative and politically neutral sources of information and analysis of how the commons are being used and abused.* Although it is neither desirable nor possible to "denationalize" all or most information about the international commons, the process of ensuring mutual accountability for commons use will be advanced if multiple sources of information coexist and compete for attention, and if in important areas of controversy there is at least one neutral international agency whose reports are available to all members of the international community.

2. *The expansion of international consultative processes—especially among those who use and those who are most directly affected by the condition of particular commons—aimed at clarifying conflicting interests and exposing the range of choices available to the parties involved and to the larger international community.* The consultative process often will start rather spontaneously among nuclei of governments, corporations, and interest groups who, for example, share the contours of an ocean basin or who are directly affected by regional atmospheric system.

But these nuclei of consultation, insofar as they involve commons that are linked into larger regional and global commons, will need eventually to expand from their initial core of directly involved local parties to accommodate a steadily widening consultative process accountable to affected constituencies more remote in geographic location and future time. This global expansion will probably require leadership from influential actors normatively committed to the principle of international accountability.

As these informational and consultative processes result in treaties of mutual restraint and obligation, such as the regional Mediterranean Plan, the Montreal Protocol on Ozone Depletion, and the contemplated global treaty on greenhouse warming, the international constituencies for these treaties are having to consider means of assuring mutual compliance that do indeed contemplate some erosion of sovereignty on the part of the participating nation states. But given counter constituency pressures and the deeply ingrained traditions of statecraft in the nation-state system, such sacrifices in national sovereignty, however minimal at the outset, will have to be phased in gradually and voluntarily if they are not to induce defections that will undermine the mutual accountability thus far achieved. International lawyer Abram Chayes (legal adviser at the State Department from 1961 to 1964), urges at least the development of "a technically competent and credible international monitoring and compliance capability" on the model of the International Monetary Fund. But Elliot Richardson (a former high official of the Nixon administration who took a leading role in the Law of the Sea negotiations) warns against agreements whose effective implementation would require delegating to multilateral organizations the power to override national environmental policies. A global Environmental Protection Agency that deployed "a legion of inspectors and enforcers," he argues, "rather than increasing compliance, could well have the opposite effect."

Clearly, world society has entered an era of intense debate not only on the material and scientific questions of the nature of the planet's ecological systems and what kinds of human induced alternations they can tolerate, but also on the structure and powers of political-legal regimes that are necessary to constrain some of these perturbations. Unavoidably, many of the political-legal regimes, simply because of the location of the ecologies, will have to be transnational, transregional, and global in membership and scope of authority. The extent to which the new regimes for ecological management can nevertheless remain congruent with the essential structure of the nation-state system is duly addressed.

Ecological Modernisation

In his celebrated study of the US conservation movement around the turn of the century, Samuel Hays (1979) describes how the popular moral crusade for conservation of American wilderness paved the way for a group of experts that, under the veil of working for conservation, advanced their own particular programme. These 'apostles of efficiency' did not share the somewhat sentimental attitude towards wilderness that was typical of the predominantly urban movement for conservation. Above all, they were interested in applying new techniques of efficient resource management in introducing new forestry practices or in constructing and experimenting with the latest hydroelectric dams. For the American urbanites wilderness had a deeply symbolic meaning. Trees and mighty rivers were the icons of the alleged moral superiority of nature that stood in sharp contrast to the bitter reality of a rapidly industrialising society. For experts like Gifford Pinchot and his colleagues, in contrast, wilderness was a nuisance and nature was a resource: trees were merely crops and rivers were to be tamed and tapped. For the urbanites nature had to be preserved; for the experts nature had to be developed.

The story is instructive in several respects. Firstly, it shows that 'our' ecological 'problematique' most certainly is not new. The negative effects of industrialisation for nature have been thematised time and again over the last 150 years. Yet characteristically the public outcry focuses on specific 'emblems': issues of great symbolic potential that dominate environmental discourse. Examples of emblems are deforestation in the mid-nineteenth century, wilderness conservation (USA) and countryside protection (UK) at the turn of the century, soil erosion in the 1930s, urban smog in the 1950s, proliferation of chemicals in the early 1960s, resource depletion in the early 1970s, nuclear power in the late 1970s, acid rain in the early 1980s, followed by a set of global ecological issues like ozone depletion or the 'greenhouse effect' that dominate our consciousness right now. Given this sequence of issues it is better to refrain from speaking of today's predicament in terms of 'our ecological crisis' (which suggests it is time and space specific) and to speak of the *ecological dilemma*.

Secondly, if we accept the thesis that environment discourse is organised around changing emblems, we should investigate the repercussions of these subsequent orientations of the debate. After all, emblems mobilise bias in and out of environmental politics. They can be seen as specific discursive constructions or 'story lines' that dominate the perception of the nature of the ecological dilemma at a specific moment in time. Here the framing of the problem also governs the debate on necessary changes. In the case of the US conservation issue the prevailing story line framed the environmental threat as a case of 'big companies; that tried to destroy the American wilderness and rob 'the American people' of something that was constitutive of its national identity. This then paved the way for the state-controlled technocrats who established 'national parks', and seized control over rivers and pastures in the name of the common good. Hays's reinterpretation of the history of the conservation movement illuminates the often disregarded fact that technocrats subsequently used their brief to implement a comprehensive scheme of 'scientific resource management' in which wildlife and nature were largely made subordinate to their concern about achieving optimal yields, thus directly going against the original intentions of the popular movement. The word 'conservation' remained central, yet its institutional meaning changed radically. Ergo: ecological discourse is not about the environment alone. Indeed, the key question is about which social projects are furthered under the flag of environmental protection.

Thirdly, the story of the US conservation movement illustrates the complex nature of what is so often easily labelled the 'environmental movement'. Here the term 'movement' leads astray. Hays's narrative is in fact about not so much a movement as a bizarre coalition that comprised at least two rather distinct tendencies: a popular tendency that was morally motivated, and a technocratic tendency organised around a relatively confined group of experts, administrators and politicians. The important thing is that both had their own understanding of what the problem 'really' was and what sort of interventions could or should be considered as solutions. Nevertheless, together they constituted the social force behind the changes that were made. Hence, instead of speaking of a movement, we would be better to think in terms of 'coalitions'. And, as the above indicates, these coalitions are not necessarily based on shared interests, let alone shared goals, but much more on shared concepts and terms. We therefore call them 'discourse-coalitions' (see Hajer, 1995).

Fourthly, in environmental debates we can often identify implicit ideas about the appropriate role and relationship of nature, technology and society that structure implicit future scenarios. Hays sees a dialectical relation between the public outcry over the destruction of the American wilderness and the implicit critique of industrial society. Nature symbolised the unspoiled, the uncorrupted or the harmonious which was the mirror-image of the everyday reality of Chicago, Detroit or Baltimore at that time. The popular movement wanted to save nature from the effects of industrialisation but did not address the practices of industrial society head on, focusing instead on the effects on nature. In the end it thus paved the way for a programme that focused on the application of new technologies and scientific management techniques to 'conserve nature'. Here the concern about the immorality of society was matched by a renewed appeal to forms of techno-scientific management that were very similar to those industrialistic practices that had motivated the moral outcry in the first place.

This chapter investigates some similar dynamics in contemporary environmental politics. It argues that environmental politics is now dominated by a discourse that might be labelled ecological modernisation. It presents an outline of this policy or regulation-orientated programme and gives a brief account of its history. Subsequently the chapter presents three ideal-typical interpretations of what ecological modernisation is about. In the fourth section of this chapter then discusses the social dynamics of ecological modernisation. Extrapolating from the developments in some countries where ecological modernisation is now put into action, it tries to grasp the socio-political tendencies in the environmental domain in the years to come.

Ecological modernisation is a discourse that started to dominate environmental politics from about 1984 onwards. Behind the text we can distinguish a complex social project. At its centre stands the politico-administrative response to the latest manifestation of the ecological dilemma. Global ecological threats such as ozone layer depletion and global warming are met by a regulatory approach that starts from the assumption that economic growth and the resolution of ecological problems can, in principle, be reconciled. In this sense, it constitutes a break with the past. In the 1970s environmental discourse comprised a wide spectrum of—often antagonistic—views. On one side there was a radical environmentalist tendency that thought that the 'ecological crisis' could be remedied only through radical social change. Its paradigmatic example was nuclear power. On the other side of the spectrum was a very pragmatic legal-administrative response. The 'Departments for the Environmental', erected all over the Western world in the early 1970s, worked on the basis that pollution *as such* was not the problem; the real issue was to guarantee a certain environmental quality. Its paradigmatic example was the end-of-pipe solution. Where ecological damage was proven and shown to be socially unacceptable, 'pollution ceilings' were introduced and scrubbers and filters were installed as the appropriate solution. Moderate NGOs or liberal politicians would subsequently quarrel about the definition of the height of ceilings and whether 'enough' was being done, but they shared with the state the conviction that ecological needs set clear limits to economic growth.

Ecological modernisation stands for a political project that breaks with both tendencies. On the one hand it recognises the structural character of the environmental problematic, while on the other ecological modernisation differs essentially from a radical green perspective. Radical greens or deep ecologists will argue that the 'ecological crisis' cannot be overcome unless society breaks away from industrial modernity. They might maintain that what is needed is a new 'place-bound' society with a high degree of self-sufficiency. This stands in contrast to ecological modernisation which starts from the conviction that the ecological crisis can be overcome by technical and procedural innovation. What is more, it makes the 'ecological deficiency' of industrial society into the driving force for a new round of industrial innovation. As before, society has to modernise, itself out of the crisis. Remedying environmental damage is seen as a 'positive sum game': environmental damage is not an impediment for growth; quite the contrary, it is the new impetus for growth. In ecomodernist discourse environmental pollution is framed as a matter of inefficiency, and producting 'clean technologies' (clean cars, waste incinerators, new combustion processes) and 'environmentally sound' technical systems (traffic management, road pricing, cyclical product management, etc.), it is argued, will stimulate innovation in the methods of industrial production and distribution. In this sense ecological modernisation is orientated precisely towards those forces that Schumpeter once identified as producing the 'fundamental impulse that sets and keeps the capitalist engine in motion' (Schumpeter, 1961:83).

The paradigmatic examples of ecological modernisation are Japan's response to its notorious air pollution problem in the 1970s, the 'pollution prevention pays' schemes introduced by the American company 3M, and the U-turn made by the German government after the discovery of acid rain or *Waldsterben* in the early 1980s. Ecological modernisation started to emerge in Western countries and international organisations around 1980. Around 1984 it was generally recognised as a promising policy alternative, and with the global endorsement of the Brundtland report *Our Common Future* and the general acceptance of Agenda 21 at the United Nations Conference of Environmental and Development held at Rio de Janeiro in June, 1992 this approach can now be said to be dominant in political debates on ecological affairs.

How should we interpret ecological modernisation ? Is it just rhetoric, 'greenspeak' devoid of any relationship with the 'material' reality of ongoing pollution and ecological destruction ? Here we have to differentiate. The empirical evidence of the developments in environmental policymaking and product-innovation in Germany and Japan, the experience of the Dutch 'environmental policy planning' approach, or the emergence of Clinton's and Gore's 'win-win' strategy in environmental and conservation issues (see for example Cockburn, 1993), shows that the least we can say is that ecological modernisation has produced a real change in *thinking* about nature and society and in the *conceptualisation* of environmental problems in the circles of government and industry. This is what I call the condition of disourse structuration. One of the core ideas of ecological modernisation, 'integrating ecological concerns into the first conceptualisation of products and policies', was an abstract notion in the early 1980s but is by now a reality in many industrial practices. Especially in OECD countries, ecomodernist concepts and story lines can now be seen to act as powerful structuring principles of administration and industrial decision-making from the global down to the local levels. It has produced a new ethics, since straightforward exploitation of nature (without giving thought of ecological consequences) is, more than ever before, seen as illegitimate.

Yet one should also assess the extent to which the discourse has produced non-discursive social effects (the condition of discourse institutionalisation). Here one has to define a way to assess social change. Three seems to be a consensus that in terms of classical indicators (such as energy consumption, pollution levels) one cannot come to a straightforward conclusion. There have been marked successes in some realms (say, curbing SO_2 emissions), but mostly they have been cancelled out by other developments (such as rising NO_x levels). Likewise, where energy consumption has gone down one may legitimately wonder whether these changes are the result of the new discourse or whether the 'achievements' should be attributed to some other processes (such as economic restructuring). Hence in terms of *ecological* indicators it is difficult to come to an assessment.

The question that we focus on here is the sort of *social* change that ecological modernisation has produced, a question that is neglected only too often in social-scientific research on environmental matters. Is ecological modernisation 'mercantilism with a green twist'? Has it led to a new form of 'state-managerialism'? Does ecological modernisation produce a break with previous discourses on technology and nature, or is it precisely the extension of the established technology-led social project ? Or should the 'ecological question' be understood as the successor of the 'social question', and ecological modernisation as the new manifestation of progressive politics in the era of the 'risk society'?

My approach here is to first sketch three different interpretations of ecological modernisation. They are ideal-typical interpretations in the sense that one will not find them in real life in this pure form. Almost inevitably all three of them draw on certain social-scientific notions. In this respect it is important to see them merely as heuristic devices that should help us define the challenges that the social dominance of the discourse of ecological modernisation produces. Each ideal-type has its own structuring principles, its own historical narrative, its own definition of what the problem 'really' is and its own preferred socio-political arrangements.

The most widespread reading of the developments in environmental discourse interprets the course of events as a process of institutional learning and societal convergence. The structuring principle of the institutional learning interpretation of ecological modernisation is that nature is 'out of control'. The historical account is framed around the sudden recognition of nature's fragility and the subsequent quasi-religious wish to 'return' to a balanced relationship with nature. Retrospectively, *Limits to Growth* here appears as the historical starting point. *Limits to Growth* first argued that we cannot endlessly exploit nature. Of course, the report was based on false premises but now we can see that the Club of Rome had a point: we should take nature seriously. Global environmental problems like global warming or the diminishing ozone layer call for decisive political interventions.

Typically, the political conflict is also seen as a learning process. 'We owe the greens something', it is argued. The dyed-in-the-wool radicals of the 1970s had a point but failed to get it through. This was partly due to the rather unqualified nature of their *Totalkritik.* The new consensus on ecological modernisation is here attributed to a process of maturation of the environmental movement: after a radical phase the issue was taken off the streets and the movement became institutionalised as so many social movements before it. With the adoption of the discourse of ecological modernisation its protagonists now speak the proper language and have been integrated in the advisory boards where they fulfil a 'tremendously important' role showing how we can design new institutional forms to come to terms with environmental problems. Likewise, the new consensus around ecological modernisation has made it possible that the arguments of individual scientists that found themselves shouting in the dark during the 1970s are now channelled into the policymaking process.

The central assumption of this paradigm is that the dominant institutions indeed *can* learn and that their learning can produce meaningful change. Following that postulate the ecological crisis comes to be seen as a primarily *conceptual* problem. Essentially, environmental degradation is seen as an 'externality' problem, and 'integration' is the conceptual solution: as economists we have too long regarded nature as a 'sink' or as a free good; as (national) politicians we have not paid enough attention to the repercussions of collective action and have failed to devise the political arrangements that could deal with 'our' global crisis. Likewise, scientists have for too long sought to understand nature in a reductionist way; what we need now is an integrated perspective. Time and again nature was defined 'outside' society, but further degradation can be prevented if we integrate nature into our conceptual apparatus. Fortunately, the sciences provide us with the tools needed: systems theory and the science of ecology show us the way. This understanding of the ecological crisis is supported by what the institutional learning perspective sees as the 'key problems'—collective action problems like the greenhouse effect, acid rain or the diminishing ozone layer. Basically, the institutional learning perspective would define ecological modernisation as the perception of nature as a new and essential subsystem and the integration of ecological rationality as a key variable in social decision-making. The hardware can be kept but the software should be changed.

The preferred socio-political arrangements in essence follow its reading of the history of ecological modernisation and its definition of the problem. Its historical narrative illustrates the strength of pluralist social arrangement. After all, ecological modernisation is the historical product of the critical interplay of opposing social forces. The fact that the World Bank has now adopted an ecomodernist stand is the best example of the radical power of rational argument: even the big institutions will change if arguments are phrased convincingly and correspond with the scientific evidence available. The institutional learning perspective would insist that we have to consider which alterations in scale and organisation we have to make to the existing institutional arrangements to improve 'communication' and make ecological concerns an 'integral part' of their thinking. On the one hand, that implies changes on the level of the firm and the nation state (that is, the stimulation of so-called 'autopoetic' or self-organising effects—for instance mineral or energy accounting in the firm, or the 'greening' of GNP and taxes on the national level). On the other hand, the need for integration finds its political translation in an increased demand for coordination which results in a preference for 'centralisation' of decision-making. Global ecological problems have to brought under political jurisdiction so what we need, above all, are new forms of global management. On the local level, ecological modernisation implies that the scenarios that have been devised to further the ecologisation of society have to be protected against the inevitable attacks from particular interests groups. Hence the possibilities for essentially selfish NIMBY (Not In My Back Yard) protests might have to be restricted.

The sciences should in this perspective search for the conceptual apparatus that can facilitate instrumental control over nature and minimise social disturbances. They should, first and foremost, devise a language that makes ecological decision-making possible. What is required is a specific set of social, economic and scientific concepts that make environmental issues calculable and facilitate rational social choice. Hence the natural sciences are called upon to determine 'critical loads' of how much (pollution) nature can take, and should devise 'optimal exploitation rates', as well as come up with ratings of ecological value to assist drawing up of development plans. Engineering sciences are called upon to devise the technological equipment necessary to achieve the necessary ecological quality standards respecting existing social patterns. In a similar vein, the social sciences' role in solving the puzzle of ecologisation is to come up with ideas of how behavioural patterns might be changed and to help understand how 'anti-ecological' cultural patterns might be modified.

In all, in this interpretation ecological modernisation appears as a moderate social project. It assumes that the existing political institutions can internalise ecological concerns or can at least give birth to new supranational forms of management that can deal with the relevant issues. Hence it is a sign of the strength and scope of ecological modernisation that the World Bank has become the manager of the Green Fund—It assumes that national governments can rethink their sectorial policies and that the network of corporatist interest groups can be altered in such a way that it becomes sensitive to ecological matters.

The interpretation of ecological modernisation as a technocratic project holds that the ecological crisis requires more than social learning by existing social organisations. Its structuring principle is that not nature but technology is out of control. In this context it draws upon the dichotomies dominant-peripheral and material-symbolic. It holds that ecological modernisation is propelled by an elite of policymakers, experts and scientists that imposes its definition of problems and solutions on the debate. An empirical example is the UN Brundtland Report. It is a 'nice try' but, as the Rio Conference and its aftermath show so dramatically, it falters because it is only able to generate global support by going along with the main institutional interests of national and international elites as expressed by nation states, global managerial organisations like the World Bank or the IMF, and the various industrial interests that hide behind these actors. Hence ecological modernisation is a case of 'real problems' and 'false solutions'. The material-symbolic dichotomy surfaces in the conviction that there is a deeper reality behind all the window dressing. Behind the official 'rhetoric' of ecological modernisation one can discern the silhouette of technocracy in a new disguise that stands in the way of implementing 'real solutions' for what are very 'real problems'.

Its historical narrative starts with the emergence of the 'counterculture' in the 1960s. The environmental movement is essentially seen as an offspring of that broader wave of social criticism. Environmentalism was driven by a critique of the social institutions that produced environmental degradation. Important icons are the culture of consumerism that forces people to live according to the dictum 'I shop, therefore I am', or nuclear power that would not only create a demand for more energy consumption but would also enhance the tendency towards further centralisation of power in society. Certainly, *Limits to Growth* is also seen as a milestone, but not for the environmental movement. Yet what *Limits to Growth* was for social elites and governments, so were *Small Is Beautiful* and *Blueprint for Survival* for the counterculture. While in *Limits* the environmentally sound alternative was largely left implicit, the latter publications showed the way towards a truly sustainable society. In this world there would be no place for the 'big government', 'big industry' or 'big science' that, incidently, dominated the Club of Rome that published *Limits to Growth*.

The technocracy critique also has a different interpretation of the significance of the environmental movement of the 1970s. The social movements of the 1970s were not ineffective 'interest groups' that shouted loud but achieved little because they did not know the nitty-gritty of lobbying and strategic action. Quite the contrary, they were embryonic examples of new alternative democratic and ecologically benign social structures and lifestyles (Cohen, 1985). In this movement one found not only 'young well-educated middle class radicals' as some analysts would have it. It also included many scientists who were disturbed by the centralist culture that penetrated the realm of scientific inquiry but who did not necessarily share the radical political agenda of some of the activists. Likewise, it attracted many housewives and farmers who again had their own motives for participating and their own understandings of what the problem 'really' was (see the by now classic article by Offe (1985)). Many a social critic looked upon the environmental movements as one of the forerunners of a new non-technocratic society. Yet rather than learn from these movements 'the state' repressed the alternative movement, either by brute force on the squares of the cities and near nuclear power plants or by 'repressive tolerance', inviting the movements to participate in its judicial inquiries where their political message was inevitably lost in the straitjacket of legalism (see for example Wynne, 1982). Consequently, in this perspective the emergence of ecological modernisation is not seen as product of the 'maturation' of the social movements. Ecological modernisation is much more the repressive answer to radical environmental discourse than its product. Now the ecological issue has been 'taken up by the apparatuses of power, it becomes a pretext and a means for tightening their grip on daily life and the social environment' (Gorz, 1993: 57). In this context it is not seen as a coincidence that nuclear power is conspicuously absent in the main text of the Brundtland Report. The debate has shifted from this politically explosive issue to global ecological issues that after all suggest that 'our common future' is at stake, thus obliterating old dichotomies and social alternatives.

In this perspective the ecological crisis is basically depicted as an *institutional* problem. The technocracy critique fiercely challenges the assumption that the dominant institutions can learn. How can it be that we try to resolve the ecological crisis drawing on precisely those institutional principles that brought the mess about in the first place: efficiency, technological innovation, techno-scientific management, procedural integration and coordinated management? Who believes that growth can solve the problems caused by growth ? Incidently, which institutional learning processes followed the Green Revolution ? Is sustainable development not the next 'top-down' model destined to bring evil while in name it intends to do good ?

This interpretation would also point at the 'structural' aspects of the problem that are left unaddressed in the discourse of ecological modernisation. What ecological modernisation fails to address are those immanent features of capitalism that make waste, instability and insecurity inherent aspects of capitalist development. Surely ecological modernisation will not end the 'leapfrog' movement of capitalist innovation whereby production equipments, generations of workers or geographical areas are 'written off' periodically ? In this perspective the fact that the World Bank is now in charge of the Green Fund is not seen as a sign of strength of the 'ecological turn' but precisely as evidence of the fact that ecological modernisation is really about the further advancement of technocracy.

Clearly, eco-software will not save the planet if capitalist expansionism remains the name of the game.

This interpretation opens the black box of society and argues that the emergence of ecological modernisation was to be seen in the context of the increasing domination of humanity by technology, where technology refers not merely to technical 'artefacts' or machines but to social techniques as well. Consequently, the *real* problem at issue is how to stop the 'growth machine'. Only then can one set about trying to remedy the very real environmental problems.

The technocracy critique argues that the sciences have in fact to a large degree been incorporated in this technocratic project. The institutional history of the discipline of systems ecology is used as a case in point (see Kwa, 1987). As historians of science have shown, it was paradigm on its way out that during the 1960s suddenly got new institutional momentum as NASA engineers and politicians showed an interest in the science that could be integrated in the context of a wider cybernetic perspective. Likewise, the consequence of the prevailing institutional framework is that engineers develop only those technologies that enhance control over nature and society rather than achieve ecological effects while making society more humane. The social sciences are similarly implicated and are called upon as 'social engineers' who only work to help achieve preconceived policy goals. Alternatively, new institutional arrangements in academia and 'science for policy' should be developed. 'Counterexperts' should be able to illuminate the 'technocratic bias' in the official scientific reports. Likewise, more attention, credit and space should be given to those engineers who have been working on 'soft energy paths' that would show the viability of decentralised alternatives. Finally, the social sciences should not work on puzzle-solving activities like changing individual consumer patterns but on the analysis of the immanent forces that keep the juggernaut running towards the apocalypse, so that it might be possible to steer it, or preferably to stop and dismantle it.

The preferred socio-political arrangements of this technocracy critique are those that can correct the prevailing bias towards hierarchisation and centralisation. Its initiatives to further a more democratic social choice centre on 'civil society' rather than on the state. Social movements and local initiatives need protection and attention. New political institutions that would facilitate this correction are the introduction of 'right-to-know' schemes (in Europe), the widespread use of referendums, and, above all, the decentralisation of decision-making and the right to self-determination. Here the differences with the institutional learning perspective come out clearly. The fight to circumvent local NIMBY protests through centralisation and 'increased procedural efficiency', indeed the mere construction of complaints as 'NIMBY' protests, are now seen as illustrations of the tendency to take away democratic rights under the veil of environmental care. Here NIMBY protests are recognised as a building stone for an anti-technocratic coalition. After all, protests that are initially motivated by self-interest often lead to increased awareness of the ecological problem-atique. Hence NIMBYs many become NIABYs (Not In Anybody's Back Yard) (see Schwarz and Thompson, 1990).

In all, ecological modernisation as a technocratic project is a critical interpretation that extends Habermas's arguments of modernisation as the 'colonisation of the lifeworld' to include Galtung's concern over the colonisation of the future. With the demise of the radical environmental movement' its hope is set on the 'triggering effect' of a few ecological disasters.

The interpretation of ecological modernisation as cultural politics takes the contextualisation of the practices of ecological modernisation one step further. Here one is reminded of Mary Douglas's classic definition of pollution as 'matter out of place'. Her point was that debates on pollution are essentially to be understood as debates on the preferred social order. In the definition of certain aspects of reality as pollution, in defining 'nature', or in defining certain installations as solutions, one seeks to either maintain or change the social order. So the cultural politics perspective asks why certain aspects of reality are now singled out as 'our common problems' and wonders what sort of society is being created in the name of protecting 'nature'.

Ecological modernisation here appears as a set of claims about what the problem 'really' is. The cultural politics approach argues that some of the main political issues are hidden in these discursive constructs and it seeks to illuminate the feeble basis on which the choice for one particular scenario of development is presently made. The structuring principle in this third interpretation is that there is no coherent ecological crisis, but only story lines problematising various aspects of a changing physical and social reality. Ecological modernisation is understood as the routinisation of a new set of story lines (images, causal understandings, priorities, etc.) that provides the cognitive maps and incentives for social action. Of course, reductions are inevitable for any effort to create meaningful political action in a complex society. The point is that one should be aware that this coherence is necessarily an artificial one and that the creation of discursive realities are in fact moments at which cultural politics is being made. Whether or not the actors *themselves* are aware of this is not the point. Implicitly, metaphors, categorisations, or definition of solutions always structure reality, making certain framings of reality seem plausible and closing off certain possible future scenarios while making other scenarios 'thinkable'.

To be sure, in this third interpretation there is no implicit assumption of a grand cultural design. Quite the contrary, environmental discourse is made up of 'historically constituted sets of claims' (John Forester) uttered by a variety of actors. Yet in interaction these claims 'somehow' produce new social orders. Foucault speaks in this respect of the 'polymorphous interweaving of correlations'. The analytical aim of this approach is, firstly, to reconstruct the social construction of the reductions, exclusions and choices. Secondly, it tries to come to a historical and cultural understanding of these dispositions. Hence it tries to reconstruct the social forces behind ecomodernist discourse, for instance by studying discourse-coalitions. Subsequently, this approach tries to facilitate the discussion on the various probabilities, possibilities and, above all, on the various alternative scenarios for development that could be constructed.

The historical narrative of this third perspective takes up the themes touched upon at the beginning of this chapter. It emphasises that the ecological problem is not new. It observed that the ecological dilemma of industrial society is almost constantly under discussion, be it through different emblems. What these discussions are about, it argues, are in fact the social relationships between nature, society and technology. For that reason this perspective calls attention to the 'secondary discursive reality' of environmental politics: there is a layer of mediating principles that determines our understanding of ecological problems and implicitly directs our discussion on social change. Hence it would investigate what image of nature, technology and society can be recognised in the 'story lines' that dominated environmental discourse at the time of *Limits to Growth*, or during the confrontation between the state and radical social movements in the 1970s, or in the consensual story lines that dominate ecological modernisation in the 1990s. What is the cultural meaning of the biospheric orientation that is central to present-day environmental discourse ? In this respect it argues that ecological modernisation is based on objectivist, physicalist and realist assumptions, all of which are highly arbitrary. Story lines on global warming, biodiversity or the ozone layer suggest the presence of the threat of biological extinction and assert that these problems should be taken as the absolute basis for an ecological modernisation of society. But do these story lines really have the same meaning and implications for all regions ?

Rather than suggesting that there is an unequivocal (set of) ecological problem(s) the third interpretation would argue that there are only implicit future scenarios. The point here is not to doubt whether environmental change occurs. Neither would this social constructivism lead to a position in which each account is equally true or plausible. The point is primarily anti-objectivist and criticises the uncritical acceptance of certain scientific constructs as the starting point of politics. Bird (1987:256) summarised this position most succinctly, writing that

> scientific paradigms are socio-historical constructs—not given by the character of nature, but created out of social experience, cultural values, and political economic structures... the actual objects of inquiry, the formulation of questions and definitions, and the mythic structures of scientific theories are social constructs. Every aspect of scientific theory and practice expresses socio-political interests, cultural themes and metaphors, personal interactions, and professional negotations for the power to name the world.

Here it departs from the more traditional understandings of social action that are implicit in the previous two interpretations. To suggest that the developments in environmental discourse between the publication of *Limits* in 1972 and Rio in 1992 should be interpreted as a process of social learning does not appreciate the cultural bias of the process nor the contingency of the present definitions. But the technocracy critique has omissions too: its proponents might also reject the naive notion of social learning, but their differentiation between the material and the symbolic indicates that they too work with a naturalist understanding of what the problems 'really' are.

Whereas the previous two interpretations in fact shared a clear idea of the ecological problem, and both had their own idea about a possible remedial strategy (respectively conceptual or institutional change, and more coordination or more decentralisation), the third interpretation holds that there can be no recourse to an 'objective' truth. It suggests that the ecological crisis is first and foremost a discursive reality which is the outcome of intricate social processes. It is aware of the ambivalences of environmental discourse and would, in the first instance, not try to get 'behind' the metaphors of ecological discourse. It would try to encircle them to be able to challenge them scientifically, and to enhance consciousness of the contingency of knowledge about ecological matters.

What is more, it would investigate the cultural consequences of prevailing story lines and would seek to find out which social forces propel this ecomodernist discourse-coalition. Once the implicit future scenarios have been exposed, they might lead to a more reflective attitude towards certain environmental constructs and perhaps even to the formulation of alternative scenarios, the socio-political consequences of which would present a more attractive, more fair, or more responsible package. Hence the central concern of this third interpretation is with *cognitive reflectivity, argumentation* and *negotiated social choice*.

The role of academia follows from this commitment to choice and open debate. They have to help to open the black boxes of society, technology and nature. The cultural politics perspective would resist the suggestion that nature can be understood and managed by framing in a new 'ecological' language, as for instance by giving priority to economics and systems ecology, on the basis that a pure language does not exist. Its aim would rather be to pit different languages and knowledges (for example expert knowledge versus lay knowledge) against one another to get to a higher understanding of what ecological problems could be about. Here it would assume that this interplay would lead to the recognition of the wide diversity of perspectives.

A more radical consequence of the cultural politics perspective for science would be that the ecological crisis would, potentially, be put upside down: the debate would no longer be on the protection of nature but would focus on the choice of what sort of nature and society we want. After all, once the deconstruction of, say, the biospheric discourse has exposed its naturalist and realist assumptions, the debate might take a different turn. If people have become aware of the political and economic motivations behind biospheric discourse, and have come to grips with the backgrounds of their own naturalism, they might become intrigued by the 'myriad ways in which we make, unmake, and remake "nature" and "human nature" (Bennett, 1993: 256). If technology is no longer seen as inherently problematic but also as a potential force to reconstitute the social relationships between nature, technology and society according to one's own needs and preferences, the debate might lose its simplistic modern/anti-modern format and a debate on the re-creation of society might result. The consequence would, of course, be that the debate would no longer necessarily focus on environmental matters: the re-creation of society might often focus more explicitly on the conceptualisation of technologies, on the conditions of application of certain techniques, and on the preferred 'socialisation of nature' (rather than the mere protection of nature as it is).

The preferred socio-political arrangements of this third interpretation follow from this analysis and focus on facilitating the discussions of implicit future scenarios. It should be emphasised that in terms of concrete ideas of how this might be organised this perspective is still searching. The most conventional suggestions follow the tracks of the republican tradition, emphasising the need for explicit choice, defence and argument, for the (re)legitimation and/or rejection of certain interventions. Like the technocracy critics it would like to bring society back in. Here we should locate the idea of a 'Societal Inquiry' which would give citizens the right of initiate—for example to re-examine the policy towards acid rain that failed to bring about results. The suggestion is that this initiative would be qualitatively different from the new democratic forms that were introduced as part of the technocracy critique. A societal inquiry does not assume a clearly defined subject matter: the point of the exercise is precisely to explore and expose the contradictions, the reductions and exclusions and to bring into the discussion the implicit understandings of technology, nature and society as well as the implicit future scenarios. Subsequently the societal inquiry would try to create the basis for focused rhetorics, for defence and argument, for relegitimation and/or rejection, and for the reorientation of political action in the light of social debate. This would also hold true for the procedures of 'symbolic law'. The idea here is that the law should no longer be seen as conclusive statement of dos and don'ts. It would rather have to be a set of normative arguments the meaning and consequences of which should constantly be rethought in the context of concrete cases. The role of government would thus be one of defending the operationalisation it has given to the normative commitments that were the outcomes of societal debates (although one may wonder whether these suggestions are not again based on a traditional understanding of politics).

A more radical version of the cultural politics perspective would break with the traditional understanding of politics as a centralised process. It would take the very process of the creation of discursive realities as its object. Rather than seek to develop arrangements that allow to 'get behind' the metaphors it would explore how new perspectives on society can be created. The issue would not be to 'free' the natural human identity that now suffocates under the hegemony of technological applications; its aim would rather be to explore the unintended potentials of new technologies to create new identities and facilitate the awareness of affinities between various distinct identities.

In all, ecological modernisation as cultural politics starts off by opening up the three black boxes of society, technology and nature and seeks to illuminate the principal openness of ecological discourse. Indeed, it would go so far as to inquire what the meaning could be of the present *ecologisation* of the risks of modernisation.

The Social Dynamics of Ecological Modernisation

In sociological theory the ecological crisis is interpreted as the confrontation of industrial society with its own latent side-effects. Zygmunt Bauman speaks about post-modernity as 'modernity coming of age'. We are, says Bauman, now able to see modernity as a 'project'. We have acquired the ability to reflect on what brought us the unprecedented wealth and we now see the (ecological) risks and dangers that we have created in the process of modernisation (see Bauman, 1991). The theory of reflexive modernisation as proposed by Ulrich Beck suggests that it is the unintentional self-dissolution or self-endangerment which he calls 'reflexivity' which has produced the ecological crisis. Reflexivity here relates to modernity as a social formation that constantly and immanently *undercuts* itself (see Beck et *al.,* 1994; Beck, this volume). He distinguishes this 'reflexivity' from 'reflection', which relates to the knowledge we may have of the social processes taking place. Beck holds that as the modernisation of society unfolds, agents increasingly acquire the ability to reflect on the social conditions of their existence. Yet whether or not the self—endangerment of society leads to reflection remains an empirical question.

The question is of course to what extent this reflection can be shown to be present in the present discourse on ecological modernisation. Furthermore, we should assess what forms of reflexivity we can discern in the project of ecological modernisation. Which processes of deinstitutionalisation and reinstitutionalisation take place in the context of the process of ecological modernisation? Which social projects are furthered under the flag of environmental protection ? Actors might now broadly share the concepts and terms of ecological modernisation but which implicit future scenarios can we discern ?

It is instructive in this respect to have a look at the regulatory efforts of some of the countries that are internationally seen as the most advanced examples of ecological modernisation, such as Germany, or The Netherlands with its comprehensive policy planning approach. In these Western European countries we now see a broad societal coalition working on the institutionalisation of ecomodernist ideas. By and large this institutionalisation is based on the premises of the institutional learning interpretation of ecological modernisation that was sketched above. Yet the social dynamics of ecological modernisation come out to be the not as predictable as that ideal-type might suggest. We can in fact observe at least four distinct lines of development.

There can be no doubt about the fact that the main *direct* effect of ecological modernisation is the *rationalisation of ecology,* through the conceptual and institutional amendment of existing bureaucratic structures and the creation of new ones, be it by the state or by new ecocorporatist associations. There seem to be good grounds to argue that there are certain parallels between the history of the US conservation movement in the Progressive Era and the development of the discourse-coalition of ecological modernisation. What started in the late 1960s and early 1970s as a concern about the lack of care for nature seems, over the years, to have given way to coalition of forces that produces social effects that are at odds with the original intentions of the environmental movement. This tendency towards rationalisation is well known and is in fact implicitly described in the discussion in the previous section, while its dynamics have been analysed elsewhere (Fischer, 1990; Paehlke and Torgerson, 1990; Hajer, 1995).

One should observe, however, that the attempt to rationalise ecological issues according to the prescription of the institutional learning paradigm does not *necessarily* produce a rationalisation of ecology. It may also produce a critical form of cultural politics. Take for instance the effects of the national political commitment to sustainable development on policymakers at the local level. They are confronted with the need to translate 'sustainable development' into new planning procedures, conservation strategies, etc. By directive they are ordered to make sustainable development their new 'cognitive map'. Yet here they are confronted with all sorts of interpretative difficulties. After all, sustainable development is merely a 'story line' that generated its global support precisely because of its ambivalence. So what happens in actual practice? Policymakers are left to themselves when it comes to the operationalisation of the notion of sustainable development. Here they have a great freedom. They can either make a few aesthetic alterations but basically continue with business as usual, or they can use sustainable development as a crowbar to break with previous commitments. In that case institutional learning produces cultural politics and opens the possibility for a more broadly defined reflection on the sort of problem the ecological crisis 'really' is.

Another interesting development in this respect are the quarrels that are beginning to erupt over the first ecomodernist practices, most notably the waste recycling programme. Whereas waste-reduction programmes have so far not proved to be successful, waste-recycling schemes are threatened precisely because of their success. This causes similar difficulties in Germany, The Netherlands and Austria. The unexpected quantity of materials (glass, plastics, metals) that consumers manage to bring together for recycling now exceeds the capacity of the recycling facilities. On the one hand this causes a renewed resistance of industrial firms to the waste-recycling schemes. On the other hand it is a case where the pragmatic solutions themselves produce the evidence that waste might require more fundamental changes, thus, potentially, enhancing the reflection on the meaning and consequence of the 'ecological crisis'.

A second tendency we can discern is the *technicisation of ecology*. Perhaps the most significant development is taking place behind the scenes in the leading ecomodernist countries—the striking but little discussed reorientation that has taken place in the strategic planning of big multinational firms such as Siemens, DASA, and BMW. They are central in the ecomodernist discourse-coalition. They strive towards a set of clearly defined eco-industrial innovations, they have a new idea of what the relevant actors are, and they carefully work towards a set of new institutional arrangements. They too can be seen using the threats of potential ecological disaster or climate catastrophes as a crowbar, but this time it is used to fulfil the promise of 'intelligent' traffic systems, 'smart' highways, 'intelligent' energy savings technologies, renewable energies, and socially engineered behavioural changes. NGOs like Greenpeace, trade unions and politicians can, albeit for varying reasons, all be seen to help push ecological modernisation in this direction. Similar developments are well under way in the United State, where the 'Big Three' car producers work together with firms like IBM, AT&T and the Federal government on multi-billion dollar plans to create this new 'intelligent' transport system. What this in fact amounts to is the amendment and extension of existing large technical systems, a tendency which will prove to be extremely powerful.

From the perspective of the technocracy critique the danger of this technicisation of ecology is that ecological modernisation short-circuits a superficial understanding of some emblematic ecological problems with a new technological commitment. Essentially, microelectronic technologies are presented as the solution for the 'juggernaut effect'. The cultural politics perspective observes that the discussion on alternative future scenarios is thus strangled in a double way: both the debates on information technology and on the ecological crisis are shifted aside to make way for 'efficient' and 'positive sum game' solutions.

Other examples of this tendency towards the technicisation of ecology are not difficult to find. Compared to the 1970s the ecomodernist policy-discourse has also caused a huge shift in the conceptualisation of environmental problems by the NGOs. The shift in thinking about strategic solutions is of such an extent that an NGO like Greenpeace that once started off opposing nuclear tests, and is well known for its protection of endangered species, could recently announce its backing of the development of a 'green car' as well as its own plan to construct a tunnel under the Oresund, creating a rail link between Sweden and Denmark. The idea behind this latter initiative is to provide a readily available solution as an alternative to the longstanding plans of the Danish and Swedish governments to build a bridge for car traffic. Similarly, efforts are now being made in Japan to apply the latest freezing techniques to conserve species that are threatened with extinction, and, as a final example, German social scientists have found that in the debate on biotechnology ecology is now used as justification for continued development in this area. Unlike in the early days, when biotechnology was still proposed as the 'Eighth day of the Creation', it is now constructed as an 'ecologically benign' technology because it would require radically less resources (see Lau *et al.*, 1993).

This technicisation of ecology recieves its social strengh of course not primarily from its beneficial effects in terms of ecological improvements. The technicisation of ecology is the translation of a social and moral issue into a market issue. It is based on the conviction that ecology is, potentially, a new ---and huge ---market which is to be created and, subsequently, to be conquered. Traditionally, sociologists would perhaps argue that this tendency is based on a great faith in the capacity to control side-effects in advance. Yet it is questionable whether that belief really was constitutive of this tendency in the first palce.

A third line of development that ecological modernisation has produced is the tendency towards the *ecologisation of the social.* This tendency is not so much part of ecological modernisation as a response to it. Ecological modernisation is a strategy that believes in further rationalisation, and in creating and maintaining the society-wide coalitions to 'fight' environmental degradation. Despite all the critique that one might advance of the Brundtland process, the fact remains that this was conceived as an essentially social-democratic and Western European project. Brundtland was in fact the third Western European social-democratic leader to head a UN commission on global integration (after the Brandt Commission on development and the Palme Commission on disarmament) (Ekins, 1992: chapter 2). The principle of international solidarity, and the social-democratic belief in modernist productionist solutions, therefore always figured prominently.

Inherent in the positive sum game format is the commitment to conceptualise solutions within the existing social system. That means going along with the further integration of world markets, and trying to *add* the social or, more recently, the ecological dimension. Hence *add* a 'social chapter' to the Maastricht Treaty, *add* an ecological paragraph to GATT, *add* the Green Fund to the World Bank. The contradictions that are inherent in this integrative thinking now clearly also produce their reactive counterparts. And here the alliance with the 'big institutions' and existing discourses of power backfires.

Here I would point to the important role of the ecological issue in what various others have called the new regionalism, the new localism, the new tribalism or the 'politics of place'. Those concerned about environmental degradation can rejoice in great interest from the circles of the German new right, which is pasting together a 'place' orientated ideology. Here the economic and political uncertainties are interpreted as being the product of globalism. This is then subsequently used to recreate a new national sense of order based on a renewed appreciation of 'place' versus 'space'.

In this discourse the national environment becomes the basis for a new national identity, and care for the environment is put forward as an argument to try to regain an allegedly natural social ecology:

> Ecology opens our eyes and shows that nations are not simply human complexes, based on shared language, attitudes, culture and history. Their evolution and their inexchangable identity is also to be understood as the product of the soil from which these complexes grew, the space in which that happened and with which they are connected.

Environmental problems are here seen as the product of a global political project in which a diffuse array of various 'insensitive' actors including the EC bureaucracy, multinational industries and democratic politicians participate. In this context the 'problem' of asylum seekers is drawn into the ecological debate. On the one hand they do not share concern for the regional environment (they do not 'feel' it); on the other hand it is argued that they are extra mouths to feed and people to house, which will require an increase in industrial production and hence cause more environmental destruction (see Jahn and Wehling, 1991, 1993). As Jahn and Wehling have shown for Germany, this new ecologisation of the social should not be seen as a clearly defined ideology that is confined to the new right. It is much more an 'argumentative formula' that can be found much more widely (see also Eder, this volume). Indeed, it is formula that can be found in mainstream politics in other countries too.

The fourth line of development is the *socialisation of ecology*. Here the debate on the ecological crisis is simply recognised as being one of the few remaining places where modernity can still be reflected upon. It is in the context of environmental problems that we can discuss the new problems concerning social justice, democracy, responsibility, the preferred relation of man and nature, the role of technology in society, or indeed, what it means to be human. This gives ecological discourse a great political importance. In a way it is completely irrelevant whether emblematic problems like global warming constitute the dangers that some people argue they present. Global warming should simply be seen as one of the few possible issues in the context of which one can now legitimately raise the issue of a 'No' to further growth. Here the philosophical imperative of responsibility can be introduced in centre-stage political decision-making through a plea for a 'No regrets' scenario on global warming targets for low energy consumption.

At the same time, the socialisation of ecology perspective would hold that the 'ecological crisis' is by no means unique. Here it elaborates on the cultural politics perspective. Indeed, there is much to be said for the integration of the debates on new technologies that are generally kept separate. If one would break with the conception that nature should be understood as something 'out there', and with the idea that nature stands for the 'authentic', the pure and the good, one might create the possibility of a more vibrant sort of debate. If technology is no longer simply seen as what threatens 'nature' (and hence society) but is also seen as something which creates, at least potentially, new opportunities and new social arrangements, one might be willing to go along and take one more step and discuss the introduction of *in vitro* fertilisation, experiments on embryos or man-animal transplants as essentially ecological issues. This socialisation perspective reflects on 'nature in the age of its technical reproducibility' as the eloquent German philosopher Gernot Böhme (1992) has put it. Rather than mourn over the end of nature we might start to think about what kind of nature we really want. The struggle to protect nature 'as it is' often brings barbed wire into the prairie while the ever more frequent attempts to bring back 'nature as it was' lead to the most bizarre engineering exercises. So rather than leave modernist commitments as they are, it seeks to save Enlightenment thought from the attempts to interpret the ecological crisis as the basis for a further centralisation of power (as in the prevailing global discourses) and from the attempts to use the ecological crisis as the basis for a new intolerant regionalism.

This challenges the boundaries of what is normally understood to be the subject-matter of ecological discourse. That is precisely the point. Ecology would here become the keyword under which society discusses the issues of 'life politics' (Giddens) in a way that allows for a rethinking of existing social arrangements. The rhetorical strength of the ecological crisis would be used to reflect on the nature of modernity.

It will be clear that the four lines of the development sketched above are by no means equal in strength. The rationalisation and technicisation of ecology are well under way while the popular critique drifts more and more in the direction of the ecologisation of the social. The issue really seems to be how to improve the strength of the fourth perspective. Yet how would one increase the reflective awareness of the possibilities of ecological modernisation ? How would we arrive at a position where reflection means more than awareness of the 'ecological crisis' alone? How would we get it to include awareness of the necessary openness of the definition of problems and solutions and, finally, how would we achieve an increased awareness of the fact that ecological modernisation should be based on a debate on the recreation of the relationships between nature, technology and society ?

It should be said at the outset that there can be no naive idea about the possibilities of bringing about this discussion on 'the nature we really want'. The sociology of technology literature has given us ample evidence of how large technical systems have their own logic of development. Nevertheless, the critical task now is to devise the discursive stages where these patterns can be discussed and democratically renegotiated. In the context of the prevailing tendencies towards a rationalisation and technicisation of ecology, and in an awareness of the dangers of a ecologisation of the social, one should seriously reflect on the need to reinvent democracy. As Bauman (1991 : 276) writes :

> What is left outside the confines of rational discourse is the very issue that stands a chance of making the discourse rational and perhaps even practically effective: the political issue of

democratic control over technology and expertise, their purposes and their desirable limits—the issue of politics as self-management and collectively made choices.

Exploring the ambivalences of ecological modernisation and trying to come to institutional forms that could accommodate the increase of cognitive reflectivity, argumentation and negotiated social choice seems one of the key issues that could reconstitute the basis and meaning of environmental politics.

4
Crisis of Nature and Nation–State

All modern industrial democracies face environmental problems of great magnitude— destruction of wildlife habitat, extinction of plant and animal species, soil erosion, air and water pollution, daily generation of tons of solid wastes, urban sprawl, land degradation, and toxic substance poisoning, to name a few. The attempt of democratic governments to address these problems falls into two stages. The first policies are aimed at conserving wildlife and natural resources and will include such measures as setting of hunting seasons and establishment of national parks. As the pace of industrialization intensifies, the government will turn increasingly to the problem of air, water and ground pollution. It will enact laws limiting the amount and kind of effluents factories can release and set up a regime for cleaning up polluted sites, rivers and air. Growing technological sophistication will result in ever larger numbers and volume of toxic chemicals and biologically engineered genetic products in the environment. Governments then will develop policies to control these threats to public health.

How do regimes that divide the policymaking power between two levels of government approach these tasks? In particular, how do three principal English-speaking federations—the United States, Canada, and Australia—tackle the challenges of conservation and pollution control? Is federalism an obstacle to effective environmental policy formulation or does it present opportunities for efficiency and effectiveness not available in unitary polities, such as France or Japan?

The analysis is divided into four parts. First, we must understand how the federal constitutions in these three nations formally allocate responsibility for environmental regulation between the constituent units—states or provinces—and the center. The formal divisions may, of course, little resemble actual practice, which will be dictated by political considerations. Among the political forces shaping environmental policy, of course, are interest groups—both those advocating and those skeptical of large development projects—political parties and public opinion—putatively a domineering presence in democratic nations. In federal regimes, however, the most important players in environmental politics are often the competing governments. As the environmental stakes continue to grow, the federation and the member states will more and more come into conflict, embroiled in disputes not easily resolved by reference to the national constitution. Part II addresses the rules and traditions that shape the intergovernmental negotiations on which the parties have come to rely to settle environmental conflicts. Frequently, however, the central government and the provinces must seek the aid of a third party to reach a resolution through adjudication. Part III explores the role of bureaucrats and judges as environmental policy actors. Judicial leadership, we learn, is not confined to issues of civil rights and civil liberties. The prominence of adjudication as a means not only of determining specific disputes between the federal and regional governments but as a forum for making environmental law completes the circle, bringing us back to the three federations' constitutions and the role of the courts in their interpretation and evolution. What are the principal findings of the eleven scholars from two continents who contributed to this volume?

The Constitutions of the United States (1788), Canada (1867), and Australia (1901) were written long before environmental protection became a salient public issue and candidates of elective office campaigned on a green platform. If any of the three federations were to remake its constitution it is likely, with the possible exception of Canada due to the influence of the provinces, the constitutive assembly would assign explicit regulatory authority over air, water, land, and natural resources to the central authority.

According to the original constitutional division of powers, however, the provinces and states are responsible for making policy governing what we now call the environment. The U.S. and Australian Constitutions enumerate the powers of the federal government and leave all residual powers to the states. Federal, or commonwealth, jurisdiction under the Australian Constitution, for instance, is confined to fisheries beyond the states' territorial limits. The states are responsible for all other heads of environmental power. The Canadian Constitution, or Constitution Act 1867, by contrast lists the powers of the provinces, leaving the residual to Ottawa. Among the powers granted to the provinces is regulation of public health, municipalities, public lands, natural resources, and civil law. The constitutional result in the three countries is virtually the same, with the general government confined largely to promotion of commerce and defense of the whole.

In practice, however, since the 1960s the federal governments have become increasingly active in enacting legislation in the environmental area. The U.S. government has been the most ambitious. Its comprehensive catalog of legislation has nearly preempted the field, leaving the states in a clearly subordinate role. In Australia and Canada, however, federal legislation on the environment is still the exception rather than the rule. The key difference between the two former British dominions is that,while the constitutional bars to a future comprehensive federal environmental regime have largely been removed by the Australian High Court, both constitutional and political obstacles remain in Canada.

Certain language in the U.S. Constitution has aided the growth of federal power there. First, the Constitution empowers Congress to "make all needful Rules and Regulations respecting the Territory or other Property belonging to the United States."Because of the pattern of western expansion, the United States today owns two-thirds of the land west of the Mississippi River. The federal government exercises plenary power over the resources of the public lands. By contrast, the Australian states and Canadian provinces own the public lands in those countries.

Second, although the central governments in each federation are responsible under their respective basic laws for promoting and regulating trade and commerce, the three national courts have differed sharply in their construction of the power's scope. The U.S. Supreme Court has read Congress's power to "regulate Commerce... among the several States" broadly—so broadly in fact that the residual category of intrastate commerce, which can be regulated only by the states, has virtually disappeared. Congress, moreover, says the Court, can regulate any activity that affects interstate commerce. Nearly all the long series of federal environmental enactments that have appeared since the 1960s, including the Clean Air and Clean Water Acts, have been exercises by Congress of its commerce power. The Australian High Court and Canadian Supreme Court, on the other hand, have given the federal government's power over commerce such a narrow construction that it is unsuitable as a basis for a general federal environmental power.

Third, the U.S. Congress relies upon its constitutional power to raise taxes, borrow money, and spend to recruit the states into voluntarily administering federal environmental programs and following federal guidelines. The costs to a state of nonconformity are usually prohibitive, given the fact that only the federal government can print money and the states must live within their means. The Supreme Court in recent decisions, however, has ruled that the federal government may not coerce the states into enforcing federal law. Similarly, the Australian High Court has sustained Parliament's use of its constitutional control over the purse strings to effect a uniform national environmental regime. Under the Australian Constitution, the states may not tax incomes or sales, leaving them dependent upon grants from the commonwealth, largesse to which strings are often attached.

Fourth, the governments of both the United States and Australia have made ample use in the environmental field of their constitutional power to make and implement international treaties. The respective high courts have construed this power to mean that a federal law that would otherwise be invalid as an intrusion upon a reserved power of the states will pass constitutional muster if presented as an implementation of a treaty. The Canadian courts, by contrast, treat the constitutional division of powers as a powerful restraint upon Parliament's ability to meet treaty obligations through domestic legislation.

In one respect, however, the Canadian and Australian Constitutions are more favorable to federal environmental initiatives. The Australian Constitution lacks a bill of Rights and the Canadian Charter of Rights and Freedoms, or Constitution Act 1982, contains no guarantees for private property. The Fifth and Fourteenth Amendments of the U. S. Constitution, by contrast, protect property owners from being deprived of their possessions without "due process of law" and stipulate that any government taking of property must be for a public purpose and be accompanied by "just compensation." The federal courts have become increasingly concerned about local, state, and federal environmental regulations that deprive owners of the full value of their property. Efforts in the 1970s by Associate Justice William Douglas to persuade his brethren on the Supreme Court to find in the Bill of Rights a constitutional right to clean air, clean water, and unspoiled wilderness areas and to give trees and other natural objects standing to sue were unsuccessful.

In addition to its constitutional responsibilities for taxing, spending and treaty implementation, the Commonwealth of Australia grounds its environmental regimen on its power under the Constitution to legislate with respect to corporations (sec. 51[20]). It used this power, for example, in the 1980s to stop a state public corporation from constructing a dam in Tasmania opposed by environmentalists. There is no analogous federal power in the U.S. or Canadian basic laws.

A potential advantage that the Canadian government enjoys under its Constitution is its responsibility for making criminal law, which in the United States and Australia is fundamentally a state matter. The fact that most environmental regimes rely on civil and administrative law, however, coupled with the Supreme Court's narrow view of the scope of the power, has stymied its development as a basis for comprehensive federal environmental policies.

Although the U.S. Constitution divides power between two tiers of government, the Supreme Court no longer regards enforcement of the boundary as primarily its responsibility. It remains to be seen whether the Court's 1995 ruling in *U.S. v. Lapez*, striking down a federal law banning weapons in public schools, is a harbinger of a judicial effort to reduce the scope of Congress's commerce power vis-a-vis the states. Because the States are represented in the federal House of Representatives and Senate, say many of the justices, the states are well positioned to look after their own interests in the political process. The attitude of the Australian High Court toward the original demarcation of powers is similar. The sheer difficulty of amending the Constitution in the three countries has encouraged expansion of the federal role in the environment by means of judicial interpretation.

Only in Canada do the provinces still play the primary role in environmental regulation envisioned by the federation's constitutive document. Much of the explanation for this fact is the presence of Quebec. Quebec nationalism has fueled the engine of province building, a machine that drives the English provinces as well, especially Alberta and British Columbia. If Quebec were to separate from Canada, the federal role in environmental protection would likely grow.

Although public opinion shows widespread support for cleaning up the air and water and, though its power to regulate interstate commerce, the U.S. Congress has the authority to enact comprehensive environmental policies, a deepening budget deficit coupled with a $4.4 trillion federal debt means that it has little money to fund them. The result is that Congress has followed the example set by the federal courts in desegregation and other civil rights cases of mandating environmental standards on state and local governments, leaving them with the tab. Federal environmental policy in the United States is the consequence of entrepreneurial politics, with its pattern of concentrated costs and distributed benefits (Wilson 1992, 436). The combination of popular support for environmental protection in the abstract and the unpopularity of tax increases has made majoritarian politics, in which both the costs and the benefits are distributed among the majority, unattractive. The dilemma that municipalities face is that when they attempt to pass on the costs of compliance with federal mandates to the taxpayers or service users, either through higher taxes and fees or reductions in other services, voters rebel.

A second problem is that the plethora of regulations issued by the myriad of federal administrative agencies tasked with enforcing environmental legislation has made it difficult for the states to comply with often contradictory expectations. The states' plight had led to demands for new mechanisms of intra and intergovernmental coordination.

Given the problems of coordination and the local nature of most environmental issues, revolving as they do around issues like hazardous waste sites and waste water treatment, relatively few environmental laws in the United States consist of national standards, federally administered. Congress prefers either a conjoint approach, in which states implement policies in accordance with federal standards, or a cooperative approach, in which state implementation is voluntary but stimulated by federal financial incentives.The last type of program, however, is becoming less common, as grants-in-aid to state and local government continue to decline.

State-level environmental administrators are often at odds with elected bodies, such as city councils, because as civil servants they are not directly concerned with the costs of complicance and freely use federal mandates and threats of federal enforcement as levers of force compliance or block action. Unlike Australia and Canada, in the United States local government is a bigger player in conflicts with the federal government than are the states. Faced with rapidly rising compliance costs and federal vetoes of development projects, such as the Two Forks Dam in Colorado, local governments are demanding more opportunities for fuller involvement in federal environmental rule making and enforcement decision making. The combination of the environmental impact statement process—encouraging participation by public interest groups—litigation, and federal regulation, for instance, had made it extremely difficult for cities, townships, and counties to open new landfills. Enactment by Congress in 1995 of a law restricting federal unfunded mandates may free local governments to pursue pollution-control objectives at a slower pace and reduce the pressure to raise local taxes.

Following a period first of state domination of the environmental field and then one of commonwealth control, coordinate federalism is the current pattern in Australia of state-commonwealth relations in the implementation of environmental policy. As a result of a series of High Court decisions favorable to commonwealth jurisdiction, the federal government makes the most important policy decisions, such as the decision to enter into an international agreement, but the states are largely responsible for their implementation. Commonwealth control over the income and sales taxes leaves the states with few sources of revenue and dependent upon the federal government for grant-in-aid. The Australian courts are no longer major players, open neither to the states wishing to challenge commonwealth decisions nor to environmental nongovernmental organizations (ENGOs) wishing to block environmentally harmful projects.

Most of the conflict that occurred in the 1970s and 1980s were between the commonwealth and the less populous Australian states—Tasmania, Queensland, and Western Australia—whose governments were engaged in client politics, owing to the power and wealth of local industries who sought concentrated benefits and distributed costs. Electoral reality, moreover, militated against the commonwealth picking fights with Victoria and New South Wales, the most populous of the states and dominant force in the federal House of Representatives. Because the prime minister serves at the pleasure of the majority party in the House of Representatives, executive federalism often means commonwealth deference to Melbourne and Sydney. The principle of separation of powers in the United States permits the Congress to impose mandates on the states without the blame accruing to the president. Such executive blame avoidance is impossible, however, in a parliamentary system, where the prime minister would be held accountable for any burden placed upon the states.

Australian Labor Party Prime Minister Bob Hawke announced in 1990 his government's commitment to a new federalism. Hawke had in mind the cross-jurisdictional nature of many environmental problems. Under the new federalism, cooperation between the two levels of government would replace efforts by the commonwealth to coerce the states. The most significant result of this initiative was the signing of the Intergovernmental Agreement on the Environment (IGAE) in 1992. The accord is consistent with executive federalism, providing for a ministerial council called the National Environmental Protection Authority. One of the consequences of cooperative federalism is that bargained solutions are more common in Australia and Canada than in the United States, where the federal government can more easily impose its will on the states. For environmentalists in Canada and Australia, the problem is not how to increase the power of the federal government, but how to persuade the federal government to use the power it has.

The Canadian provinces are much stronger than the U. S. or Australian states. The fact that there are 50 American states, in contrast to 10 Candadian provinces and 6 Australian states, explains part of the American states' relative weakness. While the American states seek to influence Washington primarily through their representatives in Congress, Candadian provinces and Australian states trust their interests to their premiers and cabinet secretaries, who frequently meet with their federal counterparts in ministerial conferences to negotiate disputes. Although increasingly under attack as undemocratic, executive federalism continues to mark the pattern of intergovernmental relations in parliamentary federations. Institutions of executive federalism have been in place in Canada for some time. The Canadian Council of Resource Ministers was established in 1964 in order to harmonize provincial and federal environmental policies.There is in fact, however less harmony in intergovenmental relations now than in the 1960s, because of the participation of mobilized environmentalists and the federal courts, which produces friction between the prodevelopment provinces and a more environmentally sensitive federal government.

Client politics, with its pattern of concentrated benefits and distributed costs, is more representative of environmental politics in Canada than is entrepreneurial politics. The provincial dominance of environmental decision making means that territorially dominant economic interests will typically prevail over objections from ENGOs articulating diffuse public interests. A number of provincial economies are highly dependent on a single natural resource, such as pulp and paper or hydroelectricity. In addition, the fear of provoking separatist sentiment in Quebec makes the federal government unenthusiastic about taking the kind of effective enforcement actions typical of the federal government in the United States. Ottawa has the will neither to impose mandates on the provinces nor to force compliance.

The popularity of environmental protection in Canada as a public policy goal affects provincial as well as federal behavior, especially in provinces such as Ontario not dominated by a single resource. Because each level of government often wishes to take credit for reducing pollution, mechanisms, such as joint delivery and financing of programs, have been developed to share credit while avoiding blame. Under the constraints of executive federalism, however—including the requirement of unanimity among the participating ministers for many decisions—federal provincial conflict continues to lead to "buck-passing,"delays, inaction, rigidity, and piecemeal solutions.

The Courts and Administrative Agencies

In the United States, the federal judiciary has become one of the most important actors in environmental decision making. The high level of judicial activity in this field is illustrated by the fact that the priorities of the chief rule making and enforcement body, the Environmental Protection Agency (EPA), are largely set by the courts through judgments and consent decrees. The courts in effect have incorporated the regulatory agencies into the judicial hierarchy, with exercises of discretion by agency heads subject to review by the U.S. District Courts or Courts of Appeal. Judges have blocked or forestalled construction of hundreds of projects, resulting in abandoned public works or costly delays. Neither the Congress nor the presidency has the will to make hard choices in the trade-off between development and conservation, sc these choices are invariably left with unelected federal judges, who are appointed for life.

Judicial activism on the environment was part of a larger sea change in the role of the courts in the review of agency discretion, known as the due process revolution of the 1970s. Courts, believing that many executive agencies, boards, and commissions had been —"captured" by the economic interest they were designed to regulate, dramatically relaxed the rules governing standing to sue, making it possible for ENGOs to litigate in the capacity of private attorneys general, who file suit in order to protect the public interest. A Democratic Congress, often at odds with Republican presidents on environmental protection and other issues, acquiesced in this judicial-ENGO partnership by authorizing award of attorneys' fees to the public interest plaintiff. Congress also encouraged environmental interest groups to achieve their goals through litigation by enacting "action-forcing" and "technology-forcing" legislation, severely limiting the discrecting of administrators by imposing on them judicially enforceable standards and duties.

The most valuable change wrought by federal judges on behalf of ENGOs was a relaxation of the rules governing access to the courts. Since the 1970s, organizations like the Sierra Club and the Natural Resources Defense Council have been able to challenge private and public projects by simply asserting an esthetic, psychological, or other immaterial interest shared with the general public. There is no need for the plaintiff to show direct, concrete, or personal harm. Congress, moreover, has even enacted legislation, such as the Endangered Species Act, that explicitly grants standing to "any person" who believes the government is in violation of the statute. Citizen suits have become an important part of the enforcement mechanism serving environmental law. To provide substance in addition to procedure, the federal trial and appellate courts elaborated the injunction as the judicial remedy of choice, especially powerful when a large construction project is proposed or even under way. Public interest plaintiffs typically request the court to enjoin the project when the defendant has failed to file an environmental impact statement (EIS) or the EIS is inadequate. Although the language in the National Environmental Protection Act (NEPA) as enacted by Congress in 1969 treated the EIS as discretionary, U.S. District Court Judge Skelly Wright in 1971 read the statute as mandating an EIS for any project requiring federal action, such as a license. Congress was reluctant to rewrite NEPA to clarify its intention because Judge Wright had read the legislation in a way unfavorable to the executive and favorable to the legislature in the eyes of public opinion. The due process revolution, at least in part, was an American response to the rise of the New Class—relatively affluent and well-educated persons with skeptical attitudes toward big business and who place a high value on such postmaterialist goods as leisure, participation, self-expression, and open processes (see Maslow 1987 : Inglehart 1990). Environmental decision making in the United States increasingly provides the kinds of symbols and processes valued by the New Class.

The parliamentary system of Canada and Australia had led to very different patterns of environmental decision making, in which the courts play a relatively minor role. Under the Westminster model, the executive dominates the legislature, with the result that Parliament typically avoids limiting the discretion of administrators. ENGOs have found Parliaments and the political parties that control them largely insensitive to their policy demands, leaving only the courts and certain portions of the civil service as potential allies in their struggle to protect the public's interest in environmental protection. Neither the Canadian nor the Australian courts, however, have the will or the means to launch a serious challenge to executive decisions. Under the maxims of equity, the injunction cannot be issued against the crown. Canadian litigation has never seriously delayed a construction project. The executive-controlled Parliament can easily reverse the decisions of activist judges, as the Canadian Parliament did in 1992 after the Federal Court of Canada had attempted to make the EIS process mandatory.

Also motivating the House of Commons was Prime Minister Brain Mulroney's desire to avoid confrontation with the provinces, especially

Quebec, over the environmental assessment process. Several of the provincial economies are dependent upon a single resource industry, such as pulp and paper in British Columbia, oil and gas in Alberta, and hydroelectricity in Quebec. The largely prodevelopment provincial governments preferred that environmental assessment be discretionary and within their control.

The Canadian Supreme Court, to be sure, has relaxed the rules of standing, permitting individuals and public interest groups to litigate on behalf of the environment, who would not have qualified under the traditional rules, but with rather disappointing results compared with the success achieved by their U.S. counterparts. By contrast, the Australian High Court has been unwilling to compromise executive discretion even by broadening access to the courts. The traditional, restrictive rules of standing remain largely in place. The primary contribution of the High Court to the judicialization of environmental politics was by legitimizing commonwealth supremacy in environmental policymaking, at the expense of the states. Once the Court, through constitutional interpretation in the 1980s, completed the project of broadening the federal powers over the environment—at the request of the federal executive—there was little opportunity for it or any commonwealth court to contribute to resolving the dispute between economic development and environmental protection. This is a question completely for the federal prime minister to make. As a result of adverse High Court decisions, the states have largely resigned themselves to their role as implementers of environmental policy made by Canberra.

Among the judiciaries in the industrialized democracies, courts in the United States play the most active role in environmental policymaking. The explanation for this phenomenon lies in a number of features of the American political system, only some of which are shared by the Canadian and Australian federations.

1. *Federalism.* Until recently, laws governing air and water pollution and degradation of natural areas were the responsibility of the state and provincial governments in Canada, the United States, and Australia. In the 1970s, the federal governments began legislating in this area and generating continuous conflict with the subnational governments. Developers, who are locally based, generally have more influence over the provincial governments than on the national government, which is more sensitive to public opinion. Because the federal judiciary serves as the "balance wheel" of the federal system, it will have opportunities to referee

in the conflict between development and environmental protection. Governments can diminish the role of the judiciary, however, by pursuing alternative modes of dispute resolution, such as negotiation conducted by first ministers or under the auspices of intergovernmental agreements. Courts in unitary systems, such as those in Great Britain, will see relatively little litigation over environmental issues fought between levels of government. There local governments are creatures of the center, on whom they are dependent for their authority and sheer existence.

2. *Judicial Review.* Another reason for the passivity of the British courts is the lack of judicial review—the power of a court to annul a statute if the judges regard it as repugnant to the constitution. By contrast, courts in the United States exercise general supervisory power over the federal and state legislatures and administrative agencies. The obverse of this authority is the power of the courts to legitimize controversial policies, promulgated by the legislature. The Australian High Court, for instance, legitimated the nationalization of environmental policy by the federal executive in the 1980s. A great influence on the judicialization of environmental law in the United States was the existence of the Administrative Procedure Act, which explicitly encouraged judicial review of agency decisions.

3. *Separation of Powers.* In a parliamentary system, the executive and legislature are melded together, with the latter being dominated by the former. Because the system encourages cooperation between the executive and legislative branches, there are relatively few instances of interbranch conflict calling for the intervention of the courts. In the United States, frequently the presidency is controlled by one political party and the Congress by its rival. Divided government is a fertile breeding ground for environmental litigation.

4. *Judicial Independence.* The more independent the judiciary is of the provincial and federal governments, the more likely judicial intervention becomes. Federal judges in the United States are the most independent, being appointed by the president for a term of good behavior. Impeachment and removal of a federal judge by Congress occurs only infrequently. Australian and Canadian federal judges enjoy a similar level of security. One difference is the existence of a mandatory retirement age in Australia and Canada, which leads to greater turnover in the judiciary and thus greater executive influence than in the United States, where federal judges serve for life.

5. *Access.* The common law rules governing standing to sue restrict

access to plaintiffs who can demonstrate concrete, personal injury, distinct from the general harm suffered by most citizens. By definition, the rules exclude environmental public interest litigants. These restrictive criteria are still intact in Australia but not in Canada or the United States, where the supreme courts have relaxed the rules to the point where nearly any ENGO opposed to a project or policy can launch a challenge in court. The decision of the U.S. Congress to authorize courts to award attorneys' fees in certain kinds of environmental litigation to plaintiffs who have advanced the public interest in effective enforcement has opened further the judicial gates.

6. *Remedies.* In civil suits, the complainant is typically demanding monetary compensation from the defendant. In environmental cases, however, the public interest plaintiff usually either wants a project stopped or wants to force the governments to take some kind of protective action. According to English legal tradition, courts may not issue injunctions against the Crown. In both Canada and Australia, courts are reluctant to intervene in construction projects for lack of a suitable remedy. In the U.S., by contrast, the Supreme Court has expanded the concept of injunctive relief since the 1950s to the point where judicial remedies available match plaintiff demands in environmental cases.

7. *Existence of Public Interest Advocacy Groups.* In each country, since the 1960s, groups of citizens have come together to form organizations dedicated to representing the public interest with regard to the environment. Federalism, with its multiple points of access to political power, multiplies such associations. Unlike their corporate and government opponents in environmental litigation, however, ENGOs have no stable source of funding. In addition to attorney's fees, these groups are dependent on membership dues, merchandise sales, private contributions, and government and foundation grants. Canada has gone the farthest in providing government subsidies to keep ENGOs afloat.

8. *Lack of Judicial Deference to Agency Decisions.* Ministerial responsibility is a central principle of parliamentary government. Ministers are answerable to their parties and ultimately to the electorate for the performance of their departments. In order not to diminish the level of responsibility, judges assume that ministers are acting in good faith and in general defer to administrative judgment. In the U. S. presidential system of separated and jealous powers, the legislature and the courts often ally against the executive, rendering the judges more willing to question administrative exercises of discretion.

9. *Career Legislators.* Loyal service to the party is the most important ingredient in a successful political career for members of Parliament. Members of the U.S. Congress and state legislatures, by contrast, campaign largely as individuals and are heavily dependent on voluntary service and campaign contributions from their constituents. In the latter system, those seeking a career as a legislator have a strong incentive to avoid taking a stand on controversial issues, for no matter which position they take they will alienate large numbers of voters and contributors. The result is that the hard choices often end up in court, to be made by unelected, life-tenured federal judges. The existence of party discipline in parliamentarian systems means that important policy decisions are made by the party leaders, or government, in the case of the majority party.

10. *Party Competition.* In one-party states, the judges belong to the same political party as the chief executive and leading legislators. In countries where control of the government alternates between two or more parties, tension and conflict between the government and the judiciary are more common and the courts are more likely to rule against government policy. All three federations exhibit party competition, with the least alternation occurring in Australia, where the Labor party has been in power for almost the entire period in which the commonwealth has legislated for the environment.

11. *Existence of Non-Discretionary Duties.* In Canada and Australia, environmental impact assessments are voluntary on the part of government. When the Canadian Supreme Court attempted to make them mandatory, the Parliament responded by enacting legislation clarifying its intention that they be a matter of administrative discretion. The federal courts in the United States, however, regard such assessments as a judicially enforceable duty. An inadequate environmental impact statement is one of the principal grounds relied on by courts for stopping a project.

12. *Existence of a Bill of Rights.* In the United States, developers fighting adverse government action motivated by a desire to enhance the environment frequently argue that the government is attempting to violate their property rights as guaranteed in the Bill of Rights. The Australian constitution, by contrast, contains no Bill of Rights, and the 1982 Canadian Charter of Rights of Freedoms provides no protection of property rights.

13. *Reliance on International Agreements.* The judiciary is less likely to play an independent role in environmental policymaking if the federal government's environmental agenda is a function of its international commitments. Lacking foreign policy expertise and not wishing to introduce

another voice into the nation's communication with other nations or impair the government's ability to keep its international promises, the courts tend to defer to the government under such circumstances. Australia has gone farther than either Canada or the United States in making environmental policy decisions through the treaty process.

14. *Judicial Activism in other Policy Areas.* Courts in the United States are the most active in the world, with the Canadian judiciary a distant second. The federal courts in the United States have played a policymaking role since the 1880s in such areas as business regulation, agricultural policy, social welfare, civil rights, and civil liberties. Activism in one areas easily leads to policy involvement in others. The courts, in fact, have gathered their own constituency, consisting of those groups often ignored by the political branches. The absence of any such record in Australia and the brief experience of the Canadian Supreme Court under the Charter of Rights reduce significantly the likelihood of judicial activism in the area of environmental protection.

Despite, or perhaps because of, federalism, the United States, Canada, and Australia are among the world's leaders in environmental protection. The quality of the environment in the three federations is as high as that of Organization for Economic Cooperation and Development (OECD) members with unitary constitutions, such as the Netherlands, Sweden, and Japan (OECD 1994). The multiplication of points of access to decision makers means that no one level or branch of government has been able when it was unsympathetic to appreciably slow the environmental movement's progress. During the Reagan-Bush years in the United States, for example, environmentalists turned away by the federal executive found success in appeals to Congress, the federal courts, and even some state and local governments.

The lack of party discipline and separation of the legislature from the administration in the United States means that Congress will be dominated by local economic interests, insuring that policy is always a curious mixture of funding for "pork-barrel" projects, such as dams and canals, and legislation, such as the Clean Water Act, severely restricting pollution and degradation. The parliamentary systems of Canada and Australia produce less discordant federal policies and are less responsive to locally based, prodevelopment interests.

Ultimately, the conflict over environmental policies and practices in federal systems does not stem from the struggle for power between two tiers of government, each sovereign in its constitutionally assigned sphere.

In many disputes, the provinces are surrogates for locally based economic interests and the federal government is a surrogates for those associations willing to put environmental protection ahead of economic growth and development. The underlying conflict is one common to all liberal democratic industrialized nations—how much is society willing to pay for uncontaminated soil, clean air, clean water and undisturbed wilderness areas? The fact that in a federation at any single time one party will control some jurisdictions and another party will hold the reins of power in the others guarantees that clashes between the interests of industry, organized labor, and environmentalists will be acted out as regional/national disputes. What could be fought as bitter contests between social classes or partisan factions, such as between the Old and New Left, takes the more legalistic and thus less destabilizing form of jurisdictional conflict.

Global Environmental Change and the Nation State

The increased seriousness of many environmental problems provides one of the most intuitively plausible reasons for believing that the nation state and the system of states may be either in crisis or heading towards a crisis. Running through much writing on the subject is the sense—sometimes explicit, more often implicit, that the state and the fragmented system of sovereign states are less and less able to guarantee the effective and equitable management of an interdependent world in general, and of the global environment in particular.

Environmental issues (and especially second generation 'global' issues) present states and the state system with new challenges of unprecedented complexity. The state is seen to be both too big and too small for dealing with these challenges: too big for the task of devising viable strategies of sustainable development which can only be developed from the bottom up; and too small for the effective management of global problems such as combating global climate change or protecting biodiversity which by their nature demand increasingly wide-ranging forms of international cooperation.

In relation to the environment there are three principal arguments that the nation state as a political form is either already in crisis or else heading towards a crisis. The first concerns the state system as a whole. From this perspective, the system of nation-states may be said to be in crisis or to be dysfunctional because it can no longer provide a viable political framework for the collective management of the global environment. Although there is little agreement on alternative paths, there appears to many to be a basic contradiction between a single integrated, enormously complex, and deeply interdependent ecosystem and our still dominant form of global political organization: a fragmented system of sovereign states, normatively built around mutual recognition of sovereignty, and politically forming an anarchical system in which cooperation has been historically limited and in which war and conflict have been a deeply rooted, and for many, an inherent feature. As the Brundtland Report put it: 'Our Earth is one, our world is not' Or, as Lynton Caldwell has suggested more recently: 'By the time, experience should have taught us that a complex planetary biosphere cannot be addressed effectively for protection or for rational management by a fragmented and uncoordinated political order'.

A second argument is that an increasing number of individual nation-states are no longer able to provide localized order and an adequate degree of environmental management within their own borders. The weakness of many states and state structures is all too evident. What is harder to discern is the degree and significance of this weakness. As we shall see, for some the environmental failings of many weak states are merely suggestive of a crisis of particular policies, or, at worst, a crisis of particular political or economic institutions. But for others they suggest something altogether more generalized and far reaching. Ronnie Lipschutz and Ken Conca, for example, believe that we are witnessing 'the emergence of a fundamental new social dynamic, with which governments, their critics, and their observers may be poorly equipped to deal'. Global ecological interdependence is leading both to 'tighter systemic binding among actors in the prevailing international system, and the simultaneous decay and fragmentation of the traditional authority structures of world politics'. Of these authority structures the position of the state is particularly shaky and they speak of 'the fundamental incapacity of governments to control the destructive processes involved'.

The third argument moves beyond the state's practical capacity to deal effectively with new challenges. On this view environmental problems may be contributing towards crisis of the nation-state by eroding the normative appeal of the state and the idea of the nation state as the primary, if not exclusive, focus for human loyalties. In part this loss of legitimacy derives from the domestic environmental shortcomings of many states. But in part it results from the extent to which increased awareness of global environmental problems and of the deep and unavoidable reality of environmental interdependence have created a new sense of planetary consciousness which is leading to new forms of non-territorially based political identity. Moreover this sense of planetary consciousness is increasingly embodied concretely in the mobilization of new social actors around environmental issues. Undoubtedly tied to other processes of globalization, the consolidation of what is loosely termed the global environmental movement seen as one of the most significant and substantial pillars of an emerging transnational civil society. On this view we are therefore witnessing the emergence of new forms of non-territorially based political identity and new mechanisms of political organization and action that go beyond the nation state and which challenge the hegemony of statist world politics.

These challenges to the nation-state do not of course stand alone, but are symptomatic of a broader reading of contemporary world politics. First, there is the extent to which the state is caught between two contradictory processes: fusion, globalization, and integration on the one hand; and fragmentation, disintegration and disorganised market is on the other side. There is the extent to which processes of globalization (economic, technological, environmental, cultural) force us to reopen questions about both the nature and limits of state sovereignty and the solidity of established identities. And third, there is the pervasive sense that the pace and scope of charge have undermined the established spatial and temporal categories around which global politics has been traditionally conceived and analysed.

The notion of 'crisis' is particularly problematic when used in relation to the environment. There are, to be sure, many examples of environmental crises that are immediate and very visible, and that have already led to sudden death or widespread catastrophe (for example, the environmental factors centrally implicated in the series of large scale African famines). But many, perhaps most, environmental problems are long-term and their effects and (especially) interactions uncertain. Here 'normality, continuing to adopt the profligate resource use and lifestyles typical of modern industrial societies and continuing to promote traditional notions of economic growth in the developing world, is fundamental to the idea of the environmental crisis. Normality in the sense of allowing existing trends to continue, is likely to consign the majority of the world's population to a bleak future of grinding poverty and worsening environmental degradation and, in the long run, may well render the planet uninhabitable. Moreover, if humanity waits until forced to change by an acute and immediate crisis, then the available range of options is likely to be drastically reduced. In these sense, then, normality itself comes to form a central element of the 'crisis'. To quote Norman Myers:

Were environmental problems to strike us like a heart attack, we would rush our ecosystems into intensive-care units and have them restored. Instead they are like a cancer, quietly undercutting our foundations, unseen and unresisted until they eventually burst forth with deep damage all too evident. Or to shift the metaphor, they are like the frog in the experiment. If you drop a frog into a saucepan of boiling water, it will respond to its acutely and suddenly hostile environment by hopping out. If then you put the same frog into a saucepan of cold water and set the pan on the stove, the frog will enjoy its benign environment for a while. It will even think is environment becomes more benign as the water warms up. It will swim around placidly, oblivious to the threat of the rising temperature. As the water gets hot, it will start to feel drowsy. Finally it will succumb to the heat and go into a coma before boiling to death. For us, it is the world outside the window that is steadily heating up.

To what extent do nation states (embodying a set of institutions exercising final authority over a given territory, claiming independence from any external authority, and forming the focus for a territorially defined national identity) and the state system (characterized by interaction between a plurality of sovereign states and by limited forms of institutionalized cooperation) prevent us from understanding what may be happening outside the window and from devising an alternative future to that of the boiled frog? There are large questions that are, at least in part, speculative in nature. This article seeks to specify the three principal arguments of those who believe the nation state to be in crisis and to unravel some of the complexities of the issues involved.

The Incapacity of the State System

Although only one aspect of global environmental management, the problem of securing a sufficient degree of inter-state cooperation remains fundamental. Indeed it is clear that the increased seriousness of environmental degradation and the emergence of a new category of global environmental problems demand a qualitatively different kind of inter-state order. Managing global environmental issues involves a dramatic change in the character and goals of international society: away from minimalist goals of coexistence and towards the creation of rules and institutions that embody notions of shared responsibilities, that impinge heavily on the domestic organization of states, that invest individuals and groups within states with rights and duties, and that seek to embody some notion of the planetary good. This switch can be characterized in different ways: in terms of Terry Nardin's distinction between a practical association on the one hand and a purposive association on the other; or Hedley Bull's distinction between pluralist and solidarist conceptions of international society; or the distinction drawn by international lawyers such as Richard Falk or Antonio Cassese between a Westphalian model of international law and a UN Charter model.

Cries of despair should not, however, be taken at face value. Indeed it is perfectly possible to provide an optimistic reading of the evolution of global environmental governance. On this view international society has begun to tackle emerging environmental problems, albeit fitfully and perhaps belatedly, by building on the common interests, common rules and common institutions of international society.

In the first place, optimists can point to the emergence of an increasingly complex structure of global environmental governance and to the increased attention given by policymakers and politicians to international environmental issues. Indeed the UNCED process has helped to crystallize an enormously important change in both popular and political attitudes towards the environment. However varied the level of concern, it is now very difficult to imagine environmental concerns disappearing completely from the agendas of governments. Not only has there been a mushrooming of environmental regimes but the time taken from recognition of a problem to international action has decreased (compare, for example, the Law of Sea negotiations with the emergence of the ozone regime and both with the signature at UNCED of the framework conventions on biodiversity and climate change).

Second, we have seen the emergence of a wide variety of new international legal concepts with which to deal with environmental problems. Legal duties to prevent environmental harm, liability for environmental harm, duties to inform and to consult, duty to undertake environmental assessments have all become firmly established. Moreover quite radical principles have appeared on the international scene, albeit usually in a 'softer' form: for example, the precautionary principal, the principle of intergenerational equity; ideas of common heritage, of shared resources, and of common concern; and the recognition by the industrial countries of a duty to help secure sustainability in the developing world through the transfer of funds and technology. Such a normative shift is undoubtedly important and needs to be seen as part of a broader shift in international legal understandings of sovereignty: away from an emphasis on the rights of states and towards a far greater stress on both duties and common interests. Such developments also bring home the extent to which sovereignty needs to be understood not as a single discrete claim based solely on state power, but rather as a historically constituted 'bundle of competences' whose exact definition depends on the changing constitution of the international legal order as a whole.

Third, optimists stress the extent to which environmental regimes need to be understood and evaluated as part of an ongoing process of management and negotiation. For the optimists it is wrong to lay excessive stress on the loopholes of a particular agreement. Rather, the effectiveness of environmental regimes derives from the extent to which states are tied into a continuing and institutionalized process: hence the importance of provisions for regular meetings and for the generation and publication of information; hence the view of regimes as frameworks around which political pressure on states can be mobilized. This sense of an ongoing process of cooperation is central to optimistic assessments of UNCED which highlight the extent to which the framework conventions create institutions for follow-up and further negotiation and which make much of the creation of new institutions such as the Commission for Sustainable Development.

Fourth, optimists can also claim with some plausibility that conflict over sovereignty has eased. Attitudes to sovereignty, particularly in the developing world, have shifted very substantially since the Stockholm Conference in 1972. Developing countries such as India or Brazil have moved away from the rigid dichotomy between environment and development visible at Stockholm. They have come to lay greater weight on the importance of protecting the environment and on moving towards more sustainable patterns of economic development. There is, then; increasing consensus on the ways in which environmental protection can reinforce economic development. There is also increased awareness of the threats posed to the South by unchecked environmental degradation. Indeed the persistent poverty in many parts of the developing world means that the South is less able to afford to put right reversible damage to the environment and also less able to manage the process of adaptation to whatever global environmental changes do occur. In addition, the South has come to accept that environmental degradation within states is a matter of legitimate interest to the outside world, being both a matter of 'international concern' (suggesting that it is legitimate for other states to become involved), and, increasingly, of the 'common concern to humankind'. Recent declarations have also acknowledged the rights of

NGOs both to involve themselves within the 'domestic' environmental affairs of developing countries and to participate in global negotiations.

Fifth, a great deal of the optimistic case depends on confidence in scientific knowledge: both to generate solutions to environmental problems, but also to promote and facilitate international cooperation. Indeed one dominant theme of the literature has been the extent to which increasing levels of scientific knowledge can work to redirect state interests, to facilitate international co-operation, and to promote 'environmental learning'. Within this context much attention has been given to the role of transnational 'epistemic communities' of scientists and experts. This is, of course, related to the greatly increased role that non-governmental groups (NGOs) have come to play in global environmental politics: in shifting public and political attitudes towards the environment and placing environmental issues high on the political agendas of an increasing number of states; in publicizing the nature and seriousness of environmental problems; in acting as a conduit for the dissemination of scientific research; in organizing and orchestrating pressure on states, companies, and international organizations; and in providing one of the most important mechanisms for helping to ensure effective implementation of environmental agreements. Impatient as ever with states, liberals are inclined to see the emergence of this transnational civil society as an inherently positive development.

Out of these various arguments a broader case can be made, namely that the environmental challenge is working, not to undermine, but rather to reinforce the centrality of the state. Dominant patterns of managing global environmental change (such as the Brundtland Report) have emphasized the importance of strengthening inter-state cooperation and the institutional capabilities of states. The environment can be viewed as an example of how perceptions of crisis can lead to the reassertion and extension of state authority and how states are increasingly willing to trade a degree of legal freedom of action for a greater degree of practical influence over the policies of other states and over the management of common problems. Moreover, there is a close and important link between inter-state cooperation and domestic political power. Thus, for example, although the Biodiversity Convention recognizes the importance of indigenous peoples for the protection of forest resources, it also gives international blessing to the authority of the state over such peoples.

Thus for modern liberals, the seriousness of environmental problems and the inescapability of ecological interdependence will increasingly force states to cooperate. James Rosenau, for example, talks of environmental issues 'impelling national and sub-national governments towards ever greater transnational cooperation'. The language of environmentalism is full of talk of 'necessities' and 'imperatives' and often rest on the idea that fear of impending catastrophe will inevitably help to bring forth reform. But, whilst it is impossible to arrive at a definitive judgement on the effectiveness of current structures of global environmental governance, there are unfortunately good grounds for scepticism, for questioning this optimistic picture, and for arguing that traditional patterns of inter-state conflict will be reproduced within the new domain of environmental politics.

In the first place, the weaknesses of many existing legal regimes are too great to be ignored. The numbers of agreements may well be large but sanctions for compliance are weak. There is a marked preference for non-binding targets/guidelines which states are free to implement at whatever pace they see fit rather than the acceptance of firm and unambiguous obligations. Indeed the agreements negotiated at Rio on Global Climate Change and Biological Diversity are peppered with caveats. qualifications, and escape holes, and lacking in clear measurable commitments. Few existing environmental treaties contain inescapable requirements that states resort to binding third-party procedures for settlement of disputes. States remain extremely keen to maintain firm control over reporting, monitoring and inspection procedures. And although much is made of the increased openness of states to NGO participation, states continue to be extremely resistant to any significant dilution of control.

The negotiations around the Earth Summit therefore illustrate the continued plausibility of realist accounts of the obstacles to effective cooperation: the weakness of most international institutions and the absence of sanctioning power; the unprecedentedly high levels of cooperation and policy coordination required to deal with many of the most pressing environmental issues; the pressures on states and state representatives to place a high priority on their immediate short-term interests and on the protection of political autonomy; the mismatch between the time horizons of politicians and political processes on the one hand and the extended time frames needed to address and deal with many of the most serious environmental problems on the other; the fact that there is no easy link between increased scientific knowledge and the growth of international cooperation; the extent to which the loose rhetoric of 'interdependence' disguises a wide variety of problems whose specific dependence structures may sometimes work to promote cooperation (as in the case of ozone) but may also militate against cooperation (as in the case of global climate change); and finally, the extent to which these difficulties have to be set against the large number of deep-rooted historical conflicts that exist between states and by the cultural, political, and economic heterogeneity of the international system. Moreover it is depressing to note the reappearance in the follow-up negotiations to UNCED of the old clashes over the political control of environmental institutions, over the amount and management of transferred resources, and over the meaning of sustainability.

Second, the concern for sovereignty remains a fundamental factor in global environmental politics in both North and South and the political acceptance of the erosion of sovereignty is less apparent than legal declarations would tend to suggest. This is well illustrated by the impasse at the Earth Summit on those critical issues that threatened to bite deeply into the sovereign prerogatives of governments: the unspoken agreement not to tackle the divisive issue of population growth; the near absolute refusal of the North to accept that sustainability might require a change in its consumption patterns and resource use, especially its use of energy and fossil fuels; or the bitter resistance of developing states to the negotiation of a convention on the protection of forests.

Third, we have to note the inapplicability of traditional techniques (and especially legal techniques) for dealing with most serious environmental issues. These have mostly depended on treating discrete aspects of the environment, often of rather narrow notions of what constitutes environmental problems. International environmental regulation has traditionally relied on separating issues and negotiating particular agreements to deal with particular problems. Yet attempting to give meaning to sustainability at the international level is necessarily about managing the environmental implications of a diverse and highly politicized sets of relationships (for example links between trade and environment, between debt and environment, between military spending and environment). Unsurprisingly international society has found this task to be a daunting one and the most notable step in this direction (the negotiation at Rio of the 400 page Agenda 21) was marked by omissions, by lack of overall coherence, and by a reluctance to prioritize and to specify any too clear link between impressive aspirations and effective action.

This leads to a final problem, which is by far the most serious, namely the capacity of the major states to coordinate the global economy in the interests of ecological rationality. Even those inclined to emphasize markets and market mechanisms as the most effective instruments for environmental policy recognize the importance of continued inter-state cooperation. On a fundamental level global capitalism has long depended on the political structures of the state system (not least for guaranteeing a stable pattern of property rights). Greater economic integration increases both the need for and the complexity of international environmental regulation (for example, in providing stable management of the links between the rules of the trading regime and national environmental policies). Moreover, these challenges will be greatly increased if the dominant reformist liberalism that characterizes so much international thinking on the environment proves to be overoptimistic. On the 'official version' (exemplified by the Brundtland Report or the 1992 World Development Report), a revitalization of global growth (albeit of a more sustainable character) is an essential part of averting future environmental catastrophe and of securing some form of 'global bargain' between the industrialized and developing world. But for those who see a deep contradiction between this continued emphasis on growth and the finite nature of the earth's ecosystem, the distributional conflicts are likely to be far more intense and politically significant than the comforting rhetoric of 'Brundtlandism' and 'sustainable development' would suggest. If the scale of human activity relative to the biosphere is becoming simply too large, then unregulated markets, however efficient they may be in increasing wealth, are unlikely to provide an adequate solution, and the zero-sum character of international politics is likely to be intensified not diminished.

As with domestic policy, the problem is not with what markets and market mechanisms *might* be able to do to secure long-term sustainable development, but rather with the weakness of the political institutions that would enable these prescriptions to be applied in practice. The central difficulty is that states may no longer possess the power to manage the international order because of the extent to which 'power' has been diffused away from states and towards both markets and the players that dominate those markets. Thus, if it is indeed the case that power in the global economy is exercised increasingly by nonstate actors and, in particular, by transnational companies, then the utility of a predominantly state-centered approach to international order is also likely to be limited. Many of the most important environmental policy 'decisions' are not taken by states, but emerge out of the production, technological and trading strategies of a relatively small number of powerful transnational companies. Equally, both the generation of many 'local' environmental problems and the capacity of states to deal with those problems is heavily influenced by the pressures and constraints of an increasingly globalized world economy—for example, linkages between structural adjustment policies and environmental degradation, or more broadly, the transmission via the market of western lifestyles, of a particular vision of modernity and progress, or of particular kinds of environmental knowledge.

If this is in fact the case, what is to be done? Many environmentalists would suggest that the choice is a stark one : either to 'bring the world economy under control' and to move to more centralized political coordination, or to try and reverse the powerful contemporary pressures towards integration and globalization, to decentralize economic and political power, and to build a sustainable future around grassroots democratic participation and locally generated economic transformation. For most environmentalists decentralization is the preferred route and the attenuation of sovereignty as part of a project of radical decentralization forms a common plank of much of the environmentalist agenda. Others, such as Susan Strange, would argue that the world economy is already effectively out of control and that state control cannot be reasserted in the traditional manner. If true, and given the incapacity of the global economy to develop a politically and ecologically sustainable order of its own, then the project of international society is indeed lost and we are faced with a pessimism as profound as that of the gloomiest realist.

The Erosion of State Capacity

But even if it were possible to imagine a world in which the process of international environmental regime creation proceeded easily and unproblematically and in which the many barriers to inter-state cooperation had been overcome, dealing with many environmental challenges would still depend on the effective capabilities of the states that make up that broader order. In an important sense the emergence of transnational environmental issues poses a severe challenge to all states precisely because solutions cannot be found solely within their own jurisdiction. Moreover, for many commentators, the expansion of economic and societal interdependence has served to empower citizens and citizen movements, to promote challenges to existing authority, and to complicate the task of governance in all parts of the world.

Beyond these general trends, it is clear that many of the most serious obstacles to sustainability have to do with the domestic weaknesses of particular states and state structures. In some cases these weaknesses stem from the limits of economic development: the fragility, inefficiency and corruption of government bureaucracies; the absence of appropriate human, financial and technological resources; the prevalence of deep-rooted economic problems; and the increasing susceptibility to international economic forces and the policies of transnational companies. But in many cases the problems are directly political: the opposition of powerful political interests that benefit from unsustainable forms of development and the difficulties of the state in regulating both itself and the many areas of economic life in which it is directly involved.

The old dichotomy between domestic order and international anarchy has therefore been recast in many parts of the world. As international lawyers never tire of pointing out, there is great deal more 'law and order' internationally than there is on the streets of an increasing number of states, unable to secure even the most minimal conditions of social order. Indeed it is becoming a truism of the post Cold War world that the problem is not the lack of legitimacy between states, but the still greater lack of legitimacy within them. In many parts of the world environmental problems such as extensive urban degradation, deforestation, desertification, water or fuel wood scarcity are helping to undermine the economic base the social fabric of many weak states. Such problems do not stand alone but interact with political instability, economic mismanagement and civil war to produce a deadly downward spiral leading towards disintegration and anarchy. Thus even if few major conflicts can be seen as exclusively 'ecological', environmental factors have come to play an important role in an increasing number of social conflicts.

The net result is to debase further the currency of statehood and to move towards a situation in which the empirical claims to statehood of many quasi-states are being gutted of any real meaning. The problems of states that are states only in name is not of course a new one; it has been central to the analysis of post-colonial politics. But the ecological fragility of many states has added a powerful new twist to an old problem. It is also important to stress that the issue of environmental management and the very complex problems to which it gives rise have forced a reassessment of commonly used distinctions between 'strong' and 'weak' states. Clearly the problem of environmental degradation is acute in many of the weakest states, such as Haiti, El Salvador or many parts of Africa. But the story of the Brazilian Amazon provides a parable of how a quintessentially 'strong' state came to grief: an extensive state-led development programme built around a powerful ideology of national integration and national development; the attempt to achieve direct centralized control, displacing traditional local elites and replacing them with new bureaucratic structures of control; the gradual erosion of the capacity of the state to control the powerful and contradictory forces that had been unleashed; the present situation in which the writ of the state has ceased to run in many, perhaps most, parts of Amazonia. Moreover the Brazilian case does not stand alone, as shown by the role of environmental degradation and environmental protest in the collapse of communist regimes in the Soviet Union and Eastern Europe. And there are worrying signs that its shaky environmental foundations may yet force a dramatic reassessment of the much vaunted 'Chinese miracle'.

Despite the rhetorical emphasis placed on sustainable development, environmental policies in many developing countries suggest little more than the illusion of action and serious attempts to implement the measures discussed at UNCED and formalized in Agenda 21 have been at best patchy. The list of problems facing developing countries is long and depressing. An inadequate summary would include: the weakness of environmentalism and environmental parties domestically; the impact of economic adjustment on public spending and increased poverty; the degree to which incomplete understanding of the long-term costs of environmental damage leads to a reluctance to assume the short-term costs of environmental reforms; the extent to which the pressing nature of existing economic, political and social problems and high levels of institutional instability make any kind of long-term planning extremely difficult to draw up, let alone implement; the impact of the debt crisis and the ascendancy of neo-liberal economics on the capacities of the state and on perceptions of long term planning; the manifold weaknesses of environmental bureaucracies, lacking technical knowledge, political and bureaucratic clout, or financial resources; the critical problems of implementation and enforcement and the fact that the writ of the central government is often confined to limited areas of the country ; the extent to which the currently fashionable ideas of democratization and decentralization may not only serve to 'empower' those seeking to improve the environment and the use of natural resources, but by the same token those (often entrenched regional elites) most directly opposed to the implementation of tighter controls over the use of such resources.

Our Own Agenda, the Latin American follow-up to the Brundtland Report provided a frank acknowledgement of the scale of the problems involved:

> Any action in the direction of sustainable development will be very difficult whilst any of these conditions prevail: authoritarianism and the incapacity to interpret signals by society; deficient representation; absence of full guarantees on the part of

> a legally constituted state and the failure to combat corruption; non-professional civil service; lack of formulation and monitoring of medium and long-term policies...

Although the seriousness of these problems varies from one country to another, their existence is widely acknowledged. What is contested, however, is what they mean. There are two broad ways of looking at the domestic crisis of ecological viability. The first sees the problem essentially in technocratic terms, the policy levers are assumed to exist and the main difficulty consists of locating the optimum mix of market based and interventionist measures. The dominant orthodoxy leans heavily on the positive role of markets, although it assigns an important role to the state in correcting market failures, ensuring the proper valuation of environmental goods (for example biodiversity or forest resources), guaranteeing the distribution of property rights among individuals and groups, securing the enforcement of environmental legislation, correcting environmentally harmful fiscal policies, and providing macroeconomic stability.

Yet in many technocratic analyses there is a fundamental ambiguity about the role of the state. On the one hand, the extent to which the state has proved to be an environmental villain is widely recognized, as are the political difficulties faced by the state in regulating both itself and the many areas of the economy in which it is involved. Indonesia's transmigration programme, Sri Lanka's Mahaweli scheme and Brazil's Polonoreste programme provide just three examples of large state-led development programmes that caused enormous environmental damage. On the other hand, the technocratic solution clearly depends on reforming the state and turning it into an environmentally more benign actor. This problem is made more acute because demands that the state 'manage' the environment come at a time when the central thrust of international pressure is to restrict the role of the state and to redefine the boundaries between the private and public sectors. How is the circle to be squared? On the technocratic view it is mostly a matter of 'institutional strengthening' and 'capacity building', together with a degree of empowerment/involvement, and a heavy dose of decentralization.

Yet it is precisely the growth of doubts about the viability of this technocratic strategy that has given rise to the alternative 'community approach' favoured by many NGOs. According to this approach, it is grassroots and peoples' organizations that need to play the predominant role in the transition towards a more sustainable society. This view has a strong anti-statist slant, arguing that the state is so implicated in the generation of environmental problems that it is unlikely to serve as the vehicle for their solution. Especially in the developing world, many doubt whether states possess the capacity to control the destructive processes involved or have access to the requistie effective policy levers, especially given the importance of many forms of environmentally destructive development for key state-society alliances.

This view, therefore, emphasizes the political obstacles that block environmental policy reform and points to the social and political conflicts that lie behind many environmental issues—conflicts over access to specific resources but also conflicts over the meaning of 'development', 'environment' and 'sustainability' and the ways in which understandings of these concepts are socially constructed. On more extreme readings, states and the state system are seen as central parts of the 'problem'. As the Indian environmentalist Anupam Mishra has put it: 'It would be a folly to think that the Brundtland Commission can find solutions within the "counter-productive framework" of governments, the United Nations, the World Bank and so on. Because the present structures have given us the disease, is it then logical that they should also provide the cure?'

The increased political importance of environmental pressure groups and NGOs has attracted a great deal of attention. The pressure for expanding the role of NGOs has come primarily from the movements themselves, born of protest at the environmental failures of states and international institutions. But they have also come from states anxious to cut their losses, to reduce their role in conformity with the new international orthodoxy, and to divest themselves of difficult problems; and from international institutions anxious to find an alternative channel for aid and a way of deflecting environmentalist criticisms. Not only is an increasing percentage of official aid being channelled through NGOs, but, in several cases governments have wanted the text of international agreements to include the wording favoured by NGOs precisely in order to increase legitimacy.

The empowerment of both individuals and communities, combined with a strong emphasis on decentralized forms of political organization, has become a major theme of environmentalist writing. Decentralization and empowerment facilitate sustainability in various ways: first, by helping to create the political conditions that would make more effective public opposition to existing environmental dangers; second, by strengthening the balance of political forces in favour of greater social equity and justice; and third, because of the extent that local groups and communities possess special knowledge of what forms of development are sustainable and provide the social organizations within which that knowledge can be effectively implemented.

These arguments are important and few would want to dispute the importance of NGOs in developing new forms of political action and social development. But there are also real limits to the role of NGOs. First, there are the difficulties of generalizing and implementing on a larger scale what may be effective and equitable grassroots projects (for example, the concept of extractive reserves in Amazonia). Much of the value of such projects lies in their small size, and they may not easily lend themselves to 'scaling up' to perform larger and more complex roles. Second, as Steve Sanderson for tackling the underlying causes of environmental destruction. 'In Latin America, the development assistance community has been much better at developing small-scale projects than it has been in addressing the more fundamental questions that make their creation necessary. Third, there is the difficult trade-off between the role of NGOs in articulating criticisms or raising environmental or political awareness on the one hand and the loss of legitimacy that can follow from their becoming too closely associated with the provision of services. As many NGOs are becoming aware, excessive expectations and moves to become the lowest rung on the state bureaucracy are likely to engender a rapid loss of legitimacy.

Finally, and most importantly, despite the rhetoric of new forms of authentic democratic action and political practice, NGOs cannot themselves fulfil the core functions of the state: including the goal of providing minimum public order or protecting property rights. NGOs can usefully supplement but only rarely supplant the state at the local level (still less the national or international), however tempting an alternative this may appear to be. If the state collapses it is all too likely that the warlords and the drug barons will move in instead.

On closer inspection many of the anti-statist arguments of the environmental movement turn out to be calls for reformed and more democratic states. Having denounced 'statism' as a cruel deception and, along with scientism and developmentalism, one of the main sources of our present predicament, Paul Ekins goes on to provide an impressively long list of the functions that states need to be pressed to fulfil:

> State power has a vital role to play in people's self-development. It must provide the basic institutions to encapsulate and frame the market so that the market mechanism may work to general advantage. It must guarantee continuing access for all people to the resources for production and developmemt, both monetary and non-monetary in nature. And it must implement basic norms of social justice which narrow differentials in society

> by progressively enabling the disadvantaged to provide for their own needs from their own resources and participate fully in its mainstream life.

This is hardly an exit from 'statism': more a call for grassroots pressure to reform and rehabilitate the state.

There are at least two reasons why the domestic failures of many weak states have far wider ramifications. In the first place, the traditional separation between the domestic and the international overlooks the extent to which domestic weakness is connected to international forces. There is no need to claim here, with crude dependency or world systems theory, that the external is all powerful and that all domestic environmental problems are the result of malign external pressures; only that both the problem themselves and the state's capacity to deal with them are the product of the interaction between domestic and global factors. Examples would include the complex links between structural adjustment and environmental degradation, or between particular sets of agricultural policies and deforestation/desertification.

Second, the capacity of the state system (and of the most powerful states that dominate that system) to deal with the most pressing environmental problems is clearly affected by the fragility of many states. Exactly in what ways, to what extent and with what consequences forms one of the most important issues in global enviornmental politics. These links are most visible when one considers the impact of domestic weakness on environmental issues that are global in the strong sense that they affect everyone and can only be effectively managed on the basis of cooperation between all, or at least a great majority, of the states of the world: controlling climate change and the emission of greenhouse gases, the protection of ozone layer, safeguarding biodiversity, protecting special regions such as Antarctica or the Amazon, the management of the sea-bed, and the protection of the high seas. Developing countries are central to many of these problems. With the exception of Australia, for example, the top twelve 'megadiversity' states are all in the developing world: India, Malaysia, Brazil, Colombia, Ecuador, Peru, Maxico, Madagascar and Zaire Equally, global climate change will be critically affected by the future decisions on energy use of major countries such as China, Brazil or India.

But it is only a matter of these more obviously 'global' problems. The scale of many problems that have often been seen as 'local' has expanded enormously over the past fifty years. According to some estimates, for example around 10 per cent of the vegetation bearing surface of the earth is suffering from moderate to extreme degradation due to human activity since 1945 (an area larger than India and China combined). Moreover, whilst many environmental issues (particularly questions of resource scarcity) appear manageable when viewed from a global perspective, it is clear that, once disaggregated, 'success' will depend on high levels of cooperation and significant levels of inter-state redistribution. Thus the number of individual countries likely to be affected by 'localized' environmental degradation and serious resource scarcity remains alarming. For example, although the 'world' may be able to feed itself, food production lagged behind population growth in 69 out of 102 developing countries between 1978 and 1989. The world's consumption of water more than doubled between 1945 and 1980 and is likely to double again in the next twenty years. Yet already 80 countries with two fifths of the world's population suffer from serious water deficits. Such examples underline the extent to which definitions of 'global' are politically constructed and hence politically contested.

It is wrong to believe, with the arch apostles of ecological globalism, that everything matters and matters equally. There are many examples of extreme environmental degradation and human misery that are unlikely to engage the political interests and humanitarian concerns of the core industrialized countries. But too mechanical an understanding of the linkages between North and South, too cynical a definition of interest, and too narrow an understanding of how and why the South 'matters', are equally misleading. For political as much as environmental reasons, it is difficult to believe in a stable international order that condemns a large part of humankind both to material deprivation and to high levels of powerlessness and vulnerability.

The ball is therefore quickly back in the court of international society. Two problems are evident: First there are the political problems connected with the management of increasing international inequality. Environmental change provides a good example of how globalization works not to erode the power of all states, but rather to create new patterns of inequality and dominance. Environmental degradation works to increase inequality since some states are manifestly more able to adapt, both because of their superior wealth and, especially, technological capabilities, and because of their ability to help frame collective solutions that reflect their own preferences and interest.

Second, increasing pressure is placed on the core capitalist states to intervene and try and 'do something' about the manifest environmental failings of those developing states which palpably affect their own interests. Part of the difficulty stems from the dubious legitimacy of external intervention. But still more arises from its questionable efficacy. There are by now enough cases of misguided and misdirected external involvement to place in doubt the capacity of the core states to find viable answers to environmetal problems. (For example, the repeated environmental catastrophes of World Bank supported projects and the difficulties of securing effective implementation of apparently impressive environmental goals). It is therefore essential to consider just what we mean when we speak of the 'power' of the most powerful industrialized states. For if the 'power' of the core industrialized states is insufficient or irrelevant, then a crisis in the periphery will rapidly become a crisis for the centre.

The Erosion of Identity

Increased environmental awareness may have affected the normative appeal of the state in two ways. The first set of challenges undermines the normative appeal of the state from within: by questioning of the ability of large-scale centralized power structures to deal with environmental problems; by arguing for the need to root solutions and identities in local knowledge and local values; by filling the void left by a retreating state wherever the latter is no longer able to perform its traditional functions. There are several powerful and persuasive examples of ecological failures which have been catalysts of a dramatic and widespread loss of legitimacy. Not only was mobilization around environmental issues central to political protest in the Soviet Union and Eastern Europe but the scale of the region's environmental problems helped to expose the hollowness of official claims and formed a major obstacle to bureaucratic reform. In many parts of Latin America environmentalism grew up as part of a broader protest against authoritarian rule and of what O'Donnell has termed 'the resurrection of civil society'.

The second set of challenges derives from the increasingly global character of many environmental issues and from the extent to which this global character has strengthened a cosmopolitan awareness or planetary consciousness. Perhaps the most important shift in the twenty years that separated the Stockholm Conference in 1972 from the Earth Summit in Rio de Janeiro in 1992 was the emergence of the paradigm of *global* environmental crisis. Dominant understandings of the most pressing environmental problems moved from the discussions of the 1970s about the impact of localized pollution and the limits to natural resources (The Club of Rome, 'limits to growth', OPEC etc.) to an increased emphasis on the notion of 'global environmental change' and on the limited capacity of the planet to absorb the wastes produced by economic activity: in shorthand, a shift from 'resource limits' to 'sink limits'. The emergence of global environmental problems and the greatly strengthened awareness of a global common interest amongst all peoples in protecting the environment and safeguarding the future of humanity have provided a powerful stimulus to the growth of cosmopolitan moral consciousness. The notion of sharing a world, the essential inter-connectedness and interdependence of the global environment, and the scarcity of the resources available to humanity that need to be distributed both within and between generations all create conditions within which it becomes much harder than in the past to accept that community ends at the borders of states. For many people, then, global environmental interdependence has given greater plausibility to visions of a cosmopolitan global community.

The essential claim here is a very important one. The sceptic has traditionally denied the importance of the idea of a global community of humankind by claiming that it is no more than the figment of the imagination, that it has no empirical referent. Attempts (for example by Charles Beitz) to root the existence of such community in the workings of the global economy were never very convincing. They drastically underplayed the difference between the *fact* of being part of a common system on the one hand and the *consciousness* of belonging to a single community on the other. To argue that a global community is coming into being solely as a result of technological change or economic integration is to succumb to technological or economic determinism.

Environmental interdependence, however, is arguably very different. First, because it is 'deeper' in the sense that no state or group of people can cut themselves off from the actions of others, unlike economic interdependence, which is, at least in principle, reversible and where patterns have oscillated over time. Second it is 'deeper' in the sense that interconnections are not simply 'external' relations. Global climate change, for example, is caused by core industrial activities and by the lifestyles of millions of citizens. In the third place, it is different because of the extent to which the global environmental movement now gives concrete political expression to the idea of a global community. Thus we have seen increased attention being given to the importance of environmental groups, not just because of their ability to influence state policies but also to create a transnational civil society and to define a new pattern of politics. This attention encompasses both the scientific community and transnational environmental pressure groups concerned with the interlinked issues of sustainable development, the promotion of grassroots democracy, and the protection of indigenous peoples. The strength of such groups rests on their ability to articulate a powerful set of human values, to harness a growing sense of cosmopolitan moral awareness, and to respond of the multiple failures of the state system, both local and globally. The ability to act in this way is clearly assisted by other aspects of globalization in that increased levels of economic globalization provide the 'infrastructure' for increased social communication—the role of communications technologies in facilitating the flow of values, knowledge and ideas and in allowing like-minded groups to organize across national boundaries.

The emerging sense of planetary consciousness is undoubtedly important and adds further complexity to the constant and confusing swirl of contemporary claims to identity. But how far does all this indicate a serious and sustained crisis of legitimacy for the nation state?

How strong are these new loyalties? It is extremely hard to judge how far environmentalism and the global environmental movement are undermining the normative appeal of the idea of the nation state. There is a large body of work on Northern environmentalism, but far less on environmental movements in other parts of the world and less still on the specifically transnational elements of the global environmental movement. What we do know suggests that its impact has increased very significantly but remains uneven, that it varies from one issue to another and can fall as well as rise. Indeed it is interesting to note how many environmental pressure groups believe their influence on outcomes at UNCED to be quite modest.

Second, there is the question of the relative strength of the various 'new' identities that have emerged to challenge the legitimacy of existing states. There are surely powerful reasons to believe that ethnic or nationalist claims exercise far greater sway over the popular and political imagination of many peoples than the arguments of the environmental movement. Such 'disintegrationist' claims may well represent a deep challenge to the stability of the state system—by reopening the criteria for membership and undermining the pragmatic compromise underlying the post-war application of self-determination (colonial self-determination combined with opposition to secession); and by undermining many of the traditional instruments of inter-state order (balance of power, spheres of influence, non-instruments etc.). But they do not challenge the centrality of the nation-state itself as the dominant political form. Indeed nationalist movements continue to be driven by the overriding goal of establishing their own state, however bloody may be the road towards that goal.

Third, much environmental thinking is characterized by an attractive combination of globalism, of solidarity, of 'one-worldism' on the one hand and of diversity, of parochialism, of the importance of small-scale community on the other. Indeed communitarian arguments that stress the importance of particular communities and emphasize pluralism and diversity take on a new dimension in the environmental field: The relationship to nature and the natural world is often a defining feature of a community's sense of itself. Environmentalism may well provide a more promising route towards the reconciliation of these conflicting identities than the ferociously divisive and deeply particularist claims of race, religion or ethnicity. But it will not be easy to achieve this reconciliation . No universal definition of sustainable development can be applied in a mechanistic fashion in all parts of the world. Environmental policies and priorities will inevitably and legitimately vary from one country (and one community) to another. This reflects the immense variation that exists in the physical world, in the nature and scope of environmental challenges, and in the different perspectives on environmental problems that come from different levels of economic development. Equally, sustainability unavoidably requires trade-offs between different priorities : between the maximum preservation of the natural environment and the pursuit of continuously high levels of economic development; between rapid economic growth and the protection of traditional cultures or improvements in equity and social justice; or between the importation of the latest technology and the safeguarding of traditional practices and cultures.

The UNCED process revealed the still very deep divisions (including within the NGO community) over the ways in which these trade-offs are managed. As Tickell notes, in many cases '[T]here is a clash of uncomprehending cultures within and between countries and peoples. For all the claims to novelty, it may well be, then, that the difference between economic interdependence and ecological interdependence is not so great. It is still very hard to move from participation in common system, even one in which there are substantial common interests, towards a shared sense of community built around a consensus either on substantive values (what, for example, 'sustainability' might actually mean) or on the procedural mechanisms (whether, for example, greater 'global democracy' would be a help or a hindrance) by which the claims of conflicting sets of environmental values can be adjudicated between different communities, states, and cultures.

The increasing range and seriousness of environmental problems undoubtedly threatens to overwhelm the already frail capabilities of many states and to undermine the extent to which they can form the 'building blocks' of a broader world order. There is a serious tension between seeing the state as both deeply implicated in many forms of environmental degradation and as the vehicle for reform and redemption. Equally the need to reconcile the scope of human activity with the carrying capacity of the biosphere is likely to require historically unprecedented levels of inter-state cooperation. Although the number and scope of international environmental agreements have indeed increased very rapidly, there is no guarantee that such cooperation will be forthcoming. The obstacles to such cooperation remain all too evident and the argument that 'necessity' will 'inevitably' bring forth such cooperation is a shallow one. States and the state system, then, remain indispensable but may well prove inadequate.

Of course global environmental order cannot be usefully understood, still less promoted, solely in terms of the actions and policies of states. On the one hand, there is the central role of the global economy; on the other, the rise of NGOs and of environmentalism. The global environmental movement has certainly become a significant political force. Transnational civil society has also become extremely important both in promoting grassroots community and development and in cultivating and extending a sense of the common world good. It would be absurd to pretend that global environmental politics can be reduced to a narrow statist perspective.

But the image of the Global Forum in Rio as a 'world community in waiting', although a seductive one, is deeply misleading. The state system may well be part of the problem but it is also an essential part of the solution. The lack of global solidarity about resources and environmental issues is not primarily rooted in the state system but in the inability of human beings to agree on the nature and seriousness of the environmental threats, on the meaning of sustainability, and on the principles of global environmental management. Unless the present international system break up in some dramatic and unexpected way, these tensions need to be managed on a global basis. Relations within ' a community of communities' (to take Herman Daly's picture of the future) would have to replicate or reinvent many of the institutions of international society. The political and moral tensions that have long been central to international society—above all between the respect for difference and pluralism on the one hand and the cultivation of an overlapping consensus on the nature of a common world good on the other—would not go away, but would merely reappear in a different form. There is no obvious reason for believing that an alternative to the state system would prove a better means of achieving this (already extremely difficult) end.

5
Political Theories of Ecology

Definition of Ecology

The distinctive qualities of ecologism arose in the late nineteenth century, and consisted of two distinct strands. One was an anti-mechanistic, holistic approach to biology, deriving from the German zoologist, Ernst Haeckel. The second strand was a new approach to economics called energy economics. This focused on the problem of scarce and non-renewable resources. These two strands fused together in the 1970s. The scientific element in energy economics gave impetus to the biologically based ecological movement, which had lost credibility because of its links with Germany. The two categories, biological and economic, had a certain degree of cross-membership. There was contact between individuals, and forefathers are still cited. It is the combination of the intensely conservative moral and cultural ecological critique with the full apparatus of quantitative argument that has rendered ecologism the powerful force it is today.

The word ecology is widely used today in the normative sense, not in the biological sense. The science of ecology is one that considers energy flows within a closed system. The normative sense of the word has come to mean the belief that severe or drastic change within that system, or indeed any change which can damage any specie within it, or that disturbs the system, is seen as wrong. Thus, ecological ideas have come to be associated with the conservation of specific patterns of energy flows. These patterns can be relatively small in scale, such as a one-acre wetland site; or it can be the weather pattern resulting from the Amazon rain forests, or larger patterns that affect the continuity of human existence.

The place of man within this hierarchy of patterns is no longer seen by ecologists as predominant. A recent theory is that the earth is not just a dead planet which contains a valuable closed system, but is itself alive. According to this belief, 'Gaia', the earth, has its own serene ecological balance, its own will to live. It is capable of preserving its own existence. It can shrug off disturbing intrusions, whether from comets or from man. Like any other species, Gaia has its own natural term. It lives and it will die.

The countries where ecological theories have been most prominent are Britain, Germany and North America. Although the intellectual community responsible for disseminating and provoking these theories included French and Russian scientists and political activists, England and Germany today present the most striking picture of mobilised environmental groups. North America has both inspired radical, alternative ideas and received them again, in somewhat altered form, from Europe.

The persistence on this 'ethnic map' of ecologists, which has been noted by several observers, deserve comment. Britain, Germany and North America all had different rates of industrialisation. In their demography and patterns of land settlement, too, they have little in common. North America in 1890 was a small town continent, as rural as Russia. Germany had many provincial capitals, the largest being Berlin. England alone was heavily urbanised overall. However, all three had a large, educated middle class, possessed of a strong liberal and Protestant culture. These cultural roots will emerge as a constant theme in my exposition.

The historical manifestations are, of course, profoundly different in the different countries under review. In Germany, there existed a dissatisfaction with and uncertainty about German identity. The shifting political and territorial boundaries of the nation led to a search for a more 'authentic', earth-bound identity. The hunt for anti-mechanistic values meant opposition to big institutions and size as an end in itself. German ecologism well predated National Socialism. It formed part of a generic cultural phenomenon that was a part diverted into the Third Reich as an underlying theme. It re-emerged, well after the Second World War, in more obviously left-oriented groups. The insecurity of German national identity had no exact parallel in Britain, but the British political ecologists also demonstrate a sense of a lost folk heritage, as well as a cultural criticism. The North American radical tradition, of which its ecologism is a native development, differs in its optimism. Theories of post-scarcity abundance, and a libertarian anarchic trend, characterise the American commune movement. In all three countries there was a sense of loss of the past, associated with, but not confined to, the passing of the old, rural world. This fused with critiques of orthodox, liberal economics and mechanistic biology to produce the ecologists, and their later flowering, the Greens.

The Ecological Critique

Many aspects of ecological ideas have now impregnated our collective unconscious. Claims which, a few decades ago, would have demanded an analytical response now quickly become cliches, part of our mental furniture. Clearly ecologism met a need.

> Ecology was the science which could interpret the fragments of evidence that told us something was wrong with the world - dead birds, oil in the sea, poisoned crops, the population explosion... What it meant was—everything links up... Here was a new morality, and a strategy for human survival rolled into one.

This was written in 1972. On the other hand, ecologists claim that the sense of something wrong has resonated over the centuries. How recent is cultural criticism ? We find the same kind of criticism in the early nineteenth century. Did it refer to the same kind of wrongness ? Or has there been, as I will argue, a change in the way in which we look critically at the world? A sense that something is wrong is not a reliable guide for constructing specific and revolutionary policies. On the other hand, it is an intuition which needs investigation. No matter how many explanations there may be for the location and growth of ecologism, they would in the last resort be irrelevant to the value of their claims.

What are these claims ? Man's vision of his place in the world, the question of the objective existence of that world and his relation to it, is fundamental to Western intellectual life, with its awareness of transience, the tension between past and future, being and becoming, ego and other. It affects the largest questions: the source of historical change, the nature of man, the why and how of man's history. It is intimately bound up with the problem of causality, affecting especially the question of the source of innovation and creativity. The validity of objective science, and the possibility of a social science, these all hinge on the stance taken towards man's place in nature.

Further, there are political implications. Over the centuries, nature has oscillated between being hero and villain. A study of the changing attitudes of nature and environment, and the vision of balance between them known as ecology, shows that the axis man-nature provides a set of political categorizations which are fruitful, useful and relevant to today's political scene. But the picture is not a simple one.

Put baldly, nature-based ideas are seen as legitimising social Darwinist, red-in-tooth-and-claw beliefs. The role of nature in German vitalist philosophy and philosophical anthropology between 1890 and 1933 has been associated with the growth of National Socialism, while irrationalist and 'cranky' movements have claimed a special relationship with Nature and Mother Earth. Conservative and reactionary movements have often looked back to the peasant-landowner relationship as a source of national strength. However, the essential characteristic of ecology, while it does not fit happily into any one ideological category, is that it draws many of its conclusions from scientific ways of thinking, and is not conservative.

Political ecology, which began towards the late nineteenth century, started as a progressive, science-based, anti-democratic movement. Kropotkinite anarchists as well as Spencerian individualists, all based their politics on recent theories about biology and physics. Between the wars, a number of positions were associated with ecological ideas, dominated this time by a fear of erosion and famine, and including, in England, the High Tory movement of Hugh Massingham and Lord Lymington. Technophiles and technophobes have always warred within ecologism. Technological optimism was more common in North America, where the late 1960s saw an anarcho-communard green movement. The most successful green movements today, though, are of the radical Left, and there are Greens today who feel unease at some of their ideological forebears.

The complexity is this; it is possible to assert that if man is part of the natural world, subject to the same laws as the animals, then he is, like them, entitled to compete to survive. Because he cannot hope to escape from his animal nature, he is justified in aggression. This is the social Darwinist argument associated by many with a politics based on nature. It assumes that man's survival cannot be taken for granted; he is never secure. The counter-image is that man is so special, so malleable and adaptable in his nature that the laws of the natural world no longer apply to him. Man's intellect and self-awareness, in this mode, meant a qualitative change in his status, and removed him from the biological law of selection and evolution. If his behaviour is not controlled by instinct, then man is adaptable enough to be made over in any image. The model of improvement through social and environmental change is generally a progressive and left-wing model.

However, one can also argue that it is precisely because man partakes of the earthly burden that he should help nurture the earth, rather than despoil it. His 'natural' role is that of a shepherd. Nature embodies stasis and harmony. Man should therefore accept, runs this argument, his limitations, and fit into the given pattern of energy flows. This is, on the whole, the ecological viewpoint, that man is the shepherd of the earth.

And an ecological conclusion has been drawn from the premise that man does not have inbuilt limitations. This conservative variant points out that it is precisely man's lack of a fixed genetic inheritance that makes stable institutions essential as a substitute. Because man's culture has to be learnt afresh with each generation, those traditions, such as the family, which embody memory and habit, must be preserved. The belief that man is born without a genetic template for, say, the Church of England, makes continuity in social institutions more important and not less; makes progressive aims more dangerous, precisely because man can be stripped of his non-genetic endowment, his cultural heritage, by well-meaning destruction of existing structures. So man's capacities for improvement and change are finite, and he should beware of attempts to strain the boundaries of what is natural to him.

Thus, it is an over-simplification of ecological politics to think that nature-based thinkers have to be social Darwinist, while believers in man's malleability must reject nature from their analysis. The political stance of ecologists has been more complex, just as other political categories shift and change over time.

Ecologists and Greens

The cultural and political criticism known as political ecology involves substantial ethical and moral claims, and proposes drastic and apocalyptic remedies. Today's Green parties have carved out a political niche which receives between seven and eleven per cent of national party votes. The European Parliament has a Green section which has more members than has the Communist Party. Green parties have flourished in Northern and Central Europe, in a wedge stretching from Finland to Austria, to Belgium. Britain, too, has a Green Party (formerly the Ecology Party, and the first to be so named, founded in 1973), and there has been growing 'entryism', especially within the Liberal Party and middle-class Labour constituencies. The Conservative Party is under considerable pressure to protect rural values, and the National Front went Green in 1984. Greens have to be moles in Britain, because of the two-and-half party system; but even so, in Britain alone some three million people are alleged to be members of environmental and other ecological groups.

The green tendency has aroused unease in some political quarters, dismissal in others. The Right today tends to be pro-American, pro-nuclear power and conservative. It suspects enthusiasm. The hard Left, despite recent efforts to capture green ground for Marxism, has tended to write off ecologists as trivial, irrelevant, or doomed to failure. One social historian describes Richard Jefferies, the nineteenth-century self-educated farmer's son and naturalist, as 'the Tory transcendentalist writer', and sees his ideas as 'a refuge from unpleasant realities'. In one typical structuralist criticism, ruralist ideas are seen as having 'a fatal flaw.....like ecological ideas, they were not made to mobilise the masses.' A fatal flaw indeed, but the evidence seems to be that the masses are being mobilized none the less. When cultural criticisms are combined with political action, it is time to examine the phenomenon seriously. The best way to start is to create a history of ecologism. Surprisingly, this has not yet been done.

For many young, uncommitted observers, the idea that ecologists pre-date the 1970s would come as a surprise. Others, working for environmental causes for decades, see the recent growth of media interest in the Greens with some cynicism, or even irritation. Ecologists themselves locate their roots variously. Some believe there has been an alternative, holistic tradition running through Western culture since the Middle Ages. There is already a substantial literature, dominated by American feminists, which propounds the virtues of an alleged pre-patriarchal, pre-exploitative Golden Age, run by female market gardeners and moon worshippers.

Academic studies usually confine their studies to one country. Armin Mohler, historian of recent German conservatism, thinks the ecological 'package-deal' (*Gedankengut*) derives from the conservative romantic reaction of the 1920s. He cites Friedrich Georg Jünger, brother of the better-known Ernst, as a key figure. The historian of geography, David Pepper, finds two main roots of environmentalism in Britain, a scientific root derived from Malthus and Darwin, and an unscientific romantic concept stemming from Matthew Arnold. The American Donald Worster, in the most comprehensive work of its type of date, concentrates on America, and the influences of Thoreau and Emerson. He also finds two strands of ecologism; and Arcadian theme and a more classificatory, dominating attitude. Juan Martinez-Alier's history of energy economics deliberately confines itself to authors who offer specific calculations of calorific values and resources. This naturally excludes biological ecologism, as well as philosophical or mystical ruralism. A standard work on modern British environmentalists, by Jane Lowe and Philip Goyder, notes the parallel developments in North America, Europe, Britain and the White Dominions, but they confine their study to British politics. There is no work which ties together the geographers, land planners and biologists in all three countries, and relates them to the present. Although the present study, too, cannot expect to be comprehensive, it will, I hope, provide a broad framework in which to consider our heritage of ecological ideas.

Almost a third of this book concerns the German connection. In one way this is not surprising. Ecology was formulated in Germany, and many 'alternative' ideas, in the field of medicine, sun-worship, vitamins and homeopathy come from German-speaking countries. During the Third Reich, refugees brought to Britain that tradition of holistic medicine, often bound up with an anti-liberal criticism surprisingly similar to that enunciated by those who remained and were thus associated with the Third Reich. But it is not this connection which will be found in the literature to date. When ecologists sit down and muse about their origins, the scope can be breathtaking but inaccurate. The place of Germany within their framework typifies this, but points to an intriguing problem. Nietzsche, for example, is frequently described as an important figure. Why should this be? In reality, he does not conform at all to the model ecologist, nor is he a German Romantic,—he espoused anti-nationalist and rationalist causes for most of his life. But misinterpretations of Nietzsche are an important force. The symbolic misuse of Nietzsche means:—values, extreme individualism, nationalism, the blood, anti-modernism, Dionysian irrationalism and the superman. It is illiberalism based on existentialism. For many ecologists, these ideas are alien. Yet still Nietzsche hovers, worrying but relevant. For he puts man in God's place, with the responsibility as well as the fun that implies. He is a forerunner of vitalism, and these ideas, attacked by the intellectual establishment, do have a perpetual appeal. They fill a lack. Goethe, Nietzsche, Bergson, Driesch and Hei-degger together form an anti-analytical, holistic canon, and escapes from the arid desert of linguistic philosophy often find themselves wandering in their epistemological ether.

Man the creator, man the destroyer; man whose touch produced light and death—what clearer image could there be of the exploitative, dominating Promethean? It was a later German philosopher, Martin Heidegger, described by George Steiner as the 'metaphysician of ecologism' who wrote a surprisingly modern-sounding critique of consumerism in 1944; he called on man to be the shepherd of the earth, to accept his humble role as part of the world, to avoid technology, domination and the role of exploiter. Clearly, a philosophical tradition which produces such opposed interpretations of man as the Promethean and the Shepherd is a complex one. It seems worthwhile, therefore, to examine the recent German nature tradition and its various strands, and its experience in tragic practice.

The question of National Socialist absorption of ecological ideas arises here. I touched on it in a previous book, where I pointed to the existence of ecological arguments so similar to today's in the Third Reich and asked whether it was significant or just an embarrassing accident.

Although I examined the issue seriously, and offered supporting evidence, still I did not do more there than outline the problem, and urge that it be taken seriously. This is a suitable work in which to re-examine the problem, with all its implications for our view of Nazi ideology, and for the future of support for the Greens. As this is not a specialized book on Nazi history, I will concentrate on two questions; why, as one historian has already asked, the Nazis were the first 'radical environmentalists in charge of a state': and secondly whether the Nazis succeeded in their attempt to keep the small farmer on the land. This is an ambition of today's Greens, especially those concerned with the Third World. So is autarky, another concern of the German agrarian radicals. It is important to separate the effects of non-specific historical phenomena from the effects of the peasant experiment. I, therefore, compare various European fascist doctrines, including those of Mosley's fascists in Britain, to see whether the ecological component in Germany can be seen as ethnically specific rather than politically contingent.

Recent years have seen an increasing trend towards the historicisation of National Socialism. Comparative studies have been carried out in fields such as welfare policy, crime, policing and architecture. Various observers, including Thomas Mann, have already pointed to the rural values lying, as a style or rhetorical tendency, behind much of Nazi ideology. There is now concrete evidence to support this intuition. However, there were distinct strands of agrarian ruralism, ecologism and agrarian modernism which need to be differentiated clearly, while it is also important to distinguish between essential and accidental similarities.

Because of the alternative nature of the ecological criticism it has already been subject to a certain degree of polemical criticism which the evidence here may help to fuel. The pacifism and hostility to nuclear power inherent in the Greens renders them the automatic enemy of today's Right. Further, today's Right fears what it perceives as an element of anti-rationalism, together with the inherently destabilizing and oppositional nature of ecologists, with their conservative moral values and non-conservative means. The frequent attacks on alternative science, medicine and evolutionary theories launched by luminaries from the scientific establishment clearly display this fear; together with its corollary, that the oppositional, anti-establishment and radical nature of the Greens could lead to revolutionary phenomena. Of its essence, the fear of anti-rational revolution is the fear of a Pol Pot as opposed to a Lenin. A Lenin is seen as working, however destructively, within a recognized and familiar Western framework. The revolt of the peasant, however, is boundless, formless and terrible. Yet ecologism is based on a belief in objective truth and values. Ecologists reject the humanist act of faith for the best of reasons – because their humanism is grounded in what they perceive as immutable natural law. For this reason alone it has been attacked under its guise of social Darwinism as sinisterly anti-progressive. An argument which is used by both establishment-oriented conservatives, together with members of the socialist academic establishment, is that ecologists are a danger because they reject reason and a danger because they believe in reason. This is either deeply wrong or profoundly right. To attack a philosophy because it claims to overthrow progressive aims through its objectivity and closer grasp or reality, and to attack it because it appears to do away with rationality, does seem to mean that there is a confusion somewhere. It may be a valuable pre-paradigm-breaking confusion, or perhaps a sign that existing institutions are under attack,—but certainly it is something that warrants investigation.

My own hypothesis is that the apparent contradictions of the ecological movement can be resolved by seeing it as forming a new political category in its own right, with a history, right wings and left wings, with leaders, followers and a special epistemological niche all to itself. In this book I seek to provide the evidence to prove this theory.

The Ecological Box

To explain what I mean by a political theory of ecology I must define an ecologist, and explain his beliefs. Then I must show how he occupies a special political niche, and what are the epistemological consequences of that occupation. One way to do this would be to assume that we are all agreed on who and what were ecologists. No such agreement exists. The history of ecologism is not only in its infancy, but what exists has largely been written by believers. Its historiography is divided into uninvolved histories and very much involved histories. This is not to criticize involvement in itself. A philosophy should affect the life of its time, while a subject is only of interest if it relates to our sense of values, whether aesthetic or political or moral, or all three. However, engagement produces problems for the historians of ideas. It means that some works are considered as subjects for academic dissection, while others are written by co-dissectors. This distinction between comrades and victims does not reflect any difference in quality, but in objective and in self-definition. In defining what an ecologist is, what he thinks is his own history is obviously relevant. Here, then, a specific historiography becomes part of the syndrome it defines.

Ecologism is a political box. It is a new box, into which many distinguished and important thinkers fit who fit only partially into other, better-known boxes. 'Thinkers' they must be, since an acquaintance with scientific ideas, available to specialists in other disciplines but not widely disseminated, is an essential part of ecologism. The box began to attain its current shape and size around 1880 in Europe and North America. Self-definition about belonging in this box arose later, in the 1920s. It was not until the early 1970s that the box acquired a proper name, and earlier ecologists saw what they had thought their very own box expropriated. Over the last hundred years the clarity of the box's outlines was obscured by the presence of other, bigger, better-known boxes, some of whose corners were tucked into our ecological box – that is, they shared policies and aims, but temporarily, and variably, since non-ecological boxes fluctuate in their degree of concern for ecologism.

How is one to define a man-made category, and how far back is one to trace its ancestry? At what stage does it cease being pre- or proto-, and become, as it were, *sapiens*? Conservatism, Socialism and Communism too go back only so far. How far is a matter of dispute, and depends on whether one accepts self-definition by members of these categories. Such self-definition is itself a constantly changing, live political issue. The argument for continuity of ecological opposition is held by many ecologists. They believe that an alternative ecological idea dates back millennia. How is one to judge the validity of such a claim? One may feel that some violence is done to a historically specific concept by linking together disparate cultures and eras, by spotting collectivism among Pythagoreans and laissez-faire ideology among the victims of Diocletian. We realize that each historical epoch is unique, and we do not, therefore, expect to find duplicates of historical phenomena in each period. At the same time, we know that there are human constants and similarities. Much of ecologism lies in looking for these. We know that continuities exist. The historian walks a tight-rope between these two conflicting realities, both of which are true. We step and step not into the same river.

However, change and development there must be. Therefore, new fusions can be created from ancient human instincts and habits. In normal terminology, the political categories mentioned earlier are confined to the recent past. We trace Conservatism and Socialism back certainly to before the exact definitions and party systems as we know them today arose. Not too far back; probably to a few decades at most, a short time before people recognized themselves as being 'it', and we allow for the fact that full-blown 'its' can still change substantially within the usable time-span, as Tories changed to Conservatives, and Marxist Social Democrats changed to liberal Socialists. By analogy, therefore, one would expect the ecologist to emerge shortly before the word became used normatively. As the first normative use of the word that I have found dates to 1915, it seems reasonable to place the creation of the ecological box in about 1880, some thirteen years after the scientific term was first coined.

Conservatism and Socialism have, in general usage, an association with the words which form their root: conserving and *sozial*. Similarly, ecologism arises from the concept of *Oekologie*. Ecologism does not involve the web of life alone; it was used originally as co-terminous with ethology, the study of animal behaviour in its environment, and with *oekonomie*, the concept of 'economical' household management. This implies that the use and conservation of resources is a moral activity as well as an economic one; and a morality closely bound up with the survival of the group.

But, although the terms rest on Greek roots – some ecologists find this link with early classical Greece itself significant – the words refer to a set of biological, physical science and geographical ideas that arose separately around the mid-nineteenth century. Biological holism showed that man and animals were interdependent in and on a balanced environment. It implied that there was a scientific truth that lay outside man's perceptions, but on which man depended. The physical sciences learned that the dissipation of energy might endanger man's existence, or even that of the planet itself. Geographers examined land settlement and use from the aspect of resources. Land itself became perceived as endangered, and its finiteness, always known as a truism, began to matter.

How and when did ecologism manifest itself? A theory about this is not provable in the scientific sense. The method I propose to follow is to describe, explain and analyse together. I start from the position that we are aware that something exists which is to be examined, using observation, common sense and empathy. The form of the examination will help to define the phenomenon. At this stage I want to sketch out the qualities of an ecologist, and show what the potential political consequences were.

The First World War brought apocalypse to a generation already intellectually alienated. It showed that real disaster, real loss, was possible. In the 1920s ecologists began to define themselves as such. It had taken about that long for the scientific roots of ecologism to merge into a political discipline, to become an ideology.

The existence of this ideology has been obscured because it took on varied political forms. Most controversially, in the 1920s and 1930s, an alternative, anti-capitalist stance meant that the apparently alternative, anti-capitalist "Third Way' National Socialist and Fascist parties attracted ecologists. After the Second World War the ideal lay dormant for a period. It then revived, still in an alternative anti-capitalist form, with similar ideas, programmes and beliefs, but with a self-defined leftwards tinge. The political shift was partly because the 'soft centre' moved from right to left during this time. It was also because American anarchists and Marxists in the late 1960s took up ecological ideas as part of 'alienation'.

Ecologists themselves are divided between those who believe that ecologism sprung up fully formed in the late 1960s, and those who see an underground, green tradition that always existed in Western history. Some place its origins in early Greek times; some in the Bronze Age. Heidegger believed that society went wrong in the transition from Greek to Latin, so that Greek concepts were translated into Latin but misunderstood. To give an account of beliefs that rationality has always battled with intuition as a source of our civilization would take too long at this stage; I will only say that it is *ecologists* themselves who argue this. The beliefs itself is a symptom of being an ecologist, and will be treated here on that level. Similarly, the hunt for a scapegoat who *made* society go wrong is a symptom of ecologism. Much of the literature consists of accusation and counter-accusation hurled to and from the scapegoats of other ecologists' Manichaean analyses. It is unusual for the historiography to be part of the subject itself.

Ecologists believe in the essential harmony of nature. But it is a harmony to which man may have to be sacrificed. Ecologists are not man-centred or anthropocentric in their loyalties. Therefore, they do not have to see nature's harmony as especially protective towards or favouring mankind. Ecologists believe in an absolute responsibility for one's actions, and for the world in general. There is no God the Shepherd; so man becomes the shepherd. There is conflict between the desire to accept nature's harmonious order, and a need to avert catastrophe because ecologists are apocalyptical, but know that man has caused the impending apocalypse by his actions. Ecologists are the saved.

As part of their sense of responsibility, ecologists know that there is no free lunch. Everything has a cost; everything a place. The saved are better able to plan man, space and the environment than existing institutions. Bureaucracies are wasteful and slothful, as Kropotkin pointed out; but man's unplanned actions are destructive and can be aesthetically unappealing.

For, although non-anthropocentric, ecologists are not passive in their stance towards the world. They care intensely about how things look, feel and are, and feel a responsibility to indicate the way to the truth. Aesthetic values, then, are vital to ecologism. But not only the sensuous pleasures of nature, the importance of which to ecologists varies from decade to decade and from country to country. There is hostility to the elaborate, the formal, despite the belief in benevolent planning. The civilization of the latifundia is resented as much as the civilization of megalopolis. The aesthetic values of the ecologists include the spiritual value of the one-to-one contact between man and object; between the history and meaning of a thing and the thing's maker, and the user or purchaser or owner of the thing. Ecologists prefer a direct link between man and object; both the object and the contact with it are then seen as more real. This opposition to 'reification', as the Marxists call it, involves in Marxist terminology the alienation between man and what he makes, and is an attack on the factory system, as well as alienability of land and property. Here, Marx was tapping a pre-capitalist vein of social criticism. But the criticism is deeper and a more spiritual one than Marx makes, and is not confined to the factory system or to capitalist society. The poet Rilke in one of his letters refers to his belief that the thingness of things was 'dying away, through mass consumerism. If there is to be no interposing mechanism between man and man, man and thing and man and nature, neither must there be any wasteful, artificial state mechanisms, no bureaucracy, no unproductive 'Thing', in Cobbett's words.

Since the ideal moral and aesthetic relationship between man and the world is what is local and intimate, trade is the part of the market economy, or indeed, any economy, that is most alien. Production can be in the form of small-scale craftsmanship, but trade cannot be anything other than a distancing between man and product. Most ecologists are opposed to trade *as such*, for moral reasons. Given that belief, programmes are erected to show that trade damages buyer and/or seller. But the belief is not dependent upon the rationale.

Some of the apparent contradictions of ecologism can be reconciled by perceiving its underlying moral stance. Ecologists are optimistic, in the sense that there is no original sin and nature is harmonious. However, they are also pessimistic, fearing waste, irreversible decline and the ruin of the environment, because nature is harsh, not man-centred and is unforgiving, as reality is unforgiving. And there is no God of the kind needed to step in and put things right.

Most ecologists are not formally religious. Ecologists who began in irreligious rebellion are sometimes converted to a 'strong' religion, but a pantheistic religious feeling is tne norm. Mediaeval Christian mystics are cited; such as Joachim di Fiore and Francis of Assisi. Ecologists often tend towards the Asiatic religions, Buddhism and the Way of Lao-Tzu. Confucius is too worldly. In a post-religious culture, some ecologists who have religious yearnings choose Catholicism, be it Roman or Anglo. The left-wards politicization of ecologism, together with its alternativeness, has brought in the Quakers. Regeneration of the countryside and Back-to-the-Land were Liberal Quaker causes in late nineteenth-century Britain.

The ecologist believes that nature embodies eternal reality, and also that the scientific method provides a means of uncovering the truth. There is a scepticism about 'traditional' science, but no rejection of objectivity. There are philosophical problems concerned with the fact that man's standpoint does not comprise that of the universe. But even if truth can only be attained incrementally, it is still possible eventually to get there. Any holy lies or golden myths that lurk in the way to the truth are seen as merely lumber.

This rejection of the existing, traditional system, whatever it might be, together with its upholders, does not seem conservative, despite the similarity in some values between the conservative and ecologist. What political beliefs reject the interposing mechanism, of owner or of state? Anarchism, of course, and individualism; a dislike of involvement in party systems, and a rejection of any existing mechanism for mediating and legitimising the claims of interest groups on the production of others. It is an alternative, apolitical stance, but placed here at the service of a larger unit than man, namely the world.

Politics can be defined in many ways. It is the legitimation of structured force, or of a monopoly of force located in one area. It is the description of the processes by which men conduct their affairs. It is the way in which men rule themselves or each other. It is the ordering of disorderly impulses. It is war by any other means. It is a way to distributive justice, the maintenance of the polity. It is the shadow on the cave. Whichever definition you may choose, ecologists go outside the political process. But, like Marxists, whose revolutionary dialectic is equally unpolitical, their non-political nature becomes itself a new political category. Ecologists strain at the bounds of ordinary political discourse, and in doing so extend it.

The categories 'Right' and 'Left', or 'Conservative' and 'Socialist', have constantly shifted in their attitude to nature, and its acceptance or transcendance, what one might call the naturist axis. The Table 1 gives an example of how the axis Nature/Transcending Nature shifted political contexts at the end of the last century. Similarly, Table 2 shows how apparently straightforward political issues, like equality, have represented different things to ecologists.

The need for an unequal, though not necessarily hierarchical society, was earlier derived from nature. Equality as a priority for human survival in a world of finite and shrinking resources is a more recent derivation. Equality used to be the progressive technocratic ideal; but a creative inequality emerges from Jacques Monod and Noam Chomsky's work as 'natural'. I am not arguing that Chomsky is either an ecologist or sympathetic to—

Table 1

Date	*Nature*	*Transcending Nature*
1860	Conservatives	Liberals, Socialists
1870	Individualists (e.g., H. Spencer)	Collectivists (e.g., T.H. Green)
1880	Socialists (e.g., Duhring)	Marxists (e.g., Engels)
1890	Scientific biologists (Haeckel, Alfred Wallace)	Scientific Utopians (Shaw, Wells)
1900	Co-operative Anarchists (Kropotkin)	Individualists (Maine)

Table 2

Date	*Nature*	*Transcending Nature*
1890-1960	Inequality	Equality
1965-80	Equality	Creative inequality

conservative, hierarchical societies. However, his work on the inbuilt, genetic language programme entails the need to develop it, with the concomitant risk of unequal development. The theoreticians of capitalism, accused for so long of relying on nature to back up their chosen form of society, now reject instinct and other—as they see it—non-rational residues in man. Libertarians such as Ilya Prigogine classify themselves as humanists. Humanism is a typically transcendentalist concept. He argues that the law of the universe, which by definition incorporates man, is one of infinite change and adaptability. He concludes that no static system, such as an eco-system, can exist, and that consequently attempts to adapt man to a static nature are useless. Third World Marxist intellectuals, perhaps as part of their rejection of Western culture and values, appropriate nature as their own special property, and with it, equality. The left wing of the ecological movement is egalitarian, demanding an equality of sacrifice and withdrawal from the exploitation of nature.

But, is it necessary to dwell on the theoretical political implications of ecologism? After all, the ecological movement does today have a voice and a movement in the shape of the Green Party in England and Germany, and similar parties and groups elsewhere. Unfortunately, things are not so simple. Party and ideology are not always the same. Ideologies change as parties acquire or approach power, and as their constituency changes. Party spokesmen may not be the most reliable or truthful sources for information on policies or their implications. It may not matter for the party faithful who their forebears are, or forebears may be useful for conferring legitimacy on difficult or apparently unideological policies. An example here is the use of Disraeli to legitimise interventionist Tory policies in Britain in the 1960s and early 1970s. Of course, it can be argued that without a party and programme ideology and forebears are irrelevant. To those who see politics purely as the mediation of interests by structures my arguments will appear meaningless. Yet, there are parties which depend more than others on ideas, and radical parties in their inception are among them. Any attempt to explain green parties it terms of their sociological component would imply that their ideas were secondary to the real question, 'who whom?' (not that I wish to attribute such a coarse phrase to political scientists). Another objection to identifying party and ideology is that the green parties have already split, and after a mere few years they have no united policy. In Germany, the Green Party first lost its more conservative component. More recently it split into fundamentalists and realists. Some 'fundos' have now abandoned party politics altogether. The green voice is fractured along lines of party, country and activity. There is not yet a homogeneous set of spokesmen, although it may develop soon. But in any case ideologists cannot always be relied upon to present their own ideology. They may not understand it; they may be lying or they may have been deceived. They may be more interested in converting than in analysing.

Forebears have been cited by today's Greens, sometimes to explain policies, more often to help express ideas; they are brought forward as if contemporaries, to bear witness. But the forebears are selected carefully.

A fear of the past has helped shape the present German green policy. For Greens may be ecologists, but not all ecologists are Greens.

Many of those who espoused ecologism, and who will be discussed here, were originally radicals of various kinds, Marxists, anarchists or National Socialists. (I will argue later that fascism did not have or attract a green component, and am distinguishing here between fascism and national socialism, a distinction not valid in all spheres but important here). These radicals managed to drop out even from their own radical allegiances. So putting one's individual judgment ahead of party allegiance, even of the most fanatical kind, is another hallmark of the ecologist. As well as being saved, he is a Protestant. As marginalised escapees from Lutheranism, that is not surprising.

The Development of Modern Ecopolitical Thought

The environmental crisis and popular environmental concern have prompted a considerable transformation in Western politics over the last three decades. This transformation has culminated in the development of new political cleavages, the formation of Green political parties, and the revision of old political platforms by existing parties. This, in turn, has generated new areas of political study and analysis as journalists, academics, and other observers seek to come to terms with these new political developments. Whatever the outcome of this realignment in Western politics, the intractable nature of environmental problems will ensure that environmental politics (or what I shall refer to as "ecopolitics") is here to stay.

How can we make sense of these new political developments ? If we look back over the ecopolitical literature of the last three decades, it is possible to discern three major ecopolitical preoccupations that can be encapsulated in the themes of participation, survival, and emancipation. To some extent, these three themes may be seen as roughly characterizing the general ecopolitical preoccupations of the last three decades respectively, although this temporal association is a loose one only and should not be pressed too far (*i.e.*, "later" ecopolitical themes are discernible in earlier periods just as "earlier" themes are discernible in subsequent periods). Indeed, the last three decades have seen a general broadening of ecopolitical dialogue as a result of the gradual interpenetration of these themes or phases of inquiry. That is, the participatory, survivalist, and emancipatory phases may be seen as representing the thesis, antithesis, and higher synthesis respectively in the ecopolitical dialogue of the last three decades.

The emergence of a general Green philosophy and Green political parties in the late 1970s and 1980s may be seen as representing this third emancipatory moment. That is, although Green political thought sometimes draws on the New Left participatory thinking of the 1960s and some aspects of the survivalist or so-called doomsday environment literature of the early 1970s, it nonetheless represents a new, ecologically inspired political orientation that has raised new political issues and called into question old political responses. Of course, the label *Green* is an extraordinarily elastic one that has been applied to, or appropriated by all, manner of environmental and political positions over the past decade. However, from the point of view of participants in the *Green* movement and in Green political parties, the word *Green* represents a distinctive body of ideas and a new political force. The development, tripartite characterization of ecopolitical thought presented in this chapter is offered as one way in which we may locate and distinguish the broad contours of a general Green (*i.e.* emancipatory) political perspective from other ecopolitical perspectives. Of course, within this broad Green ballpark there are many different and more subtle interpretations of the theory and practice of Green politics. Indeed, we shall see that Green politics has its own internal spectrum of debate, with its own competing "political wings". What is noteworthy, however, is that the most important of these wings are not the familiar left and right wings of conventional politics, although such divisions can be found. Rather, the most significant internal difference is to be found between what I shall call *anthropocentric Greens* and *ecocentric Greens*. As we shall see, this new environmental cleavage can be used to shed very new light on very old political debates.

The Environmental Problematic as a Crisis of Participation

The 1960s marked the beginning of widespread public concern over environmental degradation in the developed countries of the West. However, it took roughly a decade of persistent political agitation over such matters as pesticides, nuclear power plants, toxic waste dumps, large scale industrial developments, and pollution before an "environmental crisis" was officially recognized as a matter of local, national, and international concern. The first Earth Day celebrations in 1970, the emergence of a panoply of new environmental laws in Western countries in the late 1960s and early 1970s, the development of interdisciplinary environmental studies programs in higher education institutes, and the United Nations Conference on the Human Environment at Stockholm in 1972 all represent significant landmarks of national and international recognition of environmental problems.

Yet much of this official recognition, such as new environmental legislation, also helped to define and contain environmental problems as essentially matters of poor planning rather than as indicators that the optimistic and cornucopian assumptions of the post – World War II growth consensus might need to be revised. In particular, the notion that there might be ecological limits to economic growth that could not be overcome by human technological ingenuity and better planning was not seriously entertained until after the much publicized "limits to growth" debate of the early 1970s. As John Rodman observed in the context of the United States, environmental problems were originally perceived in the 1960s as a "crisis of participation" whereby excluded groups sought to ensure a more equitable distribution of environmental "goods" (*e.g.*, urban amenity) and "bads" (*e.g.*, pollution). This is not surprising given that the early wave of environmental activism was generally seen as but a facet of the civil rights movement in its concern for more grassroots democratic participation in societal decision making, in this case, land and resource usage. The growth in public concern over environmental problems was thus widely interpreted as being only, or at least primarily, concerned with participatory and distributional issues, that is, issues concerning "who decides" and "who gets what, when, and how". The upshot was that by the 1970s environmental problems were, as Rodman has put it,

> domesticated by mainstream political science, reduced to the study of pollution control policy and environmental interest groups, and eventually absorbed within the framework of " the policy process" and the "politics of getting".

This kind of characterization of the problem was widely shared by both policy makers and political theorists. This is not to say that new critiques, sensibilities, and theoretical paths did not emerge in the 1960s and early 1970s. Rachel Carson's *Silent Spring*, Murray Bookchin's *Our Synthetic Environment,* and, to a lesser extent, Charles Reich's prophetically titled *The Greening of America* represent three important landmarks in the emergence of a new sensibility that celebrated the living world and was deeply critical of dominant Western attitudes toward the nonhuman world. These contributions were, however, exceptions. By and large, there were few major theoretical innovations in social and political thought in the 1960s that arose specifically from a consideration of the environmental crisis. This tendency to treat environmental protest as an aspect of the wider pursuit of distributive justice and democratic planning was especially marked among socialist, social democratic, and liberal welfare theorists – a tendency that has continued through the 1980s. Perhaps the exemplar of this kind of social democratic analysis is Hugh Stretton's award winning book *Capitalism, Socialism and the Environment*, which opens with the unequivocal declaration that :

> This book is about the distribution of environmental goods : the shares that go to rich and poor in the developed democracies of Europe, North America, Japan and Australasia.

Although I must hasten to add that distributional questions remain crucial questions in any ecopolitical inquiry, to circumscribe the problems in this way can nonetheless serve to reinforce rather than challenge the prevailing view that the environment is simply a human resource (albeit a resource to be utilized more efficiently and equitably).

By virtue of the radical democratic and participatory nature of environmental protest in the 1960s, many political commentators tended to regard it as an adjunct to the New Left. Yet even this association was soon to come under challenge as a rearguard action developed against environmentalism by labor, socialist, and liberal welfare activists and theorists. The discovery of the socially regressive consequences of some environmental reforms (*e.g.*, the costs of pollution abatement being passed on as higher prices; unemployment resulting from the closing down of polluting industries) soon gave rise to the now familiar accusation that environmental protest is an elitist, middle-class phenomenon that threatens the hard won material gains and jobs of the working class. Such social conflicts provide a significant indication of the gradual realignment of political cleavages that has been taking place in the West between the so-called New Class (or New Middle Class) that furnishes the core activists of the environmental movement and the two traditional classes of industrial society, namely, the owners/controllers of capital and the working class. The growing tension that developed between the demand for environmental reform, on the one hand, and redistributive justice and economic security, on the other hand, has remained an enduring and vexed issue in ecopolitical discussion.

The 1960s and early 1970s were also a time of theoretical stocktaking and revision for socialist theory—a revision spearheaded by the rise of the New Left. In particular, Herbert Marcuse's *One Dimensional Man* and the essays collected in Jurgen Habermas's *Toward a Rational Society* played an influential role in tracing many of the problems of industrial society—including its environmental dislocations—to the dominance of instrumental or technocratic rationality. This contributed to the widening of the New Left's agenda to include questions of life-style, technology, and the exploitation of nature. The ready absorption of these ideas by the counterculture and "back-to-nature" movements of the 1960s was defended eloquently by political theorists and cultural historians such as Murray Bookchin, Theodore Roszak, and Charles Reich. Many of the issues raised by these writers, such as the importance of consciousness change and alternative worldviews, remain significant currents in modern emancipatory/ Green theorizing.

Yet, with the exception of the work of Roszak and, to some extent, Marcuse and Bookchin, none of these early theoretical developments mounted a serious challenge to anthropocentrism or argued for a new humility and compassion in our dealings with the nonhuman world. Rather, the growing concern for environmental quality was incorporated into the New Left's agenda for greater individual and community autonomy and control. After all, the overriding revolutionary goal of the New Left, as George Katsiaficas succinctly describes it in his comprehensive international study, was "the decentralization and self-management of power and resources."

To most New Left thinkers, then, questions concerning humanity's power vis-à-vis the rest of nature were dealt with in terms of who exercised such power and on whose behalf. Of course, these were (and still are) crucial questions, as I have already noted, yet they remained embedded in an essentially anthropocentric framework and were firmly wedded to the "participatory" ethos of the times. Even the innovative attacks on the ideology of "scientism" and instrumental rationality waged by Critical Theorists such as Marcuse and Habermas only partially transcended this framework (enough, however, for me to identify these theorists as emancipatory theorists, albeit in the anthropocentric rather than ecocentric stream). Their overriding concern was to open up improved channels of political communication in order to facilitate the achievement of a democratic consensus that would direct the development and use of technology toward more human liberatory ends. This was also the major thrust of William Leiss's critique of "the domination of nature." Although these critiques were innovating and provocative and remain important contributions to emancipatory thought, their overriding objective was the liberation of "inner" rather than "outer" nature (*i.e.*, human instincts or human communication rather than the nonhuman community). Critical Theory's objection to the domination of nature ultimately comes to rest on the human-centered argument that it leads to the domination of *people*.

This brief characterization and critique of the participatory theme in ecopolitical thought should not be interpreted as a rejection of the contribution of the New Left. Questions concerning citizen participation, self-management, and distributive justice remain central issues in emancipatory thought. These themes are reflected, for example, in two of the so-called four pillars upon which the platforms of many Green parties rest, namely, grassroots democracy and social justice. Yet these themes are merely a necessary—as distinct from a sufficient–condition for a proper characterization of emancipatory thought. That is, while these themes are essential aspects of Green political thought, they do not *distinguish* Green thought from other ecopolitical perspectives. The "discovery" of "ecological interconnectedness"—which was brought to public attention in the early 1960s with the publication of Rachel Carson's *Silent Spring* but did not gather momentum until the late 1970s and early 1980s—was to set in train significant theoretical innovations, the *political* repercussions of which are only beginning to be worked out in any degree of detail. As we shall see, the most significant of these has been the attempt by emancipatory theorists to revise and incorporate the principles of individual and community autonomy into a broader, ecological framework.

The Environmental Problematic as a Crisis of Survival

The "crisis of survival" theme in ecopolitics rose to prominence in the early 1970s following the publication of the Club of Rome's *The Limits to Growth* and *The Ecologist* magazine's *Blueprint for Survival*. Although evidence of widespread environmental deterioration had been steadily accumulating since the 1950s, the sensational and widely publicized findings of these two reports posed a considerable challenge to the sanguine belief that we could all continue with business and politics as usual. The mounting evidence of environmental degradation stemming from the exponential growth in resource consumption and human population was shown to pose very real threats to the earth's biological support systems. Although there were important differences between the two reports they shared the same general message. That is, the environment crisis amounted to much more than a crisis of participation : what was at stake was the very survival of humanity. The metaphor of our planet as spaceship Earth–which had become popular following the circulation of images of the "Whole Earth" taken from outer space by NASA– was widely employed to emphasize a new appreciation of the fragility and finiteness of the Earth as an "oasis in the desert of infinite space." This marked the emergence of a deeper appreciation of the *global* dimensions of environmental degradation and the *common fate* of humanity. However, some of the ecopolitical solutions offered in the wake of this new awareness of global environmental degradation and resource scarcity (such as Garrett Hardin's "life-boat ethics") did not prove to be particularly "brotherly."

Not surprisingly, the dire projections of *The Limits to Growth* and *Blueprint for Survival* (which carried the endorsement of many eminent British scientists) had a significant impact on the world's media and prompted calls for a swift and multifaceted response from national governments. (The ensuing debate was intensified by the 1973-74 oil crisis, which came as a timely reminder of the heavy oil dependence and hence vulnerability of industrialized countries). Indeed, *The Ecologist's* detailed solution outlined in *Blueprint for Survival* provided the impetus for the formation in 1973 of Europe's first Green party, the British People's Party (which later became the Ecology Party in 1975 and the British Green Party in September, 1985). This party adopted *The Ecologist's radical* "blueprint" as its basic theoretical statement. *Blueprint for Survival* has proved to be landmark publication in Green politics in foreshadowing many of the goals and policies that are found in the platforms of the various Green parties that formed in the late 1970s and 1980s.

In concentrating mainly on the physical limits to growth, however, the MIT study commissioned by the Club of Rome spawned a plethora of counterarguments to the effect that the problems were susceptible to "technological fix" and pricing solutions that would alleviate the negative ecological externalities of economic growth without the need for any fundamental changes in political values or the pattern and scale of economic activity. Moreover, the particular projections of the MIT team were criticized for containing methodological flaws and resting on unduly pessimistic assumptions.

Yet the methodological problems that have been discovered in *The Limits to Growth* have not, by and large, seriously detracted from its essential message. The Club of Rome's 1974 updated survey (prepared in response to criticisms of its 1972 report) concluded, in a slightly more optimistic tone, that growth was possible, provided it was ecologically benign :

> For the first time in man's life on earth, he is being asked to refrain from doing what he can do; he is being asked to restrain his economic and technical advancement, or at least to direct it differently from before he is being asked by all future generations of the earth to share his good fortune with the unfortunate—not in a spirit of charity, but in a spirit of survival.

Indeed many of those who have been most critical of this body of so-called doomsday literature have acknowledged that the crisis is real and that far reaching changes in both our values and institutions are required if ecological and social catastrophe is to be averted. Moreover, the basic message of *The Limits of Growth* and *Blueprint for Survival* has been reinforced by later, more refined studies of global trends in population growth, resource consumption, and ecological deterioration. For example, the major study of the world's environmental problems commissioned by President Carter in *The Global 2000 Report to the President of the U.S.* summarized its findings as follows :

> If present trends continue, the world in 2000 will be more crowded, more polluted, less stable ecologically, and more vulnerable to disruption than the world we live in now. Serious stresses involving population, resources, and environment are clearly visible ahead. Despite greater material output, the world's people will be poorer in many ways than they are today.

The annual *State of the World* reports, published by the Washington based Worldwatch Insitute, and the recent Brundtland Report (*Our Common Future*) have continued to reinforce this message.

Not surprisingly, many of the ecopolitical publications that appeared in the climate of the early 1970s—especially those that appeared in immediate aftermath of the "limits to growth" debate—shared an overriding preoccupation with human survival, a sense of great urgency, a new, practical and empirical frame of mind, and a preparedness to call for tighter governmental controls. Gone were the heady New Left calls for freedom, citizen participation, and the "good life." In their stead came sober discussions of resource rationing, increasing government intervention, centralization, and population controls. The new message, expressed eloquently by Robert Heilbroner in the closing pages of *An Inquiry into the Human Prospect* (a landmark survivalist publication that typified the mood and temper of the period), was that the individualistic Promethean spirit must give way to the example of Atlas—the spirit of fortitude, resolutely bearing whatever burdens were necessary to sustain life. Appropriately, the cover of Heilbroner's book bears a picture of a doleful Atlas, stoically bearing the load of the Earth on his shoulders.

As early as in 1968, Garrett Hardin set the tone of this phase of the discussion in his influential essay "The Tragedy of the Commons" with his warning that freedom in the unregulated commons brings ruin to all. Hardin's well-known parable of the medieval herdsmen overstocking the commons vividly demonstrates the tragic dynamic that arises when people are motivated by an economic "rationality" that has as its sole objective the maximization of individual gain in the short term. Hardin has argued that when people act according to such an economic rationality they will inevitably despoil the commons, even when they have full knowledge of the mounting public cost that the pursuit of private gain will bring. Hardin's answer to the tragedy— "mutual coercion, mutually agreed upon by the majority of the people affected"—marked this survivalist school as one whose overriding preoccupation was to find the means of warding off disaster and discover a minimally acceptable way of life rather than search for the "good life."

Hardin did not, however, extend his ecosocial contract theory (which rested on *mutual agreement* by the *majority* of the people affected) to the global population problem. His notorious neo-Malthusian "life-boat ethic" which argued against a more equitable distribution of the world's resources on the grounds that we would *all* "go under," has been widely condemned for protecting the advantages of the affluent and pronouncing a death sentence for the poor. As Richard Barnet has argued :

> The specter of the hungry mob supports Hobbesian politics, a world of struggle over inadequate resources that cries out for Leviathan, the authoritarian state that can keep minimal order. The Malthusian fantasy offers an alternative to the Leviathan state. There is no need for a civil authority to regulate scarce goods, because Nature, cruel only to be kind, periodically thins the surplus population by famine.

As we have seen, the general preoccupation with survival also stamped Heilbroner's somber inquiry, which opened with the searching question : "Is there hope for humanity ?" after exploring world demographic trends in the context of the persistent threat of nuclear war and the escalation of environmental degradation, Heilbroner reached a reluctant and pessimistic conclusion. Given "human nature" (which Heilbroner saw as fundamentally selfish), our only hope for survival lay in our obedient rallying behind a centralized, authoritarian nation—the only institutional form that Heilbroner saw as capable of extracting the necessary sacrifices, regulating distribution, and redirecting agriculture and industry along ecologically sustainable lines.

Since Heilbroner's major concern was the fundamental issue of human survival, he did not address (and, at the time, would probably have thought it a luxury to consider) the question of how to preserve and foster the more agreeable aspects of human nature, at least during the convulsive period of transition. Faced with the urgency of the interrelated crises confronting humankind (particularly the environment crisis), Heilbroner adopted an empirical frame of mind, focusing on how people are likely to behave rather than on what people might eventually become. In this context, he insisted that we cannot afford to ignore obdurate human characteristics and build a future on unrealistic beliefs. In Heilbroner's assessment, people will not willingly acquiesce in giving up a way of life, particularly where it entails the enjoyment of relative privileges. It is this premise that set the tone of Heilbroner's entire analysis.

It deserves mention, however, that although Heilbroner saw centrally planned, authoritarian states as the necessary transitional scenario, it is clear that this is not what he would personally wish for. Rather, he expressed a preference for "a diminution in scale, a reduction in the size of the human community from the dangerous level of immense nation states toward the 'polis' that defined the appropriate reach of political power for the ancient Greeks." In Heilbroner's view, however, this vision (which is the one generally promoted in *Blueprint for Survival*) was highly improbable in the short and immediate term.

Heilbroner's political conclusion that external constraints on human behavior are essential to make possible the transition from a growth oriented to a steady state society–has also been endorsed to a large extent by William Ophuls. Like Heilbroner, Ophuls also admits his preference for a smaller scaled, face-to-face democracy of the Greek city state or Jeffersonian type, which he sees as the most appropriate vehicle for the pursuit of "the good life" but he considers that "reforming a 'corrupt people' is a Herculean task" (recall Heilbroner's Atlas!). In Ophuls' view, we are ultimately confronted with a limited choice between "Leviathan or oblivion." Although Ophuls has since moderated his position by placing a greater emphasis on the need for self restraint than on the need for external coercion, he continues to maintain that the latter must be resorted to if calls for the former are unsuccessful.

Ophuls and Heilbroner may be seen as offering more interventionist variants of Hardin's call to "legislate temperance" by "mutual coercion, mutually agreed upon" in order to mitigate the ecologically and socially destructive rationality that characterizes human behavior in the unmanaged commons. Heilbroner's and Ophul's fellow Americans are seen as sharing the same characteristics as Hardin's herdsmen—"selfish hedonists rationally seeking private gain." They therefore have much in common with the model of the self-interested human who roamed in Hobbes's and Locke's state of nature insofar as they are seen as being in perpetual (Hobbes) or intermittent (Locke) conflict with the interests of the larger social and natural community to which they belong. In such a context, salvation can only come from the surrender of a considerable degree of individual liberty to a central authority. Indeed, Ophuls has frequent recourse to the social contract theories of the seventeenth and eighteenth centuries, suggesting that the constitutional limits of the central authority of the future might be struck in accordance with a new "ecological contract" that would hopefully be based on prudent self restraint and seek harmony not only among humans but also between humans and the rest of nature. However unlike the social contract of Locke (which was based on cornucopian assumptions), the ecological contract would be based on the Hobbesian premise of scarcity and would therefore require an all powerful Leviathan, not just a limited government. That is, if certain freedoms were not voluntarily surrendered by citizens, then restrictions would have to be imposed externally by a sovereign power.

> The authoritarian solutions proffered by Heilbroner and Ophuls and the life-boat ethics of Hardin have prompted a number of critics to ask just what is to be sacrificed in the name of human survival and to ponder whether perhaps the price might be too high. In particular, the dire analyses of this survivalist school have been widely criticized (particularly, but not only, by socialist theorists) for displaying an insensitivity to old conflicts such as national rivalry and the gap between rich and poor. As Andrew Feenberg has observed, this insensitivity leads to a politics of despair that would freeze the current relations of force in the world—and with them the injustices they sustain—as a condition for solving the issue of survival.

Similarly, Enzensberger has criticized those who employ the "brotherly rhetoric of spaceship Earth for conveniently overlooking the difference between "the bridge and the engine room." Others critics, reasserting the participatory theme, have argued that it is the very *erosion* of liberal democracy that has enabled powerful elites to pursue, with the backing of the State, environmentally destructive growth. What is needed is *more* rather than less participation in government; the survivalists, according to this view, have seriously overestimated the capabilities of centralized institutions and underestimated the capabilities of decentralized, democratic political institutions to respond to the crisis.

While agreeing with the need for more participation, some political theorists have expressed more deep-seated reservations about the capacity of liberal democracy to meet the ecological challenge. As Susan Leeson has put it :

If authoritarianism is the response to the inability of popular governments to impose the limits required to avoid ecological disaster, such a response merely reflects the crisis to which modern political philosophy and liberalism have led; it is not itself a solution.

What is needed these critics argue, is a fundamental reexamination of the basic axioms of liberalism such as possessive individualism, private property, limited government and market freedom. According to Leeson:

> it was the unleashing of the passion for material abundance, legitimized by Hobbesian natural right, amplified by Locke, combined with the rejection of the classical commitment to reason and proper limits that caused the ecological crisis.

It was this kind of ecological critique of liberalism that led many ecopolitical theorists to turn to the broad socialist tradition as an alternative. Yet, as well shall shortly see, other ecopolitical theorists found many of the ecologically problematic assumptions of liberalism to be also embedded in the socialist tradition. From this important dialogue between survivalists and their critics there emerged the highly contested question: is socialism ecologically salvageable or must we look elsewhere, that is, beyond liberalism and socialism for ecopolitical enlightenment?

Despite the widespread criticism of the authoritarian response to the deepening ecological crisis, it would be wrong to dismiss the survivalists' contribution out of hand. First, they have done much to draw attention to the seriousness of the ecological crisis and have challenged the widespread complacency concerning the ability of existing political values and institutions to respond to the crisis. Second, the controversial nature of the authoritarian solutions that surfaced in the wake of the "limits of growth" debate has encouraged the search for more deepseated cultural transformations along with alternative, nonauthoritarian institutions that would foster a more cooperative and democratic response to the environmental crisis. In this respect, the above authoritarian scenarios have become sobering reminders of what can and might happen if too little remedial action is taken, or if it comes too late. These scenarios have thus served as a useful foil for later democratically and ecologically oriented theorists who have sought to develop an alternative solution to the environmental crisis that incorporates yet revises and transcends the general participatory ethos of the 1960s, which had been largely premised on now discredited cornucopian assumptions.

The Environmental Problematic as a Crisis of Culture and Character and as an Opportunity for Emancipation

Many of those who were critical of the survivalist school responded by extending ecopolitical debate beyond the realm of the *physical* limits to growth to the point of questioning the very notion of material progress and lamenting the social and psychological costs associated with the dominance of instrumental rationality. Included among these costs were alienation, loss of meaning, the coexistence of extreme wealth and extreme poverty, welfare dependence, dislocation of tribal cultures, and the growth of an international urban monoculture with a concomitant reduction in cultural diversity. For those who took this step, the sanguine reliance on future "technological fixes" and better planning—seen by many other critics of survivalism as the definitive rejoinder to the "limits to growth" projections—was increasingly recognized as part of the problem rather than the solution. By the late 1970s and early 1980s, a growing number of ecopolitical thinkers were pointing to the new cultural opportunities that lay in what had hitherto been pessimistically approached by the survivalists as a dire crisis with a limited range of options. In short, this new breed of ecopolitical theorists began to draw out what they saw as the emancipatory potential that they believed was latent within the ecological critique of industrialism. Moreover, this new project entailed much more than a simple reassertion of the modern emancipatory ideal of human autonomy or self-determination. It also called for a reevaluation of the foundations of, and the conditions for, human autonomy or self-determination in Western political thought.

The general tenor of this third, emancipatory phase of ecopolitical inquiry may be best introduced in the voices of some of its leading contributors. As William Leiss has explained:

> No elaborate argument should be necessary to establish that there are some limits to economic and population growth. But everything depends upon whether we regard such limits as a bitter disappointment or as a welcome opportunity to turn from quantitative to qualitative improvement in the course of creating a conserver society.

John Rodman has sounded a similar theme in pointing out :

> to the extent that limits are perceived as external to us, they may have to be imposed on us by authoritarian governments ; whereas the more they are perceived as arising from within personal and social experience—*e.g.*, in the form of frustration resulting from

> "the limits to consumption then" the more the "limits to [industrial] growth" emerge "naturally," and the appropriate role for government appears, which is not to repress growth, but to stop forcing it... and to facilitate the transition to the steady state.

As early as 1965 Murray Bookchin argued, in a prophetic and pioneering essay entitled "Ecology and Revolutionary Thought," that the insights of ecology offered a critique of society "on a scale that the most radical systems of political economy have failed to attain." Since that time Bookchin has maintained the argument that the cultivation of an ecological society, resting on the principles of social ecology, will serve to *expand* rather than narrow the realm of freedom or self-directedness in first (*i.e.*, nonhuman) and second (*i.e.*, human) nature.

Theodore Roszak, another pioneer of this emancipatory approach to ecopolitics, has pointed to what he sees as the "vital reciprocity" between person and planet:

> My purpose is to suggest that the environmental anguish of the Earth has entered our lives as a radical transformation of human identity. The needs of the planet and the needs of person have become one, and together they have begun to act upon the central institutions of our society with a force that is profoundly subversive, but which carries the promise of cultural renewal.

Rudolf Bahro, in a somewhat ironic tone, has signalled his indebtedness to the environmental crisis because it has forced us to reexamine the question of emancipation in fresh terms. According to Bahro, if the Earth were infinite and if there were no problems of energy shortages and resource depletion, we would continue to believe (falsely, in Bahro's view) that the road to freedom lay in material expansion. Bahro has argued that the environmental crisis, which he has claimed to be the "quintessential crisis to capitalism," has forced us to reexamine not only the psychological costs of the competitive and expansionary ethos of our materialist culture but also our imperialist attitude towards other species.

In a similar vein, Christopher Stone, in his eloquent defence of the "rights" of nonhuman beings, has regarded the environmental crisis as offering an opportunity for metaphysical reconstruction and moral development. In voicing the approach taken by a growing number of ecophilosophers, stone has argued that :

> whether we will be able to bring about the requisite institutional and population growth changes depends in part upon effecting a radical shift in our feelings about "our" place in the rest of Nature.

> A radical new conception of man's relationship to the rest of nature would not only be a step towards solving the material planetary problems; there are strong reasons for such a changed consciousness from the point of making us far better humans.

Pursuing this same theme, Bill Devall and George Sessions have argued for the cultivation of new "character and culture." By this they mean the "development of mature persons who understand the immutable connection between themselves and the land community or person/planet" and who act in ways that "serve both the vital needs of persons and nonhumans."

What is common to these various responses to the ecological crisis? First and foremost, the environmental crisis is regarded not only as a crisis of participation and survival but also as a crisis of culture in the broadest sense of the terms, that is, "the total of the inherited ideas, beliefs, values, and knowledge, which constitute the shared bases of social action." Indeed, this was exemplified as early as 1972 in the manifesto of the New Zealand Values Party (the world's first national green party), which spoke of New Zealand being :

> in the grip of a new depression. It is a depression which arises not from a lack of affluence but almost from too much of it. It is a depression of human values, a downturn not in the national economy but in the national spirit.

Second, emancipatory ecopolitical theory may be understood as challenging ecopolitical discourse and widening its agenda on three interrelated levels : human needs, technology, and self-image. At the political level, emancipatory theorists have taken the claims of the ecology movement seriously and have embarked upon a critical inquiry into the structure of human needs and the "appropriateness" of many modern technologies. It is no longer considered adequate merely to challenge, say, the site of a nuclear power plant, freeway or chemical industry, or merely to insist on better safety devices or pollution filters. Instead, this third phase of ecopolitical inquiry has sought to draw attention to the more fundamental question : to what extent do we really need these kinds of energy sources, these means of transport, these industries and technologies, and the like ? Surely *more of us* (human and nonhuman) can live richer and fuller lives if humans can become less dependent on this kind of technological infrastructure and the kinds of commodities and lifestyles it offers ? As Cornelius Castoriadis has observed, whereas the working class movement has mainly tackled the theme of authority (hence its focus on participatory and distributional issues), the ecology movement is now questioning

> the scheme and structure of needs and the way of life. And that constitutes a very important transcendence of what could be seen as the unilateral character of former movements. What is at stake in the ecological movement is the whole conception, the total position and relation between humanity and the world and, finally, the central and eternal question : what is human life ? What are we living for?

Third, this theme of cultural malaise and the need for cultural renewal has meant that emancipatory ecopolitical theorists have directed considerable attention toward the revitalization of civil society rather than, or in addition to, the state. This is reflected in the concern of emancipatory theorists to find ways of theoretically integrating the concerns of the ecology movement with other new social movements, particularly those concerning feminism, peace, and Third World aid and development. This new theoretical project is concerned to find ways of overcoming the destructive logic of capital accumulation, the acquisitive values of consumer society, and, more generally, all systems of domination (including class domination, patriarchy, imperialism, racism, totalitarianism, and the domination of nature).

This is indeed a bold and ambitious theoretical project and one for which the most influential political philosophies of modern times—conservatism, liberalism, and orthodox Marxism—appear either poorly or only partially equipped. Indeed, the limitations in these political philosophies have served as general theoretical points of departure for emancipatory ecopolitical theorists.

The Emancipatory Critique of Conservatism, Liberalism and Orthodox Marxism

Although the emancipatory critique of the major political traditions has been mainly directed against liberalism and orthodox Marxism, it is useful to explore briefly the relationship between Green political thought and conservatism. This is especially so since many observers on the Left have often wrongly characterized environmentalism—and, by implication, Green political thought—as simply a new incarnation of conservatism. Now it is certainly true that there are some notable points of commonality between conservatism and many strands of environmentalism. The most significant of these are an emphasis on prudence or caution in innovation (especially with respect to technology), the desire to *conserve* existing things (old buildings, nature reserves, endangered values) to maintain continuity with the past, the use of organic political metaphors, and the rejection of totalitarianism. Indeed, these links have occasionally been manifest in the appearance of *ad hoc* political alliances between environmental activists and traditional conservatives over specific issues such as the preservation of threatened old buildings and landscapes. Moreover, some of the political tributaries that have flowed into contemporary ecopolitical thought, and in some cases Green political thought, may be traced to conservative sources (*e.g.*, Thomas Carlyle via William Morris, Edmund Burke via William Ophuls).

Yet those who have noted the correlation between conservatism and some strands of environmentalism have acknowledged that environmentalism also contains strong elements of radicalism in its call for a rapid and far-reaching response to the current crisis. This peculiar mixture of radicalism and conservatism has understandably confounded some observers and has prompted the suggestion that perhaps environmentalists could be understood as "radical conservatives" or, more precisely, ideational conservatives pushed into situational radicalism."

However, these and other general categorizations of environmentalism cannot be simply transposed onto ecopolitical thought, least of all Green political thought. In the case of the latter, one can certainly find some of the elements of conservatism already mentioned, such as a rejection of totalitarianism, caution in technological innovation, a desire to conserve threatened buildings and landscapes, and the use of organic political metaphors. However, these elements have been rewoven into a new constellation of ideas that has a distinctly radical political edge, both in the original sense of going to the root of the problem and in the more popular sense of demanding a widespread transformation of the political and economic status quo. As we have seen, Green political thought is imbued with a culturally innovative and egalitarian ethos, which puts it at considerable odds with conservatism's opposition to social and political experimentation and cultural change and its endorsement of hierarchical authority and the established order of things. Unlike political conservatives, emancipatory ecopolitical theorists are concerned to challenge and ultimately transform existing power relations, such as those based on class, gender, race, and nationality, to ensure an equitable transition toward an ecologically sustainable society. Indeed, when it comes to modern variants of political conservatism, Greens have been some of the most vociferous critics of such neoconservative ideologies as American Reaganism, British Thatcherism, and their respective successors. Not surprisingly, emancipatory theorists have passed over conservativism (traditional and neo-) as a source of political enlightenment. Whatever the similarities to be found between conservatism and Green political thought, their fundamentally different stances with regard to power relations means that conservatism may be summarily dismissed as a serious contender in the emancipatory ecopolitical stakes.

Liberalism and Marxism, however, have attracted greater attention from emancipatory theorists, although most of this has also been critical. In particular, emancipatory theorists have done much to draw attention to the similarities between liberalism and Marxism. They have noted, for example, that while social relations between humans are theoretically different under capitalism and socialism, the relationship between humans and the rest of nature appears to be essentially the same. This has also proved to be the case historically. As Langdon Winner has remarked:

> A crucial failure in modern political thought and political practice has been an inability or unwillingness even to begin… the critical evaluation and control of our society's technical constitution. The silence of liberalism on this issue is matched by an equally obvious neglect in Marxist theory. Both persuasions have enthusiastically sought freedom in sheer material plenitude.

Indeed, the international nature of environmental degradation has lent force to the broader claim by emancipatory theorists that the modern ecological crisis is the quintessential crisis of *industrialism* rather than just Western capitalism. Industrialism encompasses the "state capitalism" of communist nations as well as the largely privately controlled market capitalism of Western nations, both of which are seen by emancipatory theorists as resting upon the ideologies of growth and technological optimism. This ecological critique is therefore concerned to emphasize the shared expansionary ethos of both West and East. In the Soviet Union, this ethos was, until recently, encapsulated in the Program of the Soviet Communist Party approved in 1961 at the twenty second party Congress, which stated that "Communism elevates man to a tremendous level of supremacy over nature and makes possible a greater and fuller use of its inherent forces." One could just as easily substitute Western capitalism for communism in this confident assertion of modern humanity's technological mastery of nature.

To be sure, it was classical liberalism, underpinned by *laissez faire* economics and defended in the writings of John Locke and Adam Smith, rather than communism that originally underscored the fundamental direction of modern bourgeois political economy by basing it on cornucopian assumptions and an expanding economy. As Susan Leeson has argued :

> Lockean thought legitimated virtually endless accumulation of material goods; helped equate the process of accumulation with liberty and the pursuit of happiness; helped implant the idea that with ingenuity man can go beyond the fixed laws of nature, adhering only to whatever temporary laws he establishes for himself in the process of pursuing happiness; and helped instil the notion that the "commons" is served best through each man's pursuit of private gain, because there will always be enough for those who are willing to work.

Within this Lockean framework, the nonhuman world was seen in purely instrumental terms, that is, as no more than a means to human ends. After all, according to Locke, the Earth had been given to humans for "the support and comfort of their being;" moreover, the mixing of human labor with nature was an act of appropriation that created something valuable (*i.e.*, property) out of something otherwise *valueless* (the Earth in its state of "natural grace").

Of course, it must be noted that some influential liberal philosophers have challenged this instrumental and expansionary ethos and introduced important qualifications concerning the extent to which it is permissible for humans to dominate the nonhuman world. Scattered among the writings of J. S. Mill, for example, one can find a defence of ecological diversity and a brief but eloquent case for a stationary state economy. And Jeremy Bentham's extension of his utilitarian calculus to all sentient beings has provided the philosophical touchstone for contemporary animal liberation theorists such as Peter Singer.

Although some emancipatory theorists, such as John Rodman, have noted and discussed these byways in liberal thought, the general tendency has been to look to other political traditions for the ideals and principles that would underpin an ecologically sustainable *post-liberal* society. Indeed, the classical liberal defenders of individualism and *laissez faire* economics are seen by emancipatory ecopolitical theorists as apologists for the very dynamic that has led to the "tragedy of the commons." And, as the survivalists had shown, the logical sequel of this dynamic is authoritarianism from above rather than self-limitation from below. Moreover, emancipatory theorists largely accept the democratic socialist critique of liberalism that the exercise of economic freedom by the privileged renders the exercise of both economic and political freedom largely illusory to the mass of ordinary working people, the unemployed, and the peoples of developing countries. In particular, the exercise of the inalienable right (which confer the right of the individual heralded by liberalism, of land, labor, and capital) together with freedom of contract and market incentives, is seen as leading to the concentration of ownership of capital and of free, autonomous development for each individual. Moreover, emancipatory theorists (like democratic socialists) do not consider it an acceptable solution merely to rely on the redistributive largesse of the welfare State to iron out excessive inequalities, since this merely brings the dispossessed into the market passive consumers rather than self-determining producer (their only area of effective choice being how to spend their limited welfare checks). Accordingly, emancipatory ecopolitical theorists are concerned to reassert the New Left themes of participation and self-management, but in a new ecological (rather than cornucopian) context.

More importantly, liberal ideals were born in and depend upon a frontier setting and an expanding stock of wealth, with claims for distributive justice being appeased by the "trickle down" effect (which maintains relative inequalities in wealth and power). Emancipatory theorists point out that once the frontier becomes exhausted, the gap between rich and poor is bound to intensify and the prospects of distributive justice and a more egalitarian society will become more remote.

This combined ecological and social critique of liberalism has led emancipatory theorists to reject the philosophy of possessive individualism and turn toward alternative political theories that are more consonant with an ecological perspective or, at the very least, respectful of "ecological limits," and are better able to foster some kind of democratic, cooperative, and communitarian way of organizing social and economic life.

However the orthodox Marxist alternative, while seen by many emancipatory theorists to be *theoretically* preferable to liberal political philosophy (in seeking collective economic decision making and a fairer distribution of society's stock of wealth), was found to be ultimately wedded to the same expansionary ethos and anthropocentric framework as liberalism. Moreover, as the evidence of ecological degradation in Eastern Europe mounts, communism in practice is being increasingly regarded as an unmitigated disaster from the point of view of ecological sustainability. Orthodox Marxists, by and large, merely disagreed with liberals on how the drive to cornucopia was to be realized and on how the "spoils of progress" were to be managed and divided. Like Locke, Marx saw economic activity, the act of producing via the appropriation of nature, as essential to human freedom. And like Locke, Marx regarded the nonhuman world as no more the ground of human activity, acquiring value if and when it became transformed by human labor or its extension—technology. Where Marx differed from Locke and other liberal theorists was in his rejection of the institution of private property on the ground that it gave rise to class domination and the appropriation of surplus value from the worker.

The upshot of this critical rereading of the two most influential pillars of modern political philosophy was sobering. From Hobbes and Locke through to Marx, the nation of human self-realization through the domination and transformation of nature persisted as an unquestioned axiom of political inquiry. As Rodman has shown, in the modern era the solution to poverty, injustice, and inequality had become dependent on the abolition of scarcity via technological innovation and industrial growth—an approach that has been traced to the Enlightenment ideal of the progressive liberation of humans from all traditional and natural limits. Now, however, emancipatory theorists have carried forward the survivalist argument that the modern era must be seen as but a temporary suspension of the tradition of scarcity, as an aberrant period in human history. Some have likened it to the "pioneer" stage of ecological succession (*i.e.*, where rapid growth and aggressive exploitation takes place), which must soon phase into a more mature, steady-state climax community.

Although emancipatory theorists are in general agreement that liberalism and orthodox Marxism provide unsuitable theoretical underpinnings for an ecologically benign, conserver society, they differ markedly on the question of alternatives. This new breed of ecologically oriented theorists rapidly divided over the question as to what kind of post-liberal social and political theory could best address the interrelated social and environmental problems of the modern world : was it neo-or post-Marxism democratic socialism, utopian socialism, anarchism, feminism or some revised combination thereof ?

At a more fundamental ecophilosophical level, deep divisions also developed over the question of our proper relationship to the nonhuman world. While most emancipatory theorists agree that it is not enough simply to return to the participatory and countercultural ethos of the 1960s (with its cornucopian assumptions of an ever growing stock of wealth); serious disagreement developed as to *how far* the anthropocentric assumptions and technological aspirations of the modern world needed to be revised. This has given rise to *the* most fundamental division within emancipatory ecopolitical thought.

The Anthropocentric/Ecocentric Cleavage within Emancipatory Thought

It should be clear from the above brief introduction to emancipatory inquiry that it is best understood as representing a *spectrum* of thought rather than a single ecopolitical theory or an internally coherent bundle of ideas—a situation that reflects the current state of day-to-day Green politics. Although there are many different areas of disagreement, the most fundamental division from an ecophilosophical point of view is between those who adopt an anthropocentric ecological perspective and those who adopt a nonanthropocentric ecological (or ecocentric) perspective. The first approach is characterized by its concern to articulate an ecopolitical theory that offers new opportunities for *human* emancipation and fulfilment in an ecologically sustainable society. The second approach pursues these same goals in the context of a broader notion of emancipation that also recognizes the moral standing of the nonhuman world and seeks to ensure that it, too, may unfold in its many diverse ways. This anthropocentric/ecocentric cleavage follows the ecophilosophical cleavage that is central to the relatively new but rapidly expanding field of environmental philosophy. The centrality of this distinction is reflected in the large number of broadly similar distinctions that have been coined not only in ecopolitical thought and environmental philosophy but also in environmental history and environmental sociology. It is reflected, for example, in Arne Naess's influential distinction between shallow ecology and deep ecology; in Timothy O'Riordan's characterization of "technocentrism" and "ecocentrism"; in the "Imperialist" and "Arcadian" traditions of ecological thought identified by the environmental historian Donald Worster; in Murray Bookchin's distinction between "environmentalism" and "social ecology"; in William Catton and Riley Dunlap's distinction between the dominant "Human Exemptionalism Paradigm" of mainstream sociology and the "New Ecological Paradigm" of the "post-exuberant age"; and in Alan Drengson's distinction between the "technocratic" and "pernetarian" (*i.e.*, person-planetary) paradigms.

Although some of these distinctions bear different nuances, they all contrast a human-centered orientation toward the nonhuman world with an ecology-centered orientation. In the case of the former, the nonhuman world is reduced to a storehouse of resources and is considered to have instrumental value only, that is, it is valuable only insofar as it can serve as an instrument, or as a means, to human ends. The latter approach, on the other hand, also values the nonhuman world - or at least aspects of it - for its own sake.

While Naess's brief but fertile characterization of deep and shallow ecology has proved to be the most influential in ecophilosophical circles, I will use the more general ecocentric/anthropocentric distinction for the purposes of this inquiry since it is more immediately descriptive of the two opposing orientations it represents. Deep ecology, or (after Fox) "transpersonal ecology," may be understood as representing one very promising and distinctive *kind* of ecocentric approach.

An alternative approach to classification might have been to locate emancipatory theory on the familiar left/right political spectrum. However, as we have seen, most contributors to this third phase of ecopolitical inquiry tend, in any event, to cluster to the left of this traditional spectrum insofar as they are seeking some kind of communitarian, cooperative, or democratic socialist solution (and here, it is not clear which of these approaches are supposed to be "more to the left"). Its use as an analytical framework in this context is therefore decidedly limited.

Another dimension that might be more profitably applied to these various left-leaning emancipatory approaches is that of community versus state control. In terms of our tripartite characterization of ecopolitical theory, this dimension would shed light on the different attempts by emancipatory theorists to resolve the tension between the participatory and survivalist themes of ecopolitical thought already discussed. It would also bring into sharp relief the differences between emancipatory theorists on matters such as political organization and strategy. However, as important as these themes are to Green political theory (particularly with respect to the debates between ecoanarchists and ecosocialists) the community versus state control dimension does not highlight what is distinctive about the emancipatory approach (*i.e.*, the emphasis on cultural renewal, the emphasis on developing an ecological consciousness, and the critique of industrialism). More importantly, such a dimension does not adequately register the major *ecophilosophical* debates in emancipatory thought. Nonetheless, the community versus state control dimension can serve as a useful adjunct to the more overarching ecophilosophical dimension.

The anthropocentric/ecocentric dimension registers the major ecophilosophical differences within emancipatory ecopolitics and brings into sharp focus the novel and challenging scope of these new ideas. Moreover, it does this in a way that helps to *explain* some of the diverging *political* responses to different ecological issues adopted by different schools of emancipatory thought, as I show below in my discussion of what I identify as two "litmus test" ecological issues.

An ecocentric philosophical orientation provides the most comprehensive, promising, and distinctive approach in emancipatory ecopolitical theory. Accordingly, the various Green political theories examined in part 2 of this inquiry will be assessed in terms of where they fit on the anthropocentric/ecocentric emancipatory dimension. To the extent that they fall short of a comprehensive ecocentric perspective, they will be judged inadequate. To the extent that they point to problems associated with an ecocentric perspective, their critique will be addressed and evaluated. And to the extent that they contribute to the rounding out or further elaboration of an ecocentric political perspective, particularly on social and institutional questions where much work needs to be done, their contribution will be incorporated accordingly.

What, then, are the salient features of the ecocentric approach? In terms of fundamental priorities, an ecocentric approach regards the question of our proper place in the rest of nature as logically prior to the question of what are the most appropriate social and political arrangements for human communities. That is, the determination of social and political questions must proceed from, or at least be consistent with, an adequate determination of this more fundamental question. As exemplified in some of the quotations selected to introduce this third phase of inquiry, ecocentric political theorists are distinguished by the emphasis they place on the need for a radical reconception of humanity's place in nature. In particular, ecocentric theorists argue that there is no valid basis to the belief that humans are the pinnacle of evolution and the sole locus of value and meaning in the world. Instead, ecocentric theorists adopt an ethical position that regards *all* of the various multilayered parts of the biotic community as valuable for their own sake. (There are, of course, different degrees of anthropocentrism and ecocentrism, as will be seen in the following chapters. Here I am simply characterizing a thorough-going ecocentric perspective.)

The special emphasis given to ecological interconnectedness by ecocentric theorists is seen as providing the basis for a new sense of both *empathy* and *caution*. By this I mean a greater sense of compassion for the fate of other life-forms (both human and nonhuman) and a keener appreciation of the fact that many of our activities are likely to have a range of unforeseen consequences for ourselves and other life-forms. The magnitude of the environmental crisis is seen by ecocentric theorists as evidence of, among other things, an inflated sense of human self-importance and a misconceived belief in our capacity to fully understand biospherical processes. The ecocentric perspective is presented as a corrective to these misconceptions insofar as it underscores the need to proceed with greater caution and humility in our "interventions" in ecosystems.

It was the adoption of this thoroughgoing ecocentric perspective that most set this particular group of emancipatory ecopolitical thinkers apart from most of the influential New Left theorists of the 1960s who had addressed the problem of environmental degradation. To be sure, there has been an important re-assertion by ecocentric theorists of New Left themes (such as autonomy, self-management, and the critique of technocratic rationality) in response to authoritarian ecopolitical solutions. However, these themes have been relocated in a new ecocentric theoretical framework that draws inspiration from the insights of ecology rather than from the human-centered orientation of the New Left. Anthropocentric Green theorists, on the other hand, have maintained greater continuity with the New Left themes of the 1960s. The main point of difference, however, is that anthropocentric Green theorists have revised the cornucopian assumptions of the 1960s in the wake of the "limits to growth debate" of the early 1970s. The result is a more ecologically informed (albeit still human-centered) emancipatory theory that provides a much more comprehensive critique of economic growth and technocratic rationality.

Ecocentric and anthropocentric emancipatory theorists offer diverging responses to a range of important practical social and ecological issues. In particular, I would point to two "litmus" ecopolitical issues that highlight these ecophilosophical differences: human population growth and wilderness preservation. The ecocentric stream of emancipatory thought is noted for its greater willingness to advocate not simply a lessening of the growth rate of the human population but also a long- term reduction in human numbers. Rather than directly address the matter of absolute numbers, the anthropocentric stream tends to direct attention to the social causes of population growth and argue the case for a more equitable distribution of resources between the rich and poor. The ecocentric stream is also noted for its greater readiness to advocate the setting aside of large tracts of wilderness, regardless of whether such preservation can be shown to be useful in some way to humankind. The anthropocentric stream, in contrast, tends to be more preoccupied with the urban and agricultural human environment. Large scale wilderness preservation tends not to be supported unless a strong human-centered justification can be demonstrated.

The ecophilosophical differences between ecocentric and anthropocentric theorists should not, of course, obscure the significant commonalities between these two streams of emancipatory thought. As we have seen, both streams are distinguishable from other ecopolitical approaches in terms of their more penetrating diagnosis of environmental problems (i.e., these are seen as representing not just a crisis of participation and survival but also a crisis of culture and character). Both streams are also united in their optimistic attempt to offer a creative synthesis of the themes of participation and survival through the more encompassing theme of emancipation, which promises new opportunities for universal human self-realization. At the policy level, both streams are critical of indiscriminate economic growth, large scale organization, "hard" (as distinct from "soft") energy paths, and ecologically and socially destructive technologies. Where these two approaches differ, however, is in the way in which they integrate these critiques and in the ecophilosophical justifications they provide for their alternative approaches.

Having located the ecocentric emancipatory stream in the larger body of ecopolitical thought, the central questions to be examined in this inquiry can now be presented: (i) does an ecocentric approach have a natural ally within the existing pantheon of modern political traditions with which it can forge a theoretical link; or (ii) can an ecocentric approach be assimilated into any one of a number of different political traditions after appropriate revisions; or (iii) must ecocentric theorists develop an entirely novel political arrangement?

In order to narrow down the field of choice, it will be useful at this stage to outline a response to these questions from the perspective of emancipatory ecopolitical thought in general. This will provide the general parameters for the ensuing inquiry.

Although there is at present no unanimity among emancipatory theorists in response to these questions, definite leanings are discernible. First, as we have seen, emancipatory theorists are united by their intention of "head off" the acknowledged possibility of the survivalist solution, namely, that only a centrally planned, authoritarian State is capable of steering modern industrialized society through the convulsive process of de-industrialization into an ecologically sustainable, post-industrial society.

Second, the conservative political tradition may be ruled out as a serious contender, notwithstanding the resonances with emancipatory ecopolitical thought that have been briefly noted in this chapter. This is because conservatism's endorsement of the established order, hierarchical authority, and paternalism and its resistance to cultural innovation and social and political experimentation put it at considerable odds with the egalitarian and innovative orientation of emancipatory thought.

Third, all emancipatory theorists roundly reject "free market" liberalism and neoconservatism as giving free rein to the very dynamic that has given rise to the "tragedy of the (unmanaged) commons." This does not entail an outright rejection of entrepreneurial activity or of the market as a method of resource allocation, but it does require that the market become subordinate to ecological and social justice considerations. Beyond this, however, emancipatory theory, particularly the ecocentric stream, is still very much in its infancy and there is, so far, little agreement as to what mix of private and public economic endeavor would best secure a socially just and ecologically sustainable society. The arguments for the rejection of classical liberal philosophy have already been canvassed earlier in this chapter and will not be pursued in any detail in the remainder of this inquiry. It should be noted, however, that the emancipatory critique of liberalism has not led to an outright rejection of the entire cluster of liberal values. The (usually unacknowledged) retention by emancipatory theorists of the enduring liberal values of tolerance for diversity, basic human rights (*e.g.*, freedom of speech, assembly, and association), and (for some) limited government indicates that emancipatory political theory is decidedly post- rather than *anti*-liberal.

Fourth, although Marxist and neo-Marxist theories have also attracted their due share of ecological critiques, they have, on the whole, proved to be more resilient than classical liberal approaches. Marxism's penetrating critique of capitalist relations and its promise of universal human self-realization has continued to exert a considerable sway on the anthropocentric and, to a much lesser extent, ecocentric streams of emancipatory thought. For these reasons, Marxist and neo-Marxist responses will be critically explored in detail in other chapters (if only to demonstrate why both are ultimately incompatible with an ecocentric perspective).

Fifth, in view of the broad egalitarian and democratic ethos of emancipatory thought and its sympathy with the concerns of new social movements, feminist, democratic socialist, utopian socialist, and anarchist approaches have enjoyed widespread support among emancipatory theories of both persuasions. According, these politicial theories (or ecophilosophies, in the case of ecofeminism).

Sixth, no emancipatory theorist has been able to come up with an entirely novel social and political arrangement, that is, one that has not already been mooted in modern social and political theory. By this I am not meaning to argue that there is nothing new or distinctive about Green political thought, only that the newness or distinctiveness of Green political thought is not primarily to be found in the various social and political institutions defended by its theorists. Rather, the principal newness or distinctiveness of emancipatory thought (and this applies more to the ecocentric than the anthropocentric stream) lies in the different ecophilosophical perspective that is brought to bear upon contemporary problems, the different and more encompassing kind of critique that is applied to existing social and political institutions, and the different and more encompassing ethical and political justifications provided for the various (not unfamiliar) social and political arrangements that are proposed.

Ecology and Political Theory

The main issue in the encounter of ecology with political theory is whether ecology does undermine traditional political theories and constitutes a new theory itself. In the light of the rise of ecology are traditional political theories put into question or how should they be altered? Does ecology constitute a new paradigm through which environmental, social and political issues can be answered on green grounds? These are important questions because they determine which theoretical perspectives can help with fundamental environmental social and political concerns. There are two issues: (1) the implications of ecology for traditional political theory and (2) the possibility of green political theory.

Ecology as revolutionary for political theory: Ecologists do bring new insights to political theory. They bring in nature in two mould breaking ways. First, they show that there are natural limits to social and political life. The latter has to be evaluated in terms of natural limits and not just on social desirability. Second, they argue that there is an intrinsic value in non-humans, who should be considered to moral evaluations. These points require political theory to include natural limits and non-humans. They are revolutionary for political theory in the same way that the feminist insistence on including personal in political thinking is, because they imply the need for bringing in previously excluded issues of concern.

A green political theory? There are two main problems with the case that ecologists make for green political theory. First, it is true that some sorts of social and political arrangements are more conducive to ecological ends than others and so could be seen as green. However, these are fewer in number than many greens argue. Greens put down too broad a range of values as being green. Many of the values they propose—equality and diversity, for example—are not definitively green. Ecological stipulations do not necessarily imply egalitarian or pluralist arrangements. Some—decentralism and non-interference, for instance—are problematic on green grounds. Second, there are a wide range of problems—for example on justice, equality and liberty—which environmental criteria are not equipped to solve. On such issues older political theories are more helpful.

In short, ecology does bring mould-breaking insights to political theory. But the capacity for ecology to support a political theory can be exaggerated. With radical greens I agree that ecology is revolutionary for political theory. Against them I do not think traditional political theory is redundant or that ecology can support a new political theory. Against sceptics, however, I think that some principles and social and political arrangements (*e.g.*, centralized co-ordination and selective growth) are more adequate on green grounds than others and that ecology can, therefore, support a limited range of political theory principles. Let me explain some of these points, looking a ecology in relation to traditions in political theory such as conservatism, liberalism, authoritarianism and fascism, socialism and feminism.

Conservatism

Conservatism is a political philosophy which is averse to progressive change, oriented to the preservation of institutions and values and committed to tradition and authority. It is concerned with conservation of the best of the past and of hierarchy and the *status quo*. It should not be confused with the politics of say, the British Conservative Party which, as well as containing conservative strands, also contains strong elements of radical *laissez-faire* liberal politics. It should also not be equated with the right in general. While in the West conservatives are often right wing, conservatism in the former Soviet Union, for example, is a label attached to Communists, with right-wing free marketeers who espouse liberal economics seen as the radical progressives.

Some greens urge humans to be more humble and accommodating before nature, adapting to its laws and rhythms and putting less emphasis on exercising control over their environment and manipulating it to their own advantage. They are often sceptical and critical of Enlightenment ideas about the capacity of human rationality and the commitment to progress and innovation. This gives ecology a distinctively conservative edge, emphasizing conservation and adaptation to the existing order rather than intervention and change. Many greens hark back to the golden days of a pre-industrial past and use organic metaphors in ways also typical of conservative thought.

Naess (1989:), for instance, argues that our ignorance about the long-term consequences of our actions for the ecosystem means that the burden of proof should rest with interventionists rather than ecologists. *In the absence of convincing evidence that our encroachments on the environment are not likely to be detrimental we should opt for a conservative stance of non-interference, accommodation and restraint.* Naess echoes the holist and non-interventionist sentiments and conclusions of others like Lovelock(1979) when he argues that the awesome complexity and ability of nature to achieve balance and optimal conditions for sustaining life are sufficiently beyond our comprehension—yet to our benefit—that we are better advised to adapt to it rather than disturb it.

However, there is much in green thought which is distinctly radical and non-conservative (see Eckersley 1992:21-2 and Wells 1978). Many greens call for quite radical changes in economic priorities, political structures, social lifestyles and cultural value systems. There are also strong elements of democracy and egalitarianism in radical green thinking which are at odds with conservative emphases on authority and hierarchy. In addition, ecology brings new insights with its emphasis on natural limits and the moral standing of non-humans. Ecology does have strong conservative elements. But there are ways in which ecology is opposed to many traditional conservative tenets and brings new issues and concerns to political theory that are not accounted for in conservatism.

Liberalism

Liberalism is a political philosophy committed to the rights and liberty of the individual. It contrasts with socialism or conservatism which are seen by liberals as being too tied to ideas about the obligations of individuals to the collective and the state rather than their freedom from such institutions. As with conservatism, it should not be equated with the politics of Liberal parties which, while often embedded in the liberal tradition, are also wedded to interventionist social democratic values which go against the liberal grain.

The inclusion of nature in the ethical community can be seen as an extension of liberalism in an ecological direction because it speaks in a typically liberal language of rights and obligations. What greens can say is that they are taking the liberal language of rights to its logical conclusions (see Callicott 1980 and Nash 1985 and 1989). Rights have been extended from propertied men to slaves, the propertyless and women and through the legal, political and social spheres of society. It is the next logical step for them to be extended to future as well as present generations and to animals and other living and non-living organisms (animals, plants and maybe even rocks, stones and sand). Humans, by virtue of our relationship to nature in a wider community, have ethical obligations to it. Ecologists discuss their concerns with concepts and preoccupations of longstanding concern from liberal political theory. Influential classic liberals have, in fact, explicitly preached environmentalist virtues. John Stuart Mill (1979) was an early advocate of the stationary state economy and Jeremy Bentham (1960) of the extension of rights to animals as sentient beings.

However, there is a lot in liberal political theory that runs counter to radical ecology. Individualism, the pursuit of private gain, limited government and market freedom are contradicted by radical ecology commitments to the resolution of environmental problems as a collective good and to intervention and restrictions on economic and personal freedoms to deal with them. Liberal political economy is seen to underpin the commitment to economic expansion and accumulation and to the identification of wealth and material advancement with progress and improvement. Furthermore, the commitment to institutions of liberal democracy does not seem to fit well with strands in radical ecology which stress either decentralized participatory democracy or centralized authoritarian survivalism.

So while ecology could be seen as an extension of liberalism, there are other senses in which the two are contrary to one another. There are elements of liberalism in ecological political theory but ecology goes against liberalism as well as drawing on it. In this case ecology challenges traditional political theory. But, by drawing on it, it does not undermine it and shows that green political theory does not stand alone as a new political theory which breaks with the old traditions to support itself on environmental arguments alone.

Authoritarianism and Fascism

Ecology is often seen as conflicting with liberalism where it requires coercive solutions to environmental problems. It not only goes against liberalism in attributing environmental problems to market freedoms and the pursuit of private gain but also in suggesting that liberal principles may need to be overridden to prevent environmental degradation and the loss of human freedoms in the future as a result of worsening natural necessities. Ecology is seen by many critics as an illiberal political theory which draws on authoritarian and even fascist doctrines.

Critics suggest that green demands require excessive restrictions on human freedom. Sustainability, according to greens, requires governments to impose stiff restrictions on levels of consumption, family size and individuals' freedom to pursue their preferred lifestyle. These sorts of restrictions strike at the heart of liberal concerns. They suggest centrally imposed, co-ordinated rationing and intrusions into the most private aspects of our lives.

Writers like Heilbroner (1974), Ophuls (1977) and Hardin (1977) who propose centralized or coercive solutions fear genuinely for human survival. Fired by notions such as the Club of Rome's 'exponential growth' they feel a need for urgently effective solutions. Given conditions in which individuals are motivated by self- interest and the maximization of private gain, strong centralized state action is needed to enforce behaviour necessary for common survival. Individuals are too self-interested to pursue this by themselves. Even if human nature is transformable, the requirement for immediate action does not allow us to wait. Radical action is needed in the meantime and, in the absence of individuals' willingness to take it, has to be enacted by the state. A more liberal scenario would be preferable but pressing necessities require immediate state action to ensure survival and protect human freedom from worse future impositions on it due to disintegrating ecological necessities.

Some of the 'coercive' perspectives touch on arguments to do with population control and deal with distributions between developed and less developed countries and issues to do with immigration and race. It is in areas like this that coercive solutions are sometimes seen to be also fascist. Let me illustrate arguments put forward by some allegedly authoritarian or fascist environmentalists by looking at the proposals of ecologists like Hardin and others.

Hardin expresses many of the themes to do with private self-interest and commonly agreed coercion now to avoid worse ecological impositions in the future. He looks at population control and distributions between developed and less developed countries. His allegory on the 'tragedy of the commons' is a classic in the ecological literature (Hardin 1977).

Hardin argues that the 'tragedy of the commons' happens when herdsmen using common pasture decide individually to add animals to their herds to maximize their own gain. Each herdsman calculates that he will reap the full gains from grazing an extra animal because it will all be his but will be able to spread the consequences of the overgrazing caused by this because it affects property which is communal. On balance it is worth it for the individual. The tragedy is when all the herdsmen start to do the same thing and get locked into a spiral where each looks to their own individual interest and disregards the interests of society. The commons are, of course, subject to natural limits which do not allow them to carry the escalating level of use and they become overgrazed and eventually ruined because of the free pursuit of self-interest on common property. 'Freedom in a commons'. Hardin argues, 'brings ruins to all'(1977:20) and this, of course, is an analogy for the planet-wide situation. This is where the population question comes in because Hardin argues that the commons are safe while the population of herdsmen and cattle are kept down by war, disease and so on. But it is when population growth begins to exceed the carrying capacity of the land that the problems start.

Hardin's metaphor could be used to come to different political conclusions and is very relevant to whether liberal or socialist perspectives are more adequate to a green perspective in political theory. From the left it could be a condemnation of private ownership, market freedom and self-interested economic rationality. If the herd as well as the land was owned commonly then the communal impact of overgrazing would receive greater attention. From the right it could be an argument for private ownership of the land as well the cattle so that private decisions would have a private rather than a common impact and people would be personally liable for their decisions. This would inhibit them from pursuing environmentally damaging practices if they were to bear the full brunt of its effect and would provide a self-interest motivation for protecting the environment.

Hardin himself advocates various solutions—private property and pollution and population controls—which involve impinging on peoples' freedoms. Mutual coercion, mutually imposed, is how he envisages it. But Hardin argues that these restrictions prevent us from imposing common ruin on ourselves and safeguard our future freedom to pursue our goals. Furthermore, coercion rather than exhortation is necessary because appeals to act conscientiously do not recognize the self-interest maximizing orientation of individuals and their ability to remain stubbornly unshaken by common interests in a context where greatest value is placed on liberal individual freedoms.

Hardin's argument is powerfully evocative and many greens are convinced of the need for some measure of coercion, if only to a degree comparable to the coercions in law we already accept and in pursuit of longer-term freedoms. This is not least the case on the question of population control that most concerns Hardin. Irvine and Ponton (1988:18-

23), for example, argue that:

> Nature would eventually solve the problem to human numbers but in ways unacceptable to civilised thinking. The only alternative, therefore, is human self-restraint... Freedom is divisible... If we want to keep the rest of our freedoms, we must restrict the freedom to breed... There could be payments for periods of non-pregnancy and non-birth... tax benefits for families with fewer than two children; sterilisation bonuses: withdrawal of maternity and similar benefits after a second child; larger pensions for people with fewer than two children; free, easily available family planning; more funds for research into means of contraception, especially for men; an end to infertility research and treatment a more realistic approach to abortion; the banning of surrogate motherhood and similar practices... In terms of foreign aid, the cruel truth is that help given to regimes actually opposed to population policies is counter-productive and should cease. They are the true enemies of life and do not merit support. So too are those religions which do not actively support birth control.

Proposals such as those for the ending of fertility research and surrogate motherhood raise an issue central to many environmental proposals but often overlooked: equality {for exceptions see J. Young (1989) and Jacobs (1991)}. These proposals place the burden of population control disproportionately on one group: infertile women. Apart from this fact and the stridency of the final remarks quoted, though, what is most shocking and unsettling for many of us about what Irvine and Ponton advocate is in a cruel illiberal irony. This is that to rescue—one thing we categorize as 'nature'—the external environment—they propose manipulation of another activity we feel should be immune to interference because it is regarded as natural and private—having children.

In another controversial allegory in which he proposes this time a 'lifeboat ethic', Hardin shows how environmentalism can be turned into authoritarian or fascist proposals. He conjures up a lifeboat carrying ten people on a sea full of others drowning. The boat only has supplies for the ten. Hardin argues that to let any extra people on board would lead to starvation and the death of them as because of insufficient supplies to go round. This is easily translated into arguments against food aid to the third world on the grounds that the earth cannot supply enough for everyone and that third world peoples will have to go without, not least because they are the ones supposedly responsible for 'overbreeding'.

This is echoed in the quote from Irvine and Ponton above but is fiercely attacked by environmentalists like Trainer (1985) and Caldwell (1977). They argue that both environmental and third world problems have more to do with first world over-consumption than third world over-population. Either way it shows that environmentalist concerns with issues such as population growth and scarcity are easy prey for translation into the reinforcement of stereotypes and discrimination on the grounds of race (Pepper 1984 : 204-14).

Critiques of aid link in with solutions to population control proposed by some greens which draw on Gaia-influenced ecological ideas about the self-balancing capacity of the earth to stabilize and provide the optimal conditions for life. Aid, it is argued, removes natural checks on population growth by improving health and mortality and fertility rates. A report by the Environmental Fund (which includes environmentalists like Paul Ehrlich and Garrett Hardin) argues that: improving the nutrition of poor women increases their fertility... simply sending food assistance to hungry nations, or even helping them grow more food isn't enough. It simply makes the problem worse' (Environmental Fund 1977, quoted in Pepper 1984:210). Similar Malthusian reasoning is expressed in the journal of the green group Earth First !: 'If radical environmentalists were to invent a disease to bring human population back to sanity, it would probably be something like AIDS... the possible benefits of this to the environment are staggering' (quoted in Dobson 1990:64).

Hardin's views go on to advocacy of triage (criteria for selecting which third world countries should be eligible for aid and which not) and eugenics (improvement of the human species by encouraging breeding among its more intelligent members and sterilization of the unintelligent and irresponsible (Pepper 1984:211-12). Such discussions are based on Hardin's arguments about ecological scarcity and over-population and it can be seen here how ecological thinking can have clear commonalities with fascist political theory.

Other supposedly quite moderate liberal greens propose tight immigration restrictions to protect communities from population growth (Porritt 1986:191; Goldsmith 1988:203). This is a recipe for parochial self-protection, implying that communities should separate themselves off to look after their own interests and leave others to it. It would be made worse in the autarkic self-sufficient communities advocated by many greens. Furthermore, it does not tackle the problem which is to do with overall population levels rather than their distribution between territories. Immigration controls do not solve the over-population problem but merely displace it onto someone else. They do not relate to over-population but provide a breeding ground for xenophobia and racism.

The emphasis of many greens on self-restraint, self-policing and re-education through the state or decentralized community, and the ultimate fallback of coercion and law should moral pressure fail, all smack of the totalitarian (see Goldsmith et al. 1972:14). And there is in some ecological writing a 'romantic quasi-mystical sentimentality'(Pepper 1984:207) and a metaphysical spiritual power given to the wilderness and 'Mother Earth'(see Lovelock 1979). This is reminiscent of non-rational semi-religious notions of race and destiny in Nazi philosophy. Like fascists, many greens are preoccupied with organic and holistic notions, naturalness and the natural rightness of hierarchy and the survival of the fittest (Pepper 1984:206).

All of this is of concern to critics of fascism and authoritarianism. In considerations of population, immigration and the third world and in the concepts and rhetoric of some green thinking there are racist and fascist potentialities. In proposals for restrictions on population, consumption and lifestyle a significant loss of human freedom seems to be implied.

Ophuls (1973,1977) is a survivalist advocate of coercive solutions who tries to deal with liberal criticisms of such a position. He argues that some rights would have to be given up in a sustainable society especially rights to use private property as capital. But he suggests that restrictions on such economic rights do not imply restrictions on political rights or liberal constitutionalism. Restraints on consumption and lifestyle can be self-imposed. In fact, it is the absence of greater ecological consciousness and lifestyles rather than its imposition which is likely to lead to tyranny. Escalating resource depletion, population growth and pollution will, in line with the expectations of the limits to growth thesis, necessitate eventual recourse to even greater totalitarian and authoritarian measures by political authorities if these problems are left untouched by early action and are allowed to reach crisis point. Alternatively, nature will exert its own tyranny when extreme lack of resources and pollution place restrictions on human lifestyles. The choice is not between restrictions on one hand or freedom on the other. It is between freedom of lifestyle now or freedom from external necessity in the future and between restrictions imposed by political choice in the present or involuntarily later. Ophuls also argues that the decentralized self-reliant local communities envisaged by greens would involve less centralized power and intervention rather than more. Furthermore, greens tend to favour a freedom of local communities to adopt whatever social and political systems they prefer, with a resulting free diversity of forms rather than their imposition from above.

Some of Ophuls's arguments are powerful, particularly that failure voluntarily to change our own behaviour now stores up the possibility of greater authoritarian action in the future. But his hopes for self-imposed changes are optimistic and understate the degree of centrally imposed restrictions that are necessary. Furthermore, small-scale autarkic local communities can be authoritarian in the degree of close community control they are able to impose, whether through coercion or simply the pressure of social norms. Larger, less easily monitored and controlled communities can be less effective in this respect. And a liberal tolerance of diverse forms of political organization in different communities may be illiberal because of the authoritarian regimes it could allow to exist.

So the strength of Ophuls's arguments is mixed. But the key point is that centrally imposed curtailments on peoples' freedom now are likely to be less authoritarian than those that would be required at a later stage and so can obviate more authoritarian solutions in the future. Impositions on our freedom to pursue the lifestyle of our choice now will be nothing compared to threats to our ways of living, health and even survival if we do not make them. Greens can argue that restrictions on our freedom to pursue whatever lifestyle we choose are inevitable and that if we do not impose them politically ourselves they will be imposed in a more ferocious manner by nature. Libertarians are sensitive to the oppression of the state but at the expense of a sensitivity to possible threats to freedom from non-state sources (such as economic power or ecological necessity) and to the capacity of state to be a friend as well as sometimes an enemy of freedom (in this case intervening to pre-empt environmental crises). They are also reluctant to consider that restrictions cannot only be mutually imposed but also mutually agreed through normal channels of democratic accountability. State action can be combined with liberal and democratic institutions.

So environmentalist concern can involve appeals to authoritarian or fascist ideas. On authoritarianism, however, many environmentalist proposals do not involve a qualitative shift from democratically agreed coercions we already agree to accept mutually in liberal societies. Furthermore, coercive action now is intended to pre-empt greater restricitions on freedom in the future whether imposed by political authority or natural necessity. Mutual impositions can also be subject to mutual agreement through normal channels of democratic accountability and liberal restraints. On fascism, environmentalist ideas can be compared in some cases to elements in fascist ideology. However, fascism is possible in, rather than necessary to, environmentalism. Many values in environmentalist thinking—the valuing of diversity and equality of species, for example—also go against the sort of totalitarian and racist aspirations of fascist ideology.

Marxism and Socialism

Many ecologists argue that ecology is neither right nor left. Capitalism and socialism are seen as equally unecological because both accept the logic of industrial growth. Green thinking rejects that logic and goes beyond both. Porritt and Winner (1988:256), for instance, say that there is a 'super-ideology' which unites capitalistm, and socialism in a common pursuit of economic and industrial growth (see also Porritt 1986:44). Socialists as much as capitalists, it is argued, are committed to growth and the development of productive forces. Ecological problems in Eastern bloc state socialism have been worse than in Western capitalism. Chernobyl being the most prominent instance. Western parliamentary socialism on the other hand has envisaged growth as creating the wealth needed to finance the relief of poverty, egalitarian distribution and the welfare state.

However, there are questions on which ecology does not break so decisively with socialism. Socialists have been keen to reinvigorate their own embattled ideology by aligning it with ecology whose fortunes are seen to be more on the rise than on the wane. But the reason for seeing some common ground between ecology and socialism can not be reduced just to socialist expediency.

Socialist writers have attempted to explore the relationship between socialism and ecology with varying degrees of receptivity or hostility to green thinking. I will look in this section at the relation ecology to Marxist and socialist perspectives in political theory. Does ecology challenge such perspectives or require them to be adapted ? How much can it draw on them to further its own analysis? Does it completely undermine them and establish itself as a new and distinctive doctrine which can break with traditional political perspectives?

I will look first at positive things which could be said about Marxism and socialism in relation to ecology before turning, to a more critical assessment of their adequacy on environmental grounds. There are three main ways in which Marxism and socialism could be looked at positively in relation to ecological thought:(1) Marx had interesting things to say about the relations between humans and nature which could be useful to a green political theory, (2) Socialist political economy is a useful contributor to the analysis of capitalist and market structures that contribute to environmental problems and of institutions of socialist economic organization that could facilitate their resolution, (3) There is a decentralized communitarian tradition in non-Marxist socialist thought which is comparable to some strands in radical ecological thinking.

1. *Marx on humans and human nature*: A number of writers suggest that there are elements in the social theory of the early Marx which contribute to green political theory and an environmental theorization of the relations between society and nature. On this account, far from being undermined or surpassed by green political theory Marxism is a key contributor to it.

Dickens (1992) and Lee (1980) argue that Marx has (1) a dialectical understanding of the relations between society and nature; (2) a notion of human realization which stresses relations with nature; and (3) an analysis of capitalism which criticizes peoples' alienation from nature. All this points to the beginnings of an ecological perspective in Marx which can be used in green political theory.

Marx argues in his early writings that peoples' being is not simply psychologically internal but is constituted in their relationships with the wider social and natural world. People work on and transform their environments and the environment they are in affects what they become. More practically, people depend on nature for their material existence. Nature is 'man's inorganic body'. Marx felt that the powers and needs of humans, for intellectual, spiritual and aesthetic fulfilment, perception, interpretation, exploration and appropriation, are realized through interaction with their environment, social and natural. Without such interaction these powers are left unrealized or distorted. This is a dialectical conception which goes beyond unecological frameworks in which humans and nature are divorced or opposites. Marx argues that among the forms of alienation suffered by people under capitalism one involves alienation from nature. Under capitalism nature is transformed into something 'other' to be exploited and valued for its utility and exchange value or as a property, possession or commodity. Overcoming alienation involves restoring our relationship to nature and rediscovering it as something of value in itself.

All this sounds promising for ecological analysis. It gives a useful picture of peoples' interconnections with nature and an antidote to the idea that we can alter and transform it without this having implications for us. In the picture of human realization through interaction with nature there is a reason for humans to look after and protect the natural world. These observations suggest that, far from being made redundant by ecological political theory or transcended by it, Marxism may provide a basis for a more ecological social and political theory.

2. *Socialist political economy*: Socialist political economy suggests that environmental problems under capitalism are caused by its competitive and expansionary dynamic. Market rationality, the imperative to accumulate and the unbridled pursuit of profit produce externalities such as depletion and pollution. These do not matter in capitalist calculations which are focused on what comes up on the balance sheet. In the effort to complete and accumulate, natural resources are over-exploited and polluting side-effects created. Market rationality is driven by short-term interests in profit which triumph over consideration of the consequences for resources or pollution in the distant future. Furthermore, environmental problems are not driven just by forces of production—industry and technology—but are also related to asymmetrical relations of production. Behind environmental problems are material interests and power relations. Capitalist owners are keen to pursue their material interests and, because they own the means of production, are dominant in power relations and able to do so. It is not just environmentally damaging technology which is at fault but also material interests in wealth accumulation and power structures deriving from ownership which allow technology to be used in pursuit of such ends.

Socialist political economy suggests the need for the dilution of the profit motive and market rationality in economic decision-making in pursuit of broader and more long-term social and environmental objectives. Such a change requires a shift in relations of production in which at present those with a material interest in accumulation have disproportionate power deriving from ownership. Long-term co-ordination in the common interest, as opposed to competitive self-interest in pursuit of private gain, would require collective ownership.

States acting on behalf of the general interest through legislation and enforcement provide a more realistic prospect for environmental change than decentralization. It problematic to see market rationality or capital self-interests as coinciding with a general interest in environmental protection. Ecological imperatives imply the priority of general interests, intervention and planning over self-interests, *laissez-faire* and market capitalism. Such priorities find support in socialist political economy. My discussion has also suggested that collective ownership of the means of production is more adequate to solving environmental problems than private capitalist ownership.

3. *Decentralist socialism* : Socialism has, throughout its history, been a rich and diverse tradition but one in which its decentralist and liberal variants have been squashed by reformist statism in the form of social democracy in the West and revolutionary statism in Eastern bloc Marxism-Leninism. Decentralist versions of socialism, personified by writers like William Morris, G.D.H.Cole, J.S.Mill, Proudhon, Robert Owen and the French utopian socialists, have been the subject of rescue and revival attempts in recent times by liberal and pluralist socialists. The significant point is that the autarkic, decentralized, simple, self-sufficient commune envisaged by many greens is similar to that advocated by these socialists. What is more, some of them, Morris and Mill for example, were well aware of and concerned about environmental problems and the possible consequences for the environment of unsustainable forms of growth. Mill, ahead of his time also on socialism and feminism, even wrote, as I have mentioned on the steady-state economy.

So in Marx's theorization of nature, socialist political economy and decentralist socialism, there is a grounding for ecological theory in socialist thought. There are questions of political values on which ecological imperatives do not specify an answer and this is another area in which traditional political theories like socialism remain relevant. Ecology by itself does not make a whole politics or social programme. Questions of justice and authority, for example, cannot always be answered by environmental requirements. Ecology needs political theory and vice versa because 'we are social/political animals as well as denizens of an organic biosphere' (Ryle 1988:20). Ecological imperatives require some forms of social and political response but cannot alone determine them across the board, and structure of a sustainable society have to be judged in terms of traditional as well as ecological perspectives. This is another respect in which socialism might be required by green political theory rather than being made redundant by it.

4. *Ecological problems with socialism:* Let me look now at the extent to which ecology challenges socialist theory or requires it to adapt. I have already discussed the merits and limitations of decentralization. There are two further problems I will focus on here: (1) the usefulness of Marx for a theory of the environment; (2) the incorporation of natural limits and non-humans into socialist thought.

Marx's discussions of the environment are more ambivalent and complex than positive views of his ecological merits suggest. There are two problems: first, Marx's theory involves too heavy an emphasis on the human transformation of nature, and, second, it is concerned with humans at the expense of non-humans.

On the first, nature is seen as a medium for labour. Humans appropriate nature through labour and technological advancement. Through the transformation of nature human essence is realized. The relationship between humans and nature is certainly dialectical and double-sided with nature playing its part in transforming humans. But part of the dialectical process is also the humanization of nature by people. Human freedom is seen in overcoming the constraints of nature. Marx's philosophy of history and social transformation and his theory of human nature recognize a dialectical relationship between humans and nature but one in which humans realize and transform themselves and their successive historical forms of social organization in the transformation and exploitation of nature through labour and the development of productive forces.

Second, Marx's conceptualization of the human-nature relationship is based on human betterment and not the well-being of non-human entities or of nature itself. The significance of the human-nature relationship is that it is through this relationship that humans realize their essence. The theorization of nature as our inorganic body is not set up to provide a basis for care for nature but to show how transformation of it is part of the furtherance of human development. There is nothing here about the betterment or well-being of non-human entities. In fact animal activities are downgraded to being lowly or basic compared to human activities which are higher and more lofty and sophisticated. Common sentient being as a basis for comparing ethical treatment is not even considered.

The usefulness of Marx's dialectical conception is compromised and complicated by the view of the transformation of nature given in it and its orientation to the betterment of humans to the exclusion of concern for non-humans. The contradictions with ecological concern complicate the usefulness of Marx's framework for a theory of environmental protection as much as they contribute to it. Given that the strength of Marx's approach is in its dialectical framework it may be better to pursue such a framework through other sources or original work on dialectics rather than in the texts of the early Marx which are too complicated and contradictory on ecological concerns.

The second area in which socialist theory could be criticized on ecological grounds is for ignoring, first, natural limits and, second, obligations to the non-human world. The first of these does not stand up. Much socialist political economy is concerned with productivity, growth and the development of productive forces and their use to escape scarcity and create wealth in order to tackle poverty. It often focuses on restructuring relations of production leaving the commitment to developing the forces of production unquestioned. However, more and more socialists now question these assumptions. Growth and technological advance are seen to be subject to natural limits and susceptible to environmental side-effects. Socialist political economy is now often centrally concerned with the environmental externalities associated with market rationality and capitalist relations of production. Proposals for alternative forms of economy are based on adaptation to physical finitude and restraint in the development of productive forces and environmental exploitation. Eco-socialists recognize that a change in ownership of the means of production alone will not resolve environmental problems as these also require changes in the productivist outlook and restrictions of expansion in the forces of production. Many, furthermore, propose widening agency from the productivist industrial working class to social movements outside the labour movement.

While socialists have shown a capacity to re-orient to concerns to do with natural limits and the problems of growth they have done so because of their anthropocentric concern for the well-being of humans. Socialists have been conscious of the implications of physical finitude and environmental externalities for humans. But they have been less concerned for non-humans and have drawn back from a genuinely environmental ethic. On 'the critique of the cornucopian and anthropocentric assumptions of modern political thought', Eckersley argues, eco-socialism 'has challenged the former but made no substantive inroads into the latter' (Eckersley 1992:120).

There is some truth in this but even here changes in eco-socialism are occurring. Benton (1993), for example, attempts a socialist theory of animal rights which goes beyond both cornucopian and anthropocentric assumptions but within a distinctively socialist perspective. Eco-socialism is sensitive to natural limits and weaker on obligations to non-humans. But on both it shows a capacity to revise its assumptions, even on the latter, where it has been slower, yet on which it can alter its conception of the relation of humans to animals on the basis of a socialist theory of equality and rights. Eckersley (1992:131) considers that while eco-socialism does not go beyond the human community this is not necessary to its outlook and can be remedied within a socialist framework.

Let me summarize on socialism. While Marx is well worth returning to for a political economy of capitalism, I am not convinced of his usefulness for the interpretation of environment-society relations. Otherwise, though, green political theory does not make socialism redundant. Socialism is challenged by the need to incorporate natural limits and non-humans into its political thinking and these are adaptations socialists can and are making. Green political theory can also take a lot from socialist political economy. Furthermore, socialism is necessary to resolve non-environmental problems to do with issues such as authority, freedom and justice. Socialism is, in short, reconstructing itself in the light of green challenges and is of use to ecology. Ecology does not render it redundant. In fact it may find in it a good basis for eco-socialist alliances, theoretical and political.

Ecology and Feminism

Another area in which ecologists are influenced by and find common areas of interest with traditions in political theory is in their relationship with feminism. In recent years some feminists have shifted from the main thrust of traditional feminism. They have moved away from an egalitarian and rights based emphasis on achieving equality in a man's world to a 'difference' concern with re-emphasizing the virtues of the specifically feminine. For its advocates this means breaking with the terms of reference and undesirable values and characteristics endemic in patriarchal institutions. To its critics it means returning to a celebration of all those submissive and privatized conceptions of femininity which have been at the very basis of womens' oppression. This difference of emphasis and direction has laid out preoccupations and concerns which have defined the studies of some ecological thinkers. Many ecologists have been drawn to the insight and concepts of feminism in their analysis of the relationship between humankind and nature.

Some eco-feminists argue that ecological sustainability require placing greater value on balance and interrelationships, on biological and natural processes beyond human rationality and control and on attitudes of caring, nurturing and humility. All of these correspond to personality traits and values traditionally associated with femininity. Eco-feminists conclude that women, or at least feminine values, have a special place in change towards greater ecological sustainability.

Women are traditionally thought to have a greater sense of the worth of relationships and, as childbearers, to be closer to the rhythms of biological and natural processes. In their traditional domestic and maternal roles they are in day-to-day touch with tender, caring and nurturing concerns. Femininity is more conducive to ecological sustainability than the individualism, mechanistic instrumental rationality and dominating exploitative rationality of patriarchal masculinity.

Many feminists reject this approach for the manner in which it reproduces sterotypes of traditional femininity which have been at the root of women's oppression. It ties women to the servicing and care of men and children, equates womanhood with a dangerous and mysterious biological emotional irrationality to be controlled and mastered, and it subordinates women to roles of humility and submissiveness.

There are a couple of clarifications worth making about eco-feminism at this point, first on biology, second on men. First of all, eco-feminists do not necessarily seem to be saying that feminine values are biologically inherent to women and therefore fixed, immutable and confined to them. Femininity could be a socially constructed role which women are expected to live up to. In fact, that eco-feminists aspire to femininity becoming more generalized throughout the population as a whole suggests that they do not assume femininity is biologically determined and fixed. The biology and nature eco-feminists talk about is not the biology of genetic inheritance but of biological processes like childbearing, lactation, ovulation and menstruation. They do not generally endorse the psychology of genetically inherited personality traits or intelligence but are suggesting, rightly or wrongly, that by having special experience of childbearing women are closer to natural and biological processes of reproduction. This does not mean that men cannot have a 'feminine' sensibility but that the sexual division of labour combines with biological experience to make it more likely among women.

The second clarification to make is that eco-feminists, for good or ill, are not generally separatist, anti-men or anti-masculinity. On separatism they propose not that femininity should be expressed by women in a world of their own away from men but that the shared world of women and men should be more feminized. On men and masculinity, they seek a balance between masculinity and femininity in which men and women each share characteristics of both. They reject traits associated with masculinity such as aggressive individualism and domination but would find it difficult to reject the idea that women and men should not take from masculinity the values of being strong, assertive and making demands. In the sense of both the clarifications I have mentioned eco-feminists appear to be different from some 'difference' feminists who sometimes have a biologist or separatist ring to their arguments.

So eco-feminists argue that the 'feminine' stress on relationships and caring and women's closeness to biological and natural processes of childbearing and birth make them better equipped for the relational ecological sensitivity necessary for greater sustainability. The greater generalization of feminine traits and values among the entire population, female and male, can foster a more ecological society.

Some eco-feminists argue, in a way that Bookchin (1980) does on hierarchy in human society in general, that there is a connection between the exploitation of women and the exploitation of nature. This may be because exploitative relationships in parallel spheres take place through similar hierarchical and dominating structures or, more strongly, because women and nature are actually connected in the same process of exploitation. On the weaker argument women and nature are simply both victims in different spheres of a society based on hierarchy and domination. More strongly, it can be argued that there is some greater connection in that structures of hierarchy and domination are sustained by the same patriarchal Enlightenment rationality which emphasizes 'masculine' values of mastery and rational control (Shiva 1988). Stronger still is the argument that women and nature share common characteristics or are constituted similarly in patriarchal myths and discourse (see Merchant 1990). Both nature and women are seen as having similar negative characteristics: irrational, unpredictable, biological, mysterious and in need of control. Women and nature are not merely separate phenomena subordinate in parallel dualisms. They are subject to the same mechanistic patriarchal domination and constituted identically by it. Their exploitation is identical, and ecological and women's liberation are linked. This common identity of womanhood and nature could imply political alliances between the women's and green movements. Both, from this view, could benefit from the articulation of relational concerns and a greater value being placed on caring, nurturing and humility.

I have argued that eco-feminism does not necessarily see femininity as biologically determined nor, for good or ill, is it separatist or anti-men. It does provide a corrective to the devaluation of feminine values and traditionally female activities in patriarchal and some feminist discourses. There are two problems in eco-feminist thinking I can mention here. The first concerns the problem of identifying feminine traits and second the tactical advisability of focusing on revaluing femininity.

A first criticism is that it is difficult to identify what feminine traits are when women often exhibit masculine traits and men feminine ones. To put it another way, it is difficult to find a consistent set of traits which women share and makes them distinct from men. The problem with this criticism goes back to the clarification made earlier on biology. It operates on the level of biological sex rather than social gender. Feminine personality traits are those socially associated with the social construction of femininity. They are not traits biologically inherent to women or that women always express and men do not. Feminine traits are not any less feminine if men sometimes exhibit them. This merely demonstrates that men may sometimes be feminine, and the traits remain those socially associated with femininity and particularly expected of women. It is not that women exhibit consistent traits that make them feminine but that they are traits conventionally defined as feminine and expected of women. Most of us are fairly clear about what the core traits of femininity are on this understanding.

There is a more tactical or strategic question which many feminists, with some justification, point to. This is that the activities and traits ecological and difference feminists seek to see more positively valued—care, nurturing, humility etc.—are those which have been at the root of women's oppression for centuries, confining women to servicing and subservient roles in the private sphere. Re-emphasizing such traits is likely to get us back to a situation from which feminists have spent a lot of time trying to extricate women.

This is a strong criticism but there is an answer. Feminists can escape the reproduction of women's oppression yet still positively value feminine traits by focusing less on women's aptitude for them and more on the virtues of men expressing them. The focus can be on deconstructing masculinity and feminizing men rather than on women celebrating and expressing femininity. The latter strategy, pursued in a patriarchal society, is likely to reproduce and strengthen women's subordinate position. The former offers the possibility of promoting feminine values without merely reproducing women's confinement to traditional feminine roles.

This does not preclude women celebrating feminine values or taking strength, assertiveness and self-worth from traditional masculinity. But it does imply a tactical shift of emphasis towards changing men which can avoid a return to female submissiveness. This engages with a stumbling block facing the women's movement. Problems in the past have often been based around mobilizing women into making demands and progress outside traditional feminine spheres. An increasing problem is men's refusal to be moved from their traditional masculine sphere towards more feminine values and into traditionally feminine areas of work, such as domestic work and childcare in the private sphere and traditionally female occupations and concerns in the public. Women seeking equality in paid employment or public involvement have found that they carry a double burden because they have to combine their public roles with continuing responsibilities in the domestic sphere. These are as great as before because of the lack of movement by men towards playing a role there.

Whatever its difficulties, eco-feminism recognizes that traditionally feminine personality characteristics and activities have been devalued. This has been to the detriment both of women who have performed their tasks too single-handedly and subject to low esteem and of men who have not helped or benefited from 'feminine' work (childcare in particular). Traditional egalitarian and rights-based feminism might have been an unwitting accomplice in devaluing desirable values and characteristics and rejecting potentially rewarding and fulfilling human activities as oppressive. Feminine values and activities, some feminists argue now, need to be more positively evaluated in future, for the benefit of women and men. Childcare and domestic work becomes impoverished when it is devalued and disproportionately loaded onto women. However, given more value and more equally shared, such tasks can be a source of fulfilment for women and men alike; similarly with feminine personality traits of tenderness, caring, nurturing and concern for relationships. The absence of such traits from public life hinders ecological progress and the amelioration of conflict and inequity. In private life their greater concentration on one side of the sex divide hinders liberation and fulfilment for both men and women.

Feminism is another example of a tradition which ecology draws on rather than renders redundant. Ecology does not break off as a new paradigm with the ability to deal with environmental and social issues on green grounds alone. Just as it draws on ideas to do with obligations and rights from conservatism and liberalism and on socialist political economy, so feminist thinking is a resource for ecology rather than a tradition it transcends.

Ecology: New Political Theory or no Political Theory?

Andrew Dobson argues, when discussing O'Riordan's (1981:303-7) typology of global, centralized-authoritarian, authoritarian commune and anarchist versions of environmentalism, that:

> not all of these presentations can accurately be described as correponding to the political ideology of ecologism... the closest approximation... to the centre of gravity of a Green sustainable society is the last one: the so-called 'anarchist solution'... the Green sustainable society... will not be reached by transnational

> global co-operation, it will not principally be organised through the institutions of the nation-state, and it is not authoritarian… it would therefore be quite wrong to see ecologism as an ideology (like nationalism?) that can be either right or left-wing... its political prescriptions are fundamentally left-liberal, and if a text, a speech or an interview on the politics of the environment sounds different from that then it is not Green but something else. (Dobson 1990:83-5).

Ryle on the other hand argues that:

> 'Ecology'… does not in itself determine in a positive sense the future development of social and economic reality. A society adapted to ecological constraints… could take widely varying forms. This is… implicit in the fact that very diverse 'sustainable societies' have been projected by different thinkers.
>
> One can imagine an authoritarian capitalist or post-capitalist society... in which those at the top enjoyed ecologically profligate lifestyles… protected by armed guards from the mass of the people, who would endure an impoverished and 'sustainable' material standard of living… One can imagine a 'barrack socialism' in which an ecologically well-informed, bureaucratic elite directed the economy in accordance with environmental and resource constraints… Ecological limits may limit political choices but they do not determine them. The green movement may attempt to assess every option against ecological criteria, and may claim that all its proposals are compatible with sustainability; but we should not make the mistake of thinking that no other proposals, and no other outcomes, could be compatible. We should not assume that 'ecology' can satisfactorily define the new politics we are trying to develop. (Ryle (1988:7-8).

Dobson is arguing that there can be a green political theory and that it is left-liberal anarchism. Ryle argues, however, that there cannot be a green political theory because ecological imperatives are open to different sorts of social and political arrangements. I would argue against Dobson that there cannot be a green political theory because while ecology implies some forms of social and political arrangements rather than others it also draws on older traditions to work out which are preferable on these grounds and to answer non-environmental questions to do with issues such as justice and liberty. Where different sorts of social and political arrangements are compatible with green objectives, traditional non-ecological criteria are needed to decide which are preferable. Ecology can be part of a political theory but does not provide the basis for such a theory in itself.

However, ecology is not completely open. I have argued that interventionism and central co-ordination are implied by ecological imperatives rather than markets, capitalism or decentralization. Environmental demands do imply some sorts of social and political arrangements rather than others. Nevertheless, Ryle is right to say that many questions cannot be answered by ecology and, this being so, that a political theory cannot be constructed on green criteria alone.

Traditional political theories are challenged by ecology. Ecology requires that they are adapted to take into account natural limits and non-humans. It has further implications for political theory in that some social and political arrangements are implied rather than others by environmental requirements. However, ecology cannot provide a new paradigm through which a political theory can be constructed on green grounds. Dealing with environmental issues involves drawing on old conservative, liberal socialist and feminist analyses. Furthermore, there are non-environmentalist issues to which green criteria do not determine answers and which have to be answered by these old traditions. Ecology has to combine with other perspectives to put together a theory and politics on preferable regimes of economic, social and political organization.

Environmentalisms

Before the next chapter let me summarize the different sorts of environmentalist argument I have identified. As I have suggested in this book one issue on which different environmentalist arguments can be identified is to do with solutions to environmental problems (see Table 1).

Many greens propose technocratic solutions based on the development of environmentally friendly technologies. These might be

Table 1
Solutions to Environmental Problems: Technical or Structural

Type of environmentalism	*Solution*
technocratic environmentalist	technical
structural environmentalist	structural

'cleaner' or less polluting or can harness renewable (e.g. wind, solar power, tides) rather than non-renewable energy sources (e.g. coal, gas, oil). Other greens propose that underlying structural factors to do with social value systems and lifestyles are the basic problem to which technical solutions cannot be found. Ecological degradation will continue until we halt growth and wind down consumption and population levels.

Another distinction within green arguments between those that rely strictly on environmental considerations for certain courses of action and those that rest their case also on independent social arguments for the intrinsic desirability of such courses (e.g. frugality, self-sufficiency) (see Table 2)

Table 2
The Sustainable Society: Reasons for Proposing it

Type of environmentalism	*Arguments*
environmental	environmental
social	environmental and social

The latter category of arguments can lead to conclusions which coincide and support more specifically green arguments, but they are not themselves strictly green in content. I have suggested that environmental arguments should be distinguished from social arguments put forward by greens. Some green proposals (e.g. for lower levels of consumption and lower population levels) can be justified by recourse to environmental arguments alone. Others (e.g. the argument for decentralized self-sufficient communes) are not such clear-cut candidates for environmental justifications. Consequently green arguments for them rest more heavily on social arguments about intrinsic rewards and desirability which are not specifically green and should not be portrayed as such.

In this book I have also distinguish between different green arguments on reasons why we should care about the environment (see Table 3). Shallow ecologists argue for care for the environment on the grounds of its utility for human beings. In this sense it is humans and not the environment, itself that they are really concerned about and this is what prompts some to regard people in this category as not really environmentalist at all. Deep ecologists argue that we should care about the environment because of its intrinsic value and entitlement to the same

Table 3
Environmental Ethics: Reasons for Caring About the Environment.

Types of environmentalism	*Reasons for caring*
Deep ecologist (eco-centric)	Intrinsic value of all environmental entities
Sentient ecologist (sentient-centric)	Intrinsic value of sentient beings. Extrinsic value of non-sentient things
Shallow ecologist (anthropocentric)	Intrinsic value of humans. Extrinsic value of non-humans

sorts of rights traditionally extended to human beings. These ecologists aruge we should care about the environment for its own sake and irrespective of its usefulness for humans. Sentience advocates argue we should take special care to protect and respect all creatures who have the capacity to enjoy life and should also protect parts of the environment which have value for such creatures.

On the basis of sentient arguments such theorists extend obligations to animals as well as humans. On the basis of intrinsic value arguments deep ecologists extend them to more of the environment: sentient and non-sentient living entities (i.e. plants as well as animals) and in some cases non-living organisms as well (e.g., earth, water, rocks etc.). How far the extension of rights goes depends on the characteristics according to which entities in the environment are seen to have intrinsic value. If merely being part of the community is what counts, then all things might be seen to have value and command respect. If capacity to flourish is what gives them intrinsic value then respect may extend to plants (and in differing quantities to different species of animal and plant according to their varying capacity to flourish) but not to non-living organisms like rocks.

6

New Directions for Ecopolitics

We are entering a new era of environmental policy. We are addressing new issues, using new tools, and beginning to experience a new kind of politics. This shift is part of a broader transformation in how we do the public's business in an increasingly information-based society.

The new environmental issues transcend the current array of laws and regulations. These regulations set limits on the emissions of hundreds of individual chemicals and other pollutants, or they protect specific environmental values, such as wilderness areas, endangered species, or the local quality of air and water. This one-by-one approach to environmental protection does not always work. The future of individual species and special places depends on the health of broader ecosystems. For example, what happens to the rich variety of plants, animals, and birds in the Everglades National Park depends on how water flows through a vast area outside the park. The grizzlies, the wolves, and perhaps even the spectacular geysers of Yellowstone National Park are strongly influenced by what happens on lands outside the park. These broad ecosystems, and others that are less spectacular, are threatened by many kinds of pollution simultaneously, not to mention the stress of human visitation and occupation. There is still much uncertainty about exactly how ecosystems function, but we are learning that to protect them, we must invest in public works, research, education, and public participation. It is not enough to regulate individual pollutants or to protect individual species and areas.

We are also learning how to address new forms of pollution. Most of the laws of the 1970s and the 1980s related to large-scale point sources, including the smokestacks and pipes through which factories and water treatment plants send their wastes into the air or water. Now many firms are showing that by changing their production processes, they can prevent pollution before it reaches the smokestack; in the process, they can often reduce their costs and make themselves more competitive. We are also learning about the pollution caused by thousands of dispersed "nonpoint" polluters, such as farmers who spread chemicals on their fields, office buildings that waste energy with inefficient lighting and heating, and average Americans who drive farther each year on the trek from home to work or to the shopping center.

To take up this unfinished business—to restore and protect ecosystems, combat nonpoint pollution, and prevent pollution in the first place—we are beginning to use new tools. Regulation is still the back-bone of environmental policy, but these new issues lend themselves to nonregulatory tools, which provide information and incentives rather than sanctions.

Debates about environmental regulation have often been battles between "black hat" polluters and "white hat" protectors of environmental values. As we address the unfinished business, we will still face tough choices. Although the debate may cool down as firms stop complaining that environmental regulation is too costly—instead accepting its inevitability and learning how to profit by preventing pollution—new cleavages may be emerging. For example, some local governments complain that they cannot afford to comply with all environmental regulations and that the regulations sometimes impose costly requirements of no measurable benefit. The new tools and the new environmental agenda may add to the cost burden, at least in the short run. It certainly will be expensive to restore ecosystems, although perhaps less costly than if we let them collapse.

The choices ahead will be difficult, but they may divide us less bitterly than past fights over regulation. The battle lines are less clear cut when the polluters are more numerous (including perhaps most of the citizenry), when governments use incentives as well as sanctions, and when the parties share information about how to solve problems.

These are the changes that are beginning to emerge around the edges of environmental politics, where federal law does not reach. At the state and local levels, there was a ferment of creativity in many area of public policy, including environmental policy, in the 1980s and early 1990s. This book reviews practical evidence that has developed at the state and local levels about new approaches to environmental politics and policy. It asks:

- In states and localities, are government agencies tackling the unfinished business of environmental protection, including nonpoint pollution, the protection of ecosystems, and the prevention of pollution?

- Are states and localities using new tools like economic incentives?
- When states and localities tackle environmental problems in new ways, what happens to the process of making decisions in the political arena and inside the agencies?
- What role has the federal government played in state and local initiatives?
- Perhaps most important for the 1990s, what can federal government do to provide top-down support for bottom-up environmental initiatives?

During the early 1990s, a consensus began to develop that a new approach to environmental policy was needed. Several national leaders spoke eloquently about the need for fresh ideas. For example, Gus Speth, then president of the World Resources Institute, told the winners of the 1992 presidential election, "I don't think we will succeed in bringing our economic and environmental objectives together with the curremt set of approaches... We need to move to a new model of environmental governance." The National Commission on the Environment which included respected leaders of the U.S. Environmental Protection Agency (EPA) from both Republican and Democratic administrations, called for "radical reform ." The commission's report stated that "the U.S. statutory and regulatory regime is woefully inadequate, cumbersome, and sometimes even perverse with respect to environmental issues."

A second generation of environmental politics and policy seems to be emerging. There is no widely accepted label for the new tools, new policies, and new politics. Experts who focus on the tools often stress the importance of "market mechanisms" and "economic incentives," including fees, taxes, and tradable permits. But other tools—such as public education, technical assistance, and new ways of investing in and operating public works—are also important. Discussions of broad trends in policy often refer to "sustainable development." The key seems to be the principle of ensuring that environmental considerations—including the benefits of a clean environment, the difficulty of predicting environmental impacts, and the risks of unexpected environmental collapse—be taken into account in the millions of decisions that are made about how to invest society's wealth.

The future of environmental policy will be shaped not only by the principle of sustainable development and the new tools of economic incentives, but also by the practicalities of political and administrative processes. The story of innovation at the state and local levels in the 1980s suggests what such a politics might be like. This book calls the emerging politics and policy "civic environmentalism" and suggests that civic environmentalism is the new paradigm that many have called for. It is the process by which sustainable development might become a reality.

Command-and-Control Regulation

Since the early 1970s, environmental policy has relied heavily on what insiders call command-and-control regulation. This regime is based on federal laws that set standards for air and water quality, for emissions of materials that might harm the environment, and for the handling of dangerous substances. To obtain permits from regulatory agencies, polluters must show that they will not violate these standards. With few exceptions, federal laws do not provide for balancing economic and environmental objectives. Rather, the Environmental Protection Agency is charged with setting standards that will protect public health and other environmental values; polluters are left to cope as well as they can.

Three features of federal laws shape the patterns of traditional environmental policy and politics: federal preemption of state and local authority, fragmentation, and the combination of tough procedural requirements with ambitious goals.

Federal preemption began with a wave of federal legislation in the early 1970s. Before then, states and local governments regulated pollution as a nuisance that fell within their police powers. The federal government helped with research, technical assistance, and some funding for water treatment projects. But federal agencies did not tell states and local governments what to do. This division of responsibilities seemed clearly inadequate to deal with the pollution caused by modern industry. State and local officials were often reluctant to stand up to industries that belched smoke or fouled rivers. Faced with a choice between jobs and pollution on the one hand, or no jobs and no pollution on the other hand, pollution was accepted as the inevitable price of progress.

In the 1970s, this way of doing business was changed by the enactment of a series of tough federal statutes that set new standards and procedures for regulating pollution. Most federal environmental legislation does not prohibit regulation by states and localities, but it does set standards and procedural requirements to guide them. Federal laws also provide for the close supervision of state and local officials by federal environmental agencies.

In the words of former EPA administrator William Ruckelshaus, the federal role in command-and-control regulation is to be the "gorilla in the closet. In other words, states and localities continue to regulate pollution, but only pursuant to detailed federal requirements. When industries resist state and local regulators, the regulators can threaten to let the federal gorilla out of the closet to force industry to comply with the law.

Although the command-and-control system is essentially top-down, driven from Washington, the idea was not to weaken states but to add to their power in dealing with polluters. In *The Politics of Pollution*, J. Clarence and Barbara Davies write that federal statutes increase state power by giving them the tools to regulate more effectively and the political backing to use those tools. The federal gorilla is often kept in the closet, leaving states the task of applying federal requirements in diverse local situations. Furthermore, most federal environmental statutes set minimum standards and allow states to adopt tougher standards.

A second key feature of environmental laws is that they are fragmented. That is, they call for separate permits for different types of pollution, rather than a single, comprehensive permit. As early as 1970, it was clearly recognized that this was not the most rational approach to environmental regulation, because pollutants can move from one medium, like air, to another, like water. President Nixon told Congress in 1970, "Despite its complexity, for pollution control purposes the environment must be perceived as a single interrelated system.... A single source may pollute the air with smoke and chemicals, the land with solid wastes, and a river or lake with chemicals and other wastes. Control of the air pollution may produce more solid wastes, which then pollutes the land or water."

Notwithstanding this fine argument, the political realities dictated a different way of organizing federal environment programs. The EPA was created in 1970 by an executive order that brought together agencies that had been in different departments. There was no legislation to establish EPA or to provide it with a charter of cross-cutting, cross-medium authority. The separate programs in EPA for air, water, and waste have never been consolidated; and most subsequent legislation has focused on individual programs rather than overall management. In political terms, this means that the EPA is not a single gorilla, but a whole family of gorillas, one for each law and each program.

The third feature of federal regulation of the environment is that it is characterized by a combination of lofty goals, detailed procedural requirements, and tight timetables. When EPA was created and Congress passed the tough environmental legislation of the 1970s, both environmental advocates and members of Congress were familiar with the phenomenon of institutional capture—that regulatory agencies might come under the influence of the industries they regulated. To prevent this, each statute contained detailed procedural requirements as well as ambitious goals (for example, "fishable, swimmable," water). If EPA failed to act decisively, procedural requirements provided opportunities for congressional guidance through oversight hearings and for challenges by environmental groups in federal court. In effect, each law created not just a family of EPA gorillas but whole hierarchies of gorillas.

Furthermore, the laws encouraged confrontational politics. The lofty goals and tight timetables encouraged an air of urgency and sometimes of desperation or cynicism within EPA, and they opened the door for vigilant congressional oversight, litigation, and protest.

How to graphically how the command-and-control system works. At the top are advocates for the public's interest in a clean and safe environment. These advocates include environmental groups, congressional committees with jurisdiction over environmental matters, and sometimes the citizenry itself—for example, when citizens insist, "Not in my backyard" (NIMBY). These advocates exert pressure on EPA and other federal agencies through a variety of means. Often federal courts are involved. Sometimes the courts act almost as another independent voice for environmental values, because many environmental statutes contain clear statements of purpose and procedure while lacking guidelines about how EPA should allocate scarce personnel and political capital to accomplish its tasks. These statutes often encourage judges to issue detailed orders about how EPA should go about its business. Buffeted by these many voices for environmental values and pressured by industry, EPA watches over the states, which issue permits to polluters and monitor compliance.

Civic Environmentalism

This book describes another way of organizing environmental politics and policy, civic environmentalism. The central idea animating civic environmentalism is that in some cases, communities and states will organize on their own to protect the environment, without being forced to do so by the federal government. As we shall see, federal agencies can often play important roles in civic environmentalism, but not by forcing state or local action or by threatening to override decisions. Civic environmentalism is fundamentally a bottom-up approach to environmental protection.

Civic environmentalism emerged in the 1980s when, as we will describe in more detail in later chapters, federal environmental policy lost its momentum. There were many reasons, including cutbacks in the budget of the EPA; explicit efforts by Republican administrations to weaken environmental regulations and to turn authority over to states; and deadlocks, both within Congress and between Congress and the White House, on proposals for new environmental legislation. Stalemates and cutbacks in Washington created a vacuum into which stepped many state and local governments, as well as nonprofit organizations, citizens, and even some private businesses.

The style of policy and politics that emerged in these bottom-up initiatives is different from the command-and-control model in four ways: it tends to focus on a different set of environmental problems, uses different tools, seeks to overcome fragmentation, and searches for alternatives to confrontation.

Top-down regulation works best for large, clearly identifiable sources of pollution, like smokestacks, water treatment plants, and toxic waste dumps, rather than dispersed, small scale sources like individual homes. The command-and-control model is more difficult to implement when there are large numbers of polluters and when it is difficult to monitor what each polluter contributes to an environmental problem. It is simply too difficult for regulators to keep track of so many sources. As one Iowan put it, "It may take an occupying army to regulate the 100,000 farmers in our state."

Nor is regulation usually adequate to protect ecosystems in danger or to prevent pollution before it occurs. The environmental laws of the 1970s focus on specific results—clean air and water, safe handling and disposal of wastes, and protection of endangered species—whereas the threats to most ecosystems in danger arise from a complex mix of factors. Also, most of the environmental laws now on the books focus on results, rather than on strategies to achieve the results.

To address these problems, civic environmentalism uses a variety of tools, such as technical assistance to farmers and small businesses, subsidies, public education, and new approaches to investing in public services and facilities. These tools are being used by many organizations, including economic and community development agencies, schools, universities, trade associations, and public-private partnerships.

Civic environmentalism also tends to involve a different style of politics than command-and-control regulation. There are still strong differences of opinion, but there are fewer confrontations between black hat polluters and white hat protectors of the public trust, and there is more bargaining among a diverse set of participants. Civic environmentalism is a more collaborative, integrative approach to environmental policy than traditional regulation.

For most readers, the most familiar example of civic environmentalism might be efforts reduce household waste and to promote recycling. The polluters are numerous— in effect, everyone. For years, states and localities have been seeking to reduce household waste not by regulating how much trash we all send to the dump but with a much broader array of tools, including economic incentives, public education, and new ways of delivering public services, such as curbside recycling.

King County, Washington and Seattle, its largest city, have been leaders in promoting recycling. The story of how they became leaders illustrates how civic environmentalism can emerge from traditional regulatory policies and politics. For decades, King County dumped its trash into landfills with minimal environmental controls, until in the early 1980s, when landfills in western Washington either closed or had to spend millions for environmental controls. A landfill north of King County, which had received much of the trash from Seattle businesses, closed and became a Superfund site. The city of Seattle also closed a landfill for residential trash.

These closures put more pressure on Cedar Hills, a large landfill operated by the country. As the volume of waste being trucked to Cedar Hills began to rise, increasing the number of trucks on nearby roads and exacerbating environmental problems, homeowners who lived nearby filed several suits to force the county to clean up. The state Department of Ecology also intervened, adopting regulations that forced the county to control drainage, vent gases that were building up inside the landfill, and place plastic liners and two feet of clay under new parts of the landfill and on top of closed areas. King County eventually spent over $95 million to clean up Cedar Hills and another $29 million for remedial upgrades at four smaller rural landfills. (The state was far ahead of the federal EPA in adopting tough regulations for landfills.)

As it became more difficult and more expensive to operate landfills, and as it became clear that neighborhoods might organize to prevent construction of a new landfill when Cedar Hills filled up, both King county and Seattle began to rethink their solid waste policies. The classic environmental system of top-down, command-and-control regulation and bottom-up, NIMBY protests forced the city and the county to look for new ways to manage their trash.

Initially both Seattle and King County decided to build incinerators. Since the days of the energy crisis of the early 1970s, King County had been working on plans for "waste-to-energy" plants that would generate electricity by burning garbage. A new county executive was elected in 1986 and directed the King County Solid Waste Division to take these plans off the shelf and get to work. The county released a preliminary proposal to build as many as four incinerators in different parts of the county, and Seattle proposed to build others.

Then all hell broke loose. By designating a half-dozen possible sites, solid waste officials had aroused a half-dozen NIMBY groups, who quickly organized a countrywide federation of neighborhood groups and environmentalists who did not want incinerators or landfills anywhere. (This alliance still exists, as the Washington Citizens for Recycling, and has a small but busy office with a half-dozen paid staff members and volunteers). Solid waste management became the central issue of local politics in 1986-1987, and an important state issue as well. The protesters attended hearings and picketed meetings of the county council.

Bowing to public will, Charles Royer (Seattle's new mayor) and Paul Barden (a law-and-order Republican on the county council) led the charge. The county organized citizen task forces on all aspects of solid waste management. By the end of 1987, both the city and the county had made formal decisions that waste reduction and recycling would henceforth be the preferred choices for managing trash, with incinerators put on hold. The state legislature also went to work, passing the Waste Not Washington Act in 1989, which endorsed the same hierarchy of preferred options for managing solid waste, and directed that counties work with cities and towns to prepare comprehensive solid waste management plans consistent with this hierarchy.

Five years later, King County had succeeded in doubling its recycling rate, from 18 per cent to 35 per cent of all trash. There were four reasons for this change. First, Seattle and most suburban cities adopted curbside recycling, consisting of a separate pickup for recyclables, which homeowners separate from the rest of their trash. Second, there were economic incentives for recycling and reducing waste. The cost of garbage serviced quadrupled, and a new structure of fees was adopted in most towns, charging less to pick up a smaller "minican" and more to pick up a second or third trash can. Third, there was an extensive public education campaign, including recycling weeks, programs in public schools, brochures for homeowners on how to recycle and how to reduce waste, and technical assistance for businesses that wanted to recycle or reduce waste. Finally, the political controversy over the incinerators was itself a stimulus for recycling and waste reduction. Western Washington prides itself on being a center of environmental consciousness, and citizens can demonstrate their support for environmentalism by recycling. Recycling has become as potent a political symbol in King County as motherhood and apple pie.

The story is not over. King County has set the goal of almost doubling its rate of recycling and waste reduction again, to 65 per cent by the year 2000. Seattle aims for 60 per cent by 1998. The state will require 50 per cent by 1995. Meanwhile, as has happened in other cities where citizens are recycling enthusiastically, the markets for mixed waste paper, glass, and many other recyclables have become glutted. Seattle and King County are fortunate in having local customers for newsprint at local pulp mills. Also, because Seattle is a convenient port for Asia, over 90 per cent of the mixed wastepaper is exported to mills in Taiwan, Indonesia, and other parts of Asia. But other cities on the Pacific coast are exploring the possibility of sending their trash overseas, and in the summer of 1992, one King County trash hauling firm had to pay an Indonesian paper mill over $10 a ton to take mixed wastepaper.

Some in King County want to return to command-and-control politics. The county and many towns are lobbying the state legislature for the authority to ban the sale of products that are difficult to recycle. The leader of Washington Citizens for Recycling is active in an effort to pass federal legislation to force manufacturers to assume responsibility for the waste they generate. At the same time, there are active efforts to use other tools to solve solid waste problems. The county and the state have established programs to expand the recycling industry, and these agencies are supporting technical studies, market tests, revisions of procurement policies, and other ways to build stronger markets for recyclables. What seems to be emerging is a mixture of regulatory and nonregulatory policies to manage solid wastes in King County.

As the city and county have emphasized alternatives to regulation, and as the debate turns away from hot spots like the Cedar Hills landfill, the politics of solid waste management has changed. Many of the leaders of the protests of 1985-1987 are now active members of county advisory committees and generally supportive of county policies and programs. As one neighbor of the Cedar Hills landfill said, " We have some quibbles with what some of the suburban cities are doing, like still charging a flat rate for trash collection, but basically we think King County is doing just fine."

In the search for more tools to influence the behavior of homeowners, businesses, and others, there are more efforts to bridge the gaps between different government programs and to bring environmental values directly into forums where the primary concern is not environmental protection but other matters, such as economic development. For example, the state's Clean Washington Center, which seeks to build a larger recycling industry, is part of the state Department of Trade and Economic Development. The King County Chamber of Commerce has established a solid waste task force, whose chair also serves as chair of the county's commission on recycling.

Most of the links involve nonregulatory "carrots" like information, education, subsidies, and economic incentives. However, regulatory "sticks" are still important at times and do appear in the picture of civic environmentalism. In contrast, civic environmentalism tends to address several related forms of pollution at the same time.

The Significance of Civic Environmentalism

Civic environmentalism is not a replacement for traditional regulatory policies; it is rather a complement to those policies. Civic environmentalism is possible because the struggle to put regulatory laws in place has been at least partially successful. Polluters know that if they do not somehow reduce emissions, there may be political pressure for regulation. Also, the struggle to enact environmental legislation has helped to transform public attitudes about environmental values or, perhaps more precisely, to inform the public about the causes and nature of threats to the environment. This shift in values and knowledge is particularly important inside corporations and government agencies, which have hired large staffs of professionals whose careers are built on identifying and reducing environmental problems. As we shall see, these insiders play an important role in making civic environmentalism work.

In short, civic environmentalism is possible because it is sheltered by a forest of environmental laws and nourished by new values and knowledge. But the fact that it is derived from the command-and-control regime does not make it less significant. It is like the second stage of succession in a forest. After a forest fire, some trees and bushes grow quickly under the direct light of the sun. Later, other kinds of trees grow in the shade—species that cannot survive in the direct light and drier soil. The second-stage vegetation, like second-stage environmental policy, adds vigor and diversity to the ecosystem.

During the 1980s, it became obvious that traditional regulatory programs do not provide no-risk protection for environmental values. Civic environmentalism is not without risk, either. For example, the traditional regulatory regime in much more effective in California and Minnesota than in Louisiana and Utah. Civic environmentalism may also flourish more fully in "greener" states—those with stronger pro-environment policies.

Neither style of environmental policy and politics is a guarantee that environmentalists or their adversaries will always get what they want. However, there are examples of civic environmentalism in almost every state, and this approach does seem to be a more effective way to address certain kinds of environmental problems, including many of the problems that traditional regulations has not addressed adequately. Taken together, the two systems may provide an effective way of making decisions about how environmental values can be balanced with other values to increase the chances of achieving an economically and environmentally sustainable society.

The Federal Role in Civic Environmentalism

Now that an environmentalist has been elected as vice president, and federal policy seems to be heading rapidly to the green side, should we expect federal government to assume the leadership in civic environmentalism? This might seem to be the natural next step. States are often seen as somewhat less than equal partners in the federal system, and certainly less than equal in environmental regulation. At their most assertive, they are usually seen as "laboratories of democracy," to use Justice Louis Brandeis's phrase. For example, during the 1980s, conservative presidents often sought to limit federal intervention, which left a vacuum that many governors and mayors rushed to fill with activist policies. States experimented with education reform, welfare reform, and new approaches to economic development, as well as with new styles of environmental policy. The image of states as laboratories suggests that when such experiments prove successful, the next step might be to move the innovation into full-scale production, presumably at the federal level so that the entire nation can benefit. This is what happened to many state innovations in Justice Brandeis's time; progressive ideas like workers' compensation were tested by states before the New Deal moved them into federal policy. Is this also the likely future for civic environmentalism?

Many political activists feel that the distribution of responsibilities between states and the federal government is not a particularly interesting topic because there are no principles other than short-term political advantage at work. When I told Joe Browder that I was writing a book that would reflect on federalism and the environment, he looked skeptical and said:

> I don't think there is much to say about that. We go through cycles; sometimes the federal government is more help in tackling environmental problems, and sometimes states are. People don't care about federalism: they just want to win, and they use whatever tools they have at hand. The real change in the last thirty years is greater participation in environmental issues. Nowadays, power is accessible for almost anyone.

Browder should know what the players in environmental politics think about federalism. As a journalist in Miami in the early 1960s, he helped organize opposition to a jetport in the Everglades. Since the defeat of the jetport, Browder has been assistant to the secretary of the interior in Washington and has consulted for environmental groups, native American tribes, electrical utilities, and mining companies on how to handle environmental issues. He still is an active lobbyist for protecting the Everglades.

Browder is right. The opportunities for people to speak up for environmental values have expanded. If there is something to say about federalism and environmental politics, it might be best to start with Browder's observation that people will use whatever tools they find handy. The question, then, is whether some tools are handier at the state and local levels, than in Washington, D.C. Certainly the federal government can play an important supporting role, but most decisions, and most often the leadership, must come from the state and local levels.

In the short run, the 1992 election provided environmentalists with an opportunity for much greater influence on federal policy, and their attention is likely to focus primarily on Congress, EPA, and other federal agencies for some time. But over the long run, environmental policy and politics will involve greater leadership by states, with the federal government acting not as a gorilla but as a partner who can bring specialized resources into decisions made at the state and local levels.

7

Contemporary Ecopolitics: A Case Study of India

Man is shaped to a great extent by his surroundings. Alfred Marshall, a well-known economist, had rightly said 'environments grow children.' Environment, in the sense that which surrounds us, means not only conditions that are favourable to the maintenance of physical health, but also certain emotional and aesthetic qualities of the surroundings. We can say that man is a part of the nature and the nature is a part of our culture.

Man, unmindful of the results of his activities, has inflicted severe environmental degradation mostly by abusing technological power. Environmental degradation is a twentieth century phenomenon. The levels of environmental stresses vary from country to country depending upon the development stages. While the developed countries bother about toxic substances, nuclear hazards, waste products and other forms of chemical solutions, developing countries face poverty, unemployment, deforestation, malnutrition and various types of pollution.

Environmental awareness is not new in the present century but what is new in the decade of 1980s' is the way people are responding and the actions of government in tackling environmental issues. Media, films, seminars and reports are placing authentic pictures of the natural world and its man-made problems, thus contributing to environmental awareness. The Government is in such a position that now it can neglect environmental issues only at its peril. The new awareness has raised many fundamental questions such as – how can we solve and tackle environmental problems? Can development be possible without destroying environment? Citizens are posing questions about their right to information on environmental matters and measures taken to solve an environmental problem when it exists.

Keeping in view all these things, this study deals with 'Ecopolitics in India during the 1980s'. The fundamental question here is, what is Ecopolitics and how it is different from Green politics. Karl Deutsch defines Ecopolitics as 'it asks about the viability of ecological and social systems, singly and in their ecosocial interplay and about the possibility, desirability and limits of political intervention.' Whether we like it or not, the Government's activities are encompassing the whole life of its citizens thus leaving imprints on every sphere of their individual life. Minimal government action is not preferred especially when people face problems in social and economic sectors.

The most important duty of politics is to decide the question of "who gets what, when, how and why"—we depend on natural resources for our existence like—the food we eat, the water we drink, the air we breath, the materials with which we build and equip our shelters. Thus politics decides about and interferes in all these things. We can say that 'politics stands on the ecological foundations of society'.

Ecopolitics emerges from the recognition that to overcome the current ecological crisis, political decisions will have to be made. The response of the government and public officials to environment, people's response to the political decisions and their movements and also the matter of conflicts that exists between environmentalists and politics forms the subject matter of ecopolitics. This study concerns about ecopolitics in India which is mainly in the form of government's attitude towards environmental problems and environmentalists and the policies they adopt towards the same. Environmental politics seeks to identify and conserve critical environmental areas having ecological value. It also deals with peoples' attitude towards environmental problems and their response in conserving and protecting surroundings.

There exists not much difference in the usage of 'ecopolitics' and 'Green politics'—except a slender thread of difference. People indulge in Green politics directly to try to participate in politics with the sole aim of solving ecological crises. The Greens in the Western countries consider themselves the political voice of the citizens movements. They declare their main principles as ecology, social responsibility, grassroots democracy and non-violence. They consider nature as a holistic concept, believe in preserving nature for the purpose of future generations and believe in the creation of non-exploitable society. Ecopolitics does not comprise political parties devoted to environment. Green politics is the result of expanded activity of ecopolitics. Most of the authors use these words interchangeably. This study examines these issues in relation to India especially in the decade 1980s. This decade was earmarked with severe pressures in our political, economic and social sectors. These implications are reverberated in the environment sector such as pollution levels touching the stars, forests and natural resources depleting at faster rates, soil erosion increasing in various forms, floods and droughts becoming common features etc. This environmental degradation has also affected our development efforts, thus forming a vicious circle.

Out of these conditions and also out of global influences to some extent, emerged environmental awareness which is the marked feature in the 1980s. In the words of Khoshoo, 'the striking feature of the decade is that we have begun to unravel and understand the complexity of ecosystems.' This decade has clearly demonstrated that when policy makers fail to understand ecosystems, environmental costs are the resultant consequences. We witnessed the worst environmental disaster—Bhopal episode in 1988, and several gas leakages in various parts of the country that led to loss of lives and worst chemical and industrial pollution. This decade witnessed grass-root ecological movements, public interest litigations and widespread awareness among various sections of the society. Though we could not witness the emergence of a political party entirely for the environment, the politicians are now in a position that they can neglect it only at their peril. Government has been forced to take decisions to abate environmental degradation.

Environmental problems are very large in scale and are multi-faceted. Hence, either individuals or organizations alone cannot offer solutions. Political institutions, which have access to money, man-power and authority, have the ability to mobilise the large-scale forces necessary to tackle these issues. In India, the nature of the Union Government, in terms of power and structure, is such that people look towards it for want of activity and initiative to solve any major problem. Further, inter-dependence of the world is such that it is the government that has to deal with the global environmental problems. The government, in absence of public participation or support cannot contribute much. Government has to allay the fears of people and prove its genuine concern towards solving these problems. People, through movements and awareness, make the government to focus attention on certain problems.

Mutations in the society and native system predispose both the material and spiritual life of mankind and influence its economic, political and cultural life. Thus the importance of environmental crisis extends far beyond the mere problems of the utilisation of nature. That is why environmental problems prompt quite definite reactions from the political circles. It would be no exaggeration to say that both political and environmental factors influence each other at national as well as international levels.

Politics concerns with the study of state and government and their role in decision making. It encompasses the role of various agencies in deciding common interest. Karl Q. Deutsch opines, "politics is the making of decisions by public means thus it primarily concerns with the government that is with the direction and self-direction of large communities of the people." As for J. C. Johari the term politics has three connotations—"political activity, political process and political power." Man is the centre of politics which unequivocally influences every aspect of human life.

In today's modern world, the state and the government are said to belong to the people. True of the words of M.P. Jain, "from birth to death, from morning to evening, a citizen is overshadowed by the government and public service of the state."

In nominal sense, the terms 'state' and 'government' are used interchangeably, not withstanding minor differences. The government is one of the constituents of the state apart from territory, population and sovereignty. It is a body of some citizens while state comprises all citizens. However, it is through the government that the state is formulated, expressed and realised. The ends and purposes of the state are implemented through it.

In modern day politics, the government is expected to pay attention to welfare activities. The modern government has emerged as an active and positive agent in the direction of affairs of all communities. Through making rules, regulations, enforcing them and in using power, government leaves an imprint on the society. The conditions are such that people are not accepting minimal government actions or activities but are looking forward to it when they are facing problems. Be it economic, social, communal, religious or recently the environmental issues, the government has to show its concern and throw itself in finding solution. It is not surprising when the governments transgress the limits and the state activity encompasses the life of the common man. Dennis Clark Pirages in this connection said "contemporary political institutions have been shaped in environments of growth."

This discussion brings us to examine the relationship between politics and environment. Political Geography deals with the study of the influence of physical environment on the political activities of man and how man's political organization modifies the landscape of the area upon which his given political organisation impinges. Initially, politics had been defined mostly as a matter of who gets what, when and how. With the expansion of state activity and the dimensions of problems faced by people, the nature of politics has undergone too many changes to give validity and to examine and to solve the problems. Thus, politics has to examine and pay attention to environmental issues which are demanding constant attention. Deruent Whittlesay unequivocally emphasised the relation between politics and environment by saying, "political activities leave their impress upon the landscape, just as the economic pursuits do and deep and widely ramified impress upon the landscape is stamped by the functioning of effective central authority." Walt Anderson opines that "politics is the making of decisions by human beings about the Manipulation and Utilisation of natural environment, it is an interaction among life forms which directly or indirectly affects other life forms. Increasingly and inevitably, politics is ecology."

People's interest in the impact of environmental factors upon politics goes back to the ancient world. As early as 3rd Century B.C. Aristotle felt that "people and their environments are inseparable and that they are affected by both geographical circumstances and political institutions." Many scholars in later day periods paid attention to the influence of geographic factors upon politics. For example, Jean Bodin maintained that climatic circumstances influence national characteristics as well as foreign policies of the states. Arnold Toynbee held that civilizations are born in environments that pose difficult challenges. Recent years have witnessed major focus on this issue. The United Nations conference at Stockholm in 1972, not only recognised the crisis in environment but focussed and affirmed that these problems could be solved politically and not by specialists and experts or private individuals alone. Ten years after the Stockholm conference, there was a growing recognition that "many of the great problems of the world environment have political roots." Thus, the decade of 1980's has witnessed growing awareness of environmental crisis among political circles. In this decade scholars from different backgrounds began to examine the links between environmental and political activities of the developing countries.

The magnitude of environmental crisis has caused environmental awareness among the developed and the developing countries alike. The most striking feature of this awareness is the increasing involvement of governments at all levels in environmental protection and the environmental issues are thoroughly politicised. Every major environmental issue, whatever may be the outcome, is debated and discussed at every level. The levels of environmental awareness vary from country to country.

Most of the governments have established national environmental policies and official agencies to deal with these problems.

The peculiar nature of the environmental crises forces the modern governments to look for solution of these problems. These special features of the environmental crises are—

(1) The unprecedented expansion sometimes of environmental problems would not pertain to a specific geographic extent and often cross geographical boundaries. For example, soil waste, chemical pollution, resource depletion, etc.

(2) Maintenance—Environmental maintenance involves a colossal involvement of money, time, expertise, manpower, and co-ordination. Hence, national authority becomes imperative.

(3) Priority—It is the government that decides 'who gets what, how and why' among its citizens. It is the government that gives priority to certain issues or problems that dominate the society.

(4) The last but the most important factor is the 'wholeness' of the ecosystem. In the ecosystem, units influence each other. The interdependence of all there factors reflects on the whole ecosystem.

The modern day government is expected to take all these issues in its developmental policies. True to the words of Vanda Asthana, "in the context of environment, all modern systems of government, irrespective of their nature and form own primary responsibility in this regard as people first legitimately look to their governments for initiative." It is the government which has to decide the priority of ecological issues, to form public policy and to take other relevant steps in its action to solve problems.

This chapter mainly focuses attention of the environment politics in India during the 1980s. Here, the government's form or structure, its public policy, environmental policy, government machinery, legislative measures, executive orders, political parties and their policies etc. have been analysed.

A brief discussion about the government form or structure is requisite as on it depends every form of governmental activity. R.D. Dikshit emphasises this by saying, "it is not the government *per se* but rather the form or structure of government that is of fundamental importance in determining its effectiveness as a vocational agent." India, having adopted the parliamentary form of government, is in all terms a open society. The executive body formulates policies while the legislative body enacts such policies. Judicial activism is its other hallmark.

Public policy is nothing but the activity of the government. The government takes and follows decisions regarding certain cores of activities that concern its citizens. These decisions, besides causing prodigious costs, produce important and wide-ranging consequences in the society. Here we are concerned with the governments public policy in relation to environmental sphere. Environmental policy is commonly defined as "public policy with governing the relationship between people and their natural environment. The emphasis here is on people as part of natural system." The goal of environmental policy should be proper management of natural resources, better environmental quality and life for its citizens and overall sustainable development.

Constitutional provisions relating to environment in India—under the constitutional provisions, now it is obligatory duty of the state and its citizens to protect and improve the environment. Article 21 of the Fundamental Rights guarantees the right to life, a life of dignity. Articles 48-A of the Directive Principles declares, "State shall endeavour to protect and improve the environment and to safeguard forests and wild-life of the country. Article 51-A declares that 'it shall be the duty of every citizen to protect and improve the natural environment.'

Article 31-A provides certain immunities for environmental laws from judicial scrutiny. It provides that state is securing all or any of the principles laid down in part IV, cannot be challenged in the courts.

Article 246 provides a three-fold distribution of environmental legislative powers between the Union and the States. The Union list includes regulation and development of oil fields and mineral resources, petroleum and petroleum products, control over mines and mineral development, regulation and development of inter-state rivers and river valleys, control over fisheries, and industries of public interest. The State list has conclusive power over public health, sanitation, agriculture, water, pests and prevention of plant diseases, land, fisheries, mines etc. Union government exercises power over the matters incorporated in the concurrent list on the following lines—matters concerning protection and improvement of environment.

It is evident that, in many respects, the government has failed to fulfill the obligation of providing a life of dignity to its citizens. Pollution levels in the Metropolitan cities are growing out of proportions. For example, in Mumbai, 2300 tonnes of air pollutants are discharged in the environment every day. Calcutta has the highest count of suspended particle matter in the world—at 5-6 ug per cubic meters and Delhi has the highest level of air pollutants in the world. These air pollutants have been responsible for the spread of diseases like lung cancer, tuberculosis, brochettes etc. According to estimates every 10th person in Delhi has some or other problems related to lung. In India nearly 10 per cent of the water sources are polluted by human and industrial wastes. The level of quality of drinking water provided in cities as well as in villages is not up to the mark. It is estimated that 2133 of all illnesses in India are related to water-borne diseases such as typhoid and infective-hepatitis. Another area where the government has failed miserably is in supplying drinking water to both rural and urban areas. It is acute in rural areas. The Seventh Plan has identified nearly 1,61,722 villages as problem areas. There are another 1.5 lakh partially covered villages which have also spilled over to the Eighth Plan requiring augmentation for full coverage.

Percentage of Population with Drinking Water and Sanitation Facilities

	By the end of Sixth Plan (1980-85)	*By the end of Seventh Plan (1985-90)*
(1) Rural water supply	54	About 87
(2) Rural sanitation	About 1	About 3
(3) Urban water supply	72	8419
(4) Urban sanitation	28.40	4719

Source: Economic Survey 1990-91.

Slums, poor housing conditions and poor sanitation facilities are the major features in our present day urbanisation. According to an estimate, about 20 per cent of the country's urban population lives in the slums. The ratio is high in cities like Delhi—30.19 per cent, Lucknow—38.83 per cent, Kanpur – 40 per cent, Mumbai– 38.30 per cent. Sanitation facilities are very much below the standards. Vehicular noise levels at certain urban places often average between 92-97 decibles while the optimum noise level for human beings is between 70-80 decibles, which in turn leads to side-effects like loss of hearing power, mental tension and strain. In rural areas, measures taken for pest control also lead to environmental degradation. Other social sectors like low nutritional standards, high infant mortality rates, low literacy levels etc., show the level of development we achieved.

Legislation Concerning Environment

Legislation is one of the most direct means available for regulation or development of the physical environment. It is one of the ways to bring changes in the society. "There are about 30 major enactments related to the protection of environment now being administered by the Central and State Governments." Gopesh Nath Khanna, in his article quoted the Government of India Report 1980 as saying, "there are more than 200 Central and State laws today that can be interpreted in one way or the other to protect the environment." The government has passed several laws concerning conservation, deforestation, pollution and other aspects of environment.

Besides these laws the Penal Code considers disobedience of an order by a public authority causing danger to life, health or safety, water and air as offense. Under Criminal Procedure Code, Advocate General can make an order to install public nuisance.

Most of the environmental laws are punitive in nature but not preventive. Though we have multitude laws concerning the environment in one way or the other, the decade of 1980's especially witnessed severe environmental crises, the causes being the government and legislative incompetence. The loopholes in the legislation certainly give advantages to vested interests. Multinationals and corporate sector are the beneficiaries of this. Another major lacuna is the perceptible links between industry and government which leads to passive attitudes towards the environment. Further, overlapping powers of authorities/departments involved in supervising the safety mechanism of various companies and rejection of no objection certificate (NOC) hinders the effective implementation of environmental laws. For example, municipality may grant license to an industrial unit irrespective of the cancellation of NOC by the Pollution Board. The Comptroller and Auditor-General has recently flayed the working of the Central Pollution Control Board (CPCB)—an apex institution in the country. While pointing out that CPCB was to lay down standards for quality of water and air and quality of pollutants discharged were to be regulated by the State Boards, it said, "CPCB has not yet evolved any mandatory standards for water and air quality. It directed its efforts towards development of minimal national standards for trade effluents and sewage discharge." If the condition of an apex national institution is like that, one cannot imagine the work of the State Boards. The last, but not the least point, is that environmental laws exclude people's participation in their implementation. The environmental laws facilitate certain interests like industry that are likely to be affected by the decisions of the implementing agencies but the individual is excluded by the law which is not giving any representation or allowing one to move any court as a matter of course. He has the only recourse to the provisions available in the Indian Penal Code and other Acts, where criminal prosecution is provided.

Environment under the Plans

Environment had not received planners attention until the launching of Fourth Five Year Plan in 1968. With the establishment of National Committee on Environmental Planning and Co-ordination (NCEPC) the government initiated some action towards this. It also passed Wildlife Act 1972.

The Fifth Five Year Plan stated that, 'ensure so that the pursuit of developmental goals does not lead to reduction in the quality of life through deterioration in environmental conditions.' It laid emphasis on the close connection of NCEPC with all important industrial decisions so that environmental goals could be achieved. Co-ordination of various efforts to develop standards for the emissions of pollutants, promotion of research and development in the field of environment and priority for the construction of embankments and other connected flood protection works were emphasised under this Plan.

The Government of India appointed a committee under the Chairmanship of N.D. Tiwari in 1980 for recommending Legislative measures and Administrative machinery for ensuring the environmental protection. It formulated a draft national environment policy whose objectives are – to conserve and develop healthy environment, to upgrade the quality of life, to conserve biotic diversity, to develop environment, etc. It called upon the government to create "a quick, responsive, independent and innovative national organization with sufficient funds and manpower to implement national environmental policy."

The Sixth Plan devoted a separate chapter on environment and it considered environmental conservation as the very basis of all development. It also highlighted the causes of environmental crises. The year 1980 witnessed the creation of Department of Environment which co-ordinates all other governmental machinery.

The Seventh Plan gave emphasis on sustainable development in harmony with the environment. So all development programmes, in all sectors, are to take environmental consideration fully into account. It agreed that there was a progressive strengthening of official involvement in environmental management in India, with increased scientific, technical, administrative and legislative back-up at the State and Central levels. It pointed out the side-effects of development like mismanagement of natural resources, large scale deforestation, discharge of soiled water, indiscriminate construction and expansion of settlements. The tools and methodologies of environmental planning are primarily addressed to these problems. It felt that initiatives for tackling environmental issues must emerge from official as well as non-official agencies and individuals operating at different levels.

The Eighth Plan drafted 'national perspective on the environment', to ensure the people (1) equitable and continued access to the natural resources vital for their survival, (2) decentralize governmental control over natural resources to reverse the trend of people's alienation from nature, (3) change the prevailing unjust and unsustainable model of development and the wasteful pattern of resource use and consumption inherent in it and (4) internally integrate and coordinate governmental action to protect and regenerate nature.

This Plan also listed out the major tasks before the government and the planning process. These are – protection of environment, regeneration and restoration of degraded eco-systems decentralization of control over nature and natural resources, formulatioin of national policy on nature and natural resources, monitoring of the environment, accountability of the government and personnel to the people for their actions and inactions, development of environmentally sustainable development models, coordination of governmental action aimed at conserving and regenerating nature and natural resources, and presentation of annual natural resources budget before the Parliament.

Governmental machinery for Environment Management— Implementation of the government's policy and actions, in fact, takes the real cake. The decades 1970s and 1980s have witnessed the evolution of governmental machinery for environment management. The Department of Environment, which was established in 1980, is now known as the Department of Environment and Forests (DOE&F). It is the apex agency that coordinates and integrates the activities of various environmental institutions. It is a focal point for planning, promotion and coordination of environmental programmes. By the end of 1980s, almost every state had established its own Department of Environment. The Central Pollution Control Board (CPCB) is the apex body for assessment, monitoring and control of water, air and chemical pollution. Except Manipur, Nagaland, Sikkim, Arunachal Pradesh and Mizoram, all other states have constituted their boards.

Other agencies were established for specific purposes. The Central

Ganga Authority (CGA) was set up in 1985 to oversee the implementation of the action plan drawn up for clearing polluted stretches of Ganga. National Mission on Wastelands Development (NWDB) was established in 1985 with the aim to develop waste lands. The government rechristened it as National Technology Mission on Wastelands Development in 1985. Its main aims—check land degradation, sustainable use of waste lands, regeneration of degraded forests, promotion of farm forestry and restoration of ecological balance.

The government had also established three sub-groups to work for effective utilisation of wastes. These will identify the waste, suggest technological measures, recycling, reduction and reuse of waste and to formulate action points as a basis for executive orders to be issued by the government.

The Environmental Monitoring Committee is established to ensure effective implementation of environmental safeguards in irrigation, multi-purpose and flood-control projects. The government has also established Environmental information System (ENVIS) in 1982 to supply information to policy makers, decision makers, research workers and general public. It publishes a magazine 'Paryavaran'. It also acts as National Focal Point as well as Regional Service Centre for South Asian Sub- region of INFOTERRA (a global information network of United Nations Environment programme). The Government of India also follows Environmental Impact Assessment (EIA) method. The DOE & F with the help of inter-ministerial appraisal committees comprising experts from related disciplines assess all the projects and feasibility of plans and assess environmental impact of those projects. This system is based on the premise that the environmental issues are anticipated and incorporated in the development project at the project formulation stage itself on various aspects like siting, choke of technology, minimization of environmental damage etc.

New schemes like eco-task force, Paryavaran Vahini and eco-label were launched in 1990s. The government is planning to formulate national policies on natural resources, conservation and environment.

Despite this institutional machinery, there exists many loopholes in this system. Lack of coordination, expertise and finances, prevailing corruption and usual bureaucratic delays hamper the measures taken towards environmental problems, thus causing redundance of the government machinery. Contributing to these is the absence of people's participation.

Political Parties and their Attitude towards the Environment

It is often said that 'of all the instruments designated by man to achieve his political aims, only political parties proved endurance.' Maurice Duverger opines that the "primary goal of political parties is the conquest of power or share in its exercise and it draws support from a wider base."

In a political system, parties act as the transmitter of ideas, opinions and approaches to social needs and national goals. Their ideology is the mirror of socioeconomic, political and cultural ideals, conditions and norms of a society. In the representative form of government the existence of political parties is essential as they connect the electorate and the representative institution and the citizen and the government.

In India, party system originated in the 19th century as a response towards British colonial system. Being a reasonably open society, India, has a multitude of parties but the main national parties, apart from the Congress, are Communist Party of India (M), Bharatiya Janata Party (BJP) and Janata Dal.

Digvijay Singh claims that "among the developing countries, it is India that took the lead, when the four major parties included the environment in their manifestoes in 1980 elections." Since then national parties mentioned environment related issues along with many other issues in the subsequent elections held in 1984 and 1989. In these elections, political parties paid much attention to the issues racking the country such as economy, social justice and development. Environment related issues like energy, exploitation and management of natural resources, renewable resources, wildlife, establishment of national parks and land management were figured, but not environment *per se*.

The 1991 elections definitely reversed this trend. Every national party except CPI and CPI (M), allocated at least one page on discussing the environmental problems faced by India and thereby evolved their strategy. These parties paid attention to sustainable development and environmental management.

Thus the political parties, in tune with global awareness, started paying attention to ecological problems. The side-effects of developmental effort and impact of severe environmental degradation are responsible for these. This in turn shows the marked trend that is going on since the 1980s in our social circles, since the political parties do not show any interest in those issues wherein the electorate is unconcerned. Their manifestoes should reflect the issues that concern citizen. It is said that, "election manifestoes are a potpourri to please all sections, to be taken not with a pinch but a handful of salt." These election manifestoes are in turn addressed to literate citizens and just to appease few sections of society. Any party that comes to power is not expected that it will implement manifestoes in letter and spirit. Often, parties flout their promises or sometimes those programmes are unworkable.

Parliament

It is a forum for discussion and debate of various issues of national interest thereby contributing to the awareness of people regarding these issues. Environmental Forum was launched in 1981 comprising the members of both Lok Sabha and Rajya Sabha. This Forum subsequently organized the First National Conference of Legislators on Environment in 1982. The goals of the Forum were to raise environmental issues in the Parliament, interact collectively with the government and work for environment in their respective constituencies. Legislators Environmental Forum was launched in many States by 1984 to raise awareness among representatives.

On the whole, environmental issues have figured very rarely in the Parliament as most of the pressing problems related to economy received representatives attention. Further, most of the leaders are either completely ignorant of environmental matters or simply neglected them. However, we can say that the decade of 1980s witnessed much awareness among Parliamentarians about environmental matters as compared to previous decades.

Leaders Attitude towards Environment

The Prime Minister of this country often exercises unlimited power and dominates and influences the decisions of the government. Mrs. Indira Gandhi, who came to power through 1980 general elections, exhibited at least to some extent, concern towards environment. She attended the Stockholm Conference, 1972 and said 'Poverty is the worst polluter.' She created the DOE in 1980 and stopped the Silent Valley on account of pressures from both international organisations and the agitation from environmentalists in India. She inserted Articles 48-A and 52-A to the fundamental duties which give special responsibility for both the state the and citizen towards environmental management. She took special interest in conservation programmes. Establishment of National Parks and Biosphere Reserves received special attention.

Mr. Rajiv Gandhi who came to power in 1984, also showed concern towards environmental problems. He was instrumental in launching New Environmental Policy in 1986, Policies for Energy and Power, Action plan for cleaning the Ganga, Plan for Afforestation and Wasteland development, establishment of Island Development Authority and series of technological missions for drinking-water, universal immunization of children, flood control, etc.

During the Prime Ministership of Vishwanath Pratap Singh, Mrs. Maneka Gandhi as the Environment Minister earned applauds from various circles. She took special care in conservation and pollution. Mr. Chandra Shekhar's Ministry which followed V. P. Singh's Ministry, could not take much action as it was short-lived.

The attitudes of leaders are not at all sufficient to take care of environment, as it is evident from the fact that the decade 1980s witnessed severe environmental degradation. Leaders concern remained on papers, plans and methods but not in accomplishment. In spite of the success of programmes like Project Tiger and Project Rhino which received applauds from the world, the wildlife conservation measures proved to be futile as India's biotic diversity is on the decline. The same thing is reflected in other spheres of environment.

The Environmental Lobby

S. E. Finer, combining interest and pressure groups in Lobby, says, "Environmental Lobby comprises the sum of organizations in so far as they are occupied at any point of time in trying to influence the policy of public bodies in their own chosen direction." In India, apart from corporate elements, local authorities, government departments and research associations, non-governmental organisations (NGOs) try to influence the decisions of the government and work for the environmental awareness among people.

We can trace the origin of environmental movement to the 1970's. Within months of the Stockholm Conference, Chipko Movement was launched against the deforestation and the consequent environmental degradation in the Himalayan Region. From then, there existed many NGOs which worked for the betterment of environment. Some of these organisations receive financial support and project works from the government.

International Agreements

Since the nature of environmental problems is such that globalization of ecological issues has become inevitable, the governments of various countries are forced to come forward, hold discussions and agree to provisions for common interest. Indian government, in this spirit, signed many international agreements on open space, Marine Wealth, air pollution etc. It became a signatory to Montreal Protocol, Biodiversity Convention, Antarctica Treaty, and Climatic convention. It is a signatory to some other minor treaties. India also used international conferences to raise environmental awareness. At the NAM Conference in September, 1989 at Belgrade, the Prime Minister of India asserted the need for creating a 'Planet Protection Fund'. Even SAARC countries are also paying attention on environmental matters.

The Government of India owns, controls and develops India's forests, dams, power stations, roads, mines and a large part of its industry, thus becoming not only the protector of the environment but also the foremost destroyer of the environment. In India, everything that is required for the protection of environment such as political machinery, enforcement officers, plans of action oriented projects, non-governmental organizations, exist but the outcome of these is negligible. Political unwillingness to act and strike a blow at the root cause leads to nothing in outcome. One can easily count the number of politicians who throw themselves for environmental safeguards. Mrs. Maneka Gandhi in 1988-89, and presently Mr. Kamal Nath—Minister of Environment—are in the forefront of environmental sphere. Mrs. Maneka Gandhi earned the wrath of some businessmen and interested groups for her concern towards environment. She came to be know as 'green minister'. Mr. Kamal Nath is also taking much interest and has been able to earn goodwill from environmentalists. He recently dared to stop the work of Chilka Aquatic Farm Project though tentatively, which shows his genuine concern towards environment. Mrs. Maneka Gandhi recently launched. 'Green Political Forum'. A minor party called 'Green Party of India' was also launched. Some other politicians are paying lip service towards environment.

Thus, it shows that politicians pay attention on environment occasionally here and there. They only take interest when the so-called problem fetches them vote bank. Further, the nexus between politicians and predators of environment makes the matters worse. Adams has rightly pointed out that:

> "the consistent failure of government machinery and development agency bureaucracies and their expert employees to take adequate account of the environmental impacts of their actions is matched by their frequent blindness to the need and capacities of those they develop."

The public sector in India, which should have lead the private sector by setting norms in taking precautions for environmental safeguards, instead is involved in destroying the environmental quality by its activities.

For example, indiscriminate stripping of resources, though under the supervision of public agencies is causing environmental degradation. Limestone mining in Mussorie has threatened the existence of that town itself. Jharia coal stripping also causes soil erosion, water pollution, floods etc. Thus the national policy to control the damage of surface mining is a sham. This can be seen in other spheres of environment also.

Vandana Asthana opines that "there is almost no public policy of environmental regulations and officials maintain a silence in the political battle of economic gains versus environmental hazards." Many environmental regulations are only on paper and never come into force. Pollution boards are also helpless whenever a report on certain industry causing environmental hazards either by dumping hazardous wastes into water or causing noise or air pollution comes to it. Another major drawback is the failure on the part of government to consider relevant data thoughtfully and solve ecological problems. There also exists a major gap between intentions and achievements leading to escapist tendency among political circles.

Though India has an extensive body of environmental legislation dating back to Shore nuisance case 1853 (Bombay and Lolba), such legislation has become very difficult to enforce or to implement. The Tiwari Committee (1980) noted four basic flaws relating to environmental legislation. These are (1) Many promoted development and resource use for specific economic benefits without careful analysis of potential adverse environmental effects (2) Several state laws had potential implications for neighbouring states (3) Many laws were clearly inadequate (4) Environment as such was still widely ignored and overlooked within government departments. Thus, in spite of the existence of extensive body of pollution legislation, Indian industry has remained either reluctant to control pollution or beyond.

The DOE is overburdened and under staffed with only 237 staff and an annual budget of $16 million. On the basis of its powers, "it cannot initiate any enquiry on its own and is thus content with only passing judgements whenever asked to do so." It passed Narmada Dam project in 1987, in spite of its earlier refusals to do.

Politicians and their regionalistic interests and favour, sometimes dominate in deciding the establishment of environmental projects like refineries, dams etc. regional politics have a definite say over environment and in this process also comes the negligence of scientific opinion. Further secrecy regarding environmental matters also aggravates the situation.

For example, Menon's report on silent valley was not made public.

Further, as Ajit Kamalakar opines "as the government does not work closely with NGO s it lacks the kind of access to policy making that would give it the influence it seeks." It also ignores the rural based NGOs and works with only urban-based NGOs.

We cannot say that the government failed at every account. It did achieve in framing environmental policy, arousing environmental awareness, achieving some success in conservation field and voicing its interests over the international forums. But there is a long way to go. Our economic interests, in turn development, are tied up with environment. So, the ultimate responsibility lies with government.

It is a well-known fact that government can bring the desired social change. Its action is a crucial component towards successful solution of environmental problems. It is for the government to decide the priority of ecological issues in its public policy. It implies that political responsibility of each country is paramount for environment protection. Genuine concern, will and responsibility on the part of politicians would be the welcoming trends.

The phenomenon of environmental degradation is not unique to the twentieth century in real terms. Man has been involved in the exploitation of the nature since ancient times. With rapid advances in science and technology and industrialization, environmental exploitation also followed suit. What is unique in the present century is the unparalleled environmental degradation and the consequential fall out of the quality of life. Rudolf C. Heredia thus rightly said that, " never before has human society had such an unprecedented and so disastrous an effect on its environment as ours."

India experienced severe environmental degradation especially in the decade of 1980s. The ecological crisis itself caused diverse reactions and responses from various strands of society such as people, governmental institutions, scientific community and voluntary organisations. Ecological awareness poses many questions related to governments role, society's relationship to its sustaining environment, development strategy, people's right to information and what is to be inflicted towards solving environmental problems in the days to come.

During the post-independence period, India was preoccupied with problems such as poverty, unemployment, hunger and low standards of living. Our planners thought that heavy industrialization, on the model of western countries only, would solve all these problems. Rapid growth of population and demands for development subsequently put enormous pressures on our natural resources thereby causing environmental degradation. Despite our plans stressed on to achieve, growth with justice and growth with stability the fruits of benefits accrued to only a small section. The poor have become poorer and the rich have become richer.

People are posing questions over their conditions. They are questioning the values and relevances of our development strategies. (The view that 'development at all costs' is in shambles). The side-effects of developmental plans led to a debate of development vis-à-vis environment. Even the Planning Commission admitted that development policies have caused environmental degradation. Development policies which were adopted unmindful of environmental effects, have proved that these policies are faulty and futile.

These conditions led to an awareness in both government and the people. The government has taken many steps to solving environmental problems. Its eighth five year plan gave emphasis on sustainable development which has to become a main plank of government policies. Intellectual circles are arguing that the government should evolve 'Indian model of development' rather than following western mode of development blindly. Thus, there existed a growing recognition that development and environment are not necessarily contradictory to each other but are complemental and reciprocal.

There is a growing recognition that the government has a paramount role in combating environmental degradation. The extent, dimension and magnitude of environmental crisis is such that it is only the government with its manpower finance and co-ordination of its various organisations would solve the crisis. International organisations and political leaders are also stressing on this fact. For example, United Nations Conference at Stockholm in 1972 emphasised the role of politics and Mr. Mikhail Gorbachev, former Soviet leader 'called for environmental issues to shift up to top priority for political leaders worldwide.' He even regards the preservation of environment today as the priority for all politicians.

Prior to 1972 conference, the attention of government, public and others mainly focused on conserving wildlife without much concern for environment. It is said that most of the people who raised these issues came from the elite class-shikaries, princes and princelings of yore. The Chipko movement in 1970s focused the government's attention over issues of forest policies, exploitation of natural resources and people's conditions of the people. The decade 1980s witnessed the creation of Department of Environment and Forests, evolution of environmental machinery, national policies and laws, governments financial help to non-governmental organisations and environmental education and research.

The late Prime Ministers, Indira Gandhi and Rajiv Gandhi showed concern towards environmental protection. Other political leaders like Mr. Digvijai Singh, Mrs. Maneka Gandhi and recently Mr. Kamal Nath have considered environment as one of the most important issue. Mrs. Maneka Gandhi launched Delhi Vikas Manch – a political party with environment as its main concern. Recently, a Green Party of India has also emerged. Though these two political parties are conspicuous by their absence, but it reveals that green parties would soon emerge on the political heartland of India.

In spite of all these developments and the attention of the government, the decade 1980s could not escape from ecological crisis. Lack of will, flaws in implementation, failure to perceive the dimension of problems, close connections between the government and corporate circles and absence of holistic management of natural resources are responsible for the ecological crisis.

The adverse environmental degradation has led to peoples' reactions towards it. The worst-affected due to this problem are tribals, marginal farmers and mostly the disadvantaged section of the population. Their access to natural resources are either restricted or prohibited. They lost their sources of avenue on the wake of various development projects. Initially, people were ready to bear the cost of development policies in the hope of improvement of their standards of life. But when their hopes were belied, they are no longer ready to suffer. In this process, there occurred people's movements against deforestation, commercial fishing, mining sites; establishment of refineries and nuclear power plants, salinity and waterlogging and displacement of people due to the construction of dams. India can also boast of having a large number of voluntary organisations which are leading people in these ecological movements. The main feature of ecological movements is their local base. Grass-root ecological movements mainly focus attention towards local problems and engross themselves in the conservation of resources. Despite many weaknesses, there is a possibility of expansion and scope of these movements in the years to come.

The debate over large dams versus small dams goes back to 1950s. Indian planners paid attention over the construction of large dams. The world's six highest dams are located in India. The side-effects of large dams like displacement of lakhs of people, mostly poor, salinity, water logging, sanitation, floods, prone-ness to earthquakes, loss to wild life and architectural monuments and forests have received widespread attention in recent decades. The debate over Narmada dam is a culminating point in this respect. While the government has put forward its development view-point and announced its determination to go ahead with this project; at the same time it talks loud about its sincerity to protect the environment. Anti-Narmada activists are posing questions over human values, preservation of culture and environment, the role of bureaucracies in formulating plans and policies and the right to information of facts and figures pertaining to a problem. However, the work on Narmada, despite the stoppage of funds by the World Bank and Japan is continuing and the government is holding talks with the agitators at present.

Other area, where ecological degradation is threatening the very survival of the region is the Himalayas. Man's attempt to exploit natural resources carried him even to the ecologically sensitive areas. Illegal felling of forests, unscientific management of resources, mining, tourism and other recreation facilities and population pressure and government's failure are the main causes responsible for environmental degradation. These conditions in turn led to people's awareness and movements to protect this region.

It is perceivable that India has reached a stage where the absorptive and assimilative capacity of our ecological system has been over used and misused. Awareness in various circles lead to many attempts to solve these issues. The only way is to strike at the root of the problem. Holistic approach towards natural resources, environmental education, coordination of NGOs and government and people's participation are invaluable.

In fact, India has ancient tradition of preserving and conserving natural resources which also preached against unmindful exploitation of nature. The one way is to resource into old-wise conservation methods. For example, once we used mud cups for drinking or plantain leaves for eating which are biodegradable, western influences led us to become slaves to the use of plastic and polythene culture which threatens environments. In Medieval period, Rajasthanies preserved water by following natural techniques. But today they are facing acute water shortage because of the failure to recultivate the methods they once used. There is no harm in following age-old techniques which are nature friendly and less costly.

The need of the hour is to develop certain sets of conditions such as (1) every citizen should comprehend the state of environment and its sensitivity (2) assessment of environmental movement and persuasion of citizens who inflict damages to environment. (3) cohesiveness of environmental policy (4) we should follow the long-term orientation in our civilization as a whole, in the direction of enduring harmony with its natural environment.

The government should not neglect to think of major issues like pollution of rivers, deforestation, soil erosion, floods and droughts and growing desertification and even trivial aspects like hygiene, sanitation, drainage and drinking water supply. It should do everything in its power for the betterment of the environment. It is true that some people consider that if the government does not take action, eco-disaster would soon follow. The ultimate solution lies in the government's ability to solve ecological crisis.

The need of the hour is to respond to the call of nature thereby lending it more vivacity and a greater longevity to the humankind and this planet. We should add a dynamic component to our way of thinking defying what Einstein once remarked, "everything changes, except the human way of thinking." For maintaining ecological balance, the revolution should start from home—the basic unit of the society.

8

North-South Perspective

If we take seriously today's major environmental challenges—including global-scale atmospheric pollution, loss of biological diversity, and resource degradation in developing countries—we have to ask seriously what must be done to meet them. Finding all the answers to this question will be the work of years, but one precondition already seems clear. None of these challenges can be met without a new era of heightened cooperation and agreement between industrial and developing countries. These North-South understandings must transcend the traditional environmental agenda and incorporate initiatives in policy areas as diverse as international trade and debt, development and assistance, energy, technology transfer, and population. These agreements, once reached, would be nothing less than a global compact between North and South for environmental protection and economic progress.

Consider the North–South links inherent in today's gravest environmental problems, and the need for such understandings is evident.

Global warming now threatens to disrupt weather patterns and raise sea levels around the Earth. Containing the greenhouse effect will require major reductions in emissions of the three most prominent greenhouse gases—carbon dioxide, methane, and chlorofluorocarbons (CFCs). Carbon dioxide, still the leading greenhouse gas, highlights the difficulty of control. To control emissions, industrial countries will have to cut back on their voracious fossil fuel consumption and developing countries will need to stem the deforestation that claims more than an acre a second in the tropics. Deforestation and other land-use changes now account for about one-third of the carbon dioxide produced by human activity and some of the methane.

As a practical matter, developing countries expect industrial countries to take the first and strongest actions on global warming. These developing nations want to see the seriousness of the threat validated and they conclude correctly that industrial countries are largely responsible for the problem and have the most resources to do something about it. But carrying this argument too far could lead to a tragic stalemate. Developing countries already account for about 45 per cent of humanity's yearly contribution to the greenhouse effect, and their share will grow as they industrialize. If just China and India were to increase their greenhouse gas emissions to the global average per capita rate, today's global total would rise 28 per cent; if these two countries matched France's per capita rate, the total would be 68 per cent higher. If we are to contain global warming within tolerable limits, countries North and South will need to adopt energy and forestry strategies consistent with that end.

The loss of species and genetic variety is now proceeding at rates unmatched since the mass extinction episode 65 million years ago that wiped out two-thirds of all species. Today's losses center largely in the remaining tropical forests of Latin America, Asia, and Africa that are home to nearly half the species on Earth. Every day, another hundred species die out. Deforestation is the principle culprit, but poaching and overharvesting for food and profit also take their toll. Unless we act decisively now to reverse habitat destruction, one-fourth of the Earth's 5 to 30 million species could die out over the next few decades, leaving our posterity—and our planet—incalculably poorer.

As with preserving climate, North-South cooperation is essential to preserving biodiversity. Leaders of developing countries do not deny the legitimacy of concern about biodiversity; some share this concern strongly. But they have difficulty giving it the attention needed to reverse today's trends. New land for farming and ranching and timber for export are more immediate priorities, and the forests offer both. Fighting against poachers and homesteaders puts leaders at odds with their own people. In short, if the wealthy countries want to save threatened flora and fauna, they will have to work with developing countries to counter the forces leading to biotic impoverishment and also to create powerful new incentives favoring protection of critical ecosystems.

The decline of productive natural resources is rapidly emerging as major threat to development prospects in much of the Third World. Developing countries are many times more dependent than industrial countries on their natural resources—their soils, fisheries, forests, and minerals. And within developing countries, the poor are most dependent of all. Yet, this resources base is eroding rapidly under pressure from unprecedented population growth, deep-seated social inequities, and misguided policies.

For Third World leaders, resource deterioration is a more immediate challenge than global warming or biodiversity loss, and most are showing increased concern. But even though nascent efforts to protect the environment in developing countries are now common, lack of commitment from political leaders, limited financial resources, inadequate training, and other constraints remain the rule rather than the exception.

As one measure of what resource erosion means for the future, the United Nations Food and Agriculture Organization predicts that between 1985 and 2000, rain-fed cropland in the developing world will become 30 per cent less productive, while the number of people to be fed will swell by more than one billion. Unless the synthesis of environmental and economic imperatives called sustainable development becomes a reality, billions of people in the developing world will eventually lack the basic natural resources needed to sustain them at healthy levels.

Why should industrial countries be concerned about this looming collision between resources and population? From a humanitarian perspective, a compelling argument is that resources deterioration contributes to widespread hunger and the masses of ecological refugees that demand an international response. This moral imperative can be buttressed by considerations of national interest. When resources and population challenges go unmet, this failure can lead first to economic and social stress and then to the political instability that ultimately can jeopardize the economic and political interests of industrial countries.

Equally pertinent for the North to recognize is its sometimes unwitting complicity in resources degradation in the South. Too often, Northern investment schemes and development aid finance large-scale projects that ignore environmental settings and local needs. Making matters worse is the development assistance community's historical neglect of projects that would enhance the conservation and sustained productivity of natural assets.

Similarly, industrial country management of the Third World's external debt has riveted attention on the immediate need to provide debt servicing, to the detriment of environmental, social, and other economic concerns. It also has resulted in economic stagnation that has further marginalized the poor, intensifying pressures on erodible soils, fuelwood supplies, and other resources.

Hard Choices

Today's environmental challenges require that all nations, North and South, make difficult commitments to themselves and to each other in order to secure their common future.

Consider first the key elements of the South's contribution to solving these problems. Far-reaching initiatives will be needed to stop forest destruction, establish and manage biological reserves, pursue environmentally sustainable energy strategies, and conserve land and water resources for food production. Pursuing this ambitious agenda will require leaders to take steps with political and social risks, such as land tenure reforms, major efforts to curb population growth and improve the lot of the rural poor, and adoption of cutting edge technologies that can leapfrog the destructive industrialization patterns of the North.

The leadership to make these changes must come from developing countries themselves, but industrial countries can help. Two basic preconditions of North-South cooperation seem clear. First, joint efforts for conservation must be part of a broader commitment by the North to help developing countries realize their economic aspirations. If officials and opinion leaders in developing countries genuinely believe they can create needed jobs and meet economic objectives while addressing international and domestic environmental problems, their cooperation in solving these problems seems likely. Unfortunately, the history of development in industrial countries offers plenty of cautionary tales and few working models. A major task for both North and South is to demonstrate with cogent analyses and real-world examples that such environmentally sustainable development paths are there to be taken.

Second, developing countries will expect industrial countries to show through their own domestic and international actions that they take these environmental challenges very seriously. Yet, many industrial countries are not demonstrating such commitment. The United States is a case in point, as shown by such indicators as its energy consumptions, its forest management practices, the fate of its biodiversity, the state of its foreign aid, and, at this writing, its general lack of environmental leadership internationally.

The initiatives required of industrial countries are also far-reaching and difficult. Four areas stand out as priorities.

First, these countries must launch major national and international efforts to reduce greenhouse gas emissions. As the world's largest emitter of greenhouse gases, the United State's single most important step at this point is a national commitment to gains in energy efficiency that are large enough to push fossil-fuel use and releases of carbon dioxide steadily downward. Enacting a carbon tax would be one economically attractive way to achieve this goal, as it would stimulate improvements in energy efficiency, discourage practices and technologies that contribute to global warming, and provide needed revenues for environmental and other purposes. Indeed, such new taxes might not be so unpopular if their stated purpose were to raise funds for environmental protection.

Second, industrial nations must sharply increase the flow to the South of both new financing and new technology for environment conservation, sustainable development, and population programs. Official development assistance now amounts to some $40 billion annually, and reforms ensuring that these billions are well spent are badly needed. But neither reform nor conservation is likely to gain sufficient momentum without major new financing. Noting that the net flow of financial resources from the developing countries to the industrialized world now approaches $50 billion a year, the 1989 report of commission chaired by Helmut Schmidt, *Facing One World*, called for a doubling of official development assistance over the next five years.

A recent World Resources Institute study, *Natural Endowments: Financing Resource Conservation for Development*, identified promising ways to attract additional green funding . These include a global environmental trust, which might be funded by taxing industrial countries' greenhouse gas emissions, and an international environmental facility, which would collaborate with developing countries' governments and international aid agencies to identify the most urgent conservation needs, provide "pre-investment" funding to help generate well-designed projects to meet those needs, and bring projects into being by arranging, financing, including loan guarantees, from a variety of existing sources.

Third, industrialized nations must relieve the burden that external debt imposes on developing countries. In spite of the Brady Plan to accelerate debt reduction, debt relief for Third World countries declined from $22 billion in 1988 to $14 billion last year, according to the World Bank. Yet, increased debt relief for developing countries is essential if their economic growth is to be restored and their leaders are to find the wherewithal to meet the challenges of sustainable development and international environment cooperation. Forgiving debt outright might be the North's most reasonable response to the poorest nations, whose loans come mostly from industrial governments rather than from commercial banks.

Finally, the wealthy nations must establish new programs to provide developing countries access to technical assistance, training, technology transfer, and planning grants to increase their capacity to manage environmental and energy challenges. The United States could contribute to this goal by launching a new program of international cooperation with developing countries. Such a program would not be limited to the poorest countries, which are eligible for assistance from the U.S. Agency for International Development (AID), but would extend to middle-income countries like Brazil and Mexico, where international environmental and energy cooperation is essential.

Complementary Policy-making

Such economic and environmental initiatives can be combined in many ways to spur concerted action between North and South. Perhaps the most successful steps will be those in which one country or region reciprocates positive steps taken unilaterally by another. As mutual confidence and concern grow, the process can spread. Other steps, such as those that follow, will require at least some element of negotiation and agreement.

North-South agreements can be forged around the theme of coordinated policy reform and complementary national initiatives. For example, new Northern aid policies that limit development in certain tropical forest areas or trade policies that encourage timber imports from sustainably managed tropical forests will have maximum effect only if complemented by forest sustaining reforms in developing countries. Also, industrial and developing countries can coordinate new policies to reduce carbon dioxide emissions so that the North's efforts to reduce fossil fuel consumption reinforce the South's efforts to curb deforestation and vice versa. More broadly, a comprehensive North-South agreement on carbon dioxide emission will be needed soon. Without it, curbs on fossil-fuel use in some regions could depress world prices, thereby spurring consumption elsewhere.

One interesting example of North-South cooperation, in this case on narcotics trafficking rather than the environment, occurred last November. President Bush announced that in order to boost the economies of countries such as Colombia that are cooperating in cracking down on narcotics trafficking, the United States would eliminate selected trade barriers, offer favorable trade treatment, and seek to repair the international coffee accord that collapsed last summer. Perhaps the United States could one day use such economic initiatives to spur international environmental cooperation.

Table 1 The Debtor-Deforestation Connection

	Average annual deforestation in the 1980s (thousand hectares)	*Total external debt in 1987 (billion U.S. dollars)*
Brazil	2.323	109.5
Colombia	890	15.5
Mexico	615	82.8
Ecuador	340	10.4
Peru	270	16.6
Venezuela	245	29.0
Ivory Coast	510	10.3
Nigeria	400	28.4
Zaire	347	8.6
Indonesia	620	48.5
Thailand	379	17.6
Malaysia	255	21.1
India	147	42.9
Philippines	92	28.4

Source : Data from the UN Food and Agriculture Organization and the World Bank.

Access to substantially increased capital flows and development assistance from the North can be linked to progress by developing countries in meeting their environmental and population challenges. A system of incentives can be created by tying enhanced assistance to policy reforms and other initiatives or by ear-marking much larger sums for environmental purposes. For example, new funds generated by a carbon tax could be used to finance ecological zoning and forest management in the tropics, including investments that help provide the poor with sustainable livelihoods that take pressure off natural forest areas. The Schmidt Commission, in calling for doubling development assistance, noted that "the preservation of the environment will require very large amounts of capital." It urged that donor nations give special consideration to countries that emphasize poverty reduction programs, spend less than two per cent of their gross national product (GNP) on military expenditures, take steps toward efficient family planning policies, or implement policies aimed at environmental preservation.

Debt-for-nature swaps have already proven useful in biodiversity conservation, particularly in Bolivia, Costa Rica, Ecuador, and the Philippines. Both creditor and debtor countries could adopt policies that expand their use. Can the debt-for-nature concept be scaled up to make it relevant to other major challenges, including debt relief, deforestation, and global warming? The potential certainly exists. Half of the Third World external debt and more than two-thirds of global deforestation occur in the same 14 developing countries (see Table 1). Moreover, Brazil, Colombia, Mexico, Zaire, Madagascar, and Indonesia are home to half of all the species on Earth and account for one quarter of the developing world's debt. A bargain could be struck between North and South that would exchange debt for forest conservation on a scale large enough to make a dent in both. The global environment would receive a triple benefit if the public funds needed to purchase discounted debt from commercial banks were to come from taxes levied by industrial countries on greenhouse gas emissions. The commercial debt purchased this way would be exchanged for conservation bonds that would generate local currency funding for various environmental projects.

This arrangement is but one of many ways that large-scale debt relief could be tied to long-term agreements to conserve forest and other natural resources for sustainable production.

Beyond such arrangements, the current Third World debt situation provides other opportunities that can benefit both North and South. Broad based debt restructuring plans for debtor countries could include strong conservation provision and specific requirements for policy reform, such as the elimination of tax breaks and subsidies that encourage deforestation and energy waste. World Bank loans and other lending to support debt reduction could be tied to such reforms.

Straws in the Wind

Is the world making progress toward a new era of North-South cooperation? Words must precede action, even if action doesn't necessarily follow, so let us look first at what has been said.

To begin in the United States, what has the Bush administration said about these North-South issues in recent statements? The short answer is "not much." The president's February speech before the Intergovernmental Panel on Climate Change (IPCC) was long on calls for global cooperation but short on specifics, and he gave no indication that the administration is now prepared to promote initiatives such as those discussed above. A few weeks later, Secretary of State James A. Baker spoke on "the greening of our foreign policy" before the National Governors' Association. Although his statement broke no new ground in terms of U.S. initiatives, it did reflect an awareness of the importance of developing countries in addressing global-scale environmental challenges and of the specific need for North-South cooperation. In the most pertinent section, Secretary Baker expressed doubts about "dramatic calls by some for the establishment of new financial institutions or mechanisms to provide environmental assistance," but he did recognize "... that developing countries may need some additional aid in order to meet the incremental costs associated with fulfilling their international environmental obligations. Unfortunately, even this modest bow toward "additionality" seems to have lost out to competing views within the administration during May, as noted below.

When Europeans are involved, commitments to responsive initiatives seem closer at hand. At the Paris economic summit in June 1989, the leaders of the seven major industrial nations agreed on the North's obligation to help the developing world deal with environmental problems. The final communique of this first "green summit" declared that "to help developing countries deal with past damage and to encourage them to take environmentally desirable action, economic incentives may include the use of aid mechanisms and specific transfer of technology. In special cases, ODA [official development assistance] debt forgiveness and debt-for-nature swaps can play a useful role in environmental protection." On the subject of deforestation, the industrial countries expressed "readiness to assist the efforts of nations with tropical forests through financial and technical cooperation, and in international organizations." Whether these and other statements in this landmark communique will bear fruit remains to be seen.

Perhaps the most eloquent European proponent of increased North-to-South aid is former Prime Minister of Norway Gro Harlem Brundtland, who chaired the 1987 Commission on Environment and Development. "We continue to live in a world where abundance exists side by side with extreme need," she said in a May 1989 speech. Noting that Norway gives more than one per cent of its gross national product in official development assistance, and that the industrial countries average only 0.34 per cent (the United States gives 0.2 per cent), she called for "nothing short of a 'Marshall Plan' for the poorer nations." As part of this effort, she urged industrial countries to allocate 0.1 per cent of gross domestic product to an international fund for the atmosphere that would help finance technology transfer and reforestation projects in developing countries.

It could well be that the moment of political truth for North-South initiatives such as those urged here will be the June 1992 UN Conference on Environment and Development. In December 1989, the UN General Assembly resolved to mark the twentieth anniversary of its 1972 Stockholm Conference on the Human Environment by convening this event, to be held in Brazil. Governments of developing countries and others with a major role in drafting this resolution left little doubt that they see major North-South dimensions to both problem and solution. The resolution, for example, begins by noting that "the major cause of the continuing deterioration of the global environment is the unsustainable pattern of production and consumption, particularly in the industrialised countries," and that in the developing countries "poverty and environmental degradation are closely interrelated" and must be dealt with as essentially one issue. Accordingly, the resolution stresses that the burden of action rests most heavily on the industrial countries, which are most responsible for current problems and most able to finance remedial measures. To assist the developing countries in meeting their obligations, the resolution calls for consideration of "new and additional financial resources," "favorable access to environmentally sound technologies," and reduction of "serious external indebtedness ... in order to enable [debtor] countries to contribute fully." The process leading to the 1992 conference thus will present starkly the question of whether nations North and South are prepared to come to terms with each other in a "grand bargain" for environmental protection and economic progress.

"People and nations have always been willing to accord highest priority to meeting threats to their security," said Conference Secretary-General Maurice Strong, opening the first meeting of the Preparatory Committee. "In this case the security of our planet and our species is at risk. Surely this must be seen as the ultimate security risk which calls for the ultimate security alliance. It will clearly provide member states with an historic test of their political will and challenge the ingenuity, creativity, and diplomacy of all of those involved in the preparatory process." As Preparatory Committee Chairman Tommy Koh of Singapore remarked on the same occasion, "Time is running out. The 1992 Conference must produce more than words ... It should be possible to reach solid agreements, not mere declarations, for example, on climate change by 1992."

While key issues are beginning to surface in international discussions, there have not been many concrete changes. The international debt situation has not progressed significantly, nor has the scope of debt-for-nature swaps. In the United States, aid for developing countries seems, if anything, to be losing ground, while legitimate excitement about aiding the new democracies of Eastern Europe threatens to siphon off some existing assistance to developing countries. But there are two areas where constructive action by some industrial nations, particularly those in Western Europe, is under way: pollution taxes and increased financing to help developing countries deal with environmental problems.

Taxing pollution may be an idea whose time has come. Environmental taxes of one kind or another are levied in the Netherlands, Norway, France, Denmark, Finland, and Italy and are under consideration in Sweden, Belgium, West Germany, and the United Kingdom. In May, France levied a tax on sulfur dioxide emissions at the rate of $27 per ton. The two European countries with carbon taxes have fairly low tax rates, in part because other energy taxes are already high. For example, the Netherlands' carbon tax is designed to raise around $75 million a year, with coal taxed at $1.30 per ton and gasoline at 13 cents per 100 liters. The tax in Finland is set at $5 per ton of carbon.

Tax has been an unspeakable word in U.S. politics for a decade, but if the White House and Congress get serious about deficit-reduction, the case for pollution or energy taxes may look fairly compelling. House Ways and Means Committee Chairman Dan Rostenkowski led the way in March by holding hearings on long-term environmental strategy at which World Resources Institute researchers testified in favor of pollution taxes, particularly a carbon tax. The Congressional Budget Office estimates that such a tax would net $163 billion over five years if rates were set high enough to stabilize carbon dioxide emissions (that is, tax rates of around $28 per ton of carbon, which translates into $17 per ton of coal, $3.60 per barrel of oil, and $0.45 per thousand cubic feet of natural gas). The United States is already collecting windfall-profits taxes on CFCs and halons, expected to yield $4.5 billion over the next five years.

Financing environmental initiatives in developing countries looked to be making definite progress until early in May. In March, the United Nations Environment Programme (UNEP) unveiled a proposal that industrial nations provide $100 million to developing countries over the next three years to help them meet their obligations under the Montreal Protocol to protect the Earth's ozone layer. UNEP's concept of "fair burden sharing" is embodied in this proposed multilateral fund to make ozone-friendly technology available to developing countries. This question will be taken up when parties to the Montreal Protocol meet for the second time in London in June, and it may prove nearly as contentious as whether to strengthen the protocol by requiring phase-out of additional ozone-depleting chemicals.

Indeed, the funding question may be the most contentious issue in London if the Bush administration holds to the stance it took in early May, when it withdrew support for the fund. The *Washington Post* called this decision "a serious mistake," noting that the U.S. contribution to the fund—$25 million over three years—would be less than one per cent of the revenue raised by CFC taxes. U.S. Environmental Protection Agency (EPA) Administrator William K. Reilly, Secretary of State Baker, and other top State Department officials who support the fund were apparently overridden by White House Chief of Staff John Sununu and Budget Director Richard Darman. "They [Sununu and Darman] have simply abandoned all sense of proportion and judgement," opined the *New York Times*. "The considerable damage already done to the ozone layer has been caused by CFCs manufactured in the United States," The *Times* continued. "It's not too much to ask that Americans help less-developed countries avoid the same error." Without such new funding, significant holdouts to the ozone protection regime-including India and China, which together comprise more than one-third of the world's population—will have difficulty joining it.

UNEP Executive Director Mostafa Tolba, in a December 1989 conference in Cairo, made the best case for more North-to-South aid to deal with these related threats to the atmosphere :

> We must find the means... to facilitate increased technology transfer from North to South. Let us be quite clear. Unless developing nations are made privy to know-how and have easy access through subsidies, preferential loans or other means to acquire plant and equipment, we can forget about making any realistic preparations for an overheated world. If even only a handful of major industrializing nations press ahead with their fossil-fuel and CFC-based development plans with outmoded and outdated technologies, everything the wealthy nations do will be negated.

Earlier this year, the World Bank proposed creation of a global environment facility—a larger multilateral fund that would support developing countries' conservation initiatives on several fronts. Jointly sponsored by the World Bank, UNEP, and the UN Development Programme, this facility would begin as a three-year pilot project dispersing from about $300 to $400 million a year. The bank is most inclined toward projects that would protect the ozone layer, given the robust scientific consensus about what should be done. But the global environment facility also would address such challenges as greenhouse gas emissions, sustainable use of forests, contingency planning for marine oil spills, prevention and cleanup of toxic waste pollution in major international rivers, and debt-for-nature swaps to project habitats in biodiversity "hot spots." On the question of global warming, the bank awaits the outcome of the IPCC process. In

August, IPCC is expected to release an interim report on global warming, which will be reviewed at the Second World Climate Conference in November. Pending the outcome of this process and subsequent negotiations on a climate change convention, bank response strategies will remain tentative. Meanwhile, the bank might focus on projects that have dual benefits, such as adoption of cleaner fuels in the energy sector. Although there are many issues still to be resolved, if donors, developing countries, and others endorse the plan, it could be up and running by early next year. Again, U.S. opposition may prove to be the most serious stumbling block.

These efforts, though important, are nevertheless small compared to the global environmental deterioration that is now quite literally out of control. Countries must quickly develop better means to reach understandings and make mutual commitments that can sustain the Earth and its people. Fortunately, environmental concerns are steadily pushing nations to a sense of shared responsibility and common destiny that may soon be the most powerful force binding the world together.

Voices From the South

While governments and people of all walks of life acknowledge the urgent need to protect the global environment, the North and South are frequently at odds on how this must be accomplished. The often heated negotiations that led up to the United Nations Conference on Environment and Development (UNCED) in Rio de Janeiro in June, were no exception.

In forestry, for example, it is assumed that the natural forest is unproductive. It can be made more productive, "experts" say, by converting it to a single species that can serve as the raw material for industry. Forests that might be extremely useful ecologically and locally are of no use for industry. So genetically identical tree planations that destroy biodiversity are created. Throughout the 1980s, the World Bank pushed for monoculture as a better performing system of forestry than the actual forest. The Bank encouraged the planting of eucalyptus, which is a very good species for pulping and a hopeless species for conservation, because it destroys water and nutrient cycles. We've had major protests all over the world against such planting from local communities that have seen their streams disappear, their land grow infertile and their plant and animal life shrink.

Economic values have come to identify shrinkage of ecological diversity as growth. This is economics standings on its head. We need to put it back on its feet.

The only sustainable form of agriculture we have today is practised in parts of the Third World, in areas where the Green Revolution and chemical agriculture have not destroyed the environment. That's where communities still reward prudence rather than greed; where they reward conservation, rather than degradation. Here you have a pattern of production and consumption that could be universalized without the planet's life being totally destroyed.

The North always talks about transferring technology from North to South. But the Third World has systems of knowledge of science and technology, which we should start to respect. When a community in an extremely arid area is able to build an agricultural system that can do with very little water, we should recognize their conservation efforts, instead of calling their system primitive.

A good example is millet, which has been downgraded in the international agricultural system as a marginal or primitive cry. Yet millet is far more nutritious than wheat. It is also more diverse and water-prudent. But it grows very locally and so the food and taste habits linked to millet are very culturally specific. Huge corporations could not assume control overnight and develop consumer habits for millet like they could for white bread. So they downgraded millet production even though it is one the best crops for combating desertification. I think it's time the industrialized world recongnised that its economic paradigm in demanding too much from the earth.

The world is sick because we have forgotten to put people first. In the North, they talk of overpopulation, toxic waste, water and air pollution. And they have a right to do so. These are serious problems for the environment. But it's not the same in the South. You can't tell a poor rural woman to stop having children when she isn't sure how many of her children will survive. In developing countries, children are the only form of security a woman has. Poverty is the biggest cause of environmental degradation in the South. But until the North sees this as a problem, we will never see eye-to-eye.

If the North wants sustainable growth and a healthy planet, it has to learn to share responsibility for the world's problems. The North keeps telling the developing countries to take care of their own problems. They say, "it's not us who made you poor." I think the industrialized world could learn a lot from the South if people knew how much sweat went into the things they were consuming. I don't think many Americans, for example, realize the hazards African women go through so that they can have coffee, tea or cocoa.

The North must also recognize that it doesn't have all the answers to the world's problems. The industrialized countries look at the South as an empty body that needs knowledge put into it. They talk about the transfer of technology. But I think the North and South both could learn a lot from women who are putting their traditional knowledge to use.

In Africa, women have many talents, especially as managers. It takes a special model of conflict management, for example, to live in one room with your grandparents and other family members.

The poor women of Africa are the real farmers, the real custodians of the environment. But no one ever treats them like farmers. No one ever does anything to enhance the skills or development of these women. Women are rarely allowed to participate in policy-making.

The authorities should learn to encourage the talent, skills and traditional knowledge of rural women. We should have a mechanism of dialoguing with them, of allowing them to teach us what we don't know. There is a wealth of knowledge in developing countries and it should be used.

9

Towords a New Ecopolitical Order

Earth is the scene of constant change. The summits of the Jura Mountains in Switzerland, more than 1,500 meters above present sea level, are formed of limestone laid down as soft sediments in the bed of a warm and shallow sea about 175 million years ago. There were once forests in Antarctica and dinosaurs and ice sheets in English. As Alfred, Lord Tennyson wrote, "There where the long street roars has been the stillness of the central sea."

Such changes will always occur. Some of today's seas will be squeezed out of existence by the collision of continents to form new mountain ranges, as the Himalayas are being shaped by the collision of India and Asia. The Arctic ice may well expand again, providing the ultimate solution to the architectural problems of Europe and North America. Life forms will continue to evolve and drive their predecessors toward the extinction that is the ultimate fate of every species. On a longer time horizon as astronomer Fred Hoyle has put it, "we shall certainly be roasted" when the sun emerges from its present stable phase and expands to engulf and vaporize the Earth.

However, I am concerned with a more limited perspective. Throughout this article, I will use *tomorrow* to mean 40 years from now, in 2030, and the phrase *the day after tomorrow,* viewed through a haze of uncertainty and for that reason receiving less attention, as 40 years later, in 2070. I will address three simple question:

- What will three world be like as a habitat for life if present trends continue?
- What are the implications of these changes for humanity and for the world of nature?
- What can we do about it if we would like tomorrow to be different?

Throughout history, people have adapted perforce to the cycles of the changing Earth and, where those changes have proceeded slowly, have probably hardly noticed them. Even natural catastrophes, such as massive floods and volcanic eruptions like that of Mount Vesuvius in 78 and 79 B.C., though they left scars on the body of civilization had only a local impact on its progress. Such events doubtless caused our ancestors much suffering and social upheaval, but at least people were able of excuse themselves from responsibility, unless they chose to ascribe the disasters to the vengeful acts of a god irritated by human sin. In Java and Bali, the gods are still held responsible for volcanic eruptions. However, most of the major changes on the planet today are very much acts of humanity, and they result from the cumulative impact of two linked processes; the growth in human populations and the process that we call development.

Until the last 10,000 years, our species was a relatively uncommon animal, slowly increasing in numbers and extending its range to reach a total global population of about 500 million by 1000 A.D. The number of humans then doubled by around 1800, doubled again in the following century, and is now rising past 5.2 billion. This growth has been made possible by development, or the alteration of the Earth's environmental systems so that an increasing proportion of their nonliving resources and biological productivity serves human needs. As a result of development, some 40 pre cent of terrestrial plant productivity—the basic fixing of energy by the green mantle of the planet—is today used in one way or another by people. *Changes in ecological systems have an inevitable result of development.* Because we eat cereals and our livestock are grazers, much of our land has been deforested and converted into pasture or that highly modified grassland we call cereal cropland. To expand croplands, people around the world have greatly altered patterns of water flow, sometimes successfully in stable irrigation systems but often unsuccessfully, leading to salt accumulation and soil sterilization—which has now damaged some 60 million hectares worldwide, an area equivalent of two- thirds of China's cropland.

As agricultural methods became more dependable, people not directly involved in the business of subsistence were able to create objects and ideas that enriched the total community. Such craftsmen applied increasing skill to the use of nonliving resources in buildings, metal goods, and other artifacts and transformed areas of the physical environment with mines, quarries, and other structures. As people began to smelt metals, the movement of these elements through the biosphere inevitably increased, just as their agricultural and fuel burning habits increased the fluxes of carbon, nitrogen, and sulfur. Development, by permitting the dominance of our species, has inevitably altered the world both by the nature and the scale of the transformations involved.

In recent years, some so-called environmentalists in developed countries have spoken of development as if the world were dirty. That is nonsense, as the World Conservation Strategy, prepared in 1980 by the World Conservation Union (IUCN) in partnership with the World Wildlife Fund and the United Nations Environment Programme, makes plain. Development has been essential to the evolution and expansion of human civilizations, and more will be needed to help millions of people escape from today's poverty and squalor and to feed tomorrow's added billions. What we have to be concerned about is the nature and quality of development and the social and political structures needed to bring it about. It is clear from the destruction that has been the price of today's uneven and unsatisfactory development that the world cannot afford much more of the same. We need something different. To use today's catch-word, we need development that is sustainable—that is, it must not overcrop soil, pastures, forest, or fisheries or create products that spread from a beneficial activity, like industry, to blight other essential one, like agriculture, the supply of drinking water, or the stability of the world's ecosystems.

When we demand that development should be sustainable, we must be clear about our meaning. We do not mean that the growth in a human activity, such as the cultivation of new land, must be capable of indefinite extrapolation—little such growth will be. Rather, we mean that the changes we make in our environment must not only improve the yield of a useful product today but also go on supplying that product tomorrow, without side effects or unforeseen consequences that undermine other essential environmental functions. If overuse has such an impact, we may have to accept adjustment to a lower level of sustainable production. To quote the World Commission on Environment and Development, sustainable development means "meeting the needs of the present without jeopardizing the ability of future generations to meet their own needs." For IUCN, conservation means preserving the world's natural resource base as the indispensable foundation for the future.

As we look to the possibilities of sustainable development, we would be wise to remind ourselves of three *basic features of the Earth as a habitat.* First, the Earth is a rather small planet with finite resources, and it receives a *finite* amount of energy from the sun. Its living and nonliving systems have interacted over time to create the habitats within which humanity evolved. Interactions between living and nonliving elements still operate in a fashion that regulates the overall environment in a manner analogous to the *self-regulatory mechanism of a living being.* James Lovelock pointed this out when he named the planetary organism after the Greek goddess of the Earth. Hindu scholar Gaia had the same idea 2,000 years ago. *There can be no sustainable development that does not preserve that essential planetary system on which all life depends.*

Second, 70 *per cent of the Earth's surface is ocean, used only to a very limited extent by land animals.* Although the plants in the sea fix about as much carbon annually as do those on land, humans only take from the sea about 100 to 120 million tonnes of assorted fishery products annually. Although I expect that our descendants will cultivate more marine plants and animals in shallow waters, most of the human future is going to depend on how we use the land.

Third, land will remain highly *heterogeneous* as a habitat. People living in different regions cannot expect to enjoy anything approaching environmental equality. It will always be easier to live comfortably off the produce of the temperate zones like western Europe than off the arid sands of the desert or the dry grasslands of the savannas. The broad pattern of life on Earth will prevail tomorrow as well as today, even though the detailed ecological pattern within those biomes will change. Biological diversity is and will remain concentrated in the tropics. Therefore, the nations of the world cannot be made environmentally equal. This would be true even if national frontiers had been drawn in an environmentally logical way. Instead, many boundaries bisect natural units like river basins and make it difficult for governments to manage in an integrated way the resources that support their populations. The implication is that, if humanity is to have a sustainable future on this diverse planet with many environmental inequalities, it can only be through a process of international cooperation that transcends anything we see today. To state that is immediately to pose an immense challenge if we are to seek success in as short a time as 40 years. And we have to contend with certain trends arising from the nonsustainable nature of the current development process that aggravate our problems and are likely to prove unstoppable on a 40-year time scale. I am particularly concerned with six of these trends.

The first is population growth . I have already mentioned the dramatic increase in the world's population from around 1 billion people in 1800, to 2 billion in 1900, to over 5. 2 billion today. Although the rate of population growth has slowed somewhat from a peak of nearly 2 per cent per year in 1970 to round 1.66 per cent now, a cautious medium projection suggests that by 2030 there will be more than 8 billion people in the world and that our descendants will be lucky if, by 2070, stability has been achieved at around 10 billion. The trend is unstoppable because in many countries half the population is still under reproductive age. Even if these people only have two children per marriage, a near doubling is inevitable. Forty years from now, most of those people presently under 16 years of age will still be alive and their children will be between 10 and 35 years old— and some of them will themselves have children. Common sense tells us that not all people will limit their family size to two children per couple by 2030, and it will obviously require an immense change in attitude for this to happen by 2070. The total population achieved in a number of countries will depend on how many children survive, as well as on how many are born.

Today's population explosion is a tribute to the medical profession, which has greatly increased the average life expectancy in both developed and developing countries. Clearly, this advance could continue if the effectiveness of medicine is not undermined by malnutrition or social disorder and if new diseases do not appear suddenly to exploit the wonderful habitat represented by so much healthy human tissue. My own guess is that new diseases will indeed appear because the ecological niche is there for rapidly evolving viruses, which are likely to exploit the particular means of dispersal provided by human behavior—as AIDS has exploited the unique human habit of transferring blood from person to person, a parasite's dream. However, I doubt that new diseases will limit the growth of human populations, because I have great faith in the resilience' of medicine.

On the other hand, malnutrition will limit population growth in areas where water supplies are inadequate, the soil is overexploited, and there are no new reserves of fertile land. Agricultural science, along with medicine. has been a major supporter of population growth. But in large areas of Africa and parts of India, per capita food production has been declining recently even though total food production has been increasing. Countries with high population growth, limited rainfall, and a hot climate will be at risk until population increase is curbed by measures more humane than famine. It is important to look now at places where people are on a collision course with their environment because these are the places that need the most help. We have learned the lesson of the recurrent tragedy of famine from Ethiopia and parts of the Sahel. We have also learned that food and medical aid cannot do more than stave off such misery.

Moreover, people are understandably reluctant to sit still and starve. Now, as in the past, if populations really deplete their environmental resources regularly and over significant areas, they are likely to migrate, and finding a frontier here or a different government there is unlikely to deter them. As an increasing number of people come up against environmental limits, real threats to the peace and stability of nations may arise. The only alternative is to accelerate programs of sustainable development that meet human needs and, at the same time, provide the means and the *incentive for stabilizing human numbers*, country by country, in the areas of greatest risk. Clearly, these programs will require levels of international assistance beyond anything available today, and politicians in the countries concerned must recognize that population pressure is a genuine and urgent problem—something that a number of governments are presently reluctant to accept.

The second trend is deforestation, which, I suggest, is also unstoppable because of the need to feed more people, especially in the developing world. Moreover, I do not think it is honest to present all tropical deforestation as an environmental disaster. There are parts of the tropics—including areas of the Amazon basin—where conversion of forests to well-managed agriculture, particularly agroforestry, could be a perfectly acceptable pattern of development, though the governments concerned are fearful about the damage caused by present methods. Further deforestation in the tropical regions of South America, central Africa, and South-East Asia is virtually certain. The governments concerned should steer the process in the direction of sustainable agricultural systems, while halting destructive deforestation of areas that are especially valuable as reservoirs of biological diversity, that are essential to regulate local climate, or that protect the land from erosion. Looking beyond 2030 to 2070, my prediction is that the great forests of Earth will by then be concentrated in the boreal zone, in the more rugged uncultivable mountains of the tropics, and in tracts of sparsely populated tropical lowlands where the soils are poor, I also foresee significant but relatively small patches of natural forest in the temperate zones and in the densely populated and heavily utilized tropical lowlands. We may not like that pattern, but it is the one that I suspect our descendants will have to live with.

Another trend that is unstoppable is desertification or land degradation. I do not refer to the advance of the Saharan dunes but, rather, to erosive soil loss, salinization, and declining fertility as a result of poor or inadequate irrigation—which has, for example, affected some 60 per cent of the cropland in Pakistan. However, because of some good science in recent years, there are signs of a cure. In the Sahel, for example, food production has increased steadily over the past 20 years despite a lower average annual rainfall than in the preceding two decades. In Pakistan, measures to improve the quality of irrigation, to control salinization, and to plant crops that are resistant to salt are gaining ground. Accordingly, I do not expect the maps of the world to show more desert areas in 2030 than they do today, and by 2070 this phenomenon may have been brought under control or even reversed.

Fourth, I believe that the continuing loss of the planet's biological diversity is unavoidable. Before every conservationist starts jumping up and down and shouting, let me explain at once that I do not imply that destruction of biodiversity should continue at its present rate or that we should complacently accept this trend. We are, however, almost bound to lose a significant number of species from the Earth as a consequence of the development process impelled by the imperative of human need. Such loss is a logical necessity because, as I have said, it will be impossible to stop tropical deforestation. About 50 per cent of the species believed to exist on Earth are insects and other small organisms living in the canopies of tropical rain forests. A significant number of these species are bound to disappear if the forests are destroyed. Islands, which are also significant reservoirs of unique species, are vulnerable to invasion by mainland life forms, which are increasingly spread around the world by today's unparalleled ease of transport.

The question we have to ask ourselves—and it is one that wildlife conservationists understandably shirk—is whether these losses will matter. My own answer is yes, they do matter, especially to those who can afford to care. But we must not oversell the disaster. The losses matter if you believe that species other than our own have a right to exist as a part of natural creation. They matter if you believe that the rich diversity of life maintains the **equilibrium of Gaia**, the planet, in ways we do not fully understand and that reducing diversity brings risks we do not comprehend. The losses also matter because there may be many species and genotypes in the wild that are or could be of considerable value to humanity and that will act as the genetic basis for evolution in response to future change. Despite all this, a sense of proportion is needed. The United Kingdom, for example, supports about 1,700 species of vascular plant, 25,000 invertebrates, 12 reptiles and amphibians, 54 freshwater fish, 50 mammals, and 200 birds. This is an extremely impoverished biota by world standards, yet I think we would regard it as one that is able to maintain essential ecological functions—even though people would soon grumble if their diet was based only on what they could grow or gather there. I am not arguing for impoverishing all of the world's ecosystems to the extent. It is always better to maintain a system with the widest possible range of ecological functions and the greatest practicable reservoir of genotypes. But I suggest that some loss of biological diversity does not inevitably bring collapse. The problem is that we do not know how much loss of what kinds of organism is tolerable, figuring that out is one of real challenges to science.

My final two unstoppable trends are quite different from the others. Trend five concerns pollution. Some kinds of damaging pollution are unstoppable over a 40- year time scale because they are already present in the environment and cannot be eliminated by 2030. For instance, polychlorinated biphenyls and other persistent chlorinated organic substances are widely dispersed in the ocean and in biological food chains, even though the most damaging kinds are no longer produced. Even if the production of chlorofluorocarbons (CFCs), which are responsible for depleting ozone layer, ends by 2000, as many scientists wish, the persistence of these substances in the atmosphere is such that the ozone "hole" will not begin to fill in less than 40 years, and the ozone layer will not be fully restored even by 2070.

The buildup of greenhouse gases is also most unlikely to be stopped by 2030; at best, the upward trend in carbon dioxide emissions will have been slowed, CFCs will no longer be released, and emissions of other greenhouse gases will be limited. Thus, the sixth and last unstoppable trend is climate change. Because of the many greenhouse gases already emitted there is every reason to believe that by 2030 the world will be between 1° and 2° C warmer than it is now. Temperatures are likely to increase by more than this average in the higher latitudes of the Northern Hemisphere in winter, by slightly more than the global average in the temperate zones, and by slightly less than the global average in the tropics. Wet areas may get wetter, dry areas may get drier, and the force of storms may increase. By 2030, sea level may rise by 10 to 20 centimeters. As for the climate in 2070, much depends on how successful people are in curbing greenhouse-gas emissions. If they are not—if politicians drag their feet—then the world could be 2° to 4° C warmer, and sea level could rise 20 to 40 centimeters, posing severe risks to burgeoning human populations, especially those in the coastal zones of the tropics.

Because about half of the world's population lives in coastal zones, a 1-meter sea-level rise, which is greater than most experts consider likely, could spell disaster. Such a rise in Bangladesh would inundate nearly 15 per cent of the country and displace some 10 million people. In Guyana, 95 per cent of the population and 90 per cent of the agriculture are concentrated on a 3-mile-wide coastal strip that already stands near sea level and is protected only by slender barriers. The plight of fertile and densely populated deltas and low-lying coral atolls with most of their surface below the one-meter level is obvious.

Climate change also threatens the ways of life of many inland people. Each 1° C rise in temperature effectively displaces the limits of tolerance, or ranges, of species (including crops) by about 100 to 150 kilometers toward the poles or 150 meters vertically. Temperature changes may well prove less important than changes in amounts of rainfall, but these figures do demonstrate the kinds of dislocation that could occur. The disruption of natural systems would be aggravated because the shifts in limits of tolerance could occur much faster than species of trees and other dominant plants would be capable of matching through natural dispersion. The spectacle of trees being 'left behind' by their optimum habitats and, at the same time, ceasing to be able to maintain themselves by reproduction in considerable parts of their present range has been sketched out by many ecologists. The fact of the matter is, however, that scientists do not know how the world's living systems would respond to drastic change, and finding out is a major challenge that is only now being undertaken. There is little doubt that agriculturalists could help people grow new varieties of crops adaptable to the changed environment, but there would be considerable social stress nonetheless, especially if people had to change long-established dietary habits.

Why are these trends unstoppable over such a long time scale as 40 years? All six trends have two features in common. First, all are caused by the innumerable small actions of a very large number of people who do not see their actions as detrimental. Second, there is a substantial *lag time between cause and effect for each trend*. Let me prove my point by referring to one form of pollution I have not listed as unstoppable—acid rain. This phenomenon is stoppable because of two factors. First, the time lag between the emission of the sulfur as sulfur dioxide and its deposition as acid rain is quite short— only two or three days. Consequently, once emissions are reduced, acid depositions quickly decline, and the acidified ecosystems can begin to recover. Second, because the greatest proportion of the sulfur emissions come from a relatively small number of large point sources, specifically commercial power stations that burn coal, there is good reason to believe that by 2030 these sources can be cleaned up and acid rain will have been stopped.

However, the situation for greenhouse gases is quite different. CFCs enter the atmosphere from such products as leaky refrigerators, old-fashioned aerosol cans, industrial solvents, and the materials used to expand plastic insulating foam expand. The only solution here is to end CFC production and use in favor of less harmful substitutes. Even then, because of the 80- to 100-year residence time of CFCs in the atmosphere, the problems they cause will take decades to cure. Similarly, carbon dioxide, the principal greenhouse gas, is inevitably produced whenever forests are cleared or coal, oil, gas, or wood is burned in power stations, industrial heating plants, domestic stoves, or vehicles. Although carbon dioxide and other greenhouse gases, such as nitrous oxide and methane, which come from livestock, cultivation, fertilizers, and fuel combustion, do not have as long a residence time in the air as do the CFCs, the process of their absorption by green plants or by the oceans and freshwaters is not rapid. The greenhouse gas problem is intractable because of the multiplicity of sources, the fundamental importance of fuel burning and agriculture in human life, and the significant lead time between curative action and restorative effect.

Neither the causes nor the potential impacts of the trends are evenly spread throughout the world. In developed countries like those of Western Europe, population growth is not a problem (even if we might prefer less crowded conditions) and forest areas are actually increasing (although the species being planted are not those that naturalists or environmentalists would welcome most and may not be the most tolerant of climate change). Desertification is not a problem either, although soil loss and improper irrigation techniques can be problematic, and losses of biological diversity, though unwelcome, are not as heavy as in other parts of the world. However, all of these trends are grave concerns in the developing world. Rapid population growth is correlated with poverty and is, at the same time, an impediment to the economic growth that might end poverty and provide people with the means and the incentive to limit the size of their families. Moreover, the pollutants that threaten to perturb global climate, destroy stratospheric ozone, and accumulate in living systems come overwhelmingly from the developed countries of the Northern Hemisphere, and their spread imposes extra burdens on the nations experiencing the worst of the other trends. Put crudely, the poor are in a mess, and the rich are making that mess worse.

The solution to these problems, which are growing increasingly graver, does not lie in science or in technology, but in politics. Of course we need more and better science to understand the planetary systems more fully and to manage our use of them more wisely of course we need a better understanding of the factors that determine human behavior; of course we need better medicine, better agriculture, better forestry, more efficient use of energy, technology that produces essential products without generating intractable pollution, and products that are environmentally benign and that use scarce resources more economically. All of these are necessary, and much more as well. But the lesson of the recent decades is that scientific understanding and technological capacity are not the limiting factors. The *blockage lies in human perception and the willingness of people to change how they behave at the individual, group, and national levels.*

Many world leaders would reject a great deal of my argument, and some would say that it is a typical manifestation of the obstructive and negative thinking that prevails in developed countries, where fear of over-population, arguments against deforestation, demands for the conservation of biological diversity, and calls to halt the production and use of global pollutants are deliberate devices to hold back the development of the Third World and to maintain the present inequalities among nations. These leaders would argue that the real problem of the global environment is chronic poverty, which has been imposed and aggravated by the economic dominance of developed countries that grew rich by exploiting the raw materials of poorer countries and that continue to consume more than their fair share of those resources, to control commodity markets in favor of their own terms of trade, and to depress the growth of the Third World by issuing loans that benefit the lender far more than the recipient.

These arguments can be put eloquently and, indeed, at one level, are true. I am less sure that the environmental speeches of leaders of developed nations are dishonest and actually designed to supply justification for keeping the rich rich, the poor poor, and the latter dependent on the former. However, it does not matter whether such a view is true or false. What matters is that it exists, and this argument will be heard a lot more as the United Nations prepares for the 1992 World Conference on Environment and Development. If we are seriously concerned about the future of the world as a habitat, with the quality of life for the people of tomorrow, with the peace of the world, and with the stability of the global economic system, we have to face this gap in perception and the suspicion that goes with it.

Perhaps the first thing to do is to let facts about the world environment speak for themselves. This means openly sharing all available scientific knowledge and letting the professional community in each country evaluate the significance of those for itself. This is already happening to a considerable and increasing extent. There are internationally accepted compendia of environmental data, produced, notably, by the United Nations Environment Programme. There are many international bodies that bring together governments, nongovernmental organizations, and individual specialists from developing and industrialized countries. Some problems, such as climate change and ozone depletion, are accepted almost universally as serious and in need of concerted action. In both of these areas, the developing world wants and expects the developed countries to continue to share their knowledge; to help developing countries evaluate the unavoidable trends over the next 40 years; to take steps to reduce output of CFCs and greenhouse gases, which are already overtaxing the capacity of the environment and are leaving no room for development in the Third World; and to transfer alternative materials and technologies that will allow the Third World to develop without creating new environmental risks.

The costs of these four actions would all fall on the developed world. But is that unreasonable, when the causative agents of the ozone depletion and the greenhouse effect stem especially from the activities of developed nations? Unless the developed world shows itself willing to take these actions and shoulder a significant part of the costs, the credibility of its leaders as sincere advocates of action designed to benefit the whole world will be at stake. Any attempts by leaders of developed countries to sell the essential new technology at a profit or to transfer it on terms that add to the burden of debt that already hampers the capacity of the developing world to deal with other intense problems of sustainable development will be seen as proof of insincerity. Such attempts will make it more difficult to persuade the leaders o fthe Third World to treat the issues of population growth, deforestation, and loss of biological diversity with equal seriousness. Similarly, if the developing countries are going to conserve their biological diversity, promote sustainable use of forests and rangelands, and experience positive trends in economic and social conditions that will favor population stability, they will need money, which today is largely concentrated in the developed North.

Convincing world leaders that they must talk and think as one community is essential, but I fear that it is the easiest of the tasks that lie ahead. Indeed, it is already half accomplished. For whatever suspicions and accusations they have, the leaders of the world do talk about the importance of the environment and have done so with increasing frequency since the first United Nations Conference on the Human Environment, held at Stockholm in 1972. Indeed, given the burgeoning number of international bodies, the almost incessant conferences, and the more than 100 international conventions, agreements, and action plans that now deal with world environment it might be deduced that action was well in hand. The problem is, as one of my colleagues put it recently, that "thunderstorms of rhetoric are followed by droughts of inaction." Words are cheap and action plans are easy to put on paper. Because such agreements create the cozy, inexpensive illusion of a problem solved, they are dangerous.

How do we turn the words into actions? Clearly, each international agreement must be the culmination of a process thoroughly built from within each nation so that, in signing the convention or plan, the leaders concerned know that they express the will of their people and can commit themselves to putting the agreement into operation— either by acting within their own territory or by giving aid to other countries where the need is greatest. How can such a process be ensured? Within any particular country there are three components of certainty: a sound understanding of the problems and of the means to solve them; good organization and administration; and the backing of a well-informed, committed public. None of these components can succeed without the others. Unfortunately, in many nations, environmental concerns have been grasped slowly and addressed half-heartedly through governmental measures that often lag behind public awareness and will. For example, most governments that have created ministries to address the environment have added them as new sectorial entities alongside the older establishments that deal with agriculture, energy, industry, defense, and local government. Many environmental ministries have been used primarily to govern national parks and nature reserves. However, if the environment is actually the fundamental resource base on which all development rests, then surely it is proper to see it as a country's "natural capital"— to use a term that is now widely used among economists. In other words, the environment is real national wealth, as precious or more precious than the manmade wealth guarded by treasuries and analyzed by finance ministers in annual budgets.

Managing the environment as a national treasure would unite science, economics, and government in a new way. Science would be needed to understand both the potential of using the natural environmental capital for sustainable development and the sensitivity of the environment to various impacts; the techniques for doing this already exist. Economics is needed to place financial value on the resource and to convert the material income yielded by the environment into cash terms. Again, the techniques for more precise economic evaluation of environmental assets and for evaluating the true costs and benefits of alternative options for their development are now well advanced. Government is needed to define how the state's managerial system then proceeds to get best value for its money out of those resources. Government must also ensure that individual sectorial departments do not undermine the whole system by the pursuit of narrow and often traditional policies.

However successful such national plans may be and however enlightened government administrations may become (and I would add that I know of no government in the world that has yet structured itself to deal properly with environmental issues), nothing will be accomplished without the support of the governed. This fact seems obvious in terms of the six unstoppable trends. For example, experience in China suggests that it is difficult for even an authoritarian and determined state to bring population growth rapidly under control. The power of governments to control pollution, desertification, deforestation and human-induced climate change is obviously limited, and it is expressed only by altering the behavior of individuals through education, training, incentives, help, and deterence of those individuals who nonetheless insist on seeking their own ends, regardless of wider interests. In the end, the problem and the solution are matters of perception.

Our ancestors viewed environmental disasters as "acts of God" and either tolerated them or sought to prevent them by appeasing affronted deities. Today, we are prone to regard such disasters as something done by someone else, which another, "they", such as the authorities, must put right. Meanwhile, the chemicals we use, the gasoline we waste, the fumes we generate, the heat we let escape through poorly insulated walls and roofs, the litter we create, and the environmentally unfriendly pesticides we buy because they are cheap seem so trivial in proportion to the size to the problem that altering our behavior does not seem worth the effort—even if we can find alternatives to buy and places to send items for recycling. The perceived benefit is all too often of less value that the perceived cost. Yet, unless millions of people are helped, guided, and advised to alter their behavior, the unstoppable trends will not stop and the day after tomorrow will be dark.

There is some indication that the 1992 United Nations Conference on Environment and Development could be a scene of conflict between the leaders of developed and developing countries, fueled by self-interest and greed, for bigger slices of a finite cake. To avoid this disaster, all countries need to review and be prepared to adjust their strategies and policies so that the six unstoppable trends— and other apocalyptic horsemen— do not bring the roof down over our heads. We need to devote great effort to slowing or reversing the damaging trends, but real changes in direction are also needed if we are going to build a world in which humanity lives in enduring harmony with nature. Willingly, or perforce, many people face life-style changes, and many industries may face a smaller profit margin. But unless we begin to travel with hope we shall certainly never arrive, and unless we start quickly, we shall face regression rather than progress. Let us, therefore, begin to develop practical measures that will enlist the aid and inventiveness of all the world's peoples to make their contribution to tomorrow's world.

Towards a New World Order

While postmodern culture has contributed to the dissolution of all opposition to the latest and most rampant force for environmental destruction—global capitalism dominated by transnational corporations and financial institutions, and controlled by a new international bourgeoisie—it has exposed some of the most basic cultural structures on which Western European civilization in general and modernity in particular have been based. This has provided the conditions for a radical critique of Western civilization. However, despite the insights which have been gained, and despite some effort to develop a new political philosophy, those engaged in this critique, the poststructuralists, have not provided the means to come to terms with the situation confronting us. What is required is a new postmodernism which not only negates the cultural forms of modernity, but which can replace these forms. The development of postmodern science based on process philosophy, a philosophy which supports poststructuralist or postmodernist attacks on the reification of abstract entities, could provide the foundation for such a cultural movement.

But it is not enough to defend a new cosmology in opposition to the cosmology which has underpinned modernity. It is necessary to articulate this in such a way that it can effectively challenge the hegemonic culture, so that it can orient people in practice, in their daily lives, to create an environmentally sustainable civilization. To do this it will be necessary to construct a new grand narrative, a grand narrative formulated in terms of the cosmology based on a philosophy of process.

One of the consequences of the postmodern loss of faith in grand narratives, and all narratives to some extent, is to have revealed the importance of narratives for the constitution of subjects, social organisations and societies. It has shown how we only know what to do when we know what story or stories we find ourselves a part of. If this is the case, then to know what to do about the environmental crisis requires the creation of stories which individuals can take up and participate in, which will reveal to them why there are the problems there are and how they arose, how they can be resolved and what role individuals can play in resolving them. The bio-regional narratives called for by Cheney are important in this regard; but given the way the world-economy functions, more is required. What is clearly lacking are stories of sufficient power and complexity to orient people for effective action to overcome environmental problems, to relate the multiplicity of social and cultural forms implicated in or affected by environmental destruction, to reveal what possibilities there are for transforming these and to reveal to people what roles they can play in this project. Environmental problems are global problems and their causes are global; it will be impossible for stories to effectively orient individuals for effective action to overcome these problems unless the stories pertaining to people's individual lives and to local problems can be integrated with broader narratives, and ultimately with a grand narrative revealing the relationship between the lives of individuals and the dynamics of the global political and economic order.

In order for such stories to 'work', to inspire people to take them seriously, to define their lives in terms of them and to live accordingly, such stories must be able to confront and interpret the stories by which people are at present defining themselves and choosing how to live in an environmentally destructive way. It is also important to reveal the way power operates, and show why those individuals who are concerned about the global environmental crisis are unable effectively to relate their own lives to such problems. The new grand narrative must enable people to understand the relationship between the stories through which they define themselves as individuals and the stories by which groups constitute themselves and define their goals, ranging from families, local communities, organisations and discursive formations, to nations, international organizations and humanity as a whole. Quite apart from the need to relate individuals to the dynamics of the world economy, a new grand narrative is required to comprehend and reveal the inadequacies of the grand narratives which have dominated societies in the past, and which are still operative in the present.

While it can be acknowledged that all previous grand narratives were oppressive, this can be avoided. Past grand narratives were essentially 'monological', narratives in which all participants were subordinated to the rule of one, non-reflexive perspective. However Mikhail Bakhtin has identified a second kind of narrative, a polyphonic, dialogical narrative in which a multiplicity of perspectives are represented, where through dialogue the narrative reflects on its own development and, as Julia Kristeva put it, 'constructs itself through a process of destructive genesis'. A polyphonic grand narrative in the form of a dialogic discourse could take into account the diversity of cultures and multiplicity of local stories by which humanity has formed and is forming itself, and allow that any totalizing perspective utilized to give coherence to the narrative must only be accepted provisionally, that it has rivals and that it is always possible that in the future some better alternative might be developed.

What gives coherence to narratives is the interpretations of the world on which they are based. Even the simplest stories assume one or more relatively coherent ways of interpreting the world, of defining the possible relationships between people and between humans and nature. The evaluations of what futures are possible and what futures are most worth realizing are tied up with such ways of interpreting the world. Grand narratives have always embodied a cosmology, a conception of the nature of humanity and the place of humanity in the cosmos. The grand narratives which have dominated European civilization, which have conceived of history as progress towards some final catastrophe which will inaugurate an ideal future state, or as the education of humankind and the advance of reason, or as the liberation of humanity from bondage or as the domination of nature through technology, embody the cosmology formed through the synthesis in Ancient Rome of neo-Platonic philosophy and Hebraic religious thought. The grand narratives dominating modernity embody the transmutations of this cosmology which was effected in the seventeenth, eighteenth and nineteenth centuries with the rise of modern science. The orthodox formulation of Marxism is a grand narrative which embodies a radicalised versions of the cosmology of Christian neo-Platonism—and is only a modification of the dominant grand narrative of progressive domination of nature. It is by virtue of the cosmologies of neo-Platonic Christianity and mechanistic materialism and the basic assumptions about the nature of existence on which these are based that it has been possible to construct the complex order of narratives which have constituted European civilization. While it is these interpretations which must be challenged, this is only possible through the construction of a new complex of narratives, integrated into a grand narrative founded on an alternative cosmology.

As an alternative cosmology, a philosophy of process gives a place to beings who partially create themselves by constructing narratives, and provides a way of interpreting the world on the basis of which new, polyphonic, environmentally sensitive narratives can be constructed. The two dimensions of the problem are solved together. Science based on mechanistic materialism lent itself to being identified with technology and its development. Its central problem was that while serving as an instrument for dominating the world, it made agency inconceivable, and finally reduced people themselves to things to be controlled. While it has permeated social life through the narratives of technological advance which have been formulated in terms of it, it has made it impossible to account for the way people are able to create themselves as human beings through constructing narratives. Conceiving of the world as a process of creative becoming consisting of a multiplicity of different types of processes in various complex relations, each making its own unique contribution to the becoming of the world, which must be understood at least to some extent as an immanent cause of its own becoming, can allow that humans create themselves through culture, and in particular, through being enacted by, reformulating and then enacting stories about themselves and their place in the world. It can allow for people having intentions formulated in relation to the stories by which they define themselves, and through realizing these intentions, coming to embody within the world, in the relationships between people, in the relationships between individuals and society and in the relationships between humans and nature, the interpretations of the world on which these stories are based. With its rejection of reductionism, it lends itself to being formulated into a dialogical rather than a monological grand narrative, and thereby enables the achievements of all communities, societies and civilizations of the world to be appreciated.

Once the world is conceived of as a creative process of becoming, the notion that the meaning of anything is given by the end which it helps to realize, the notion which as Nietzsche pointed out is the ultimate source of the nihilism of European civilization, can be abandoned. Each individual process or sub-process within the universe is like a melody singing itself within a symphony. While it must be evaluated in terms of its contribution to the whole symphony (which in the case of the cosmos is never complete), a symphony cannot be evaluated in terms of its final outcome, its end. The whole duration of a symphony matters, and each melody within the symphony, each note within the melody, are significant in themselves as parts of this duration. People understanding the world and themselves in such terms should be able to appreciate processes ranging from atoms, molecules, clusters of galaxies, galaxies, stars, planets, global eco-systems and species, to individual organisms, societies and cultures, as having an intrinsic significance as contributions to the unfinished becoming of the world. They should be able to appreciate the significance of their own lives and each decision and action as contributions to the world as a whole as well as to the cultures, societies and ecosystems of which they are part. But they should also be able to appreciate the intrinsic significance of their own lives as such, and that part of the significance of cultures, societies and eco-systems and the world as a whole is as conditional causes of their own becoming, for having made it possible for them to live an intrinsically significant life.

Formulating stories about the lives of people and the history of societies in these terms will enable people to be understood in the context of and as part of nature, as destructive or constructive contributions to the eco-systems which sustain the conditions of their existence. However, such narratives must have a more complex form than the narratives which have dominated European civilization in the past—and must abandon the Oedipal form of narrative which legitimates present suffering as the unavoidable path to some final reunification of the world. Since the world is conceived of as consisting of a multiplicity of processes and subprocesses, each partially autonomous yet inseparable from a multiplicity of other processes which are the conditional causes of its existence, it is impossible to accept a linear narrative in which all but the history of the main subject is treated as a passive background of the drama. For any individual, whether this be a person, an institution, a movement, a class, a nation, a civilization or humanity as a whole, what is required is a multi-dimensional narrative at least acknowledging thousands of different temporal and spatial orders, both within the becoming of humanity and within the rest of nature. Such a narrative should then highlight the way the becoming of any individual is promoting or stultifying other processes.

Conceiving of narratives in this way would avoid the tendency noted by poststructuralists of reducing people differentiated from the protagonists of a story to the 'Other'. For instance, it would avoid the tendency of history to focus on the rise of Western civilization and to deny a story to societies subjugated by it, those whom Eric Wolfe described as the 'people without history', to characterize 'women' and Orientals not in terms of their unique histories, but only in opposition to or as a counterpart to the history made by males of European descent. This does not mean that a history of humanity should not grant a central place to the rise and world domination of Western civilization; but rather than conceiving of this as progress, it should be understood as analogous to the situation in China in the third century BC. The Ch'in, founded on the mechanistic philosophy of Legalism, had by their ruthless aggressiveness ended the period of the warring states by unifying China under an extremely oppressive social order. Western civilization has through its ruthless aggressiveness united the world into one economic system. In ancient China the Ch'in were overthrown and replaced by a much more benign rule inspired by the philosophies of Confucianism and Taoism. What is required of a new grand narrative is an account of how we arrived at the present global environmental crisis, and a characterization of the challenge now confronting humanity as the replacement of the oppressive and destructive civilization which has united the world by a new global civilization based on a more adequate world-orientation in which nature, the oppressed, non-Europeans and women throughout the world are accorded due recognition.

Lyotard argued that even if a new grand narrative were formulated, there is no reason to assume that people will accept it. To begin with, this is certain to be the case. Postmodern culture is so fragmented and fragmenting that to get a new grand narrative taken seriously is far more difficult than was the case when people at least accepted the need for some grand narrative. People defining themselves and orienting their lives through a new grand narrative will be like the Christians in the last years of the Roman Empire described by St. Augustine, strangers in the societies in which they must live their everyday lives. But like these Christians, those adhering to the new narrative must become the seeds which will crystallize a new post-European civilization. Given the immediate threat to the global environment, it is not enough for those adopting the new narrative to withdraw into monasteries to wait for the collapse and total disintegration of the present order, as Alasdair MacIntyre suggested in *After Virtue*. It will be necessary to begin to build this new civilization while the old civilization, despite its nihilism and the fragmentation of its culture, is still vigorous and powerful; more powerful than any civilisation which has ever existed. For a new grand narrative to be efficacious under these circumstances it must be articulated so as to be able to inform political action. But this raises the question of what kind of political action can be efficacious in a postmodern world ?—a world in which discursive formations are proliferating and augmenting their own power at the expense of individuals and in which the global economy now transcends the reach of even the most powerful states ? My contention is that it will be necessary to develop an environmentalist form of nationalism to subordinate the discursive formations which are dominating people's lives, to counter the power of global capitalism, and to move large numbers of people to action. That is, it will be necessary to reconstruct narratives about regions which will enable all members of this region to identify themselves as participant agents committed to conserving and preserving the environment of their region. Then to articulate this, to provide the basis for decision-making, it will be necessary to develop a science of humanity which can analyse the complex power relations between social, political and economic processes and provide an alternative to the mainstream social sciences, particularly economic theories, as a basis for formulating policies and programmes of action.

Postmodern culture has been profoundly anti-nationalistic. The theoretical opposition to nationalism, utilizing poststructuralist philosophy, has come from 'subaltern historian', that is, historians of the Indian subaltern classes. The consequences of this are now with us. Anti-nationalism has enabled the New Right to break down efforts to control national economies, and because of the success of the New Right in the 1980s, the world is now facing the most severe depression since the 1930s. As in the depression of the 1930s, the extreme right has been granted almost exclusive rights to the banner of nationalism. This has facilitated the rise of racist, fascist political parties throughout the world. The only alternative offered to this racism and to the ethnic violence associated with the breakup of the communist countries of Eastern Europe and the Balkans has been a vapid internationalism.

While environmental problems require a global orientation, and while the development of institutions to represent and foster such an orientation is an essential part of the environmentalist struggle, in a world in which even most national governments in the economic centres have failed effectively to confront their own environmental problems it is hardly likely that actions taken by international organisations will have much success unless backed by strong local organisations. The struggle against global environmental problems is only likely to succeed through the development of strong nation-states committed to subordinating the operations of the market to politically defined ends—notably the conservation and preservation of the environment, and which can effectively represent local environmental concerns within broader regional and international organisations. To be successful, environmentalist will have to struggle for representation of the environment in both national and regional politics, and then use the environment as a focus to mobilize people to liberate themselves from the destructive imperatives of the world economy. What is required is an environmentalist nationalism which can harness the legitimate anger against global capitalism to carry out the massive transformations necessary to create an environmentally sustainable civilization.

At the same time, the promotion of nationalism is required to recreate the sense of community and personal identity, to overcome the fragmentation of postmodern culture which is undermining any concerted opposition to existing trends. In the modern world, radical political movements, including Marxist movements, have only ever been successful where they have been more or less explicitly fused with local cultural traditions as nationalist movements, and nationalism has been central to the struggles of every other country which has been at all successful in overcoming its subjugation by the world-market. As Dudley Seers argued in *The Political Economy of Nationalism*, only by cultivating nationalist sentiments will it possible to mobilize people to bear the costs of the struggle for regional control over economic life, to generate concern by people for justice for their compatriots, to inspire them to develop forms of life which conserve resources and to develop institutions powerful enough to tackle broader environmental problems. Only through nationalistic struggles has the hold of the consumer-oriented culture of the economic cores been broken, forms of relationships between people transcending commodity fetishism been developed, the organizational basis and the cultural conditions for confronting the long-term problems associated with the environment created and the possibility of transcending capitalism altogether revealed.The point is that except for professional intellectuals, pure cosmopolitanism is too rarefield an orientation in the struggle for justice. Most people need to feel that they will be recognized and taken into account at a more immediate level before they will define their own lives in terms of the struggle for justice.

Nationalism must continue to be fostered in the Third World. Environmental limitations have exposed the illusion that present hardships in the Third World are just stages on the way to affluence and that it is possible for everyone in the world to live the lifestyles of people in the affluent North. They have revealed the cost to peripheral nations integrating into the world-economy to be the loss of their reserves and the destruction of their resources. Those people who have overcome their poverty have been those who have relied on their own efforts. As Denis Goulet argued on the basis of a study of strategies for development in Guinea-Bissau: 'Paradoxically, the lesson of greatest importance is that the best model of development is the one that any society forges for itself on the anvil of its own specific conditions. So, as James Lamb argued:

> Development should be a *struggle* to create criteria, goals, and means for self-liberation from misery, inequity, and dependency in all forms. Crucially, it should be the process a people choose,

which heals them from historical trauma, and enables them to achieve a newness on their own terms.

This has been the secret of the success of Kerala in India and Zimbabwe in Africa. For the sake of humanity Third World people should recognize this, and struggle through local, national and regional organisations to preserve their environments from exploitation by the economic core regions. Given the location of most environmental destruction in the Third World, this struggle for liberation should be recognized as the most important struggle for the preservation of the world environment.

The primary goal of environmentalists in the affluent core economies should be the termination or radical reduction of the economic links between their countries and Third World economies, an end to the exploitation of Third World reserves and resources, an end to the importation of agricultural products and timber and an end to interference in governments or support for oppressive governments in the Third World. What is needed is action by states and other political organizations to break up the power of transnational corporations and international finance, and most importantly, to reduce the voracious appetite for materials by the core zones. As Stephen Bunker argued: 'Ultimately the need is to slow the flow of energy to the world centre. But this struggle should not be thought of in purely altruistic terms. It should be seen as part of and linked to the struggle to stop the bankrupting of farmers and the deindustrialization and associated unemployment and subsequent impoverishment of people in these core zones. For all regions of the world, to avoid exploitation, to escape the vicissitudes and pressures of the international capitalist system and to gain democratic control over their economies, to turn the advantages of improved technology to bettering the conditions of life, as far as is possible regions should aim at economic self-sufficiency. As John Maynard Keynes argued in 1933: 'Ideas, knowledge, science, hospitality, travel—these are the things which should of their nature be international. But let goods be homespun whenever it is reasonably and conveniently possible, and above all, let finance be primarily national.' With recent developments in technology, such localization of production is now more possible for most goods than ever. The task ahead of people in the economic core zones and semi-peripheries is to escape their enslavement from the dynamics of the international capitalist order, to create steady-state economies for their own benefit, for the benefit of people in the Third World, for the benefit of all future generations and for the benefit of all other forms of life. The most potent ideological weapon in the struggle for such economic and political autonomy is nationalism.

Nations as Narratively Constituted Imaginary Communities

It would appear then that the liberation of life will be achieved through the development of a reformulated nationalism or it will not be achieved at all. But in the past nationalism has been linked with imperialism, wars of aggression and the persecution of minorities. So just what is nationalism? How does it mobilize people ? And are its destructive tendencies inevitable? Nationalism is essentially ' a territorial ideology', while modern states are territorial political institutions. Nations are both cultural and political phenomena. As Benedict Anderson has argued, the nation is 'an imagined political community' which is created through being imagined. The type of imagination which made nationalism possible was created by the rise of the novel and the newspaper, allowing, for an 'anonymous' community with members conducting their affairs simultaneously, yet independently and without awareness of what other members are doing. In the modern world, nationalism, affirming the community of people in a region despite the fact that only a very small proportion of these people know each other personally, provides people with an identity as part of this community. It relates both to the traditions of the people in a region, and to the future, the common destiny of these people. In short, nationalism situates people as part of an unfinished story of the people of a region.

Nationalism serves to coordinate people's actions and lives, to mobilize them for action, and to legitimate the institutions of the state—at least insofar as the state represents the nation. It serves the state by strengthening the institutional relationships between the state and civil society, by furthering the internal unification of culturally and economically diverse regions into a more homogenous state territory, determining the geographical boundaries of the state and dividing one political community from another accordingly. Conversely, by affirming the existence of community, nationalism legitimates demands that the state itself be just and that it put to rights injustices perpetrated against its members, that is, that the state properly represent all members of the nation. As John Breuilly argued on the basis of his exhaustive examination of the history of nationalism: 'an effective nationalism develops where it makes political sense for an opposition to the government to claim to represent the nation against the present state.'

Nationalism has taken a variety of forms. To begin with, nationalism emerged in Spain, England and France as the merchant classes of these societies struggled for political representation in the new absolutist states which had emerged from the late feudal kingdoms. While this nationalism developed through the cultural unity engendered by the development of new print-languages, culture was not an issue in its development, and the nations involved were assumed to correspond to the territorial boundaries of the state. Such nationalism was identified with the democratization of government. The growth in power of England and France was a stimulus for the development of two other forms of the European nationalism—the separationist nationalism of the Irish, of Belgium and Norway, and the unificationist nationalism of Itlay, Germany and Poland. In each of these cases the promotion of national cultures was central and preceded the emergence of national states. Outside Europe, nationalism first developed among European colonies in the struggles for independence, then a 'reform' nationalism developed in countries threatened by European imperialism, notably in Japan, Turkey and China. Towards the end of the nineteenth century and culminating in the Second World War, European nationalism was extended to include the working class in the community of the nation, but at the same time, at least among the major powers, it became more authoritarian and expansionist. It came to be associated with a rejection of the right of every nation of political self-determination and independence and the assertion of the privileged position of one's own nation—the 'chosen nation'. However, there were other European states in which a new reform nationalism developed to mobilize people against the vicissitudes of the world capitalist economy without his chauvinist quality. Such reform nationalism, associated with the development of the social or liberal corporate states, became increasingly influential among small European nations after the Second World War. There also emerged at this time a post-colonialist nationalism in the Third World, in some cases serving to unify inherited political divisions, in others to separate regions from inherited state structures or to combine regions across state boundaries. Finally, a new set of nationalist movements have emerged within Europe striving for independence from old states, for instance in Scotland, Flanders, Croatia and Estonia.

While the fostering of nationalism has led to greater justice and vast improvements in the quality of life of those who are united by it, it is undeniable that nationalism is associated with tendencies to deny justice to racial minorities and outsiders. Morishima wrote of the Japanese:

> there are two quite different yardsticks governing the behaviour of the Japanese, one applied to those within one's own circle, and another applied to those outside it. In this sense neither have the Japanese been logical, nor have they shown any sensibility towards the precepts of universal justice.

This seems to be typical of nationalist societies, and such double standards have been responsible for some of the most devastating wars and persecutions the world has known. It is these destructive tendencies of nationalism which have been used to justify the claim of cosmopolitan intellectuals that nationalism is essentially pathological. But are double standards and their consequences inevitable ? Benedict Anderson has argued that they are not. He reminds us that far from being a concomitant of nationalism, racism is a throwback to notions of class. As he put it:

> The fact of the matter is that nationalism thinks in terms of historical destinies, while racism dreams of eternal contaminations, transmitted from the origins of time through an endless sequence of loathsome copulations: outside history... The dreams of racism actually have their origin in ideologies of class, rather than in those of nation: above all in claims to divinity among rulers and to 'blue' or 'white' blood and 'breeding' among aristocracies.

The ideology of nationalism is more consistent with quest for universal justice. One case which illustrates this relationship is the nationalism promoted in the 1930s in Sweden.

Up until the 1930s, Sweden was dominated by the export-oriented fraction of the bourgeoisie. This group was defeated during the Great Depression when the workers, in alliance with farmers' interest groups and manufacturers producing for the home market, gained power. This alliance recast Swedish political culture through the concept of 'peoples' home' (*folkshemspolitik*). Göran Therborn described the role of this concept:

> The Peoples' Home had an implicit connotation of 'family'—rather than 'house'—of family community and equality with 'no favourites or stepchildren'. It connoted common concern and caring for each other and had its focus on society rather than on the state and particular institutions.

This universalism transcended the notion of individuals' social rights, and replaced it with a *Weltanschauung* of national solidarity. In accordance with this, Alva Myrdal presented the case for social security not as a question of social insurance, but as a question 'of social policy, as a productive social policy—as common investment by the nation in its future welfare—with its accentuation of family policy and of preventative measures.'

It is notable that the Swedes defined their ideals in terms of a conception of people as essentially creative social beings rather than as consumers. The Social Democratic Party did not formulate the goal of equality in utilitarian terms, but as equal freedom for people to shape their future, 'to develop their inherent talents and fully express themselves in society.' This enabled them to create the most egalitarian society of the modern world. Correspondingly, the Swedes more consistently and successfully addressed environmental problems than virtually any other nation (although most of their environmental problems had causes outside Sweden), and despite their cold climate, they used only one half as much energy per head of population as people in the USA.

Such reform nationalism has been emulated by a number of countries since the Second World War in their efforts to mobilize against the vicissitudes of the international economy. And it would seem that it is a suitable model for at least small core or semi-peripheral nations. However, Partha Chatterjee has condemned nationalism in the colonial world as a foreign doctrine that has facilitated the emergence of Western-oriented elites. To avoid such tendencies, a new kind of nationalism is required. It is necessary to develop a multi-levelled nationalism, one in which extended nationalisms are developed to unite weaker states against the state of the economic core zones and the global economy, so relieving the pressure to exploit sub-regions, while simultaneously sub-nationalisms are developed in sub-regions of states to gain or regain local control over their administration.

In relation to major regions of the world, the role of the black African block in opposing South Africa, the Islamic block in opposing international imperialism, the European Economic Community in moving against the domination of the world politico-economic order by the USA, and the Latin American block in supporting Argentina during the Falklands/ Malvinas war, suggest the increasing role that an extended form of nationalism might play in the resistance to domination and exploitation and in the promotion of justice within these regions. This is likely to be important in the near future for South America, since it is only by following the sort of advice given by Jacobo Schatan—to collectively refuse to recognise that part of its debt deriving from the rise in interest rates and the decline in the prices of its resources—that the present debt crisis will ever be resolved. This will require unity on the part of all Latin America against US bankers and their representatives in the US government if it is to be successful.

At a local level, the sense of community promoted within the 3,000 communes, 192 districts and 22 cantons of Switzerland illustrates the role local or sub-nationalism can play. Through a commercial code which allows companies to choose their shareholders, set limits to the number of shares held by any one shareholder and to refuse to register shares, the Swiss have been table to prevent the takeover of their companies by outsiders and to ensure that shareholders are in a weak position relative to 'stakeholders'—bondholders, employees, customers, suppliers and members of the local community. This has enabled cantons as moral communities to take responsibility for their members in a way which has virtually eliminated poverty and unemployment, and prevented the enforced migration of people to the major cities. Switzerland is virtually free of the large regional divisions in prosperity which afflict most capitalist countries, particularly Great Britain, the USA and Italy. Associated with this subordination of the economy to the community, there is minimal private conspicuous consumption (at least compared to the United States) which, along with the greater decentralization of the population, has resulted in a rate of consumption of energy per head of population one-third of that within the USA, despite their higher standard of living.

Nationalism and Cosmology: Postmodern Nationalism

The question is then, how can a form of nationalism be promoted which mobilizes people to preserve and conserve their environments and to accord with the struggle for international justice, rather than to expand their economies, and without the tendencey towards racism, ethnic violence and militarism? As we have seen, the development of nationalism first requires a struggle for the cultural independence and the development of a sense of cultural identity in the regions in which people live. For this reason Dudley Seers argued for the development of national cultures. To this end he called for education in the traditional arts subjects, arguing that 'the centre-piece of education is history, the history of the nation *in relation to its continent and the world,* ranging right up to the present.' And he argued for the importance of 'making people familiar with their nation's cultural heritage—myths, fables, songs, dances, carvings and sculpture, buildings, etc.—which expresses national experience and can help inhibit the growth of cultural dependence.' These are important. But such an education by itself is too passive. There is no reason to suppose that the culture of any region will be adequate in its existing form for what is an on-going dialogue so that they can become critical participants in the formulation of the story of the nation of which they are part and define their own lives in terms of participation in this story, and to achieve this it is necessary to see cultural development and nationalism in terms of a theory of culture, a cosmology and a general philosophy.

The philosophy of process provides this perspective. The culture of a region can be seen as part of the process of a people's self-creation, part of their on-going struggle (with varying degrees of success) to orient themselves, practically and theoretically, in relation to nature, to each other, to their society and to outsiders; to recognize and appreciate nature's, their own and each other's significance and potentialities, and to work towards realizing these potentialities. At the same time each culture can be seen as a contribution to life and to the culture of humanity, as part of humanity's and the world's self-creation. All such self-creation is genuine creation, not entirely determined by past and present conditions, and yet is dependent on its environmental and material conditions, including the cultures of others in the past and in the present. By highlighting the point that only through some cultural diversity is it possible for unique situations to be appreciated, different possibilities explored and the limitations of each culture revealed, this conception of culture enables the unique significance of one's local culture and all its sub-cultures (and the members of one's society bearing and developing this culture) to be better appreciated, while at the same time providing a critical perspective on this and all other cultures, allowing individuals to assimilate aspects of other cultures to their own culture. By seeing this cultural development in terms of the new cosmology, this struggle for national independence can be seen as a struggle within nature, as part of the world's struggling to become conscious of itself in all its diversity and to reveal and realize its potentialities. The study of the local environment is part of the development of culture, and by fostering a recognition of the relationship of society to its environment in the past, present and future, nationalism can be fused with the commitment to conserving and preserving the integrity of this environment.

Nationalism can then be redefined as the commitment by a regional community, through the stories by which it defines itself, to justice within the region, where justice is understood as the appropriate recognition and acknowledgement of all beings—individuals, communities, animals and eco-systems, in thought and action. It is the commitment to preserving and developing the potentialities of beings—natural, cultural, social and individuals—for survival, for a full life and for contributing to society, to humanity, to local and world culture and to life itself. Above all, as the ultimate condition of all potentialities, nationalism must involve a commitment to preserving and conserving the local environment, its fertility, the genetic diversity of its fauna and flora, the integrity of the eco-systems which maintain these and its mineral reserves; and to preserving and developing built-up environments which provide the conditions for the maintenance and development of local culture, society and its individual members.

By providing a way of thinking about one's place in the world which neither atomizes the world nor dissolves each part into the totality, the new cosmology makes it possible to formulate a multi-levelled nationalism, to acknowledge the significance and partial autonomy of the community of one's local region while seeing this as participating in a national community which itself has a partial autonomy, which is in turn participating in a broader regional community with some partial autonomy (such as South America or Western Europe), which again is participating in a world communities which is more than the sum of all the particular communities which compose it. Individuals can then be simultaneously nationalistic in relation to their local region, to their country and to a major region of the world, while at the same time being committed to international justice and to the subordination of national interests to the interests of humanity and to non-human life where appropriate. The question then is one of justice, of appropriately acknowledging the uniqueness and significance of each level of the communities of which people are part.

Nations can then be evaluated according to their generativity or decadence, according to whether or not their members are willing and able to realize their highest ends or are 'falling away' from these ends; that is, whether they are participating creatively rather than destructively in the becoming of the world, whether they are producing rather than undermining the conditions for the becoming of other people, other societies and other life forms. The prime duty of governments must then be seen as striving to preserve and develop the potentialities of the society—its members, its organizations and its environment—to participate creatively in the becoming of the world, and any government which is not striving for this must be regarded as corrupt. Environmental nationalism must then be seen as the struggle to maintain, to transform or to create power structures, from the local to the international level, which appropriately recognize the people of a region, their future generations, non-human forms of life and the general environment, which effectively articulate the needs, concerns, potentialities and aspirations of these people, whatever their race or ethnic origins, and which at least strive for the conditions for generativity.

Policy Formation and Political Economy and the Social Sciences

Even when people are mobilized by a commitment to justice they are unlikely to have much impact unless they can formulate clear social, political and economic policies and programmes. One of the most important requirements for translating nationalist sentiments into effective action to create a new, environmentally sustainable social order is the means systematically to formulate such policies and programmes. At present, government policies and programmes are overwhelmingly formulated on the basis of neo-classical economic theory, in which the economy is treated as a closed system, driven by greed, tending towards equilibrium, and in which nature is treated as nothing but a passive resource. Evaluation is generally based on some version of cost-benefit analysis. Cost-benefit analyses, extending the logic of commodity fetishism, assume that the world can be understood as a collection of actual or possible states of affairs and events which can be evaluated by measuring people's preferences. Such analyses cannot take into account the complex interdependencies of the world, and replace democratic procedures by a managerial approach in which decisions are taken on the basis of quantification procedures. But a simple alternative strategy and policy-making procedure exists which assumes a dynamics, active world, which accords with the conception of people as creating themselves through constructing narratives within which they can situate themselves, and which tends to democratize decision-making rather than concentrating it in the hands of 'experts'. This is 'retrospective path analysis' which has been developed by Cliff Hooker.

Retrospective path analysis is essentially a means for constructing narratives to live by. It consists in, first, the selection of macroeconomic goals by considering a variety of end-points forty to fifty years in the future, and then second, examining various paths to the desired future state. This procedure departs from the normal approach in calculating a course of action retrospectively from some future date, specifying 'those key transitions in social structure and functioning generally which, taken in proper sequence, will lead from the present to the desired future social condition'. Such an approach focuses attention on the conditions necessary for achieving the desired future states, on the tendencies inimical to the realization of such ends and on the crucial social decisions at the branch-points of different possible paths of development. Recognizing the limits of knowledge, such decisions must take into account how much room for manoeuvre they give to different actors during the process of reaching desired ends, and they must be constantly open to re-examination and reformulation. Furthermore, since the ends must ultimately include the way people think, relate to each other and the world, these must be incorporated into the path analysis. This means that retrospective path analysis does not attempt to reduce people involved in realizing ends into predictable instruments. It opens up for discussion the question of what sort of future we want, which can include questions of what sort of people we wish to become, what sort of relationships should exist between people and what kind of narratives people should define themselves in terms of. It can contribute to transforming people's attitudes to a process world-orientation, from seeing themselves as beings standing outside the world trying to control it to experiencing themselves as processes of becoming actively participating in the becoming of the world.

Formulating policy in this way requires the development of a social science which subordinates abstract analyses to narrative, which can analyse existing economic processes, cultural forms, power relations and social dynamics, and reveal what paths to the future are possible. While cost-benefit analyses implicitly assume a crude positivistic theory of science in which knowledge amounts to the ability to predict the probabilities of the occurrence of different future states and events, retrospective path analysis requires of social science that it identifies and comprehends the dynamics of and interrelationships between a multiplicity of semi-autonomous processes. It requires a social science which does not objectify social reality which does not blind people to its becoming and to the reality of their own participation within this becoming. The philosophy of process provides a conceptual framework for such a social science, at the same time overcoming the divisions between the natural and the social sciences, between the sciences and history and between theory and practice. By conceiving of the goal of science as the development of understanding and by providing a unified conceptual framework for analysing the relationships between the dynamics of the physical world, the biological world and the complex of processes which make up the social world, and which at the same time can situate conceptually and analyse the structures of the life-worlds of people, the philosophy of process promises to provide a thermodynamically and ecologically based socio-political economics which can relate problems into an integrated perspective. Through such a social science, people—conceived of as situated but partly self-creative processes of becoming within the processes of becoming of the world, as participating in this becoming with each thought and action—could be provided with the means to extend and deepen their understanding of themselves and their potentialities as embodied subjects participating in the becoming of the world.

All social science is evaluative, with evaluation being grounded in the conception of humans and their place in nature on which this science is built. What is required of social science is that this be acknowledged, that the conception of humanity underlying specific research be open to revision or to replacement, rather than, as with the assumptions about humanity of prevailing social science, being presupposed. This would reincorporate questions of evaluation into the realm of rational discourse. With the process conception of humanity as the reference point for evaluation, social science would first of all evaluate societies in terms of their contribution to the stability and resilience of the world's eco-systems and their sustainability, and in terms of the quality of the life-worlds generated by them. These life-words and the social relations, institutions and social dynamics based on them would be judged in terms of the adequacy of the conceptualizations of the world embodied and reproduced by them, that is, in terms of whether they facilitated or stultified the dialectical patterns of representation, recognition and labour through which people are striving to orient themselves in the world, develop their identities and gain control over their destinies.

Social science should be more than just analysis and evaluation of the social world. Social science should also provide an orientation for action. The development of such a social science should be seen as a part of culture and subordinate to history, that is, as part of the process of humanity's self-formation. By trying to illuminate the present in the light of the past, it should aim to contribute to the construction of the future, to enable people better to comprehend the different tendencies within the world, the extent to which their own ends are being frustrated or facilitated by these and what part they could play in furthering or inhibiting these tendencies. It should aim to facilitate deeper understanding of the world so that its significance and the significance of different possible projects can be judged, and thereby to orient people to live better lives. This requires more than just exposing the failings of the existing order. One only refutes what one replaces. And as Rom Harre pointed out: 'people create themselves and their patterns of interaction by virtue of the psychological and social theories to which they subscribe'. Social science should be providing people with new ways to conceive themselves, their society and the world to make possible new relationships between people and between humanity and nature to replace the forms of life being revealed as defective.

To some extent environmental economics, Marxist and institutionalist political economy and various schools of anti-mechanistic thought in sociology and psychology are providing such theories; but these developments need to be seen as only stages towards a more radical reformulation of the human sciences and a more radical transformation of society. A social science based on philosophy of process would confront the commodity fetishism of capitalism. However, rather than simply oppose the reification of abstractions, it is necessary to replace the categories of economic theory, the 'forms of existence' of capitalist societies. 'Labour-power' would be replaced as the dominant concept defining work relationships by a concept which acknowledges the full needs and potentialities of people as creative social agents and the dynamics and intrinsic value of other forms of life. Podolinski's energy theory of value and the associated reformulation of the concept of 'surplus value' would replace the neo-classical concept of exchange value, and Cobb and Daly's 'index of sustainable economic welfare', taking into account all that contributes to or undermines a good life, and how potentialities for achieving the good life in the future are affected by economic activity, would replace the notion of 'gross national product' in order to situate the money economy within the environment and to focus on the real contribution of economic activity to the conditions of life—both human and non-human.

However, it is not only particular concepts which need to be transformed, but along with this, the 'images' of societies. There will always be an image of society dominating any community, and this will always function to some extent as an ideal. One of the most important tasks at present is to replace the analogy of the machine which underlies prevailing economic thought and which provides the dominant image of society with an auditory analogy, to create an ideal which does not reduce the present to a means for realizing the future, which does not promote the destruction of life and spontaneity, which assumes that human life is participation in the becoming of nature and culture. At the same time it is important to promote some variant of Wallerstein's notion of world-system, since quite apart from its role in revealing the causes and extent of economic exploitation, political oppression and environmental destruction, such a notion contributes to the construction of a world community by creating an image of it. To achieve all this, social science needs to transcend the disciplinary boundaries which at present dominate the study of humanity.

These disciplinary boundaries are so at odds with the complex interdependencies within social reality that the general population are being blinded by prevailing social science rather than informed by it. As James O'Connor argued:

> as social theory becomes more specialized, the economy, society, and polity become more unified... Hence, never before has it become so essential to invent, however crudely and provisionally, a method which combines historical interpretation, ideology critique, political economy, economic sociology, and political sociology.

At most, two broad disciplinary boundaries might be regarded as acceptable within the human sciences: psychology and a radically redefined economics, although even these should be related through philosophical anthropology and should be in constant interaction; and all studies of humanity should be historical, while all history should be theoretically informed. Psychology should conceive of its object of study, the individual subject, as being essentially biological, social and cultural as well as personal, and therefore incapable of being totally abstracted from the study of the dynamics of societies, while economics, or rather political economy, dealing with the processes and structures associated with and emerging from people's transformations of their physical, biological, socio-cultural environments, reformulated in terms of the philosophy of process and encompassing geography, sociology, politics, law and cultural studies, should assume a conception of humans and then continually revise this in the light of advances in psychology. These sciences should strive to understand people, from individuals to humanity, as a whole, in the broader perspective of the world eco-system, as a complex of dissipative structures ultimately maintained by the condition of far from thermodynamic equilibrium produced by the sun in which all power is ultimately control over the transformations of usable energy.

Such a science of humanity would not be able to provide a transparent representation of the social world, since it is impossible to reduce social reality to a single plane of becoming. As Foucault argued (reflecting the influence of Braudel, and ultimately, of Bergson):

> It's not a matter of locating everything on one level, that of the event, but of realising that there are actually a whole order of levels of different types of events differing in amplitude, chronological breadth, and capacity to produce effects. The problem is at once to distinguish among events, to differentiate

> the networks and levels to which they belong, and to reconstitute the lines along which they are connected and engender one another.

This means that it is impossible to formulate a social theory that enables the dynamics of society to be totally predicted. Rather, social inquiry and social theory should acknowledge the irreducible complexity of social reality, and that at most, only trends can be identified. But this does not mean that abstract models implying predictability of the kind used in economics cannot be of use to the social sciences. What is required of social scientists is that when focusing on any particular aspect of this complex reality, they always acknowledge the level of abstraction involved in its study; that they make use of abstractions, including abstract models, but never mistake these abstractions for reality, that they never commit the 'fallacy of misplaced concreteness'. Nor should social scientists presuppose a privileged perspective within this process of becoming of humanity. In place of prevailing economic thought which tacitly presupposes the perspective of governments and businesses in the economic centres of the world, the new social science should aim to provide the means for people to define and orient themselves to the world from their own particular situations, whether they be businessmen, workers, peasants or unemployed, males or females in any part of the world, representatives of governments in core, semi-peripheral or peripheral regions of the world, representatives of international or local organisations, or whatever. Social scientists should see themselves as servants of the general public, as only contributing anything of value to the world if they can provide insights which can be appropriated by all members of society.

Through analysis of the various tendencies within the existing societies, social scientists should also be directed to mobilizing people to replace prevailing concepts and images by revealing the commonality of interests between those who are oppressed by the present system, by presenting images of the future worth striving for, and by giving some idea of the paths which people, individually and collectively, could take to help realize this future. As Marx argued, the validity of social theories can only be judged by whether people take them up and define the world accordingly, and then by whether the promise of these theories, the potentialities they purport to reveal, are realized in action: 'Man must prove the truth *i.e.*, the reality and power, the this worldliness of his thinking in practice.' To prove the truth of this social science goals must be formulated in terms of it. Social science based on the new cosmology could give a place to people as agents forming policies and programmes of action, while at the same time it could provide the means for situating policy analyses of any group or organization within the broader socio-economic and cultural dynamics of particular societies and of humanity as a whole. It could also facilitate the consideration, and balancing of different claims to justice, of acting upon such policies. It would facilitate and require of policy-making that it not only deal with people in interaction with their physical and biological world, but that it situate economic processes of nations or regions in relation to the political and socio-cultural dynamics of societies, and situate these dynamics in turn in relation to the economic, political and socio-cultural dynamics of the whole of humanity. Having situated policy formation, such a social science could then provide a means for formulating policy and strategy analyses for the broader socio-cultural dynamics of particular societies and of humanity as a whole, so that each organizational actor and his or her modes of thought, policies and strategies could be seen and considered in the context of these broader dynamics.

Provided with such a means for interpreting the world, retrospective path analysis could be developed beyond macroeconomics to deal with multiple levels of decision-making by diverse groups and organizations. It would be possible to consider what sort of future we want for the whole of humanity, and to project goals several hundred years in the future, and then to consider shorter-term goals of different nations, of economic and political sectors in these nations, of particular political movements and of local pressure groups in terms of their contribution to realizing these longer-term goals. In this way, people would have the means to work out a complex of narratives, embodying an image of the future ranging from the short term to the long -term, from local communities to the whole of humanity. In terms of these they could then situate their own lives and activities in relation to the communities and organizations they belong to, in relation to different nations and regions, in relation to humanity as a whole and in relation to the dynamics of nature. It is such a form of policy formulation which is required to confront the present environmental and cultural crises in all their complexity.

To become an effective political force environmental movements need to articulate the problems and aspirations of people in the short- term with intermediate and long-term problems and aspirations, the problems and projects of local areas with regional and world problems and projects, the immediate problems and goals of individuals with national problems and goals and with the problems and goals of humanity. First, using retrospective path analysis it is necessary to work out what form of world-society and civilization could provide the best conditions for people to live in while preserving the environment. This can be posited as something to be aimed at several hundred years in the future, and the paths which must be taken from our present situation to realize that goal can then be examined. In the light of this general project, it should then be possible to consider each region in the world and for each nation to consider in more detail what paths they need to take if humanity is to achieve a sustainable world-order. In this way it should be possible to formulate regional and national goals for a hundred years or so into the future, and then to consider how different locations, institutions and organizations can be developed to realize these goals. These goals could be developed as part of nationalistic struggles to provide the conditions within each country for people to contribute as much as their abilities will allow to their nation, to humanity and to life itself. It is then necessary to examine the immediate problems of societies and of individuals from within this general framework to relate these to the broader problems of civilization and the world eco-system. It is particularly necessary to identify forms of oppression which are preventing the realization of such national goals and the long-term goals of humanity so that struggles against this oppression can be integrated with nationalism, humanism and the struggle to preserve the world eco-system. As each more local and immediate goal and path is worked out, this should then enable broader and longer-term goals and their associated paths to be revised. Developing an image of the future in this way should involve a constant shifting of focus between the general and the specific and between the short- term and the long- term. Ultimately it should enable individuals to construct narratives which can relate their own lives to a new grand narrative, the global struggle for an environmentally sustainable civilization.

Policies for the Present

Environmentalism has become a growth industry, and like many other growth industries which have sprung up since the early 1970s, it has, absorbed people's time and money without producing much effect. If academic work on the environment is ever to become more than the mass production of high-sounding platitudes, it needs to be related to people's immediate situations. It seems only fitting then that I should end this work, which is essentially an effort to explain the nature of a culture which makes so much of the environment, treatment of animals, poverty, gender relationships, exploitation of the Third World, and yet generates so little action, with some consideration of what people should do immediately.

However, it follows from what I have been arguing that it is impossible to prescribe for everyone what should be done. To this extent, postmodern political philosophy is right. What is required is a 'politics of the rhizome' in which everyone, every community, every nation and every major region comes to terms with the uniqueness of their situation and acts accordingly—and realizes that it is only by vast numbers of people, of groups and organizations acting in accordance with the possibilities of their situations that the environmental crisis will be solved. The actions required of different regions and different nations will differ according to their situations within the global economy—according to whether they are cores, semi-peripheries or peripheries of this economy. What is required of Eastern European in the wake of the collapse of communism is different from what is required of Western Europeans, and what is required of Japanese is different from what is required of Brazilians.

Despite this, it is still necessary to identify forces at work affecting all individuals, all nations and all regions, and to see diverse actions as contributions to the broader project of overcoming these forces and creating an environmentally sustainable civilization. A knowledge of the dynamics of the global system of capitalism is required by everyone. Such knowledge should alert East Europeans to the likely costs to their integration into the economic operations of the global economy, and alert those in the Third World of the impossibility of ever participating in the benefits of capitalism. However it is the situation of people in the affluent nations which I wish to address; and in particular the situation of environmentalist members of the middle class; the salariat, self-employed professionals, artists and writers, and the few fraction of the petite bourgeoisie, the service class.

It is clear from the very limited influence of environmental movements in times of maximum public support, that is, in boom times, and the rapid decline of support for environmental issues in times of recession, that nothing much will be achieved unless environmental concerns are integrated into a broad strategy for dealing with the loss of state control over national economies. Environmentalists should respond to the existing economic crises with a struggle for political hegemony over all those groups who are being adversely affected by the globalization of the market—farmers, workers, the salariat and the new petite bourgeoisie. As family farms go broke and blue-collar workers decline as a proportion of the work-force, it is the middle class which will decide the future of these societies. Members of the middle class are now losing their niches within society, heralding the end of their honeymoon with the new international bourgeoisie. The services offered by them are less valued by those with money to pay, and they are beginning to face the same economic insecurity and social devaluation long accorded to members of the proletariat, who for a while also claimed special skills. Unless members of this class overcome the fragmentation of their culture and mobilize themselves into an effective political movement to wrest control of the economy from the new international bourgeoisie, they will continue their downward slide and will sink into permanent semi-employment, insecurity and impoverishment.

To prevent this, the cosmetic environmentalism of this class must now be forged with nationalism into a new ideological force able to inform political praxis. This means refomulating and rejuvenating the narratives defining nationhood. Nationalism should be identified with the struggle for democratic control over the financial institutions, transnational manufacturing and agribusiness companies which are at present destabilizing the world-economy, breaking down democratic institutions and creating economic and political pressures forcing people to wreck their environments to stay alive. Similarly, in order to provide the conditions for the development of institutions able to plan for the long-term future and with the power to subordinate the functioning of the market to long-term national and international interests and goals, nationalism should be identified with the struggle to erect economic barriers to break up the world economy and to control the flow of capital. In their struggle for this power environmentalists should redefine the very meaning of economics from the promotion of money-making to managing, preserving and developing the national household, with the environment—the foundation of this household—at the centre of concern. They must formulate their goal as the creation of full employment through the redirection of economic life towards preserving and improving the environment, and their long-term aim as improving the quality of life through the reduction of material throughputs in these economies by eliminating wastage, simplifying life and radically reducing the power and incomes of the wealthy.

Correspondingly, environmentalists should spearhead the attack on the policies and the institutional changes effected by the champions of greed as a nationalist struggle against global capitalism and its quislings. In the immediate future they need to formulate policies to reduce the power of shareholders in companies relative to stakeholders as the first stage towards the decentralization and democratization of industry. Most importantly, to undermine the concentrations of power in society, to free people from the tyranny of the market, to put an end to conspicuous consumption and to allow some people to devote their lives to the long-incomes—that is, with 100 per cent marginal taxation beyond a certain level.

In this struggle, it is necessary to create and maintain an image of and a sense of belonging to a just community committed to realizing people's potentialities, a community with which people can identify, can commit themselves to and can look to for support. In opposition to the ruling hegemonic ideology, it is necessary to develop an image of nations as 'people' homes,' committed to recognizing the significance of all its members, its future generations and also the organisms and eco-systems of its environments. To support such images, it is necessary to cultivate a reorientation in thinking, not only from the mechanistic world-orientation of those who at present dominate society, but also from the woolly-minded relativism and consumerism of postmodern culture to a process world-orientation, both in thought and in practice. Environmentalists should attack not only the ideological despotism of economists and pedants, but should also strive to counteract the nihilistic decadence which is now undermining civilization. In the process they must strive to create an image of the future not as the triumph of any particular movements, class or nation, but as the triumph of life. It is around this image of the future that they must elaborate a new grand narrative.

BIBLIOGRAPHY

ADAMS, W.M. (1990a). Green Development: Environmental and Sustainability in the Third World. London: Routledge.

ADAMS, W.M. (1990b). How Beautiful is Small? Scale, Control and Success in Kenyan Irrigation. World Development 18, 1309-1323.

AGARWAL, A. (1988). Beyond Pretty Trees and Tigers in India. In The Future of the Environment. The Social Dimensions of Conservation and Ecological Alternatives (D.C. Pitt ed.) pp. 93-125. London: Routledge.

AGARWAL, A. and NARAIN, S., EDS (1985). The State of India's Environment, 1984-85. The Second Citizens' Report. New Delhi: Centre for Science and Environment.

AGARWAL, B, (1990) Social Security and the Family: Coping with Seasonality and Calamity in Rural India. Journal of Peasant Studies 17, 341-412.

AGARWAL, B. (1988a). Neither Sustenance nor Sustainability: Agricultural Strategies, Ecological Degradation and Indian Women in Poverty. In Structure of Patriarchy: State, Community and Household in Modernising Asia (B. Agarwal ed.) pp. 83-120. London: Zed Books.

AGARWAL, B. (1988b). Who Sows ? Who Reaps ? Women and Land Rights in India, Journal of Peasant Studies 15, 531-581.

AGARWAL, B. (1989). Rural Women, Poverty and Natural Resources: Sustenance, Sustainability and Struggle for Change. Economic and Political Weekly 24 (43), 46-65.

AHMED, A.G.M. (1987). National Ambivalence and External Hegemony: the Negligence of Pastoral Nomads in the Sudan. In Agrarian Change in the Central Rainlands: A Socio-economic Analysis (M.A. Mohamed Salih ed.) pp. 129-148 Uppsala: Scandinavian Institute of African Studies.

ALLEN, B, and CRITTENDER. R. (1987). Degradation and a Pre-capitalist Political Economy: The Case of the New Guinea Highlands. In Land Degradation and Society (P. Blaikie and H. Brookield eds.) pp. 145-156. London: Methuen.

AMBIO, ROYAL SWEDISH ACADEMY OF SCIENCES (1983). Nucleas War: The Aftermath. Oxford: Pergamon Press.

ANDERSON, A.B. (1990). Smokestacks in the Rainforest : Industrial Development and Deforestation in the Amazon Basin. World Development 18, 1191-1205.

ANDERSON, J.N. (1987). Lands at Risk People at Risk: Perspectives on Tropical Forest Transformations in the Philippines. In Lands at Risk in the Third World: Local Level Perspectives (P.D.Little and M.M.Horowitz eds) pp. 249-267. London: Westview Press.

ANDERSON, R.S. and HUBER.W.(1988). The Hour of the Fox Tropical Forests. the World Bank, and Indigenous People in Central India. London: University of Washington Press.

ANGELI, D.J.R. COMER. J.D. and WILKINSON, M.L.N., Eds. (1990). Sustaining Earth Response to the Environmental Threat. London: Macmillan.

BAHUGUNA, S. (1985). People's Response to Ecological Crisis in the Hill Areas. In India's Environment : Crises and Responses (J. Bandyopadhyay, N. D. Jayal, U. Shoettli and C. Singh eds.) pp. 215-226. New Delhi: Natraj Publishers.

BASSETT, T.J. (1988). The Political Ecology of Peasant-Herder Conflicts in the Northern Ivory Coast. Annals of the Association of American Geographers 78, 453-472.

BAUMAN, ZYGMUNT (1991). Modernity and Ambivalence. Cambridge: Polity Press.

BAUTISTA, G.M. (1990). The Forestry Crisis in the Philippines: Nature, Causes, and Issues. The Developing Economics 28, 67-94.

BECK, ULRICH (1995). Ecological Politics in an Age of Risk. Cambridge: Polity Press.

BECK, ULRICH, GIDDENS, ANTHONY and LASH, SCOTT (1994). Reflexive Modernization: Politics, Tradition and Aesthetics in the Modern Social Order. Cambridge: Polity Press.

BECKER, L.C. (1990). The Collapse of the Family Farm in West Africa? Evidence from Mali. Geographical Journal 156 p. 313-322.

BEINART, W. (1984). Soil Erosion, Conservationism and Ideas about Development: a Southern African Exploration. 1900-1960, Journal of Southern African Studies 11, 52-83.

BEINART. W. (1989). Introduction: The Politics of Colonial Conservation Journal of Southern African Studies 15. 143-162.

BEINART. W. (1990). Empire, Hunting and Ecological Change in Southern and Central Africa. Past and Present 128. 162-186.

BENNETT. JANE (1993). 'Primate Visions and Alter-tales' in Jane Bennett and William Chaloupka (eds) In the Nature of Things, pp. 250-66.

BENNETT, JANE AND WILLIAM CHALOUPKA (eds.) (1993). In the Nature of Things: Language, Politics and the Environment. Minneapolis: University of Minnesota Press.

BENTON, T. (1989). Marxism and Natural Limits: An Ecological Critique and Reconstruction New Left Review 178, 51-86.

BERNSTEIN, H. (1990). Taking the Part of Peasants ? In The Food Question: Profits Versus People ? (H. Bernstein, B. Crow, M. Mackintosh and C. Martin eds) pp. 69-79. London: Earthscan.

BERRY, S. (1988). Concentration Without Privatization: Some Consequences of Changing Patterns of Rural Land Control in Africa. In Land and Society in Contemporary Africa (R. E. Downs and S.P. Reyna eds) pp. 53-75. London. University of New Hampshire.

BERRY, S. (1989a). Access, Control and Use of Resourses in African Agriculture: An Introduction, Africa 59, 1-5.

BERRY, S. (1989b). Social Institutions and Access to Resources. Africa 59, 41-55.

BESHIR, M.O., Ed (1984). The Nile Valley Countries: Continuity and Change, Khartoum: University of Khartoum, Institute of African and Asian Studies, Sudanese Library Series No. 12.

BIRD, ELISABETH ANN R. (1987). 'The Social Construction of Nature: Theoretical Approaches to the History of Environmental Problems,' Environmental Review, 11 (4): pp 255-64.

BLAIKIE, P. (1985). The Political Economy of Soil Erosion in Developing Countries, London: Longman.

BLAIKIE, P. (1988 a). The Explanation of Land Degradation in Nepal. In Deforestation: Social Dynamics in Watersheds and Mountain Ecosystems (J. Ives and D.C.Pitt eds) pp. 132-158, London: Routledge.

BLAIKIE, P. (1988 b). Environmental Crises in Developing Countries: How Much for Whom and by Whom? An Introduction and Overview. In Environmental Crises in Developing Countries (P. Blaikie and T.Unwin eds) pp.1-6. London: Institute of British Geographers, Developing Areas Research Group. Monograph No. 5.

BLAIKIE, P. (1989 a). Environment and Access to Resources in Africa. Africa 59, 18-40.

BLAIKIE, P. (1989 b). Natural Resources Use. In A World in Crisis? 2nd edn, (R.J.Johnston and P.J.Taylor eds.) pp. 125-150. Oxford: Basil Blackwell.

BLAIKIE, P. and BROOKFIELD, H (1987 b). Defining and Debating the Problem. In Land Degradation and Society (P. Blaikie and H.Brookfield eds.) pp.1-26. London: Methuen.

BLAIKIE, P. and BROOKFIELD, H. eds (1987 a). Land Degradation and Society: London: Methuen.

BLAIKIE, P. and BROOKFIELD. H. (1987 c). Approaches to the Study of Land Degradation. In Land Degradation and Society (P. Blaikie and H. Brookfield eds.) pp. 27-48. London: Methuen.

BLAUERT, J. (1988). Autochthonous Development and Environment Knowledge in Oaxaca. Mexico. In Environmental Crises in Developing Countries (P. Blaikie and T.Unwin eds) pp. 33-54. London: Institute of British Geographers, Developing Areas Research Group. Monograph No. 5. Boado,

E.L. (1988). Incentive Policies ad Forest Use in the Philippines. In Public Policies and the Misuse of Forest Resources (R. Repetto and M.Gillis eds) pp. 165-203. Cambridge: Cambridge University Press.

BÖHME, GERNOT (1992). Natürlich Natur—Die Natur in Zeitalter ihrer technischen Reprodu-zierbarkeit. Frankfurt am Main: Suhrkamp.

BRANFORD. S. and GLOCK. O. (1985). The Last Frontier:Fighter over Land in the Amazon. London: Zed Books.

BROWDER, J.O. (1988a). The Social Costs of Rain Forest Destruction: a Critique and Economic Analysis of the 'Hamburger Debate'. Interciencia 13, 115-120.

BROWDER, J.O. (1988b). Public Policy and Deforestation in the Brazilian Amazon. In Public Policies and the Misuse of Forest Resources (R. Repetto and M.Gills eds) pp. 247-297. Cambridge: Cambridge University Press.

BROWDER, J.O. ed. (1989). Fragile Lands of Latin America: Strategies for Sustainable Developing. London: Westview Press.

BROWN, J.W. (1990). US Policy in the Crucial Decade Ahead. In In the US Interest: Resources,Growth, and Security in the Developing World (J.W. Brown ed.) pp. 165-201. London: Westview Press.

BUDIARDJO, C. (1986). The Politics of Transmigration. Ecologist 16, 111-116.

BULL. D. (1982). A Growing Problem. Pesticides and the Third-World Poor. Oxford: Oxfam.

BUNKER, S. G. (1982). The Cost of Modernity: Inappropriate

Bureaucray, Inequality, and Development Program Failure in the Brazilian Amazon. Journal of Developing Areas 16. 573-596.

BUNKER, S.G. (1980). The Impact of Deforestation on Peasant Communities in the Medio Amazonas of Brazil, Studies in Third-World Societies 13, 45-60.

BUNKER, S.G. (1984). Modes of Extraction, Unequal Exchange, and the Progressive Underdevelopment of an Extreme Periphery: the Brazilian Amazon. 1600-1980. American Journal of Sociology 89, 1017-1064.

BUNKER, S.G. (1985b). Misdirected expertise in an unknown environment: standard bureaucratic procedures as inappropriate technology on the Brazilian 'planned Frontier'. In Change in the Amazon Basin, Volume II: The Frontier after a Dacade of Colonisation (J. Hemming ed) pp. 103-118. Manchester: Manchester University Press.

BUNKER, S.G.(1985a). Underdeveloping the Amazon: Extraction, Unequal Exchange, and the Failure of the Modern State. Urbana: University of Illinois Press.

BUTTEL, F.H. (1989). How Epoch- making are high technologies? The case of biotechnology: Sociological Forum 4. 247-261.

BUTTEL, F.H. (1990). Biotechnology and agricultural development in the Third World. In The Food Question: Profits Versus People? (H. Bernstein, B. Crow, M. Mackintosh and C. Martin eds.) pp.163-180. London: Earthscan.

CALDWELL, L.K. (1988). Beyond Environmental Diplomacy the Changing Institutional Structure of International Co-operation. In International Environmental Diplomacy: The Management and Resolution of Transfrontier Environmental Problems (J.E. Carroll ed.) pp. 13-27. Cambridge: Cambridge University Press.

CARNEY, J. and WATTS, M, (1990). Manufacturing Dissent: Work, Gender and the Politics of Meaning in a Peasant Society. Africa 60. 207-241.

CHAMBERS, R. (1983). Rural Development: Putting the Last First. London: Longman.

CHAMBERS, R. (1987). Sustainable Livelihoods, Environment and Development: Putting Poor Rural People First. Brighton: University of Sussex, Institute of Development Studies, Discussion Paper No. 240.

CHAMBERS, R. and LEACH, M. (1989). Trees as Savings and Security for the Rural Poor. World Development 17, 329-342.

CLARKE, W.C (1990). Learning from the Past: Traditional Knowledge and Sustainable Development, Contemporary Pacific 2. 233-253.

CLIFFE, L. and MOORSOM. R. (1979) Rural Class Formation and Ecological Collapse in Botswana. Review of African, Political Economy 15/16,. 35-52.

COCKBURN, ALEXANDER (1993). "'Win/Win" with Bruce Babbitt: The Clinton administration meets the Environment', New Left Review, 201: 46-59.

COHEN, JEAN A. (1985). 'Strategy or identity: New Theoretical Paradigms and Contemporary Social Movements', Social Research, 52(4): 663-716.

COLBURN, F.D. ed. (1989). Everyday Forms of Peasant Resistance. London: M.E. Sharpe.

COLCHESTER, M.(1986). Banking on Disaster : International Support for Transmigration, ecologist 16,. 61-70.

COLLINS, J.L. (1986). Smallholder Settlement of Tropical South America: the Social Causes of Ecological Destruction. Human Organization 45, 1-10.

COLLINS, R.O. (1990). The Waters of the Nile: Hydropolitics and the Jonglei Canal, 1900-1988. Oxford: Clarendon Press.

CONROY, C. and LITVINOFF, M. eds. (1988). The Greening of Aid:Sustainable Livelihoods in Practice. London: Earthscan.

CORBRIDGE, S. (1986). Capitalist World Development: A Critique of Radical Development Geography. London: Macmillan.

CUMMINGS, B.J. (1990). Dam the Rivers, Damn the People: Development and Resistance in Amazonian Brazil. London: Earthscan.

DANKELMAN, I. and DAVIDSON, J. (1988). Women and Environment in the Third World: Alliance for the Future. London: Earthscan.

DAVISON, J. (1987). Without Land We are Nothing: The Effect of Land Tenure Policies and Practices upon Rural Women in Kenya, Rural Africana 27.19-33.

DEUTSCH, K.W. (1977). Some Problems and Prospects of Ecopolitical Research. In Ecosocial System and Ecopolitics: A Reader on Human and Social Implications of Environmental Management in Developing Countries (K.W. Deutsch ed.) pp. 359-368. Paris: UNESCO.

DINHAM, B. and HINES, C. (1983). Agribusiness in Africa. London: Earth Resources Research.

DOGRA, B. (1985). The World Bank vs. The People of Bastar, Ecologist 15, 44-48.

DOVE, M.R. (1986). Peasant Versus Government Perception and use of the Environment: A Case-study of Banjarese Ecology and river basin development in South Kalimantan. Journal of Southeast Asian Studies 17, 113-136.

DRUCKER, C. (1985). Dam the Chico: Hydropower development and tribal resistance. Ecologist 15. 149-157.

DRYZEK, J.S. (1987). Rational Ecology: Environment and Political Economy, Oxford: Basil Blackwell.

DURNING, A.B. (1990). Ending Poverty. In State of the World 1990 A Worldwatch Institute Report on Progress Toward a Sustainable Society (L.R. Brown ed.) pp. 135-153. London: Unwin Hyman.

EKINS, PAUL (1992). A New World Order: Grassroots Movements for Global Change. London: Routledge.

EMEL, J. and PEET, R. (1989). Resource management and natural hazards. In New Models in Geography: The Political Economy Perspective, Volume 1 (R. Peet and N. Thrift eds) pp. 49-76. London: Unwin Hyman.

FALKUS, M. (1990). Economic History and Environment in South East Asia. Asian Studies Review 14, 65-79.

FEARNSIDE, P. M. (1986). Agricultural Plans for Brazil's Grande Carajas Program : Lost Opportunity for Sustainable Local Development? World Development 14, 385-409.

FERNANDES, W. (1990). Forest Policy: a solution to tribal deprivation? Indian Journal of Social Work 51, 35-56.

FISCHER, FRANK (1990). Technocracy and the Politics of Expertise. London: Sage.

FOX, R.C. (1988). Environment, tribe, politics and policy in Eastern Province, Kenya. In Environmental Crises in Developing Countries (P. Blaikie and T. Unwin eds.) pp. 83-110. London: Institute of British Geographers, Developing Areas Research Group, Monograph No. 5.

FRANKE, R.W. and CHASIN, B.H. (1980). Seeds of Famine: Ecological Destruction and the Developing Dilemma in the West African Sabel. Montclair, NI, Allanheld Osmun.

GALTUNG, J. (1982). Environment, Development and Military Activity Towards Alternative Security Doctrines. Oslo Universitetsforlaget.

GARCIA, R.V. (1981). Volume 1: Nature Pleads Not Guilty. Oxford: Pergamon Press.

GEORGE, S. (1985). 1II Fares the Land: Essays on Food, Hunger and Power. London: Writers and Readers.

GEORGE, S. (1988). A Fate Worse Than Debt, London: Penguin.

GIDDENS, A. (1979). Central Problems in Social Theory: Action, Structure and Contradiction in Social Analysis. London: Macmillan.

GILL, S. and LAW, D. (1988). The Global Political Economy: Perspectives. Problems and Policies. London: Harvester Wheatsheaf.

GILLIS, M. (1987). Multinational Enterprises and Environmental and Resource Management Issues in the Indonesian Tropical Forest Sector. In Multinational Corporations, Environment, and the Third World: Business Matters (C.S. Pearson ed.) pp. 64-89. Durham, NC: Duke University Press.

GILLIS, M. -(1988a). Indonesia: Public Policies, Resources management, and the tropical forest. In Public Policies and the Misuse of Forest Resources (R. Repetto and M. Gillis eds.) pp. 43-113. Cambridge: Cambridge University Press.

GILLIS, M. (1988b). Malaysia:public policies and the tropical forest. In Public policies and the Misuse of Forest Resources (R. Repetto and M. Gillis eds.) pp. 115-164. Cambridge: Cambridge University Press.

GILLIS, M. and REPETTO, R. (1988). Conclusion: findings and policy implications. In Public Policies and the Misuse of Forest Resources (R. Repetto and M. Gillis eds.) pp. 385-410. Cambridge: Cambridge University Press.

GLADWIN, T.N. (1987). Environment, Develoment and multinational enterprise. In Multinational Corporation, Environment, and the Third World: Business Matters (C.S. Person ed.) pp. 3-31. Durham, NC: Duke University Press.

GODANA, B.A. (1985). Africa's Shared Water Resources: Legal and Institutional Aspect of the Nile, Niger and Senegal River Systems. London: Frances Pinter.

GOLDSMITH, E. and HILDYARD, N. eds (1986). The Social and Environmental Effects of Large Dams, Volume II, Wadebridge, Cornwall: Wadebridge Ecological Centre.

GOLDSMITH, E. and HILDYARD, N.(1984). The Social and Environmental Effects of Large Dams, Volume I. Wadebridge, Cornwall: Wadebridge Ecological Centre.

GOODMAN, D., SORJ, B. and WILKINSON, J. (1987). From Farming to Biotechnology: A Theory of Agro-industrial Development. Oxford: Basil Blackwell.

GORZ, ANDRÉ' (1993) 'Political Ecology: Expertocracy versus Self-limitation', New Left Review, 202: 55-67.

GUHA, R. (1985). Forestry and Social Protest in British Kumaun, c.1893-1921. In Subaltern Studies IV: Writings on South Asian History and Society (R.Guha ed.) pp. 54-100, Delhi: Oxford University Press.

GUHA, R. (1989a).The Unquiet Woods: Ecological Change and Peasant Resistance in the Himalaya. Delhi: Oxford University Press.

GUHA, R. (1989b). Saboteurs in the Forest: colonialism and peasant resistance in the Indian Himalaya. In Everyday Forms of Peasant Resistance (F. D. Colburn ed.) pp. 64-92. London: M. E. Sharpe.

GUHA, R. (1990). An early environmental debate: The making of the 1878 Forest Act. Indian Economic and Social History Review 27, 65-84.

GUHA, R. and GADGIL, M. (1989). State Forestry and social conflict in British India. Past and Present 123, 141-177.

GUIMARAES, R. P. (1989). The ecopolitics of development in Brazil. CEPAL Review 38, 89-103.

HAENER, J.A. and APICHATVULLOP, Y. (1990). Farming the forest: managing people and trees in reserved forests in Thailand, Geoforum 21, 331-346.

HAIL., A. (1987). Agrarian crisis in Brazilian Amazonia: The Grande Carajas programme. Journal of Development studies 23, 522-552.

HAIL., A.L. (1989). Developing Amazonia: Deforestation and Social conflict in Brazil's Carajas Programme. Manchester University Press.

HAJER, MAARTEN A. (1995) The Politcs of Environmental Discourse: Ecological Modernisation and the Policy Process. Oxford: Clarendon Press.

HAMIITON, L.S. and PEARCE, A.J. (1988). Soil and water impacts of deforestation. In Social Dynamics in watersheds and Mountain Ecosystems (J. lves and D.C. Pitt eds.) pp. 75-98. London: Routledge.

HARAWAY, DONNA (1991). Simians, Cyborgs, and Women: The Reinvention of Nature. London: Free Association Books.

HART, G., TURTON A. AND WHITE B.eds. (1989). Agrarian Transformations: local Processes and the State in Southeast Asia. London: University of California Press.

HARVEY, DAVID (1993). 'The Nature of Environmental: Dialectics of Social and Environmental Change', in Ralph Miliband and Leo Panitch (eds) Socialist Register 1993. London : Merlin Press, pp. 1-51.

HAUGERUD, A. (1989). Land tenure and agrarian change in Kenya!, Africa 59, 61-90.

HAYNES, K.E. AND WHITTINGTOM, D. (1981). International management of the Nile—Stage three? Geographical Review 71, 17-32.

HAYS, SAMUEL P. (1979 (1959)). Conservation and the Gospel of Efficiency: The Progressive Conservation Movement, 1890-1920. New York: Atheneum.

HEALEY, P. AND SHAW, T. (1993). The Treatment of 'Environment' by Planners: Evolving Concepts and Policies in Development Plans. Working Paper No. 31, Department of Town and Country Planning, University of Newcastle upon Tyne.

HECHAT, S.B. ANDERSON. A. B. and MAY. P. (1988). The subsidy from nature: shifting cultivation, successional palm forests, and rural development, Human Organization 47, 25-35.

HECHT, S. B. (1985). Environment, development and politics: capital accumulation and the livestock sector in eastern Amazonia, World Development 13, 663-684.

HECHT, S.B. (1984). Cattle-ranching in Amazonia: political and ecological considerations. In Frontier Expansion in Amazonia (M. Schmink and C.H. Wood eds.) pp. 360-398. Gainesville. University of lorida Press.

HECHT, S.B. and COCKBURN, A. (1989). The fate of the Forest: Developers, Destroyers and Defenders of the Amazon. London: Verso.

HEIXUND, H. (1979). Contradictions in the peripheralization of a pastoral society: The Massai. Review of African Political Economy 15/16, 53-62.

HETINE. B. (1990). Development Theory and the Three Worlds London: Longman.

HIRSCH, P. (1990). Forests, forest reserve, and forest land in Thailand. Geographical Journal 156, 166-174.

HIRSCH, P. and LOHMANN, L. (1989). Contemporary politics of environment in Thailand. Asian Survey 29, 439-451.

HONG, E. (1987). Natives of Sarawak: Survival in Borneo's Vanishing Forests. Penang: Institut Masyarakar.

HOROWITZ, M.M. (1986). Ideology, policy, and praxis in pastoral livestock development. In Anthropology and Rural Development in West Africa (M.M. Horowitz and T.M. Painter eds.) pp. 251-272, London: Westview Press.

HOROWITZ, M.M. and LITTLE, P.D. (1987). African pastoralism and poverty: Some implications for drought and famine. In Drought and Hunger in Africa: Denying Famine a Future (M.H. Glantz.ed.) pp. 59-82, Cambridge: Cambridge University Press.

HOROWITZ., M.M. and SALEM-MURDOCK, M. (1987). The Political economy of desertification in White Nile Proince. Sudan. In Lands at Risk in the Third World. Local-Level Perspectives (P.D. Little and M.M. Horowitz eds.) pp. 95—114. London: Westview Press.

HORT. AF ORNAS, A. and MOHAMED SALIH, M.A. eds. (1989). Ecology and politics. Enviromental stress and Security in Africa Uppsala: Scandinavian Institute of African Studies.

HOWELL P., LOCK, M. and COBB, S., eds. (1988) .The Jonglet Canal: Impact and opportunitry. Cambridge: Cambridge University Press.

HURST, (1990). Rainforest Politics: Ecological Destruction in South-East Asia. London: Zed Books.

JAHN, THOMAS and WEHLING, PETER (1991). Ökologie von Rechts—Nationalismus und Umwelischutz bei der Neuen Rechten und den Republikanern. Frankfurt am Main: Campus.

JAHN, THOMAS and WEHLING, PETER (1993). 'Ausweg Öko-Diktatur? Umweltschütz, Demokratie und die Neue Rechte', in Politische Ökologie, 34: 2-6.

JAIN, S. (1984) Women and people's ecological movement: A case-study of women's role in the Chipko movement in Uttar Pradesh Economic and political Weekly 19, 1788-1794.

JODHA, N.S. (1986). Common Property resources and rural poor in dry regions of India. Economic and Political Weekly 21, 1169-1181.

JOHNSTON, R.J. (1989). Environmental Problems: Nature, Economy and State. London: Belhaven Press.

KASTEN JR., R.W. (1986). Development banks:subsidizing Third World pollution. Washington Quarterly 9, 109-114.

KEMF, E. (1990). Month of Pure Light: The Regreening of Vietnam. London: The Women's Press.

KENNEY, M. and BUTTEL, F. (1985). Biotechnology: prospects and dilemmas for Third-World development, Development and Change 16, 61-91.

KJEKSHUS, H. (1977). Ecology Control and Economic Development in East African History: The case of Tanganyika, 1850-1950. London: Heinemann.

KLOPPENBRUG, J. R. (1988). First the Seed: The Political Economy of Plant Biotechnology, 1492-2000 Cambridge: University Press.

KULKARNI, S. (1983). Towards a social forest policy. Economic and political weekly 18, 191-196.

KWA, C. (1987). 'Representations of Nature Mediating between Ecology and Science Policy: The case of the international biological programme'. Social Studies of Science. 17: 413-42.

LAU, CHRISTOPH et al., (1993). Risikodiskurse-Gesellschaftliche Auseinandersetzungen um die Definition von Risiken and Gefahren. Report of the German Federal Minister for Research and Technology.

LAUREN, P.G. (1982). War. Peace and the environment. In international Dimensions of the Environmental Crisis (R. N. Barrett ed.) pp. 75-90. Boulder: Westview Press.

LE PRESTRF, P.G. (1989). The World Bank and the Environmental challenge. London. Associated University Presses.

LEIFFERINK, J.D., LOWE, P. and MOL, A.P.J. (eds.) (1993). European Integration and Environmental Policy. London: Belhaven.

LEONARD, H.J. (1985). Political and economic causes of Third-World environmental degradation. In Divesting Nature's capital. The Political Economy of Environmental Abuse in the Thrid World (H.J. Leonard ed.) pp. 93-136 London:Holmes and Meier.

LEONARD. H.J. (1988). Pollution and struggle for the world product: Multinational Corporation, Environmental, and International comparative Advantage. Cambridge: Cambridge University Press.

LITTLE, P.D. AND HOROWITZ, M.M. eds. (1987). lands at Risk in the Third-World Local Level Perspectives. London: westview Press.

LOHMANN P. (1990). Commercial tree plantation in Thailand: deforestation by any other name. Ecologist 20 (1), 9-17.

MAATHAI, W. (1986). The Green Belt Movement. In The Living Economy: A New Economics in the Making (P. Ekins ed.) pp. 289-295. London: Reutledge and Kegan Paul.

MACKENZIE, F. (1986). Local Initiatives and national policy : gender and agricultural change in Murang's district, Kenya, Canadian Journal of African Studies 20, 377-401.

MACKENZIE, F. (1989). Land and territory: The interface between two systems of land tenure, Murang's district, Kenya. Africa 59, 91-109.

MACKENZIE, J.M. (1988). The Empire of Nature: Hunting, Conservation and British Imperialism. Manchester: Manchester University Press.

MAEGERLE, ANTON (1993). 'Wie das Thema Umwelt zur Modernisierung des rechtsextremen Denkens missbraucht wird', Frankfurther Rundschau, 21 December, p. 6.

MANDEL, R. (1988). Conflict over the World's Resources: Background, Trends, Case-Studies, and Considerations for the Future. Westport. Conn: Greenwood Press.

MARSTON, S.A. (1983). Natural hazards research towards a political economy perspective. Political Geography Quarterly 2, 339-348.

McCRACKEN' J. (1987). Colonialism, capitalism and the ecological crisis in Malawi: a reassessment. In Conservation in Africa: People, Policies and Practice (1). Anderson and R. Grove eds. pp. 63-77. Cambridge: Cambridge University Press.

McDOWELL, M.A. (1989). Development and the Environment in ASEAN Pacific Affairs 62, 307-329.

MEKVICHAI, B. (1988). The Teak Industry in North Thailand: The Role of a Natural-Resource-Based Export Economy in Regional Development. Ph.D. Thesis, Cornell University.

MESSERLL, B. (1990). The Himalayan dilemma: Crisis, Pseudo-Crisis, or Supercrisis. Paper Presented at the Conference on International Environmental and Resource Issues in the Ganges-Brahmaputra Basin, School of Oriental and African Studies, London.

MIES, M. (1984). Capitalism and Subsistence: Rural Women in India. Development 4, 18-24.

MISCRE, P.M. (1989). Ecological Security and the Need to Reconceptualize Sovereignty. Alternatives 14, 339-427.

MORTIMORE, M. (1989). Adapting to Drought Farmers, Famines and Desertification in West Africa. Cambridge: Cambridge University Press.

MYERS, N. (1984). The Primary Sources. Tropical Forest and Our Future. London: W.W. Norton and Company.

MYERS, N. (1989). Population Growth, Environmental Decline and Security Issues in sub-Saharan Africa. In Ecology and Politics: Environmental Stress and Security in Africa (A. Hjort af Ornas and M.A. Mohamed Salih eds) pp. 211-231. Uppsala: Scandinavian Institute of African Studies.

NADKARNI, M.V. (1989). The Political Economy of Forest Use and Management. London: Sage Publications.

NEILANDS, J.B, ORIANS. G.H., PFEIFFER, E.W. VENNEMA, A. and WESTING, A.H. (1972). Harvest of Death: Chemical Warfare in Vietnam and Cambodia, New York: Free Press.

O' BRIEN. J. (1985). Sowing the Seeds of Famine: the Political Economy of Food Deficits in Sudan. Review of African Political Economy 33, 23-32.

O'CONNOR, J. (1989). Uneven and Combined Development and Ecological Crisis: A Theoretical Introduction. Race and Class 30, 1-11.

OFFE, CLAUS (1985). 'New Social Movements: Challenging the Boundaries of Institutional Politics', Social Research, 52 (4): 817-68.

OMVEDT, G. (1989). Ecological and Social Movement.In Sociology of 'Development Societies': South Asia (H.Alvi and J. Harriss eds.) pp. 288-296, London: Macmillan.

OROTH-OGENDO, H.W.O. (1989). Some Issues of Theory in the Study of Tenure Relations in African Agriculture. Africa 59, 6-17.
Paehlke, R.C. and Torgerson, D. (eds.) (1990) Managing Leviathan: Environmental Politics and the Administrative State. Peterborough (Ontario): Broadview.

PAINTER, M. (1987). Unequal Exchange: The Dynamic of Settler Improverishment and Environmental Destruction in Lowland Bolivia. In Lands at Risk in the Third-World: Local Level Perspectives (P. D. Little and M.M. Horowitz eds). pp. 164-191. London: Westview Press.

PEARSON, C.S. (1985). Down to Business Multinational Corporations, the Environment, and Development. Washington, D.C: World Resources Institute.

PEARSON, C.S. ed. (1987). Multinational Corporation, Environment, and the Third World Business Matters. Durham, NC. Duke University Press.

PEET, R. (1985). The Social Origins of Environmental Determinism. Annals of the Association of American Geography 75, 309-333.

PELUSO, N.L. (1988), Rich Forests, Poor People and Development: Forest Access Control and Resistance in Jave Ph.D. Thesis, Cornell University.

PELUSO, N.L. and POFFENBERGER, M. (1989). Social Forestry in Java: Reorienting Management System, Human Organization 48, 333-34.

PETERS, P.E. (1984). Struggle Over Water, Struggles Over Meaning: Cattle, Water and the State in Botswana. Africa 54, 29-49.

PINTZ, W. (1987). Environmental Negotiations in the OK Tedi Mine in Papua New Guinea in Multinational Corporation. Environmental, and the Third-World: Business Matters (C.S. Pearson ed.) pp. 35-63, Durham. NC: Duke University Press.

PITTOCK, A.B. HARWELL, M. A. et al. (1985). Environmental Consequences of Nuclear War. 1. Physical and Atmospheric Effects II Ecological and Agricultural Effects 2 vols. Chichester, UK. John wiley and sons.

POMPWEMAYER, M.J. (1984). Strategies of Private Capital in the Brazilian Amazon. In Frontier Expansion in Amazonia.

PORTER, G. WTTH GANAPIN JR. D.J. (1990). Resources, Population and the Future of the Philippines. In the US Interest: Resources, Growth and Security in the Developing World (J.W. Brown ed.) pp. 59-88, London: Westview Press.

RAMOS, A. R. (1984). Frontier expansion and Indian peoples in the Brazilian Amazon. In Frontier Expansion in Amazonia (M. Schmink and C.H. Wood eds.) pp. 83-104. Gainesville: Universityof Florida Press.

RAVENHILL, J. (1990). The North South balance of Power. International Affairs 66, 731-748.

REDCLEFT, M. (1987). Sustainable Development: Exploring the Contraditions: London: Methuen.

REDCLIFT, M. (1984). Development and the Environmental Crisis: Red or Green Alternatives? London : Methuen.

REPETTO, R and GILLIS, M. eds. (1988). Public Policies and the Misuse of Forest Resources. Cambridge: Cambridge Univercity Press.

REPETTO, R. (1988a). The Forest for the Trees? Goverment Policies and the Misuse of Forest Resources. Washington D.C. World Resources Institute.

REPETTO, R. (1988b). Overview. In Public Policies and the Missue of Forest Resources (R. Repetto and M. Gillis eds) pp. 1-41. Cambridge: Cambridge University Press.

RICH, B.M. (1985). Multi-lateral Development Banks: Their Role in Destroying the Global Environment. Ecologist 15, 56-68.

RICHARDS, P. (1983). Ecological Change and the Politics of African Land Use. African Studies Review 26 (2), 1-72.

RICHARDS, P. (1985) Indigenous Agricultural Revolution: Ecology and Food Production in West Africa, London: Hutchinson.

RICHARDS, P. (1990). Local Stategies for Coping With Hunger: Central Sierra Leone and Northern Nigeria Compared. African Affair 89, 265-275.

SACHS, W. (ed.) (1992). The Development Dictionary: A Guide to Knowledge as Power. London: Zed Books.

SACHS, W. (ed.) (1993). Global Ecology : A New Arena of Political Conflict. London: Zed Books.

SALDANHA, I.M. (1990). The Political Ecology of Traditional Farming Practices in Thana District, Maharastra (India) Journal of Peasant Studies 17, 433-43.

SCHELSKY, H. (1965). 'Der Mensch in der wissenschaftliche Zivilisation', in Auf der Suche nach Wirklichkeit. Düsseldorf/Köln. pp. 439-80.

SCHENDER, A. eds (1989). Deforestation and Development in Canada and the Tropics: The Impact on People and the Environment. Sydney. Nova Scotia: University College of Cape Breton Centre for International Studies.

SCHMINK, I.M. (1982). Land Conflicts in Amazonia American Ethnologist 9, 341-57.

SCHMINK, M. (1988a). A Case study of the closing frontier in Brazil. In power and povety: Development and Development project in the Third-World (D.W. Attwood, T.C. Bruneau and J.G. Galaty eds) pp. 135-153, London: Westview Press.

SCHMINK, M. (1988b). Big Bussiness in the Amazon. In People of the Tropical Rain Forest J.S. Denslow and C. Padoch eds.) pp. 163-74. London: University of California Press.

SCHMINK, M. and WOOD, C.H. (1987). The 'Political Ecology' of Amazonia. In Lands at Risk in the Third-World: Local Level Perspectives (P.D. Little and M.M. Horowitz eds.) pp. 38-57 London: Westview Press.

SCHUMPETER, J.A. (1961 (1943)) Capitalism, Socialism and Democracy. London: George Allen and Unwin.

SCHWARTZMAN, S. (1989). Extractive Reserves: The Rubber - Tappers, Strategy for Sustainable Use of the Amazon Rainforest. In Fragile Lands of Latin America: Strategies for Sustainable Development (J.O. Browder ed.) pp. 150-165, London: Westview Press.

SCHWARZ, M. and THOMPSON, M. (1990). Divided We Stand: Redefining Politics, Technology and Social Choice. London : Harvester Wheatsheaf.

SCOTT, J.C. (1985). Weapons of the Weak: Everyday Forms of Peasant Resistance: London: Yale University Press.

SHAMMUGARATNAM, N. (1989). Development and Environment. A View From the South. Race and Class 30, 13-30.

SHENTON, B and WATTS, M. (1979). Capitalism and Hunger in Nothern Nigeria. Review of African Political Economy 15/16, 53-62.

SHIV, V. (1988). Staying Alive: Women Ecology and Development. London: Zed Books.

SHIVA, V. (1987). People's Ecology: The Chipko movement. In Towards a Just World Peace Perspectives from Social Movements (S.M. Mendlovitz and R.B.J. Walker eds) pp. 253-270, London: Butterworths.

SHIVA, V. and BANDYOPADHYAY, J. (1988). The Chipko Movement. In deforestation: Social Dynamics in Watersheds and Mountain Ecosystem (J.Ives and D.C. Pitt ess) pp. 224, London: Routledge.

SHIVA, VANDANA (1993)·'The Greening of the Global Reach', in W. Sachs (ed.). Global Ecology. pp. 149-56.

SKOCPOL. T. (1985). Bringing the State Back in Strategies of Analysis in Current Research. In Bringing the State Back In (P.B. Evans, D. Ruschemeyer and T. Skopol eds). pp. 3-37. Cambridge University Press.

SMIL, V. (1984). The Base Earth Environment, Degradation China London: Zed Press.

SMIL, V. (1987). Land Degradation in China: an Ancient Problem Getting Worse. In Land Degradation and Society (P. Blaikie and H. Brookfield eds.) pp. 214-22, London: Methuen.

SPAARGAREN, G. and Mol, A.P.J. (1992), 'Sociology, Environment, and Modernity: Ecological Modernisation as a Theory of Social Change', in Society and Natural Resources, 5: 323-44.

SUSMAN, P. O' KEEFE, P. and WISNER, B. (1983). Global Disaster: A Radical Interpretation. In Interpretations of Calamity from the Viewpoint of Human Ecology (K. Hewitted.) pp. 263-283 London: Allen and Unwin.

TEUBNER, GUNTHER (ed.) (1994). Ecological Responsibility. London: Wiley & Sons.

THOMSON, J.T. (1985). The Politics of Desertification in Marginal Environments the Sahelian Case in Diverting Nature's Capital: The Political Economy of Environmental Abuse in the Third World (H.J. Leonard ed.) pp. 227-62, London: Holmes and Meier.

TIMBERAKE, L. (1988). Africa in Crisis: The Causes of Environmental Bankruptcy, 2nd edn. London: Earthscan.

TOLBA, M.K. (1987). Sustatainable Development: Constraints and Opportunities. London: Butterworths.

TOURE, O. (1988). The Pastoral Environmental Management: the Ecological Dimension. Political Studies 3, 129-55.

UYER, J. I. and PETERS, P.E., eds. (1987). Conceptualizing the household: issues of theory and policy in Africa. Development and Change 18(2) (Special issue).

VON PRITTWITZ, V. (ed.) (1993). Umweltpolitik als Modernisierungsprozess. Opalden: Leske & Budrich.

WALKER, K.J. (1989). The State and Environmental Management: The Ecological Dimension. Political Studies 37, 25-38.

WATERBURY, J. (1979). Hydropolitics of the Nile Valley Syracuse, NY: Syracuse University Press.

WATTS, M. (1983B). Silent Violence: Food, Famine and Peasantry in Northern Nigeria, Berkdey: University of California Press.

WATTS, M. (1984). The Determine of Moral Economy: Food and Famine in Sudano Sahelian Region in Historical Perspective. In Life Before the Drought (E. Scott. ed.) pp. 12-148. London: Allen and Unwin.

WATTS, M. (1990). Peasants Under Contract Agro Food Complex in the Third World. In The Food Question: Profits Versus People? (H. Bernstein, B. Crow, M. Mackintosh and C. Martin eds.) pp. 149-162, London: Earthscan.

WATTS, M.(1983a). On the Povety of Therory: Natural Hazards Research in Context. In Interpretation of Calamity From the Viewpoint of Human Ecology (K. Hewitt ed.) pp. 231-62, London: Allen and Unwin.

WEALE, ALBERT (1992). The New Politics of Pollution. Manchester: Manchester University Press.

WEBER, T. (1987). Hugging the Trees: The Story of the Chipko Movement. New Delhi: Viking.

WESTING, A.H, ed. (1985). Explosive Remnants of War: Mitigating the Environmental Effect. London: Traylor and Francis.

WESTING, A.H,ed. (1984b). Environmental Warfare: A Technical, Legal and Policy Appraisal. London: and Francis.

WESTING, A.H. (1976). Ecological Consequence of the Second Indochina War. Stockholm: Stockholm: International Peace Research Institute.

WESTING, A.H. ed. (1986). Global Resources of War: Mitigating the Environmental Factors in Strategic Policy and Action. Oxford: Oxford University Press.

WESTING, A.H., ed. (1984a). Herbicides in War: The Long Term Ecological and Human Consequence. London: Traylor and Francis.

WESTING, A.H., ed. (1990a). Warfare in a Fragile World: Military Impact on the Human Environment. London; Trylor and Francis.

WHITENEAD, A.(1990). Food Crisis and Gender Conflict in the African Countryside. In The Food Question: Profits Versus People? (H. Bermstein, B. Crow, M. Mackintosh and C. Martin eds.) pp. 54-68. London: Earthcan.

WHITTINGTON, D. and HAYNES, K.E. (1985). Nile Water for Whom? Emerging Conflict in Water Allocation for Agricultural Expansion in Egypt and Sudan. In Agricultural Development in the Middle East (P. Beaumont and K. Mdachlan eds.) pp. 125-149 Chichester: John Wiley and Sons.

WIJKMAN, A and TIMBERLAKE, L. (1984). Natural Disasters: Acts of God or Acts of Man? London: Earthscan.

WOOD, C.H. and SCHMINK, M. (1979). Blaming the Victim Small

Farmer Production in a Amazon Colonization Project Studies in-Third World Societies 7, 77-93.

WORHY, E. (1988) Livestock Policy and Development Ideology in Botswana. In Power and Poverty: Development and Development Project in the Third World (D. W. Attwood. T.C. Bruneau and J.G. Galaty eds.) pp. 155-180. London: Westview Press.

WORLD COMMISSION ON ENVIRONMENTAL AND DEVELOPMENT (1987). Our Common Future. Oxford: Oxford University Press.

WYNNE, BRIAN (1982). Rationality and Ritual : The Windscale Inquiry and Nuclear Decisions in Britain. Chalfont St Giles: The British Society for the History of Science.

ZAMAN, M. (1989). The Social and Political Context of Adjustment to Riverbank Erosion Hazard and Population Resettlement in Bangladesh. Human Organisation 48, 196-205.

ZILLESSEN, HORST et al. (eds) (1993). Modernisierung der Demokratie—Internationale Ansätze. Opladen: Westdeutscher Verlag.

INDEX

Adams, 82
Adidas, 52
Africa, 289
AID (Agency for International Development), 280
Agarwal, A., 93-94
Agarwal, B., 93, 97
Alberta, 137
Alfalta, 14
Amazon, 80
Amazon basin, 296
Amazonian ecosystems, 83
American Assembly Report, 65
American Commune Movement, 172
Amnesty International, 60
Anderson, Benedict, 314, 316
Anderson, J.N., 79
Anderson, R.S., 92
Anderson, Walt, 257
Anti-democratic movement, 174
An Inquiry in to the Human Prospect, 194
Apichatunllop, 94
Argentina, 317
Aristotle, 257
Arnold, Mathew, 176
Asaham River, 20
Australian Labour Party, 139
Austria, 127
Availability of man made Capital, 50
Azarya, 40

Bahro, Rudolf, 200
Bangladesh, 93,298
Barefoot Economics,15
Barnet, Richard, 195
Basic Forestry Law, 20, 30
Batak People, 18-20
Bauman, Zygmunt, 125
Beck, Ulrich, 125
Beitz, Charles,. 167
Berry, S, 76
Bhopal, 43
BJP (Bhartiya Janta Party), 265
Blaikie, P.,76-77
Blueprint for Survival, 192
Bodin, Jean, 257
Bohme, Gernot, 130
Bolvia, 281
Bookchin, Murray, 189, 191, 200
Brandt Commission, 129
Brahmaputra-Jamuna floodplain, 93
Brayant, 49
Brazil's Polonoreste Programme, 161
Brighton beach, 35
Britain, 44, 55

British Colombia, 145
British Forestry Commission, 44
British People Party, 193
Browder, Joe, 250-51
Brown, Janet Welsh, 69,72
Brundtland Commission, 102
Brundtland Report, 149
Bryant, Raymond, L., 10
Bunker, Stephen, 313

Caldwell, Lynton K., 106
Canada, 133
Canadian Council of Resource Ministers, 140
Capitalism, Socialism and the Environment, 190
Capres, Fritjof, 9,16
Carson, Rachel, 103, 189
Casta Rica, 281
Cauca, 17
CGA (Central Ganga Authorty), 264
Chamber, R., 89
Chatterjee, Partha, 317
Chayes, Abram, 108
Chernobyl nuclear plant, 104
Chernobyl reactor, 42
China, 55,164-65
Chipko Aandolan, 46
Chipko movement, 26, 95, 267
Clarke, W.C., 35
Clean Water Act, 147
Clear Air Act , 44
Clinton, Bill, 40
Colchester, M., 32
Cold War, 58
Colombia, 15,17
Commission on Global Governance, 65-66
Community Initiative Study and Development Group, 21
Communist Party of India (M), 265
Constitution Act, 134
Cole, G.D.H., 227
Commonwealth of Australia, 136
Convention on the Prevention of Marine Pollution, 39
CPCB (Central Pollution Control Board), 263

Dahl, Robert, 25
Denmark, 128
Delhi Vikas Manch, 272
Deutsch, Karl, 254
Devall, Bill, 201
Dikshit, R.D., 258
Dobson, Andrew, 234
Douglas, Mary, 120

Earth Day, 188
Earth Summit, 73,102,106,155-56
Ecador, 164, 281
Ecological diversity, 53
Ecological modernisation, 109
Ecology, political theories of, 171
definition of, 171
ecological box, 79
Ecopolitics, new directions for, 239
Economic structure of, 33
Eholich, Paul, 221
EIA (Environmental Impact Assessment), 264
EIS (Environmental Impact Statement), 142
Ekins, Paul, 34, 163
Environmental Forum, 266
Endangered Species Act, 141
England, 35
EPA (Environmental Protection

Agency), 108,141
Everglads National Park, 239
Environmental Change, Sources of, 79
Environmental Impact Analysis, 28
Environmental Monitoring Committee, 264
Environmental movements, 34, 65
Environmental Problem in the Political Context, 9

Facing one World, 279
Finer, S.E., 267
First National Conference of Legislators on Environment, 266
Forester, John, 121
France, 42, 55
Framework convention on Climate Change, 36

Gandhi, Mrs. Indira, 46, 266, 272
Gandhi, Mrs. Maneka, 267, 272
Gandhi, Mr. Rajiv, 266, 272
Gardner, Richard, 58
Garhwal Himalaya, 46
GATT (General Agreement on Tariffs and Trade), 30-31
Germany, 42, 44, 113
German green Policy, 187
German New Right. 129
Giddens, A., 78
Gillis, M., 79, 88
Global Environmental Change, 148
Global Environmental Protection, 49
Global neighourhood, 65
Global networks of digital technology, 54
GNP (Gross National Product), 14-15
Goodman, 83
Goldsmith, Edward, 57
Goldworthy, 25
Gorbachev, Mr. Mikhail, 271
Goult, Denis, 312
Goyder, Philip, 176
Great Britain, 318
Green Belt Movement, 95
Green Fund, 129
Greenhoue gases, 104
Greenhouse Gas Emissions, 276
Green Party of India, 268
Green Politics: The Global Promise, 9
Green Political Theory, 209
Green regimes, 68
Green Revolution, 288
Guha, R., 89
Guyana, 298

Habermas, Jurgen, 190
Habinsaran, 19
Haeckel, Ernst, 171
Haugu Declaration, 54
Hardin, Garrett, 193
Harianboho Protection Forest, 19
Harre, Ram, 323
Hawke, Bob, 139
Hays, Samuel, 109
Heidegger, Martin, 177
Heibroner, Robert, 194
Heredia, Rudolf, 270
High Tory Movement, 174
Hirsch, P., 89
Hooker, cliff, 321
Hutagalung village, 19

Ideological structure, 33
IGAE (Inter governmental

Agreement on the Environment), 139
Indonesia, 20, 183
Indonesia Legal Aid Foundation, 28
Indonesia National Tropical Play, 31
Industrial and Technological Revolution, 104
Information Technology Revolution, 54
International Conferderation of Free Trade Union, 21
International Tropical Timber Organisation, 24
International Red Cross, 21
International Whaling Commission, 73
IPC (India Penal Code), 261
Island Development Authority, 267
Italy, 318
ITTO (Inernational Tropical Timber Organisation, 30-32
Ivory Coast, 80

Jain , M.P., 256
Jakarta, 21
Janta Dal, 265
Japan, 112
Jefferies, Richard, 176
Johri, J.C., 256
Joachin di Fiore, 184
Johnston, R.J., 57
Jura Mountains, 291

Kamalakar, Ajit, 270
Katsiaficas, George, 191
Keohane, Robert, 60
Khanna, Gopesh Nath, 261
Khoshoo, 255
Koh, Tommy, 284
Korea, 52
Kubernao, 22
Kulkarni, S.,79
Kybernan, 22

Labour supply, 50
Lake Toba, 18-20, 26, 35, 41, 45
Lamb, Jame, 312
Laszlo, Ervin, 59-60
Laski, Harold, 62-63
Leeson, Susan, 205
Legislation concerning environment, 260
Legislators Environmental Forum, 266
Leiss, William, 199
Leonard, H.J., 89
Limite to Growth, 114,117
Lohman, P., 32, 89
London Conference, 38
Lovelock, James, 294

Maastricht treaty, 129
Mac Intyre, Alasdains, 310
Mackenzie, J.M., 89-90
Madison, James, 62
Malaysia, 31
Marcuse, Herbert, 190
Marshall, Alford, 253
Mathews, Jessica Tuchman, 105
Maynard, 313
Max-Neef, Manfred, 14
Mendlowitz, Saul, 59
Maxican Environmental Movements, 95
Miedo ambiente, 17
Mill, John Stuart, 205, 217
Mishra, Anupam, 162

Mississippi river, 135
Montreal Protocol on Ozone, 38
Mohler, Armin, 176
Morris, William, 227
Mount Vissuvius, 292
Mulroney, Brain, 142
Mussorie, 269
Myrdal, Alva, 316

Nadkarni, M.V., 89
Narmada Dam Project, 269
Nath, Kamal, 268
National Commission on the Environment, 241
National Focal Point, 264
National Environmental Protection Authority, 139
National Pront, 175
Natural Endowments Financing Resource Conservation for Development, 279
Natural Resources, 50
Natural Resources Defence Council, 141
NCEPC (National Committee on Environmental Planning Co-ordination), 262
NEPA (National Environmental Protection Act), 142
Netherland, 42, 55
New Environmental Policy, 266
New Political Theory, 239
Newzeland Value Party, 201
Nile watershed, 82
NIMBY (Not In My Back Yard), 116, 120
North Sumatra, 18
Norway, 101
Notoriou Air Pollution, 112
NWDB (National Mission on Wastelands Development), 264

OECD (Organisation for Economic Co-operation and Development), 147
Oekologie, 181
Ohmae, Kanichi, 51-52
Okoth- ogando, 90
One Dimensional Man, 190
Ophuls, William, 196
Ornas, Hjortaf, 81
Ottawa, 140
Our Common Future, 194
Our Synthetic Environment, 189
Owen, Robert, 227

Pakistan, 296-97
Palme Commission, 129
Paper tiger, 64
Paris Economec Summit, 283
Paryavaran, 264
Paryavaran Vahini, 264
Papua New Guinea, 31
Peluso, N.L, 89
Peter, P.E., 89-90
Philippines, 79
Pinus merkusii, 19
Planefary Security, 65
Planetary Protection Fund, 268
Plus Valia Ecologica, 18
Political ecology, 49
  globalization, 57
  political ecosystems, 52
  nation-state, 55
  federal option, 61
  United Nation Reform, 64
Pol Pot, 178
Porter, G., 35
Potter, David, 9

Poulantzas, Nicos, 25
Policies for Energy and Power, 266
Porter, Gareth, 69
Power structure, dimensions of, 33
Prigogine, Ilya, 185

Quebec, 137, 140, 143
Queensland, 139

Rodman, John, 205
Redclift, M., 94-95
Reebok, 52
Reich, Charles, 189, 191, 199
Repetto, R., 79
Richardson, Elliot, 108
Rio, 36
Rio Conference, 116
Rio Earth Summit, 76
River Asahan, 19
Rodman, John, 189, 205
Restenkowski, Dam, 285
Roszak, Theodore, 200
Rubber-tappers movements, 95
Ruckelshows, William, 242
Russia, 172

Salik, Mohamed, 81
Salim, Emil, 28
Samosir Island, 19
Santa Barbara Channel, 103
Schatan, Jacobo, 317
Schmidt Commission, 281
Schmidt, Helmut, 279
Sehweitzer, Albert, 14
Scientific Resource Management, 110
Scott, J.C., 91
Second World Climate Conference, 287
Seers, Duddby, 312
Shanmugaratnam, 82
Shekhar, Chandra, 267
Shell Oil Company, 21
Shiva, V., 89-90
Sierra Club, 141
Silant spring, 189,192
Singh , Digvijay, 265
Singh, V.P., 267
Silent Valley, 266
Smith, Adam, 204
Singer, Peter, 205
Soviet Communist Party, 204
South Africa, 60
Spetnak, Charline, 14
Sri Lanka, Mahawedi Schame, 161
State of the World Report, 194
Steiner, George, 177
Stockholm conference, 166, 266
Stone, Christopher, 200
Stretton, Hugh, 190
Strong, Maurice, 102,104
Swedney, 104,128

Tasmania, 137
Toybee, Arnold, 257
TFAP (Tropical Forest Action Plan), 31
The Borderless World, 51
The Greening of America, 189
The Global 2000 Report, 194
The Limits to Growth, 192
The Political Economy of Nationalism, 312
The Politics of Pollution, 243
Therborn, Goren, 316
Third World Envionmental Change, 88

Third World Environmental
Movement, 95, 97
Third World Political Ecology, 77
Thompson, Francis, 53
Tianamin Square, 60
Tiwari Committee, 269
Tiwari, N.D., 262
Tolba, Mostafa, 286
Torrey Canyon, 103
Totalkritik, 114
Toward a Retional Society, 190
Tropical Forestry Action Plan, 21

UN Brundtland Report, 116
UN Conference on the Human
Environment, 188
UN Food and Agriculture
Organisation, 21, 31, 277
UN Economic Commission , 44
United Kingdom, 297
United States, 133
Utopian, 75

Waldsterban, 112
Walker, K.J., 79
Waste Not Washington Act, 247
Waterbury, 82
Watts, M., 89
Wealth of Nations, 49
Wealth, Marine, 267
Weber, T., 95
Whittlesay, Deruent, 257
Wilches, Hinstons, 9
Winner, Langdom, 204
World Commission on
Environment and
Development, 101
World Conservation Strategy, 293
World Conference on Environ-
ment and Development, 102, 301
World Council of Churches, 21
World Development Report, 157
World Order Models Project, 59
World War I. 181
World War II, 172, 182, 189, 315, 317
World Wildlife Fund, 293
Wright, Skelly, 142

Yellowstone National Park, 239

Zimbabwe, 313